Half Savage
and Hardy
and Free

Wesleyan University Press
Middletown, Connecticut

Half Savage and Hardy and Free

Women and Rural Radicalism in the Nineteenth-Century Novel

Judith Weissman

For Daniel

"If the King had no son, they would desire to live on crutches
till he had one."

The Winter's Tale

Chapters 2 and 9 were originally published, in somewhat different form, in
Women & Literature, volume 4:1 and volume 5:1. Chapters 3 and 8 were
originally published in the *Midwest Quarterly*, volume 19:4 and volume 18:4.
Chapters 5 and 10 were originally published in the *Colby Library Quarterly*,
volume 12:4 and volume 11:4.

LIBRARY OF CONGRESS CATALOGING-IN-PUBLICATION DATA

Weissman, Judith.
   Half savage and hardy and free.
   Bibliography: p.
   Includes index.
   1. English fiction—19th century—History and
criticism.   2. Women in literature.   3. Radicalism
in literature.   4. Rural conditions in literature.
5. Feminism in literature.   I. Title.
PR868.W6W4   1987   823'.8'09352042   87-2153
ISBN 0-8195-5179-1

All inquiries and permissions requests should be addressed to the Publisher,
Wesleyan University Press, 110 Mt. Vernon Street, Middletown, Connecticut
06457.

Distributed by Harper & Row Publishers, Keystone Industrial Park, Scranton,
Pennsylvania 18512.

Manufactured in the United States of America

FIRST EDITION

Contents

Acknowledgments

I do not have the usual panoply of acknowledgments because I am essentially solitary and do not rely on institutional aid. I owe whatever is good in this book to two groups of people: the friends whose faith in me has kept me going—Wendell Berry, Robert Bly, Raymond Carver, Tess Gallagher, Douglas Unger, Toby Wolff; and my dear neighbors on Maryland Avenue, who could not care less if I write a book, and who have convinced me that Kropotkin is right.

Half Savage and Hardy and Free

"I wish I were out of doors—I wish I were a girl again, half savage, and hardy, and free; and laughing at injuries, not maddening under them!"

—EMILY BRONTË, *Wuthering Heights*

Introduction

"The idiocy of rural life"[1] is one phrase from the *Manifesto of the Communist Party* that most literary critics assent to—whether or not they call themselves Marxists. The dominant literary voices of Victorian England also agreed with this characterization: Dickens, Thackeray, and George Eliot criticized urban life and occasionally indulged in sentimental re-creations of an imaginary country life from the past, but they never considered looking for intelligence and radical politics in the rural life of their present, in England. The possibility that both brains and passionate radicalism could survive in the country, and that rural life could even be the basis of a political stand against the injustices of capitalism, is hardly taken into account by literary critics who seek to represent nineteenth-century literature in the present. In a strange way, this fragment of opinion that Marx and Engels expressed in 1848, in a single document, has ironically won the minds of those who write on Wordsworth and Hardy. The reality of rural life is usually simply ignored, displaced by topics such as narrative voice, structure, language, intellectual movements. Trees and cows are but scenery in a literary text, not the stuff of literary, intellectual, and political meaning.

When Marx wrote about the destruction of rural life in *Capital* he did not call it an "idiocy" from which workers should be "rescued." There the expropriation of land is no inexorable economic process to be contemplated cheerfully as one looks forward to a coming dictatorship of the proletariat. "Hence, the historical movement which changes the producers into wage-workers appears, on the one hand, as their emancipation from serfdom and from the fetters of the guilds, and this side alone exists for our bourgeois historians. But, on the other hand, these new freedmen became sellers of themselves only after they had been robbed of all their own means of production, and of all the guarantees of existence afforded by the old feudal arrangements. And the history of this, their expropriation, is written in the annals of mankind in letters of blood and fire."[2] The blood and fire of such a struggle in rural England has escaped bourgeois literary critics and bourgeois historians alike.

Marx acknowledges that the people of rural England had not been wholly dominated by the politically unjust hierarchies of feudalism. "Communal property—always distinct from the State property just dealt with—was an old Teutonic institution which lived on under cover of feudalism. We have seen how the forcible usurpation of this, generally accompanied by the turning of arable into pasture land, begins at the end of the 15th and extends into the 16th century. . . . The advance made by the 18th century shows itself in this, that the law itself became now the instrument of the theft of the people's land, although the large farmers made use of their little independent methods as well. The parliamentary form of the robbery is that of Acts for enclosure of Commons, in other words, decrees by which the landlords grant themselves the people's land as private property, decrees of expropriation of the people."[3] Crimes were committed against the people of rural England in the interest of capitalism. Rural life had been *good.* "As Thorton rightly has it, the English working-class was precipitated without any transition from its golden to its iron age."[4] The Marx of *Capital* does not sneer at the idiocy of rural life; this Marx writes about rural life with passion and a sense of tragedy.

This is Marx the Jewish prophet, the heir of Jeremiah, a Marx who has been obscured in our century by the horrors of the Gulag and the Khmer Rouge, by the frigidity of Lenin and the lunacy of Althusser. I believe that this is the true Marx, who belongs to the generous, hopeful, angry, humane radicalism of the nineteenth century. The rich have stolen the land from the people; the state has betrayed its own poor. *Capital* is certainly a book of political economy, but it is also a jeremiad. And in the nineteenth century, no one would have found the union of these two genres incongruous. Wordsworth and Shelley, Emerson and Thoreau, Morris and Kropotkin all assumed that science and justice belonged together.

This is the Marx whose voice and whose vision have been kept alive in the work of English radical historians such as Christopher Hill, E. J. Hobsbawm, E. P. Thompson, to whose great book, *The Making of the English Working Class*, all of us who work in the English nineteenth century are forever grateful. This is also the Marx of the American historian Christopher Lasch and of the English literary critics Raymond Williams and Terry Eagleton. This Marx remains part of a living radical voice, but a voice that appears rarely in American literary criticism and very rarely indeed in literary criticism that concentrates on works by and about women.

Yet the Marx of *Capital* can be seen as part of a genuine tradition in English literature itself, a tradition to which too many literary critics have been blind. It is in *King Lear* and *The Winter's Tale* where peasants can stand up to the unjust power of the state. It hovers around the edges of Pope and Fielding in the eighteenth century. And in the nineteenth, when Marx unhappily thought that the battle had been lost, that "the very memory of the connexion between the agricultural labourer and the communal property had, of course, vanished,"[5] a group of writers took up the fight to defend what they believed might still be saved. Wordsworth, Austen, Emily Brontë, Hawthorne (in America), Trollope, Hardy, and Forster, as well as the straightforwardly Marxist political writers Morris and Kropotkin, were in a tradition of radical protest; all saw agricultural communities as a place to take a stand for economic and social justice. These poets and novelists are not "Marxist" writers; nor are they in absolute agreement about what was most valuable in rural life, or about what form ideal justice should take. They are linked with the Marx of *Capital* and with each other by their vision of the economic threat to rural England and by their conviction that the lives being destroyed were supremely valuable, supremely worth saving. They can share Marx's insights without being orthodox "Marxists." A quite different kind of writer, Fernand Braudel, has recently said, "The same process can be observed everywhere: any society based on an ancient structure which opens its door to money sooner or later loses its acquired equilibria and liberates forces that can never afterwards be adequately controlled. The new form of interchange disturbs the old order, benefits a few privileged individuals, and hurts everyone else."[6] The writers I have chosen still believed that all those "everyone else's were worth fighting for." But they differed from Marx in believing that something of the old life was still alive. After all, the sixteenth-century farming calendar of Thomas Tusser was still being used in schools as a source of information about agricultural work, not as an antiquarian oddity.[7]

What the radical novelists bring uniquely to this tradition of rural resistance is character and personality. The human individuals they create belong particularly to their threatened communities; they deserve a reader's passionate concern. Though Emily Dickinson will not appear later in this book on nineteenth-century novels, the self-declared "rural man" is part of this tradition. Rural, distinctly not idiotic, intellectual, rebellious, resisting, even revolutionary, she is unusual but not anomalous, a genius but not a sport. The rural identity of Emily Dickinson has been virtually invisible to twentieth-century admirers overwhelmed by her poetic originality and power, but the rural identity exists, a deep part of the poems. As a rural woman—who sometimes adopted the persona of a rural man—she combined domesticity and radical vision, attachment to her community and deep inwardness. The union of opposites, a constant tension between the individual spirit and the outside world, characterizes most of nineteenth-century poetry; Dickinson is unique only in the extremity of the oppositions and the resolute determination to make them one.

It is no rural idiot who can write both

822

This Consciousness that is aware
Of Neighbors and the Sun
Will be the one aware of Death
And that itself alone

Is traversing the interval
Experience between
And most profound experiment
Appointed unto Men—

How adequate unto itself
Its properties shall be
Itself unto itself and none
Shall make discovery.

Adventure most unto itself
The Soul condemned to be—
Attended by a single Hound
Its own identity.

and

1082

Revolution is the Pod
Systems rattle from
When the Winds of Will are stirred
Excellent is Bloom

But except its Russet Base
Every Summer be
The Entomber of itself,
So of Liberty—

Left inactive on the Stalk
All its Purple fled
Revolution shakes it for
Test if it be dead.[8]

The most private sense of self, attachment to the daily life of the earth and an actual human community of neighbors, and an uncompromising belief in the absolute good of liberty are all part of one lonely rural woman's mind. She has nothing to do with the strictly economic theories of Marxism; she has a lot to do with the spirit of nineteenth-century radicalism that values country life. Once we remember how small a town Amherst was, and how immersed this poet was in the life of her family, her neighbors, her friends, we have a place to stand from which we can move a world of literary criticism that has read the nineteenth century through the assumption that rural life was idiotic.

Both rural England and rural America in the nineteenth century contained all kinds of strange and individual characters, both men and women. We can glimpse some of them in the often badly spelled but always moving documents with which E. P. Thompson weaves the history of the rural people who became England's working class. If we are willing to see it, we can find plenty of evidence that in the nineteenth century rural communities were a hospitable environment for individuality, brilliance, and radicalism.

Nineteenth-century novels are full of female characters who are spiritually connected with Emily Dickinson, or at least with the self-created poetic character that is all we really know of her. Both women and men—Austen and Emily Brontë, Hawthorne, Trollope, Hardy, and Forster—pick up the particularly English form of Romantic radicalism that begins with Wordsworth and *The Lyrical Ballads*; they create fictions in which female characters take a stand in defending a viable economic rural life, the life that Marx declared had been stolen from the people of England. These heroines are part of a serious radical literary tradition. They are not figments of nostalgic sentiment for days gone by. The most serious radical and rural novels of the nineteenth century, as the most serious of Wordsworth's poems, create fictional worlds that include a genuine understanding of economic realities and demand from the reader both stricken concern and even, possibly, political action. Novels such as *Wuthering Heights* and *Tess of the D'Urbervilles*, unlike the pastoral poems of Theocritus or even the rural elegies of Gray and Goldsmith, invite not mourning but resistance, not fantasy but ferocity. These fictions engage the reader in a new political awareness, not a sweetly melancholy dream.

In this book I emphasize the meaning of the radical tradition of resistance for rural women. Wordsworth's radical poetry has female characters, but they do not predominate; in the novels that follow him rural heroines come into their own. I hesitate to call these novels *feminist*, since that word has been appropriated by a different radical tradition; they are merely heroic. They offer to the women of the nineteenth century—and, I believe, to the women of the present—a vision of political radicalism that is tied to an agricultural economy, and to forms of labor that can evade the oppressive and unjust structures of capitalism. They do not offer freedom from labor and action, a life of pure leisure and pleasure. They demand action that we stand up for a threatened and valuable economic system which is a genuine alternative to both the capitalism of industry and the capitalism of the kind of farming which reduces laborers to degraded paupers.

These novels do not offer women an English version of the Eleusinian mysteries, a celebration of some ineffable link between women and "nature" or the Earth Mother, ideas that have been the subjects of certain books in the last fifty years, from Margaret Murray's *The God of the Witches*[9] to Pamela Berger's recent *The Goddess*

Obscured: Transformation of the Grain Protectress from Goddess to Saint.[10] These novels show women a more prosaic meaning, about their possible place in a real agricultural economy. In all the novels I have chosen, none of them political tracts, female characters can see and fight against the wrongs of an increasingly powerful bourgeois capitalism. They are guaranteed no happiness and success. In some they endure the tragedy of suffering and failure. In all of these novels women are involved in some version of the real economic battle of the nineteenth century; all offer radical hope to anyone willing to join the fight.

Another strong, radical, and quite different tradition in nineteenth-century English and American literature has formed the basis of what is now called feminism. While Wordsworth was settling in the Lake District and trying to defend its inhabitants, Shelley was traveling in Europe, detached from the land, trying to extirpate all tyranny by rearranging such oppressive sexual customs as monogamous marriage. At his best, in *Prometheus Unbound* and "The Witch of Atlas," Shelley gives us the most far-reaching and joyful anarchism in all of English poetry, a dream of pure freedom approached only by Ariel's songs in *The Tempest*. Of all the nineteenth-century novelists, only Hawthorne could approach such a vision in fiction. Other novelists, like George Eliot and Charlotte Bonté, do not fulfill this vision of freedom; their romantic radicalism is centered in the spiritual and sexual liberation of the individual, and in a mysterious spiritual progress of the race only vaguely, indefinitely connected with any economic system.

Shelley's spiritual radicalism, loosed from any moorings in land or an economic system, was far more malleable than Wordsworth's. Writers who called themselves radicals transformed him in their own ways; strangely, so did some conservatives. In Dickens and Thackeray the tremulous, sensitive, spirit becomes part of the saintly, passive Victorian heroines who have become objects of horror for feminist historians and literary critics. Shelley's highly theoretical and far-reaching radicalism is also reborn straightforwardly *as* terror in *Frankenstein* and *Dracula*. In itself, as pure poetic anarchism, it did not deserve such fictional vituperation; as a source of liberation and transformation for women, perhaps it did.

The dominant tradition of radical feminism that has lived from Charlotte Brontë and George Eliot through the recent work of Adrienne Rich, Sandra Gilbert and Susan Gubar, and Nina Auerbach has its roots in Shelley. The unifying inherited assumption is that the basis of women's oppression is sexual and personal, to be changed by removing patriarchal injustice, familial constraints, and various forms of false consciousness. Patriarchy, the great, all-inclusive evil of much feminist literary criticism, is a sexual term; it can coexist with any number of economic systems. A recent volume of theoretical essays, *Women and Revolution: A Discussion of the Unhappy Marriage of Marxism and Feminism*,[11] offers permutations on the theme without providing a convincing answer to the question of whether capitalism and patriarchy are necessarily connected, or the question of how they should be combatted for the good of women. Shelley hoped, as a poet certainly has a right to hope, that an end to sexual oppression would so transform human hearts that an end to political and economic oppression would necessarily follow. Still, the precise mechanism of connection has remained elusive almost two hundred years later.

Yet in women's literary criticism Shelley's radicalism remains powerful. Patriarchy is everywhere, and agriculture is nowhere. The mythic meanings and spiritual sources of "empowerment" are the centers of a radical tradition persuasively presented by writers who look to Charlote Brontë and George Eliot as inspiring sources. From seminal essays such as Adrienne Rich's "*Jane Eyre*: Temptations of a Motherless Woman" and Hélène Cixous's "The Laugh of the Medusa," through wide-ranging recent works of criticism such as Gilbert and Gubar's *The Madwoman in the Attic* and Nina Auerbach's *Woman and the Demon*, the theme is individual, spiritual, sexual *power*, freedom from patriarchal bondage. What matter, for Rich, that the married Jane and Rochester live in a supposedly uninhabitable house in a damp wood, talking all day long? "It is not patriarchal marriage in the sense of a marriage that stunts and diminishes the woman; but a continuation of this woman's creation of herself."[12] Rich pales beside Cixous, who declares, looking toward women's future, "If there is a 'propriety of woman,' it is paradoxically her capacity to depropriate unselfishly, body without end, without appendage, without principal 'parts.' If she is a whole, it's a whole composed of parts that are whole, not simple partial objects, but a moving, limitlessly changing ensemble, a cosmos tirelessly traversed by Eros, an immense astral space not organized around any one sun that's any more of a star than the others."[13] Self-creation, souls, stars, limitless astral spaces—such thoughts begin in Shelley.

Such ideas form the intellectual basis of many important feminist readings of nineteenth-century novels. Gilbert and Gubar state the purpose of their massive study: "Dis-eased and infected by the sentences of patriarchy, yet unable to deny the urgency of that 'poet-fire' she felt within herself, what strategies did the woman writer develop for overcoming her anxiety of authorship? How did she dance out of the looking glass of the male text into a tradition that enabled her to create her own authority?"[14] Auerbach too uses the literary texts of the nineteenth century in England as a place to search for women's mysterious power: "The demon that accompanies the women of my title exists in the broadest sense: as that disruptive, spiritual energy which also engorges the divine. This demon is first of all the woman's familiar, the source of her ambiguous holiness, but it is also the popular—and demonic—imagination that endowed her with this holiness in defiance of three cherished Victorian institutions: the family, the patriarchal state, and God the Father."[15] Four recent examples only suggest and certainly do not prove a tradition, but the emphases and exclusions are clear enough. Women become their true selves by developing secret, inward sources of energy, power, demonism, sexuality; in becoming their true selves, they escape from the psychological hurt of patriarchy, authority, men's language, men's family, men's religion. This can be called radical, but it is a radicalism that can be discussed without reference to labor, economics, ecology, the production or consumption of material goods.

Even recent feminist historians who have provided valuable anthologies of nineteenth-century women's documents have often acquiesced in this belief that the battles were more sexual than economic and so have been blind to the possibility that the agricultural community could give women a place from which to resist capitalism *and* the kind of oppression that appeared to be endemic in the nineteenth-century urban noncommunity. For example, the anthology *Victorian Women* begins, "In the ferment about sex roles and the family that characterizes our own time, men and women still define themselves in terms of the Victorians, either living out ideas and defending institutions that came to fruition in the nineteenth century or reacting against these ideas and institutions, and against

Victorian 'repression.' "[16] Janet Murray's more daring *Strong-Minded Women* fulfills its purposes of bringing to light the many kinds of women whose lives are obscured by the selectivity of fiction, but she too neglects the agricultural tradition and the possibility that those women who lived in rural communities in nineteenth-century England still had something precious to save. She begins with the assumption that this world was gone and that the "pre-industrial and pre-capitalist world . . . had all but disappeared by the early nineteenth century."[17] She goes on to pursue the ways women thought they could fight for better lives *within* an industrial and capitalist culture.

I can only guess at the reasons why a radicalism that originated in Shelley rather than in Wordsworth has become preeminent in women's literary studies. It cannot be the sheer number of nineteenth-century women authors who embraced each: Charlotte Brontë and George Eliot are no more than Jane Austen and Emily Brontë. I believe that Shelley's tradition rather than Wordsworth's has triumphed in feminist literary criticism and in much feminist popular culture because in spite of its genuinely radical origins it has been easily compatible with urban, industrial capitalism. "In spite of its political implications it has been primarily personal and nonsocial."

Myths, spirits, demons, self-creation, empowerment are easily transportable commodities, as much at home in a suburban house as on a working farm, as available to a young female executive as to a woman fighting for her land. What the authors of *Women and Revolution* have called the unhappy marriage of feminism and Marxism might well be called the happy marriage of feminism and capitalism. In the hands of some nineteenth-century women novelists and their twentieth-century critics, Shelley's radical anarchism often becomes a dream of personal power that offers opposition to the economic system which in fact holds the power in our world. Such dreams have made a relatively small number of women, those lucky enough to have prestigious jobs or husbands with power, part of that system; they have not been worth much to the increasingly large group of economic victims.

Literature and literary criticism have become almost the sole property of the rich and privileged and powerful—and urban, of course—in the twentieth century. Once Eliot and Pound and the

Modernists turned their backs on the radical egalitarianism that most nineteenth-century writers at least aspired to, the serious possibility of rural resistance has been largely ignored by the readers of novels, most of whom are sequestered in the English departments of universities, hardly hotbeds of economic rebellion. The evidence of this rural and radical tradition has been dismissed, relegated to the category of artistic invention or background scenery.

I can give only the same skeptical and consciously partial answers to possible questions about the theoretical grounding of a long study that cannot absolutely answer the question of why one radical tradition seems to have triumphed over another, and a better, one. Fifteen years ago I would not have had to defend my topic, my language, my method. Today I do. I have willfully, consciously, and with full knowledge of the alternatives chosen the tradition of English Romanticism and English Marxism that begins in Wordsworth and continues through E. P. Thompson and Raymond Williams, a tradition that steadfastly affirms "the real language of men" rather than the jargon of specialists. I have avoided the current modes of French Marxism, French psychoanalytic theory, French feminism, and French linguistic theory that includes Althusser, Lacan, Cixous, Derrida, Barthes, as well as a multitude of followers in France, England, and America. (I occasionally use a bit of Foucault, for he is the one of the French pantheon who sometimes makes sense to me.)

This entire complex of thought has been dignified by the name *theory*, with all other modes of thought castigated in the academic establishment as *non*theory, mere "application." A few voices are finally being raised against this general proposition.[18] The name *theory* has become a weapon in an internal academic war which is rapidly removing literature from popular discourse. Though the ideas of the French Marxists can be called theories, they are no more "theoretical" than the ideas of Plato or Hume. I do not believe, however, that anyone has stated this forcefully enough: French Marxism and its appendages have no more right to call themselves theory than biochemistry has the right to call itself science or Judaism has the right to call itself religion. The proponents of one narrow set of theories have attempted to lure/persuade the academic community into acquiescing into a hierarchical intellectual structure rather like that of the best physics departments, in which "theorists" are usually acknowledged to be the most brilliant and innovative of members. But no physics department contains only theorists; none dismisses all experimenters. Also, scientific theorists submit their theories to the test of experiment, with the assumption that they may be proved wrong.

The large structure of this book is a descriptive history of three phases of Romantic radicalism in nineteenth-century English poetry and novels (with one trans-Atlantic addition, Hawthorne): a first phase of wide-ranging hopefulness, a second phase of reaction and destructive transformations, and a third phase of more modest and yet more dogged belief in the limited radicalism of agricultural resistance. This history covers roughly a century; most of these writers thought of themselves as part of the nineteenth century, as the heirs of Wordsworth and Shelley.

Virtually every important word of the last paragraph, the words with which I have defined my large structure, has been "called into question" by French Marxist criticism. Foucault has challenged us with "What Is an Author" and has declared that we can legitimately speak only of the "author function."[19] Barthes has denied the autonomy of texts and the idea that one text can influence a later author's mind, thereby playing some causal role in the production of another text. "Every text, being itself the intertext of another text, belongs to the intertextual, which must not be confused with a text's origins. To search for the 'sources of' and 'influence upon' a work is to satisfy the myth of filiation. The quotations from which a text is constructed are anonymous, irrecoverable, and yet *already read.* They are quotations without quotation marks."[20] So much for the literary influence in which the authors of the nineteenth century themselves believed.

These authors also believed in themselves as authors, minds, creators. They had not had the chance to read Lacan and find out that they were deluded, "subjected," into believing that they were thinking "subjects."[21] "The signifier, producing itself in the field of the Other, makes manifest the subject of its signification. But it functions as a signifier only to reduce the subject in question to being no more than a signifier, to petrify the subject in the same movement in which it calls the subject to function, to speak, as a subject."[21] They imagined that they were thinking selves who could communicate discernible meanings to other selves. They did not see communication itself as part of an imprisoning structure of thought, as Catherine Belsey sees it. "Thus author and reader (even when these are conceived as ideal types created by the formal strategies of the text) no longer present the symmetrical poles of an intersubjective process understood as communication. Instead critical practice is seen as a process of releasing the positions from which the text is intelligible. Liberated from the fixity of the communications model, the text is available for production in the process of reading."[22]

The fashionable modern positions on the nature of literary creation and literary influence are unanswerable, in their own terms. It is impossible to prove to anyone else that you are a thinking self. The French and their followers make one set of declarations; those of us who remain in the tradition of English skepticism and empiricism make ours.

I have chosen major texts by major authors; such texts are now disparagingly called "canonized," as if some invisible college of cardinals had the power to choose what we read and what we like. The argument of Althusser and his followers such as Fredric Jameson in *The Political Unconscious*,[23] that books are called "great" because they reinforce the dominant ideology, or "reinscribe the dominant codes," is worth taking seriously. So is the work of such critics as Elaine Showalter, whose *A Literature of Their Own*[24] brings back into our line of vision a group of women's texts that had been lost, perhaps because they were too subversive. Such books, however, have not altered the fact that if you want to see what literary texts have been and still are culturally significant, a good place to start is with "the canon." Granted that famous works are not the only works of literature and that the special status of some is a consequence of their support of the interests of a ruling class; still, there is no reason why they should not remain important subjects for literary analysis.

Once you have decided which texts to write about, what should you do with them? It depends on what you want to find out. The "theorists" write: "When the record is scrupulously and disinterestedly examined these [humanist] traditions will not be found to contain covert radical sensibilities waiting for post-structuralism, deconstruction, psychoanalytical criticism, feminism, or marxism, to give their disparate perceptions a local habitation and a name. Indeed, methodologies which naively favour plural 'approaches' or a multiplicity of 'readings' generated from within the essentialist individual critical consciousness as a form of 'unbridled subjectivity' are wholly inadequate as responses to the challenges now proposed by theoretically informed modes of criticism."[25] If you want to find out that texts are ideological constructs with no author and think that you should not look for meaning but should "interrogate" the texts, looking for lacunae or contradiction, you will not find a world congenial that remains large, difficult, puzzling, hard to know.

My chapters are each analyses of one or two major literary texts; the analyses are informed by the "theoretical" approach of the English Marxists, a theory of historical inquiry both skeptical and empirical, one wary of intellectually constructed categories. As E. P. Thompson says in the preface to *The Making of the English Working Class*, "By class I understand an historical phenomenon, unifying a number of disparate and seemingly unconnected events, both in the raw material of experience and in consciousness. I emphasize that it is a *historical* phenomenon. I do not see class as a 'structure', nor even as a 'category'; but as something which in fact happens (and can be shown to have happened) in human relationships."[26] Every word is, as the theorists would say, ideologically informed by assumptions. "I" is a conscious being capable of "understanding." There is a discernible external world in which events did or did not happen. Facts can be isolated, demonstrated, proved or disproved. These are the theoretical assumptions of empiricism.

The evidence offered to a reader of literature is naturally different from that available to the historian. The elements of a literary text have already been selected and transformed by a human mind. Nevertheless, I remain indebted to Thompson's method. I have tried to re-read the "evidence" within these texts—language, plot, characterization, narrative voice, structure—as part of what is "happening" in class relationships in the nineteenth century. That is really another way of saying that I read these novels as a replaying of two dominant radical traditions—traditions based on the assumption that class relations are unjust. I am working on the assumption that the authors themselves were capable of radical consciousness and that as a critic the best I can do is to bring those literary qualities that give evidence of radical consciousness to the foreground. In the preface to *The House of the Seven Gables* Hawthorne humorously distinguishes between his moral, "the folly of tumbling down an avalanche of ill-gotten gold, or real estate, on the heads of an unfortunate posterity, thereby to maim and crush them," and his method. "When romances do really teach anything, or produce any effective operation, it is usually through a far more subtle process than the ostensible one." Bringing to light that subtle process is one of the functions of criticism.

I also owe to English Marxism the method of the interweaving of these fictions with the available evidence provided by historians, primarily Thompson and Hobsbawm. To make this distinction between fact and fiction and to claim that the external world can be used as a test of the truthfulness of the created world are both the methods of empiricism, and contrary to the methods of Derrida and Althusser, who claim that it is a bourgeois act of self-subjection to "privilege" an external world. Catherine Belsey has announced that we can say good-bye to what we used to call history, since "Althusser's own concepts, produced in the process of reading Marx . . . have removed the centre from history."[27] Her history, and Althusser's, and Macherey's, is a matter of mental structures. It is, in fact, nothing other than what Marx himself attacked as idealism in Hegel. Althusser, in a revealing, infrequently quoted, passage of *Reading Capital*, says outright that his nonempirical methodology goes beyond the "ideological" (i.e., bad) concern with "the workers' cause, their labour, their sufferings, their struggles, and their experience" to the really important work of establishing "a scientific conception of practice."[28] My historical interest lies in precisely those areas scorned by Althusser and Belsey, in labor, suffering, and experience as they have been recovered by recent radical social and economic historians.

The historical facts of previously hidden lives of common people can serve a literary critic in several ways. They can expose an author's willful falsehood. What Thompson tells us about the history of the Luddites exposes George Eliot's picture of the workers who want to stop the railroad in *Middlemarch* as an act of literary hostility to intelligent men engaged in a plausible cause. More often, at least for my purposes, newly unearthed historical facts affirm the truthfulness of these fictions. Even some of the most grotesque espisodes can gain new life. Who could have believed that London really contained people like old Mrs. Brown, who abducted and stripped little girls like Florence Dombey? Anyone who has read the recent reissue of Henry Mayhew's *London Labour and the London Poor*, which has a whole section called "Child Stripping."[29] The lonely, tormented life of the female urban child out of which Dickens builds his ideal woman is no fairy tale, after all.

Even a simple object can gain new literary meaning from the new histories. The old box bed in *Wuthering Heights* in which poor Lockwood is possessed by his nightmare of Catherine Earnshaw is a virtual symbol of the peasant life that Catherine was still part of. Pierre-Jakez Helias, born a Breton peasant, now an intellectual, swears he could no longer sleep in such a bed because "I'm no longer in a state of grace; moreover I would have the impression that I was offending the Manes, Lares, and Penates."[30] If Helias can speak seriously about his bed and his Lares, maybe even Catherine's ghost can begin to tremble into the realm of possibility.

History must be used in different ways, depending on the precise genre of the novel. A book like *Middlemarch* that claims to be scientific is to be read differently from a romance like *The House of the Seven Gables* or a horror-fantasy like *Dracula*. Common sense and critical delicacy can determine the best way to use history. Reading *Dracula*, no one should ask Is this vampire real? But you can ask whether the young inhabitants of Stoker's London were historically specific for the end of the century, and whether the bureaucratic mechanisms by which the count gets himself and fifty large boxes of Transylvanian dirt into England are those that other unwelcome aliens might use.

The issue of truthfulness is particularly important in this set of readings because so many of the books point toward a utopian, radical ideal. If they offer us joy and hope beyond our daily lives, we have to ask whether we can trust them. In order to trust the radical, utopian edge of these novels, we must venture, intellectually, beyond them. For many years before the neo-idealism of the French poststructuralism attempted to shatter "reality" as a viable category, *belief* had already been a difficult and embarrassing question for literary critics. All modes of formal criticism have implicitly demanded that we put aside the question of whether we ourselves really believe or care about the meaning of a work of literature. Henry James put us all on our guard back in 1888, with the concluding exhortation in "The Art of Fiction": "As for the aberrations of a shallow optimism, the ground (of English fiction especially) is strewn with their brittle particles as with broken glass. If you must indulge in conclusions, let them have the taste of a wide knowledge. Remember that your first duty is to be as complete as possible—to make as perfect a work. Be generous and delicate and pursue the prize." None of the novels I deal with meet

James's criteria. I think the criteria are wrong. No one wants shallow optimism, but how about profound optimism?

The radical tradition that informs these novels is not merely aesthetically pleasant or morally attractive. Very hesitantly I suggest that we might indeed believe in it, believe that nineteenth-century literature can give us glimpses of lost truths. From Rousseau through Kropotkin, radical philosophers combined revolutionary fervor with the scientific study of human instincts and with environmental theories about the social conditions under which our instincts might live. With the aid of the new sciences of anthropology and sociobiology we just might be at the threshold of a new confidence in Wordsworth's belief that the true human passions could best survive in a rural community, and that these passions can enable people to live together in reasonable tranquility and mutual helpfulness—neither Hobbes's war of all against all nor a sterilized pastoral prettiness.

The natural environment does not provide moral examples to follow, but it does provide a check to human madness. This is one of the few ideas on which Wordsworth and Shelley agree. In "Mont Blanc" Shelley says that the mountain is a voice "to repeal/Large codes of fraud and woe" (lines 80–81). Wordsworth, recovering from the horrors of the French Revolution, suggests in *The Prelude*

> 'Twas proved that not in vain
> I had been taught to reverence a Power
> That is the visible quality and shape
> And image of right reason; that matures
> Her processes by steadfast laws; gives birth
> To no impatient or fallacious hopes,
> No heat of passion or excessive zeal.
> (Bk. 13, lines 19–25)

This is a modest faith, merely that nature restrains excess. But if you couple it with a belief that as biological creatures we tend to get along with each other, at least to avoid genocidal slaughter, it is not a bad one. It is good enough to offer hope to the writers of the nineteenth century.

This hopeful trust never quite dies out. We find it at the end of the nineteenth century in Kropotkin's anti-Darwinian theory that we are biologically inclined to practice mutual aid; in 1969 Ronald Blythe reasserts it, after spending time in the forgotten village of Akenfield. People bound to the agricultural world, he says, "are committed to

certain basic ideas and actions which progress and politics can elaborate or confuse, but can never alter. . . . Such inevitability cuts down
ambition and puts a brake on restlessness."[31] Since most of the
human world has been horribly confused by both progress and politics, to remember what we have been in our agricultural past is to
hope for what we might be again.

Nature itself cannot guarantee the survival of human solidarity
or human instincts or human restraint; the evidence seems to be that
we need a social system connected with our natural environment,
though both the system and the environment can vary endlessly
without destroying our humanity. Colin Turnbull has found both
human peace and human horror, something worse than what even
Hobbes thought we were, in the "nature" of Africa. If there has been
an Eden on this earth, it is in the forest of the Congo, where Turnbull
found the pygmies living in "a world that is still kind and good . . .
And without evil."[32] These are people who identify themselves as
"People of the Forest. . . . When the forest dies, we shall die." Leaving
them, Turnbull heard for the last time "the chorus of that great song
of praise: 'If Darkness *is*, Darkness is Good.' "[33]

And for those who have doubted the existence of hell, Turnbull
has found that too in Africa, among the Ik in Uganda. Displaced from
the land where they had been accustomed to living as hunter-
gatherers, forcibly removed to a new environment and a new economy, they have lost the instincts that we like to consider inalterably
human. They laugh at the old and sick, steal food from children,
loathe each other—rather as we do. "For the individuals one can only
feel infinite sorrow at what they have lost; hatred must be reserved
for the so-called society they live in, the machine they have constructed to enable them to survive."[34] They have become crueler than
any group of animals.

Our animal selves are not our best selves, but they are not our
worst selves either. Some of the helpful female social structures of
Trollope's Barsetshire can be found in the great apes of Sarah Blaffer
Hrdy's sociobiological study of primates, *The Woman That Never
Evolved*.[35] We are just beginning to understand what we are biologically, and how much goodness we may have lost to what Blythe calls
politics and progress. As Philip Kitcher said recently "Sociobiology,
like other young sciences, should not be chided for failing to deliver
flawless answers to the questions it addresses."[36] Perhaps it will all

come to nothing; perhaps it may give support to the sentence of Rousseau's that began the radical movements of the nineteenth century: "Man is born free, and everywhere he is in chains." The youngest sciences may continue to give strength to the radical beliefs of the nineteenth-century novelists who followed Wordsworth. Whatever remains of an ancient rural life is what keeps us in touch with our true humanity. We must fight for it. If we can win the fight, we may yet resist the injustices and inequalities that a capitalist economy is forcing upon us.

Part 1
Beginnings

1. Romantic Poetry: Souls and Stones

"In the make of the great masters the idea of political liberty is indispensable," said Walt Whitman in the preface to the 1855 *Leaves of Grass*. He was wrong, of course; political liberty was hardly indispensable to Chaucer or Yeats. But looking back only a generation, to his own poetic great masters, the English Romantics, Whitman was right. The importance of the idea of political liberty is a central truth about English Romantic poetry—a truth treated as a commonplace until recently. In the last few years it has become the critical fashion to declare that Romantic poetry was never truly radical at all, but the fashion is wrong, for both the internal evidence of the poetry and the historical evidence about how it was received support Whitman.[1]

Yet even the literary criticism that acknowledged the radicalism of Romantic poetry has not made it central. Other ideas have been uppermost in the minds of scholars—nature and beauty, language and spirit, community and the individual, primitive people and the future. And indeed there is no direct evidence of the poet's concern with political liberty in many of the best known Romantic poems. Not liberty but a new vision of a spiritually animated nature connects Coleridge's "Eolian Harp," Wordsworth's "Tintern Abbey," Shelley's "Ode to the West Wind," and Keats's "To Autumn." Not liberty but a new celebration of the individual soul links Byron's *Childe Harold's Pilgrimage* and Wordsworth's *Prelude*. Different as the souls are, they are similar in being, for the first time, central

subjects of long poems. That Romantic self has a new power, visionary Imagination, not the wayward and deluding imagination of
Shakespeare and Swift, but a new power that links the individual
with divine truth. The barest list of apparently nonpolitical subjects
goes on and on: pure, wordless joy in "The Idiot Boy" and "To a
Skylark"; the perceptions of children in *The Lyrical Ballads* and *The
Songs of Innocence and Experience*; morbid sexuality in "Manfred"
and "Christabel"; sympathy for mad people in "The Thorn" and
"Julian and Maddalo"; fascination with the Middle Ages in "The
Eve of Saint Agnes" and "The Ancient Mariner." And the forms of
the poetry are different—more richly visual, more colloquial, less
finished, more fragmentary, more mythic, more musical.

Yet, still, all this richness leads back to political liberty. Morbid
sexuality, colloquial language, even the lost intensity of the Middle
Ages all subtly serve the purpose of redefining human nature in
Romantic poetry; the multiplicity of subjects contributes to the
definition of a new Romantic person, someone different from the
person for whom Rousseau and Paine had sought the political liberty
of the eighteenth century. As a whole, Romantic poetry implicitly
demands a subtler, more complicated form of political liberty that
frees the spirit and the heart as well as the mind and the body. What
makes the Romantic redefinition of human being unique and politically liberating is that it is radically egalitarian. Because we have all
experienced the perceptions of childhood and can all see nature with
an inward eye, we can all attain a spiritual *level*. The Romantics
retain the radical inheritance of the Enlightenment—Voltaire and
Rousseau, Jefferson and Paine—and they make it new.

The French Revolution forced them to make it new. The revolution by which the French tried to put the ideas of the Enlightenment
into action was first a joyful inspiration and then a source of horror in
England. The Romantic poets had to make the radical ideas of the
Enlightenment new, test them, recast them, because those ideas had
failed in experience. They had to renew in poetry what had failed in
politics, just as Milton had done 150 years before. That they followed
Milton in withdrawing from politics and making revolution personal, individual, and spiritual is another commonplace; it is, however, not entirely true. The political withdrawal, particularly that of
Wordsworth and Coleridge, does not negate the continuing spiritual

power of what they thought in their youth, the hope they found on this earth, this side of the grave. And in the strongest poems of the young Romantic poets, they made poetry a power that could change the world.

Rewriting the French Revolution was not enough. For with the same cast of characters it would always be a tragedy, or worse. The poets had to re-invent the characters—the natural man, the oppressive enemy—and redefine the ultimate goal of liberty. The Romantic poets could agree that the people of England were in chains, and they could agree that the poet had to bless and free them. But the nature of the chains, the nature of the men, the nature of the poet's liberating voice, and the nature of liberty itself—these questions separate the poets whom the idea of liberty brings together. The answers that have most influenced us belong to Shelley and to Wordsworth. It is Wordsworth's radicalism that survived best in the nineteenth-century novel; it is Shelley's that has survived and triumphed in the feminism of the twentieth century. Though Blake has assumed great importance in the twentieth century, he was so little known in the nineteenth that hardly any subsequent literature can be said to show his influence. And the others—Keats barely began to write moral poetry in "The Fall of Hyperion" before he died; Coleridge turned most quickly and resolutely from politics and Christian philosophy; and Byron at his most radical is least Romantic, closest to the rational politics of the Enlightenment.

Wordsworth and Shelley are the two most important voices of Romantic radicalism because they are the two poets who most consciously analyze the French Revolution. They preserve the principle of liberty but give liberty new roots, in the hope that they could nurture a tree without poison fruit. Though the influence of these two on later thought leads in different directions, they come close to agreeing in their vision of the French Revolution: as the product of mind without love, a hope for the future wrongly cut off from the past, the work of men without women.

In retaining their hope for a better revolution in England, both had to take their stand against their increasingly reactionary countrymen. As a nation the English were tempted to use the wrongs of the revolution in France to condemn liberty at home, from the Combination Acts of the late 1790s to the Peterloo massacre of workers in

1819. Wordsworth took his stand in *The Prelude* (which he wrote and read to friends early in the century, though he did not publish it till 1850):

> When a taunt
> Was taken up by scoffers in their pride,
> Saying, "Behold the harvest that we reap
> From popular government and equality,"
> I clearly saw that neither these nor aught
> Of wild belief engrafted on their names
> By false philosophy had caused the woe,
> But a terrific reservoir of guilt
> And ignorance filled up from age to age
> That could no longer hold its loathesome charge,
> But burst and spread in deluge through the land.
>   (Bk. 10, lines 470–80)

Shelley makes the same point in *Prometheus Unbound*, when the Furies try to tempt Prometheus into cynicism by reminding him of what has happened to the latest manifestation of the revolutionary spirit he embodies:

> See a disenchanted nation
> Springs like day from desolation;
> To Truth its state is dedicate,
> And Freedom leads it forth, her mate;
> A legioned band of linked brothers
> Whom Love calls children—
>   'Tis another's:
>
> See how kindred murder kin:
> 'Tis the vintage-time for death and sin:
> Blood, like new wine, bubbles within:
>   Till Despair smothers
> The struggling world, which slaves and tyrants win.
>   (Act 1, lines 567–77)

This is the voice of tyranny; the answer Prometheus finally comes to is that the imperfect embodiment of revolutionary liberty does not negate the goodness of the unembodied impulse. The problem for both Wordsworth and Shelley is to separate the idea of liberty from what had made it go wrong in France; they turn their rage on neither liberty nor France but on ignorance, guilt, and the habit of tyranny, the ancient evils that pervert the impulses of goodness. In their angry sonnets Wordsworth and Shelley sound more similar than they do in any of their other poetry:

London, 1802

Milton! thou should'st be living at this hour:
England hath need of thee: she is a fen
Of stagnant waters: altar, sword, and pen,
Fireside, the heroic wealth of hall and bower,
Have forfeited their ancient English dower
Of inward happiness. We are selfish men;
Oh! raise us up, return to us again;
And give us manners, virtue, freedom, power.
Thy soul was like a Star, and dwelt apart:
Thou hadst a voice whose sound was like the sea:
Pure as the naked heavens, majestic, free,
So didst thou travel on life's common way,
In cheerful godliness; and yet thy heart
The lowliest duties on herself did lay.

England in 1819

An old, mad, blind, despised, and dying king—
Princes, the dregs of their dull race, who flow
Through public scorn,—mud from a muddy spring,—
Rulers who neither see, nor feel, nor know,
But leech-like to their fainting country cling,
Till they drop, blind in blood, without a blow,—
A people starved and stabbed in the untilled field,—
An army, which liberticide and prey
Makes as a two-edged sword to all who wield,—
Golden and sanguine laws which tempt and slay;
Religion Christless, Godless—a book sealed;
A Senate,—Time's worst statute unrepealed,—
Are graves, from which a glorious Phantom may
Burst, to illumine our tempestuous day.

England is in chains, the chains of spiritual decay, economic injustice, political corruption. But in the last lines of the sonnets Wordsworth and Shelley part company and declare their beliefs in utterly different kinds of hope. Wordsworth's lowly duties and Shelley's glorious phantom lead to two distinct traditions of Romantic radicalism.

Shelley's mysterious phantom, part of the realm of spirit in which the self-proclaimed atheist believes, is not unreal; it demands from the reader a whole new conception of reality, as Blake's epics do. When Shelley wrote his furious sonnet on the state of England in 1819 he was himself nowhere near his home; he had long since begun the life of a wandering traveler in Europe. Physically removed from the land he felt free to castigate, he also felt free to put his faith in a metaphysical realm beyond the earth and beyond known history. Liberty will burst out of history, out of earthly decay and wrong; it will bring a world of light that will lift humanity beyond the bonds of matter. His ancient enemies transcend historical and economic particularities in most poems. They are mental states: jealousy, vengefulness, the constricting bonds of traditional marriage. He is a true follower of his second father-in-law, William Godwin, who also saw marriage as a destructive impediment to the joyful and free development of the precious individual soul. In "Epipsychidion" (1821) Shelley puts these poetic and political cards on the table:

> I never was attached to that great sect,
> Whose doctrine is, that each one should select
> Out of the crowd a mistress or a friend,
> And all the rest, though fair and wise, commend
> To cold oblivion, though it is in the code
> Of modern morals, and the beaten road
> Which those poor slaves with weary footsteps tread,
> Who travel to their home among the dead
> By the broad highway of the world, and so,
> With one chained friend, perhaps a jealous foe,
> The dreariest and the longest journey go.
>
> True Love in this differs from gold and clay,
> That to divide is not to take away.
> Love is like understanding, that grows bright,
> Gazing on many truths; 'tis like thy light,
> Imagination! which from earth and sky,
> And from the depths of human fantasy,
> As from a thousand prisms and mirrors, fills
> The Universe with glorious beams, and kills
> Error, the worm, with many a sun-like arrow
> Of its reverberated lightning. Narrow
> The heart that loves, the brain that contemplates,
> The life that wears, the spirit that creates
> One object, and one form, and builds thereby
> A sepulchre for its eternity.
>
> (Lines 149–73)

Here, as in the more graceful poems such as "To a Skylark" and "The Witch of Atlas," the key words are *light, love, imagination*; the poem invites us to contemplate sex as part of a larger joy, a spirit of play, a life without bonds. As an ideal it is a form of utopian politics, but a form of politics that avoids material questions.

Even as sexual politics the utopian liberation of "Epipsychidion" is self-revealingly crude. It is a man's theoretical plea for the rightness of exactly what Shelley and many other men have practiced—self-indulgent promiscuity. The consequences of this philosophy were dire for the women Shelley chose as lovers and wives; nevertheless the ingredients of his Romantic radicalism have been transmuted and adopted by women writers in both the nineteenth and twentieth centuries. And though Shelley himself always maintained a connection between the liberation of the soul for varied joys and the philosophical anarchism that would spell an end to political tyranny, the connection exists so entirely in the world of spirit, so little in the world of matter, that it has proved easy for women writers to break. Philosophical anarchism is distinctly on the wane; the cult of the liberated self is culturally dominant.

The attack on the constricting bonds of marriage and the belief that the heart and brain and spirit should seek the greatest possible variety of pleasures are cornerstones of today's feminism. These beliefs have had no power to oppose an increasingly strong capitalist economy; rather they have become an essential part of that economy. The separation of families has been a source of new, movable, expendable laborers, and the cult of the individual has fueled the enormous economy of consumerism. The liberation of the individual self for fulfillments, discoveries, pleasures, and joys, and the definition of oppression as mental and emotional constraints—jealousy, self-inflicted tyranny, repression, fear: this combination existing at the heart of Shelley's Romantic radicalism remains basically unchanged in later feminist writers. The goodness of a free self for women and the badness of "patriarchal" oppression are new modern bottles for Shelley's old wine. And the power of the state—Shelley's declared enemy—has not merely proved untouched by these ideas. It has thrived upon them.

Wordsworth hardly looks like a revolutionary. He and Coleridge both gave up their radicalism as they grew older; but the radicalism of

Wordsworth's early poetry was not negated. It has rarely been taken seriously by literary critics; recently it has been denied altogether. Most literary critics, men and women alike, have assumed that Marx's disparagement of "the idiocy of rural life" was right. The possibility that Wordsworth could be both rural and radical has not occurred to them.

The Lyrical Ballads, Wordsworth's first consciously radical volume, was a response to wrongs in England more economic than political. These poems are not responses to laws, governments, wars; they go deeper, to the changes that were happening at the bottom of English culture. E. P. Thompson describes the social situation of late eighteenth- and early nineteenth-century England:

> Thus working people were forced into political and social *apartheid* during the Wars (which, incidentally, they also had to fight.) It is true that this was not altogether new. What was new was that it was coincident with a French Revolution: with growing self-consciousness and wider aspirations (for the "liberty tree" had been planted from the Thames to the Tyne); with a rise in population, in which the sheer sense of numbers, in London and in the industrial districts, became more impressive from year to year (and as numbers grew, so deference to master, magistrate, or parson was likely to lessen): and with more intensive or more transparent forms of economic exploitation. More intensive in agriculture and in the old domestic industries; more transparent in the new factories and perhaps in mining. In agriculture the years between 1760 and 1820 are the years of wholesale enclosure, in which, in village after village, common rights are lost, and the landless and—in the south—pauperised labourer is left to support the tenant-farmer, the landowner, and the tithes of the Church. In the domestic industries, from 1800 onwards, the tendency is widespread for small masters to give way to larger employers (whether manufacturers or middlemen) and for the majority of weavers, stockingers, or nail-makers to become wage-earning outworkers with more or less precarious employment.[2]

These threatened, dispossessed people are Wordsworth's subjects in *The Lyrical Ballads.*

Ballads and sentimental poems about vagrants and madwomen and other rural victims had already become part of English popular literature when Wordsworth wrote *The Lyrical Ballads.* His originality and his radicalism inhere in the way he addresses his rural subjects as a speaking poet, and in the response he expects from his readers—who are not all rural people. His rural subjects are not pathetic cases for the rich to weep over; they are resilient, imaginative, sometimes joyful, sometimes mysterious, human beings who may be better than we are. He extends a hand of equality, and he asks his readers—which includes us—to question their own assumptions about how and where to live a good life in an advanced and civilized country. He asks us to consider abandoning our stake in what is called progress, if that progress will mean the destruction of these people. He even asks whether we might not join them. And that would truly be a revolution. If a few people move to the country to hide, that is an escape. If a few induce a great many to abandon their places in the urban centers of economic power and to take their stand in a different economic order—that is a revolution.

The Lyrical Ballads is a radical volume, in spite of some poetic precedents for the subjects, in the lucid simplicity and colloquialism of language and form and in the intimacy and equality between the poet and the poetic subject, and the reader. Of all the poems, perhaps the most maligned, both in the nineteenth century and today, is "The Idiot Boy"; it can, in fact, reveal the poetic courage of Wordsworth's volume. This particular idiot boy and this particular poverty-stricken mother are anything but the objects of the poet's pity. They are living mysteries, whose emotions the poet can only guess at; they are fully human, perhaps more human than the reader, because they live in a fellowship of joy.

> And Johnny burrs, and laughs aloud;
> Whether in cunning or in joy
> I cannot tell; but while he laughs,
> Betty a drunken pleasure quaffs
> To hear again her Idiot Boy.
>
> And now she's at the Pony's tail,
> And now is at the Pony's head,—
> On that side now, and now on this;
> And almost stifled with her bliss,
> And few sad tears does Betty shed.
>
> She kisses o'er and o'er again
> Him whom she loves, her Idiot Boy;
> She's happy here, is happy there,
> She is uneasy every where;
> Her limbs are all alive with joy.
>
> She pats the Pony, where or when
> She knows not, happy Betty Foy!
> The little Pony glad may be,
> But he is milder far than she,
> You hardly can perceive his joy.
>
> (Lines 377–97)

Idiot, mother, pony—and at the end their once-bedridden friend Susan Gale, who has recovered in the effort to find the lost boy—meet the poet and the reader on a new common ground. The common ground here is not Paine's common sense or Rousseau's instincts of self-preservation and pity but love and joy. If a too-sophisticated reader rejects this equality, these characters, this balladlike form, the poet is not to blame. Wordsworth has anticipated Whitman's injunction that the artist, in the service of liberty, should "stand up for the stupid and crazy" (preface to the 1855 *Leaves of Grass.*)

The walking, observing, speaking poet tries to comprehend another hidden, mysterious mind in "We Are Seven," another mind that no earlier poet had taken seriously. He violates the reader's expectation in the very first line:"—A Simple Child." The absence of the expected first feet—"One day I saw a simple child"—transforms fact into vision, apparition. And although we rationally agree with the poet as he tries to argue the child into admitting that if two of her siblings are dead, then she is only one of five, Wordsworth lets us hear her words last:

> "But they are dead; those two are dead!
> Their spirits are in heaven!"
> 'T was throwing words away; for still
> The little Maid would have her will,
> And said, "Nay, we are seven!"
> (Lines 65–69)

She may not win the argument, but she wins the poem, and us; why shouldn't we too begin to break down the boundaries between rationality and memory, adulthood and childhood, life and death, earth and heaven? And shouldn't we begin to wonder whether a city child, whose dead brother and sister were in a cemetery instead of graves outside their home, would feel the same way?

Another topic of sentimental-Gothic ballads, the madwoman, is also transformed radically in "The Thorn." Here too the speaker, the poet, is baffled by the country man he meets. He learns, but not what he and we expected him to.

XIX

> "But what's the Thorn? And what the pond?
> And what the hill of moss to her?
> And what the creeping breeze that comes
> The little pond to stir?"

"I cannot tell; but some will say
She hanged her baby on the tree;
Some say she drowned it in the pond,
Which is a little step beyond:
But all and each agree,
The little Babe was buried there,
Beneath that hill of moss so fair.

XXI

"And some had sworn an oath that she
Should be to public justice brought
And for the little infant's bones
With spades they would have sought.
But instantly the hill of moss
Before their eyes began to stir!
And, for full fifty yards around,
The grass—it shook upon the ground!
Yet all do still aver
The little Babe lies buried there,
Beneath that hill of moss so fair.
(Lines 199–209, 221–31)

The country speaker who tells the story of Martha Ray, her lover, her child, her continuing madness does not *know* the inquisitive poet; the poet, for all he knows, may try once again to call in the law, to dig up the grave, to investigate a possible murder. But the poet discovers he would have no luck. He discovers that what might be called superstitious imagination among Martha's neighbors has protected her in the past and will go on protecting her from the authority of the state. More interesting than the archetypically Wordsworthian land-scape or the too common story of desertion, pregnancy, madness, infanticide is the mind of the speaking country man. He has his wily ways of telling and evading. He too is standing up for the crazy, the crazy neighbor woman Martha Ray. Even if she has killed, she is not going to kill again, and this country community can take care of its own.

Wordsworth's preface to the second edition of *The Lyrical Ballads* emphasizes the human value of these characters, not their value as picturesque poetic subjects:

Humble and rustic life was generally chosen, because in that condition the essential passions of the heart find a better soil in which they can attain their maturity, are less under restraint, and speak a plainer and more emphatic language; because in that condition of life our elementary feelings co-exist in a state of greater simplicity, and, consequently, may be more accurately contemplated and more forcibly communicated; because the manners of rural life germinate from those elementary feelings, and from the necessary character of rural occupations, are more easily comprehended, and are more durable; and, lastly, because in that condition the passions of men are incorporated with the beautiful and permanent forms of nature.

The poet has chosen these people as poetic subjects because their minds are good and because they are in danger. Men are leaving the country for the city, leaving the place where Wordsworth believes they can be their truest human selves:

> A sense of false modesty shall not prevent me from asserting that the Reader's attention is pointed to this mark of distinction, far less for the sake of these particular Poems than from the general importance of the subject. The subject is indeed important! For the human mind is capable of being excited without the application of gross and violent stimulants; and he must have a very faint perception of its beauty and dignity who does not know this, and who does not further know, that one being is elevated above another in proportion as he possesses this capability. It has therefore appeared to me, that to endeavour to produce or enlarge this capability is one of the best services in which, at any period, a Writer can be engaged; but this service, excellent at all times, is especially so at the present day. For a multitude of causes, unknown to former times, are now acting with a combined force to blunt the discriminating powers of the mind, and, unfitting it for all voluntary exertion, to reduce it to a state of almost savage torpor. The most effective of these causes are the great national events which are daily taking place, and the increasing accumulation of men in cities, where the uniformity of their occupations produces a craving for extraordinary incident which the rapid communication of intelligence hourly gratifies.

The idea that peoples' minds can actually flourish in villages, on farms, among illiterate neighbors, is out of style; but perhaps these passages of Wordsworth's are still right. E. P. Thompson thinks he was:

> The Industrial Revolution, which drained the countryside of some of its industries and destroyed the balance between rural and urban life, created also in our own minds an image of rural isolation and "idiocy". The urban culture of 18th-century England was more "rural" (in its customary connotations), while the rural culture was more rich, than we often suppose. "It is a great error to suppose," Cobbett insisted, "that people are rendered stupid by remaining always in the same place." And most of the new industrial towns did not so much displace the countryside as grow *over* it. The most common industrial configuration of the earth 19th century was a commercial or manufacturing centre which served as the hub for a circle of straggling

industrial villages. As the villages became suburbs, and the farmlands were covered over with brick, so the great conurbations of the late 19th century were formed.[3]

The economic processes by which men were "accumulating in cities" and also the nobility of mind Wordsworth found—or at least believed he found—in the country are clearest in a poem he added to *The Lyrical Ballads* in their second edition, "Michael." This poem is so far from the metaphysics of Romanticism, so far from what Meyer Abrams calls the Natural Supernaturalism of poems like "Tintern Abbey" and *The Prelude*, that it is often neglected. If ever Wordsworth wrote a political poem, or a passionate poem, or a radical poem, or a dangerous poem, this is it. What it most definitely is not is a sentimental or a nostalgic poem, for it forces upon the reader the demand for continuity. The stones of the sheepfold that the shepherd Michael built in the hope that his son Luke would return, remain. The poet sees them, knows what they mean, and tells his tale for "a few natural hearts" and

> for the sake
> Of youthful Poets, who among these hills
> Will be my second self when I am gone.
> (Lines 37–39)

He is not writing for youthful poets somwehere else, but for youthful poets who will stay and try to keep the rural community alive.

Michael is most definitely not a visitor to the country, not a poet, not a sightseer. He is a shepherd and subsistence farmer, and his wife is a cottage laborer, a spinner. They are not joyful, merely dignified. And Wordsworth's poetry demands that these people be seen as what they are, not symbols, not emblems, not types. The words are as simple and solid and unambiguous as the stones of Michael's half-built sheepfold. Michael lives on his land as no poetic visitor could. He does not feel the Spirit of "Tintern Abbey" rolling through all things; he is attached, attached as only the people we call primitive are still attached to their land.

> And grossly that man errs, who should suppose
> That the green valleys, and the streams and rocks,
> Were things indifferent to the Shepherd's thoughts.
> Fields, where with cheerful spirits he had breathed
> The common air; hills, which with vigorous step
> He had so often climbed; which had impressed

So many incidents upon his mind
Of hardship, skill or courage, joy or fear;
Which, like a book, preserved the memory
Of the dumb animals, whom he had saved,
Had fed or sheltered, linking to such acts
The certainty of honourable gain;
Those fields, those hills—what could they less? had laid
Strong hold on his affections, were to him
A pleasurable feeling of blind love,
The pleasure that there is in life itself.

(Lines 62–78)

More than any single character in the first edition of *The Lyrical Ballads* Michael and his wife embody the human feelings by which Wordsworth believes people could live in the liberty of what Marx calls unalienated labor. They know how to do the things that will feed and house and clothe themselves, and in knowing and doing become both powerful and loving.

Michael certainly deserves the name of patriarch, so hateful in feminist literature, since he is the owner of the land, the head of his family. But Wordsworth reveals what an agricultural patriarchal family might be: Michael, his wife, and his son work together in a spirit of independence and equality. If Isabel cooks for Michael, he repairs the tools she needs. In this poem we have a vision of an ideal agricultural woman of pre-Victorian England; if this is oppression, Wordsworth makes the most of it. Isabel certainly works harder than the women portrayed in Victorian novels; but the work she does is worth something. She does not have the ease of a Victorian Urban matron, but neither is she trapped in silks and the constraints of sainthood.

Are these two characters a mere pastoral fantasy, an idealized memory of an age long dead? Most historians and literary critics would agree with E. J. Hobsbawm, who says flatly that "by 1750 . . . it is certain that we can no longer speak of subsistence agriculture."[4] Wordsworth himself believed, however, that he was taking an active political stand on a living issue. "Writing to C. J. Fox about 'Michael' and 'The Brothers,' included in the new Volume of 1800, he asked the liberal statesman to intervene for the purpose of conserving old ways and an old class of modest yeomen."[5] And E. P. Thompson again is closer to Wordsworth than to contemporary literary critics and historians; he too thinks that Michael's cause was not yet lost, though it was losing. The people who were gaining power at the expense of farmers like Michael recognized the revolutionary potential of his class: "The Wars saw not only the suppression of the urban reformers but also the eclipse of the humane gentry of whom Wyvill is representative. To the argument of greed a new argument was added for general enclosure—that of social discipline. The commons, 'the poor man's heritage for ages past,' on which Thomas Bewick could recall independent labourers still dwelling, who had built their cottages with their own hands, were now seen as a dangerous centre of indiscipline. Arthur Young saw them as a breeding-ground for 'barbarians,' 'nursing up a mischievous race of people'; of the Lincolnshire Fens, 'so wild a country nurses up a race of people as wild as the fen.'"[6] Wildness and barbarism are bad to the eyes of a profit-minded civilization; in the eyes of a Romantic poet, wildness and barbarism could be called solitude, strength, self-sufficiency, independence. In taking care of himself a farmer like Michael exists outside of the state and the state's economy; in existing outside, he becomes a threat. And that is why he is a hero worth saving to Wordsworth the radical poet.

One of the few literary critics who takes seriously the experience Wordsworth portrays in "Michael" is Raymond Williams; he understands both attachment to the land and the economic necessity that drives people away from their homes.

I know these feelings at once, from my own experience. The only landscape I ever see, in dreams, is the Black Mountain village in which I was born. When I go back to that country I feel a recovery of a particular kind of life; which appears, at times, as an inescapable identity, a more positive connection than I have known elsewhere. Many other men feel this, of their own native places, and the strength of the idea of settlement, old and new, is then positive and unquestioned. But the problem has always been, for most people, how to go on living where they are. I know this also personally: not only because I had to move out for an education and to go on with a particular kind of work but because the whole region in which I was born has been steadily and terribly losing its people, who can no longer make a living there.[7]

"Michael" is the first great poem of protest in the nineteenth century against the economic forces driving people out of rural England, driving them away from the attachment to their homes that gives them their truest humanity. Williams is a rare voice among literary critics; few others recognize that "Michael" might not only be a political poem in its own time, but might retain its revolutionary potential even for us. The writers of literary criticism and feminist theory have virtually banished from serious consideration the kind of life people like Michael and Isabel live, and the kind of labor they do.

Yet in other books—and even in an occasional film or television show—not addressed specifically to students or feminists we can find living evidence that neither the men like Michael nor the women like Isabel have yet perished from the earth. For example, in Akenfield Ronald Blythe found tough, resilient, independent rural working women in the late 1960s, women who are more like Wordsworth's Isabel than like the ideal women of any contemporary feminist theory. Blythe describes a seventy-nine-year-old nurse living in an old farmstead: "She is unsentimental yet at the same time un-matter of fact: one instinctively realizes that a great part of her genius or triumphant personality—call it what one will—lies in her simple belief that each individual is different and that so much difference as a community of 300 souls is likely to display in a working life of forty years, such as she has experienced, must dispel most of the convenient conclusions."[8] Independent, self-sufficient rural women wander in and out of the reminiscences of James Herriot too: "Two maiden ladies farmed a few acres just outside Dollingsford village. They were objects of interest because they did most of the work themselves and in the process they lavished such affection on their livestock that they had become like domestic pets."[9] These people— men and women—have been virtually invisible to political and feminist theorists for the last two hundred years. And yet they remain, closer to Wordsworth's "Michael" than to Marx's rural idiots.

"Michael" is a warning, not a eulogy. The shepherd loses his son and his farm and leaves only a heap of stones, an unfinished sheepfold, behind. What destroys this family is the sudden need for what Michael has not got, cash. Having signed a promissory note for his brother's son, Michael has to sell his land or send his son to the city, for the life of a subsistence farmer does not produce the cash that the economy of the city needs.

> "If here he stay,
> What can be done? Where every one is poor,
> What can be gained?"
> (Lines 253–55)

The city, in this poem, is not wicked, seductive, corrupt, sinful; it is simply the location of a new economic and social life with which

Luke is spiritually unprepared to deal. Wordsworth denies us the melodrama of Luke's bad end:

> Meantime Luke began
> To slacken in his duty; and, at length,
> He in the dissolute city gave himself
> To evil courses: ignominy and shame
> Fell on him, so that he was driven at last
> To seek a hiding place beyond the seas.
>
> (Lines 442–47)

Luke is the kind of person urban economic centers need—dispossessed laborers whose disappearance does not concern their employers.

Farmers like Michael were not—and are not—dying natural deaths; they are dying, as farmers, because someone else needs what they have—the labor of their sons, or their land, or their water. To stand up for farmers like Michael is also to stand against other things—the kinds of work that need dispossessed young men like Luke, the shopping malls and factories that need land and water. Luke's transformation from land-owning subsistence farmer to expendable laborer is the tragedy of the nineteenth century in rural England: "The people were subjected simultaneously to an intensification of two intolerable forms of relationship: those of economic exploitation and of political oppression. Relations between employer and labourer were becoming both harsher and less personal; and while it is true that this increased the potential freedom of the worker, since the hired farm servant or the journeyman in domestic industry was (in Toynbee's words) 'halted half-way between the position of the serf and the position of the citizen,' this 'freedom' meant that he felt his *un*freedom more.[10]

Yet even in this poem of tragedy and protest there is a seed of economic hope. Michael is not autochthonous, no primitive man whose ties to his land could not possibly be duplicated. He has been working all his life to pay off his mortgage: the land was bought within recorded, remembered time. And land can be bought again by anyone who believed then or believes now that Wordsworth is offering us political and economic hope as well as political and economic protest. The fact that his character is so clearly part of an ideal English past does not invalidate him as a part of a radical vision of the future. Even Shelley and Rousseau looked to the pasts of Sparta, the

Roman republic, and Athens for hope; Wordsworth looks to a past that is still partly a present. Farmers like Michael, in 1800, were lost not so much in English life as in English thought; in his poem Wordsworth brings these characters—Michael, Isabel, Luke—back to the *minds* of his readers. The poem is a source of radical hope.

Defending the potential radicalism of Wordsworth's later protest against the factory system and his defense of cottage industry in *The Excursion*, Thompson writes that "the mistake, today, is to assume that paternalist feeling must be detached and condescending. It can be passionate and engaged. This current of traditionalist social radicalism, which moves from Wordsworth and Southey through to Carlyle and beyond, seems, in its origin and in its growth, to contain a dialectic by which it is continually prompting revolutionary conclusions. The starting-point of traditionalist and Jacobin was the same. 'What is a huge manufactory,' exclaimed Thelwall, 'but a common prison-house, in which a hapless multitude are sentenced to profligacy and hard labour, that an individual may rise to unwieldy opulence.'"[11] The liberty of a poem like "Michael" is not a theoretical construct, not an abstract ideal like the liberties of Rousseau or Wollstonecraft or Shelley; it is a hard, demanding, living possibility of liberty based on economic independence. To take a stand in favor of this form of liberty is not primitivism; it is not a retreat from thought and learning. Though in the years after Wordsworth wrote "Michael" the same economic forces that took labor from the country also took much culture and much learning, this terrible fact does not prove an inherent incompatibility between culture and rural life. The biblical cadences of Michael's speech are movingly echoed in even the angriest of the semiliterate documents Thompson quotes, remnants of the minds of the now-disparaged rural laborers. "You do as you like, you rob the poor of their Commons right, plough the grass up that God send to grow, that a poor man may feed a Cow, Pig, Horse, nor Ass. . . . What we have done now is Soar against our Will but your hart is so hard as the hart of Pharo."[12]

Rural voices keep returning in the nineteenth-century novel, bearing radical messages that have been too little heard and too little heeded by twentieth-century readers. The radicalism later writers inherit from Shelley has been much easier for us to recognize and call radicalism, since it takes the forms of individual self-development, quests for pleasure, boundless personal aspirations, rebellion against domestic oppression. The radicalism rooted in the earth and in an agricultural economy is out of fashion now, but it had a vigorous life in the nineteenth-century novel and gave birth to an astonishing collection of heroic female characters. These characters embody a varied and changing vision of radical hope, but the change always contains a return to the possibility of an economic life that subverts the destructive powers of the capitalistic state.

The development of the economy in nineteenth-century England, and the effects on women and artisans, small farmers and folklore, children and domestic animals is not unknown, though it is conspicuous by its absence in too much "women's" scholarship. The economic and social history of nineteenth-century England is the subject of E. P. Thompson's monumental *Making of the English Working Class*; it is here that we can find the truest and broadest context for both the hopes and the sufferings of women in the nineteenth century. This is the genuine history of Romantic radicalism in England, the history of a battle with nameable heroes and nameable enemies, not a history of vague yearnings and the ineffable enemy of "patriarchy." It is the history of degradation of which women are an essential part. "Over the period 1790–1840 there was a slight improvement in average material standards. Over the same period there was intensified exploitation, greater insecurity, and increasing human misery. By 1840 most people were 'better off' than their forerunners had been fifty years before, but they had suffered and continued to suffer this slight improvement as a catastrophic experience."[13]

Romantic radicalism remained alive in all who fought for the poor against the rich during this national catastrophic experience. This larger history of the radical impulse of Romanticism is reflected in the nineteenth-century novel. It is reflected in many ways: both narrators and created characters can echo the feelings and ideas of Romantic radicalism. Some authors applaud and some decry but none entirely escape. No novel is the equivalent of a poem or a political statement, but in the nineteenth century the three are often closer than in either the eighteenth or the twentieth centuries. They are closer because the entire nineteenth century was colored with the light of Romanticism, in the most dreamy prose of Pater, in the most urgent demands of the Luddites.

The influence of Romantic radicalism in the novel is not random.

It has its own history, not as an exact reflection of events in the English and American world, but as a critical counterpoint to those events.[14] In the first half of the century, as England slid into an increasingly conservative reaction to the French Revolution, and as big business became an increasing threat to Jefferson's hopes for America, four novelists remained entranced by the radical hopes of Romanticism and specifically offered these hopes to women. They were Jane Austen, Charlotte and Emily Brontë, and Nathaniel Hawthorne. What separates these four from all later nineteenth-century novelists is the freedom and fervor of their Romantic hopes. They combined the radicalism of resistance to a new and destructive economy with far-flung hopes that men and women might find new power and new joy in the world. They move between the agricultural radicalism of Wordsworth and the more theoretical, spiritual, sexual radicalism of Shelley; in these novels no road seems closed. A bright new world for women lies before us. These four writers keep the many-sided hopes of Romanticism alive in their fiction, making radicalism persuasive to their reluctant English and American audiences.

Austen, Emily Brontë, and Hawthorne anchor their dream of freedom for women in a larger vision of economic justice for the people who were being squeezed by the growing power of industrial capitalism. Charlotte Brontë detached extravagant, radical hopes for women from the economic struggle, yet it is her vision that has influenced later women writers in the nineteenth and twentieth centuries; the far-reaching radicalism of the others has left no literary or political descendants.

The second stage in the history of Romantic radicalism in the novel is the fiction of reaction. The reaction to Romantic radicalism centers in Thackeray, Dickens, and Eliot, the three preeminent figures in Victorian fiction. It actually begins, however, in Mary Shelley's *Frankenstein*, the first nineteenth-century novel to assert that women and Romantic radicalism were eternal enemies. Shelley's implacably angry stand against all Romantic hopes for change is matched in absoluteness only by another horror novel, Stoker's *Dracula*, which closes this episode of literary history. In the three central figures the opposition between women and Romantic radicalism is by no means simple and absolute; it is, rather, subtle and complicated. Dickens and Thackeray offer their readers a new vision of woman as the Angel in the House, the apparent antithesis of all that is radical or Romantic. And yet even their saintly heroines are the step-daughters of Romanticism's radical inclusion of new kinds of sensibility among the human possibilities. Their heroines, created by men for adoption by women, still have secret affinities with the movement to which they are opposed. Eliot, on the other hand, brandishes many of the words of Romanticism in the name of the spiritual progress of the world; yet she too is part of the Victorian reaction, since she separates that progress from women in a most resolute way.

These five writers are connected by more than the fact that they deny women Romantic radicalism. They are connected also by their detachment from the economic and spiritual life of agricultural England. Mary Shelley spins her tale in a fictional world detached from any earthly economy; Dickens, Thackeray, and Stoker choose the city, the new home of economic power in England, as the place where fictions should be located. Even Eliot, despite the self-consciously sentimental pastoralism of her early novels, in the end rejects rural life, rural work, and hope for women all together, in *Middlemarch* sweepingly and viciously. From Eliot, as from Charlotte Brontë, women have inherited the idea that they are best kept apart from rural work. The superficial radicalism of Eloit's narrative voice is betrayed by her fictional vision; she is one of the originators of the false feminism of the present, which declines involvement in large-scale struggles for economic justice.

Romantic radicalism, however, comes back to life once more in the nineteenth-century novel. Trollope, contemporary of Dickens and Eliot, and then Hardy and Forster recapture not the endless hopes of the first generation of Romantic novelists but the determined resistance that those novelists inherited from Wordsworth. Trollope, Hardy, and Forster all reverse the choices of the reactionary novelists: instead of preferring the city to the country and denying radical hopes to women, they declare that the economic life of agricultural England should be saved, and that a primary reason why is that it has allowed, and could still allow, women to be their freest and best selves. Through the social and economic worlds in which their fictions exist and also through their extraordinary heroines they defy Victorian conformity, Victorian repression, Victorian economic "progress." They defy the power of the people who were taking over England for the sake of the poor, for the sake of women, for the sake of the land and the people who live on it. They return to the Romantic radicalism of Wordsworth, the radicalism of resistance. And they offer women a truly radical hope for free and strong lives connected to a larger vision of economic justice.

The resisting, rural radicalism of these novelists is still valid as a true form of political struggle. In his moving memoir *The Horse of Pride: Life in a Breton Village* Pierre Jakez-Hèlias declares the radical value of folklore in a way that illuminates the continuing radical value of these rural novelists. "Actually, most of our contemporaries are essentially folkloric individuals. By that I mean: they are unable to bring themselves to give up certain ways of life that correspond to their deepest inclinations. I also mean that folklore is timeless. And finally, I mean that it is a defensive reaction against a future which, despite all of its promises, cannot help but trouble the sons of man. I believe that folklore has become a process of continual protest, which it never was in the past."[15] A process of continual protest. That is exactly what the rural novels of the nineteenth century are, and, in making women part of that protest they have given us a heritage we have been wrong to refuse.

2. Jane Austen: Loving and Leaving

Jane Austen's work has not been a source for radicals or for feminists. Her famous families in their country villages seem so tame, so decorous, so much emblems of the quiet and polite life of the privileged classes that would-be radical women from Charlotte Brontë to Sandra Gilbert have called her an enemy. She, the common story goes, did not write about the Napoleonic Wars; she lived through the same crises that stirred the Romantic poets to such passion and nevertheless kept her serene style, her cool composure, her unruffled view of the world. But the common story is wrong. Jane Austen lived through both the time of revolutionary hopes that the Romantic poets shared and the time of repression that embittered the poets; she explored both hopes and repression, not in the surfaces of her novels but in their underlying assumptions.

Austen perfected her form in her early novels, *Northanger Abbey, Sense and Sensibility, Pride and Prejudice.* In her last three, *Mansfield Park, Emma,* and *Persuasion,* she explored three dominant philosophical views of her time and invented three different types of heroines through whom she could offer hope to women. A feminist of the Charlotte Brontë type she is not, but a radical she is, in both *Emma* and *Persuasion.* She does not reflect historical change in any simple way; she makes ideas her own, traveling a path that defies anything that could be called the national temper. She makes the repressive ideas of the postrevolutionary years intellectually plausible in *Mansfield Park*, celebrates the threatened life of agricultural England in *Emma*, and ends with the single soul in *Persuasion*. As she says of her own last heroine, "she learned romance as she grew older" (*Persuasion*, vol. 1, chap. 4).

The battles of Austen's first novels are against theories of literature; the battles of her last are for theories of life. Even as an adolescent, writing burlesques, Austen showed she knew nonsense when she read it; she went after the excesses of Gothic and sentimental fiction—improbable coincidences, love at first sight, instant intimacy, black-hearted villainy. Her single greatest target is the cult of Sensibility, an idea that degenerated from its delicate embodiment in Lawrence Sterne's *Sentimental Journey* into a belief that the more violent, irrational, and overpowering an emotion was, the better, and that emotions and intuitions alone could provide adequate insight into character and adequate basis for action. In her early burlesques, in her Gothic parody *Northanger Abbey*, and in her first true novel, *Sense and Sensibility*, Austen issues a firm warning to all the Marianne Dashwoods of the world who try to live by untrammeled emotion.

Austen wins her literary battle against sentimentality in *Pride and Prejudice*, where she recaptures much of the faith of the eighteenth century of Johnson and Fielding. The fools and the knaves all survive, controlled, but just barely, by the intelligence, warmth, and moral exertions of the other characters. The fools and knaves— Wickham, Mr. Collins, Mrs. Bennet, Lydia—do not represent a historically new threat; nor do the intelligent and good characters represent radically new hope. When Elizabeth Bennet rebukes her unwelcome suitor, Mr. Collins, with "Do not consider me now as an elegant female intending to plague you, but as a rational creature speaking truth from her heart" (chap. 19) she is not claiming anything new for women. She is merely saying that she has the same mental faculties as a man and that reason is the highest one. This is still the reason of Pope and Johnson, not the reason of Jefferson and Paine. It can contain and control folly and knavery, but it is not about to turn the world upside down. The world *is* nearly turned upside down in *Mansfield Park*, begun in 1811, fourteen years after *Pride and Prejudice* was finished, in 1797. The French Revolution had become the Reign of Terror; the English, afraid of both a French invasion and internal revolution, had passed repressive legislation; the country was in the grip of a new kind of political fear. That new fear permeates *Mansfield Park*. Its world is no longer balanced between the wise and good and the foolish and knavish; reason can no longer be trusted to exert its power. The subtly shifting classes reflected in the fictional world of *Pride and Prejudice* have settled here into a new hostility. E. P. Thompson describes the new England of the early nineteenth century: "In the decades after 1795 there was a profound alienation between classes in Britain, and working people were thrust into a state of *apartheid* whose effects—in the niceties of social and educational discrimination—can be felt to this day."[1]

The new, mobile, city-bred middle classes threaten to corrupt England in *Mansfield Park*, more than the working class does. No worker here resembles Darcy's old housekeeper in *Pride and Prejudice*, who can speak so eloquently to Elizabeth about her master's character. The servants are silent, banished from the fiction, a perpetual problem in the Price household at Portsmouth. In this fictional world there is no accommodation among classes; what the good characters in the book desire is simply to preserve the upper class, the family of Sir Thomas Bertram at Mansfield Park. This fictional drive to preserve one class at the expense of the others creates a tone and texture unique in Austen's fiction. *Mansfield Park* truly belongs to the period of English repression; its grim glory is that Austen makes a philosophically coherent, fictionally persuasive case for a fearful, repressive view of the world.

Mansfield Park is a story of contagious evil, not mere folly or wrong. In a climactic moment near the end, the heroine, Fanny Price, exclaims, "It was too horrible a confusion of guilt, too gross a complication of evil, for human nature, not in a state of utter barbarism, to be capable of!" (vol. 3, chap. 16). Such language is not what a reader of Austen's other fiction would expect; nothing in her earlier novels—or in most other English novels—is ever that bad. Yet Austen is serious. Her heroine's horror is justified. The plot and characters of *Mansfield Park* are not radically different from those of other novels, but as a narrator Austen makes sure that these characters are made of elements different from those we expect. It is a new fictional world, one that demands a new kind of heroine.

Rot is in the air. For the first and only time in her fiction, Austen tells us that the tendency of the world is to decay. There is the filth of poverty-stricken Portsmouth, where "the tea-board [was] never thoroughly cleaned, the cups and saucers wiped in streaks, the milk a mixture of motes floating in thin blue, and the ·bread and butter growing every minute more greasy than even Rebecca's hands had first produced it" (vol. 3, chap. 15); there is the turkey of the wealthy Mansfield parsonage that "cook insists being dressed to-morrow" (vol. 2, chap. 4) since it is about to go bad.

The characters too are all about to go bad. In *Mansfield Park* Austen has carefully created a decaying social world inhabited by human beings whose innate characteristics leave them vulnerable to corruption and grant them almost no power to regenerate themselves. It is a world that demands the strange and unpopular heroine, Fanny Price, to guard it with her rigid Christian principles. In spite of her pale and tremulous personality, she is a true heroine, a stronger soul than any female character in Austen's earlier fiction, because so much depends on her. She is not a radical heroine but a repressive one, for repression is what the world of *Mansfield Park* needs.

Austen asks us to believe that this fictional world is decaying for specific historical reasons and for reasons based in eternal qualities of human nature. Sir Thomas Bertram's departure from Mansfield Park and from his traditional position of moral authority; the education of his children; and the new ideas the Crawfords bring to the English countryside from London—these are all particular causes belonging to the beginning of the nineteenth century. The human faculties that make the characters susceptible to new and corrupting historical conditions are eternal. It is through the convincing presentation of this combination that Austen makes this fiction of repression persuasive.

Sir Thomas leaves Mansfield Park to oversee his investments in Antigua: he is no longer making agriculture the center of his economic life. E. J. Hobsbawm describes England's new connection with the third world in the early years of the nineteenth century: "overseas the creation of economic systems for producing such goods [new items like sugar for trade] (such as, for example, slave operated plantations) and the conquest of colonies designed to serve the economic advantage of their European owners."[2] Expansion and empire are taking the guardians of England away from their post.

Sir Thomas has also neglected his traditional duty in the education of his children, particularly of his daughters. He has given his daughters, Maria and Julia, over to the care of his sister-in-law, their

Aunt Norris. She adds personal cruelty to the permissive educational theories adopted by the wealthy English in the late eighteenth century. Lawrence Stone describes this new educational system: "the girls were brought up permissively at home by nurses and governesses and not taught to curb their tempers or their tongues."³ When the Bertrams bring their poor young relative, Fanny Price, into their family, Mrs. Norris adds abuse of her to indulgence of the Bertram girls; she encourages them to call her stupid and to pride themselves on their superiority to her. "Such were the counsels by which Mrs. Norris assisted to form her nieces' minds; and it is not very wonderful that with all their promising talents and early information, they should be entirely deficient in the less common acquirements of self-knowledge, generosity, and humility. In everything but disposition, they were admirably taught" (vol. 1, chap. 2). In another novel Mrs. Norris would be a comic character, the bossy female busybody; here she is a source of evil because the Bertram girls have no innate goodness. They need positive moral training because nothing in their minds or hearts resists bad influences. Austen's narrator simply tells us they should have been *trained* in Christian virtues—self-knowledge, generosity, humility; These virtues must be *acquired*, for the human character is born with a tendency to sin.

Having been spoiled from childhood, Maria and Julia degenerate further when, as marriageable young women, they meet the Crawfords. Henry and Mary Crawford, relatives of Dr. Grant, the negligent clergyman of Mansfield parsonage, represent the threat of internal corruption, the threat of external revolution that the English feared in 1811. They are not the eternal fools and knaves of eighteenth-century fiction, but a new historical element, a new class, irreligious, mercenary, and city bred. They are connected with the navy, about which Hobsbawm writes, "That very commercially-minded and middle class organization, the British Navy, . . . contributed even more directly to technological innovation and industrialization."⁴ The navy, which both fought against France and extended the British Empire, is the institution on which Sir Thomas's commercial ventures in Antigua depend. His absence from England and the Crawfords' corrupting presence at Mansfield Park are historically and economically connected.

Henry and Mary have been brought up by their uncle, an admiral, who combines the mercenary qualities of his class with open sexual immorality, "a man of vicious conduct, who chose, instead of retaining his niece [after his wife's death], to bring his mistress under his own roof" (vol. 1, chap. 4). Henry and Mary Crawford enter the secluded country community of Mansfield Park bearing all the evils of modernity; they are spoiled, selfish, extravagant, mercenary, and sexually predatory. They openly espouse the self-seeking ethics of the urban economy: Henry's moral theory is, "I never do wrong without gaining by it" (vol. 2, chap. 7); Mary's is "the true London maxim, that everything is to be got with money" (vol. 1, chap. 6). They possess the intelligence and quickness of speech that become wit in the characters of Austen's earlier fiction; but instead of laughing at folly, they laugh at marriage, sexual immorality, death, and Christianity. "Certainly, my home at my uncle's brought me acquainted with a circle of admirals. Of *Rears*, and *Vices*, I saw enough. Now, do not be suspecting me of a pun, I entreat" (vol. 1, chap. 6).

Particularly serious is Mary's mocking attack on the tradition of family prayers. "The obligation of attendance, the formality, the restraint, the length of time—altogether it is a formidable thing, and what nobody likes; and if the good people who used to kneel and gape in that galley could have foreseen that the time would ever come when men and women might lie another ten minutes in bed, when they woke with a headache without danger of reprobation, because chapel was missed, they would have jumped with joy and envy" (vol. 1, chap. 9). Mary is not an eccentric in these opinions; she bears the message of modernism, for "the general decline in religious enthusiasm in the late seventeenth and eighteenth centuries carried away with it the role of the husband and father as the religious head of the household, symbolized by the regular assembly of all members, often twice a day, to hear him lead the family in prayer and obtain his blessing."[5] And in the years between 1811 and 1814, when Austen was writing *Mansfield Park*, words like Mary's were inflammatory. England was in the middle of a religious revival, a response to both the atheism of revolutionary France and the growing religious cynicism of the population at home. In Mary Crawford, Austen makes the new religious cynicism a convincing threat, for we see how much harm she and her brother can do to people who have not been trained in religion.

Austen takes great pains in *Mansfield Park* to convince her readers that characters like Henry and Mary and their modern code are indeed dangerous, and that only a strange heroine like Fanny Price could resist them. In careful, clear, consistent detail she demonstrates the inexorable progress of the Crawfords' power, until, in a time of disaster, Fanny Price is proven right. The heart of the Crawfords' power is their inscrupulous sexuality; they lure the three Bertrams who are at home into passionate love, and into a private theatrical production of exactly the kind of play the English Evangelical movement opposed—Mrs. Inchbald's translation of Kotzebue's *Lovers' Vows*. This sentimentally radical, openly sexual play is the external emblem of the Crawfords' sexual powers.

In *Mansfield Park* sex has little to do with joy or vitality; it is a dangerous passion, a weapon in the arsenal of evil. What makes the gloomy repressive message of *Mansfield Park* persuasive is Austen's fictional rigor; we understand the steps by which the Bertrams are seduced in order that we may finally understand the sincerity of Austen's fictional experiment with the theories of political and religious repression. Henry begins his seductions with Maria, who is engaged to pathetic Mr. Rushworth, and with Julia. "Thoughtless and selfish from prosperity and bad example, he would not look beyond the present moment. The sisters, handsome, clever, and encouraging, were an amusement to his sated mind" (vol. 1, chap. 12). He particularly wants to lure them into the immoral play because "in all the riot of his gratifications it was yet an untasted pleasure" (vol. 1, chap. 13). Words such as "sated" and "riot of gratifications" are harsh indications of the corrupt nature of Crawford's sexuality; its corrupting power quickly creates both passion and jealousy. "The sisters, under such a trial as this, had not affection or principle enough to make them merciful or just, to give them honour or compassion" (vol. 1, chap. 17). Although they are intelligent, the Bertrams cannot resist unscrupulous sexuality because they have not been prepared by serious moral training; once they feel desire, their undisciplined minds and corrupt hearts degenerate.

The poison of the sexual spell continues even after Crawford leaves. Maria marries Rushworth to get "all the comfort that pride and self-revenge could give" (vol. 2, chap. 3), adding two more sins to her growing collection. When she eventually meets Crawford again and snubs him, in angry, frustrated desire, he is compelled to "exert himself to subdue so proud a display of resentment." He is, as Austen's narrator says, "entangled by his own vanity" and "went off with her at last, because he could not help it" (vol. 3, chap. 17). The point of the detailed psychological portraits in *Mansfield Park* is that once people allow the evils of the modern world to touch them, they can no longer help what they do. Help must come from authority; Sir Thomas banishes Maria and her Aunt Norris from Mansfield Park once the affair with Crawford is over because in this fictional world good characters must be protected from bad ones. Julia, who marries a fool in her panic over Maria's imminent punishment, can remain in the community, but in her too the poison of Crawford's power has produced a lasting harm.

The true horror of *Mansfield Park*, however, lies in the Crawfords' power over characters who are better than Maria and Julia. Henry Crawford chooses the challenge of "forcing" Fanny Price to love him. His social and economic eligibility so impress Sir Thomas, his wife, and even Edmund Bertram that the three are united in informing Fanny that her resistance must be evidence of a "diseased mind." Her correct moral revulsion is powerless in this decaying world.

Edmund, meanwhile, has fallen in love with Mary, in spite of his "excellent nature," his intelligence, his good education. Austen's narrator tells us cynically and emphatically that in this world love is not a trustworthy feeling; the emotions on which the cult of Sensibility was founded are exposed as foolish and frail. "A young woman, pretty, lively, with a harp as elegant as herself; and both placed near a window . . . was enough to catch any man's heart" (vol. 1, chap. 7). The hearts of young men are easy to catch, and once caught, the heart affects the mind. Edmund keeps excusing Mary's flaws until the very end, when she jokes cynically about the elopement of Henry and Maria. Even then Edmund has a hard time giving her up, for her beauty, liveliness, and sexual vitality have dulled his will to act on his moral insights. Neither the heart nor the mind can lead the will and the passions straight, once they have gone wrong, in *Mansfield Park*.

In this corruptible world, in which the representatives of the urban middle class can carry all before them, a heroine like Fanny Price is necessary. Shy, sickly, moralistic, humorless, she does not win our hearts easily. We must understand her intellectually and choose her morally, just as she understands and chooses good over evil. She is different from the angels who inhabit the houses of Victorian fiction a generation later, for her character is part of the tough, consistent intellectual fabric of *Mansfield Park.* She does not save weak and sinful men by her long-suffering, stupid sweetness; she has no power at all to affect people but gains her ineffectual moral insights from the economic and emotional poverty of her life. She is made of the same elements as her cousins; she "felt his [Crawford's] powers" when he was courting her; she is protected because "she thought as ill of him as ever." Her *thoughts* also protect her from Mary, whose mind she recognizes as "darkened yet fancying itself light." Intellectual and moral knowledge of sin, given by religious training, in turn protects Fanny.

Personality is not a value in *Mansfield Park.* Fanny is a heroine because of the principles she stands for and lives by. Categories such as *feminist* and *antifeminist* do not apply to her. In the fictional world of *Mansfield Park* men and women are equally agents and victims of evil. Fanny is the moral center of the book not because she is a woman, but because she is poor and has been cut off from the worldly pleasures that have weakened her rich relatives. Both Fanny and her sister Susan, who has remained at home in Portsmouth, have benefited morally and intellectually from hardship: "Never was there any maternal tenderness to buy her [Susan] off. The blind fondness which was for ever producing evil around her, *she* had never known" (vol. 3, chap. 9). Fanny and Susan have not been harmed, as the Bertrams have, by what Lawrence Stone describes as the new parental indulgence in England: "In some high professional and landed circles in England by the late eighteenth century, there had developed an astonishingly permissive style of child rearing. As a result, some parents were obliged to cajole their adolescent children instead of ordering them about."[6] At the end Sir Thomas recognizes that his newfangled indulgence toward his own children has been harmful; he is compelled to acknowledge "the advantages of every hardship and discipline, and the consciousness of being born to struggle and endure" (vol. 3, chap. 17). Because she has grown up assuming that she can have no share in the fashionable world of her cousins and the Crawfords, she has no motive to excuse the moral deficiencies of that world. Her example finally brings Sir Thomas to a recognition of his own responsibility for the wrongs committed by his daughters: "He feared that principle, active principle, had been wanting, that they had never been properly taught to govern their inclinations and tempers, by that sense of duty which can alone suffice. They had been instructed theoretically in their religion, but never required to bring it into daily practice" (vol. 3, chap. 17).

Fanny, though the heroine, almost fades from our sight at the end of *Mansfield Park*; she has brought her uncle and her cousin Edmund, the clergyman, back to their ancient responsibilities. The marriage of Fanny and Edmund is not a topic on which Austen spends much time, for love in *Mansfield Park* is less important than moral discipline and Christian authority. It is hard for us, as readers, to like the life of the saved remnant. The remains of the Bertram family are locked into the safe little world of the estate, where "if tenderness could be ever supposed wanting, good sense and good breeding supplied its place" (vol. 3, chap. 8). No other classes enter this world. Londoners, tradespeople, agricultural laborers, country shopkeepers are all banished. This is truly a reactionary novel; its heroine stands for the oldest and strictest of Christian values. The novel is reactionary; still, it is neither unintelligent nor unconvincing. As a moral and political argument it is tougher and tighter than anything Austen's contemporary, Burke, ever wrote. The characters operate according to a psychological and spiritual model that we may dislike but cannot absolutely disprove; if it is true that only the moral power supported by the well-trained mind can restrain the corruptible heart and sexual passions and will, then the immoral code of the commercial classes that the Crawfords bring into Mansfield Park is indeed a threat. In Fanny Price, Austen has created a heroine for counterrevolutionary England, whose strict Christian values are proved necessary by the decaying world she inhabits.

Fanny Price is as far as a heroine can be from the Romanticism and the radicalism of late nineteenth-century novels; yet the care with which Austen has drawn her and the consistency of the philosophical fabric in which she has embedded her serve to illuminate the strength and the meaning of Romantic radicalism in both *Emma* and *Persuasion*. *Mansfield Park* reveals that Austen could consider seriously the counterrevolutionary theories of England in 1814; *Emma* and *Persuasion* reveal that she could emphatically and joyfully reject them.

Emma Woodhouse and Anne Elliot, Austen's last two heroines, belong to different sides of Romantic radicalism, different visions of the social world of England, different ideas of human nature. Emma belongs to the fertile land of England; Anne must leave the land for love. It is Anne who points toward the Romantic heroines of Charlotte Brontë and George Eliot (though feminists do not acknowledge her); Emma belongs to Wordsworth. Like Shelley's West Wind, Austen can be both a destroyer and a preserver: Emma, like "Michael," is a luminous discovery of the goodness that can still be found and saved in rural England; *Persuasion* is a fictional leap away from a pathetically dying rural world into a new, free future.

If there is an earthly paradise in nineteenth-century English fiction, it is Emma's home, Highbury, a gentle village only sixteen miles from London, yet uncorrupted. It takes Emma—and us—the whole novel to learn that home is heaven; by the end the realization dawns that we have seen a world without evil, the only such world in Austen's fiction, a serious, radical vision of human goodness. Emma has to give up the false Romanticism of improbable fictions, the long-lost nobleman she imagines to be the father of her illegitimate friend Harriet Smith, and the false Romanticism of the spurious philosophy that has elevated imagination to preeminence among the mental faculties. When Emma finally relinquishes the imagination with which she has gleefully invented sexual relationships for everyone around her, she finds something much more than the reason of the eighteenth century; she discovers a world where reason is joined to the gentlest kind of love, where people can live freely on the fertile earth.

The central, unseen figure with whom Emma must come to terms is Robert Martin, one of Mr. Knightley's tenant farmers. The action of the book pushes her into accepting him as the proper husband for her friend Harriet and a good friend for her husband, Mr. Knightley. He is the goal of her moral and mental change. Robert Martin takes care of the earth in *Emma*; the heroine must learn to accept his class, and must learn that Mr. Knightley is perfectly justified when he says, "I never hear better sense from anyone than Robert Martin. He always speaks to the purpose; open, straightforward, and very well judging" (vol. 1, chap. 8). In Highbury good sense is common property, not the sole possession of the strictly disciplined rich.

Robert Martin the farmer is central to the fictional world of *Emma* as no agricultural laborer could be central in *Mansfield Park* because the earth itself is different. It is not a place ignored by aristocrats; it is not a place where everything is about to rot. Austen does not show us much of the earth as landscape, but what she does show us, during Mr. Knightley's strawberry-picking party, is very important. She writes that "The considerable slope, at nearly the foot of which the Abbey stood, gradually acquired a steeper form beyond its grounds; and at half a mile distant was a bank of considerable abruptness and grandeur, well clothed with wood; and at the bottom of this bank, favourably placed and sheltered, rose the Abbey-Mill Farm, with meadows in front, and the river making a close and handsome curve around it. It was a sweet view—sweet to the eye and the mind. English verdure, English culture, English comfort, seen under a bright sun, without being oppressive" (vol. 3, chap. 6). This English earth not only looks sweet; it tastes sweet, in the form of strawberries. Mr. Knightley is not making his money from slave labor on Antigua; he makes his money from the land of England. And *Emma* is one long feast of food shared with friends, sent as gifts to neighbors. The sweetbreads and asparagus Mr. Woodhouse is afraid to let his guests eat, the eggs and pork of Hartfield shared with the poor, the roast mutton and rice pudding prepared for Emma's nephews, the apples and strawberries of Donwell Abbey, the walnuts Robert Martin brings to Harriet, the goose Robert Martin's mother sends to Mrs. Goddard, the turkeys stolen from Mrs. Weston—all are good. None are rotten.

Hobsbawm says that all visitors to England in the eighteenth century "would immediately be struck by the greenness, tidiness, the apparent prosperity of the countryside, and by the apparent comfort of 'the peasantry.'" He quotes the French visitor who, in 1749, was "struck with the beauties of the country, the care taken to improve lands, the richness of the pastures, the numerous flocks that cover them, and the air of plenty and cleanliness that reigns in the smallest villages."[7] Though the agricultural world was threatened in 1816, when Austen published *Emma*, the richness and fertility Austen conveys in her fiction are still in the realm of the possible. The agricultural economy of *exchange* is also more than a nostalgic dream; describing the food riots in the years just before Austen wrote Emma, Thompson says, "Hence the last years of the 18th century saw a last desperate effort by the people to reinforce the older moral economy as against the economy of the free market."[8] The exchanges of food that seem so good, so easy, so natural, in *Emma* were, for radicals, a cause worth dying for.

The social world of *Emma* does not have the naturalness and ease of the agricultural world. Emma, as a heroine, must save it by learning to love the right man and to value her neighbors. *Emma*, like "Michael," is about a good world that is in danger. Danger does not predominate here, but it is present, both in an occasional narrative comment and in certain conditions of the social world—evidence of economic weakness in the village and of an encroaching, undesirable economic world, embodied in Mr. Elton and his bride.

Austen's sharpest narrative comment is about the new schools which are creating a new kind of fashionable woman: "Mrs. Goddard was the mistress of a School—not of a seminary, or an establishment, or anything which professed, in long sentences of refined nonsense, to combine liberal acquirements with elegant morality upon new principles and new systems—and where young ladies for enormous pay might be screwed out of health and into vanity—but a real, honest, old-fashioned Boarding-school, where a reasonable quantity of accomplishments were sold at a reasonable price, and where girls might be sent to be out of the way and scramble themselves into a little education, without any danger of coming back prodigies" (vol. 1, chap. 3). Austen shows us a woman of this new type when Mr. Elton brings his rich bride to Highbury. She speaks in affectedly modern slang; she brags of her accomplishments and resources for solitude, patronizes everyone, and professes a kind of fraudulent feminism: "I always stand up for women." She visits no poor; she gives and receives no food; she is part of a new world and a new economy. Her feminism is as phony as the rest of her; the only woman she really stands up for is herself. She and the women produced by new schools are threats to the true feminism of *Emma*, the feminism that is part of the existing social fabric, a feminism that Emma recognizes as "the duty of woman by woman."

The social fabric of exchange and duty is threatened not only from external invasion, but from internal weakness. Highbury is less well populated than it was when the inn with the ballroom was built; we see more old people than young in the village at the beginning. It needs new life, and one of the lessons the heroine must learn is that social change need not take the form of people like Mrs. Elton. People from the world of the city and commerce can be accommodated in

Highbury and can, in fact, enrich it. The family of John and Isabella Knightley visits frequently from London, bringing children; the commercial Coles are quickly becoming parts of the community, though Emma is too snobbish to welcome them. Classes are mobile in a healthy way. Emma's former governess, Miss Taylor, has married Mr. Weston, "a native of Highbury, and born of a respectable family, which for the last two or three generations had been rising into gentility and property" (vol. 1, chap. 2). An internal process of regeneration is at work in Highbury, a bulwark against the threatened invasion from the likes of the Eltons; the task of the heroine and the reader is to recognize and celebrate this regeneration of the old moral economy, the old social fabric of duty.

Regeneration is threatened in the course of the novel. Though it ends with three marriages and the promise of more babies to join Mrs. Weston's, all three of the love affairs have to survive the misperceptions and misunderstandings caused by Emma's misguided imagination. Blunders abound here; not evils, not sins, not corruptions, but mistakes. These mistakes are all correctible, but in order to convince us that hope survives in rural England, she must guide us, through her heroine, out of a morass of false ideas and into a radical true one. The false ideas are those of literary Romanticism—sexual intrigue, imaginations, intuitions; the true one is politically radical in 1816—the idea that human beings can govern themselves without constant guidance from authority figures in the family, the church, and the state.

Mr. Knightley is unmarried and childless, and hence has no one over whom to exert authority; Mr. Elton, the clergyman, is a newcomer and an arrogant, mercenary fool who utters not a word of Christian advice in the entire novel; Mr. Woodhouse and Mrs. Weston, once Emma's governess, are too gentle and mild to control or even influence the misguided heroine. Emma has been harmed by her freedom and youthful power and has become arrogant, self-centered, and bossy. She has separated herself from the rest of Highbury and must be reeducated into seeing the value of the humble community she disdains. Because this is Highbury, however, the heroine's need of moral improvement does not reflect badly on the people who have neglected to govern her. Mrs. Weston cannot be blamed for her gentleness, nor Mr. Woodhouse for his weakness, lack of intelligence, and querulous hypochondria. The way Austen's narrator treats Mr.

Woodhouse, who might be a blameworthy, negligent father in another novel, is a key to the moral tone of *Emma*. We must learn to share the love that his odd, elderly neighbors feel for him because the narrator essentially commands us to. She forbids us to mock or dislike him when, after he has made a sweet and courtly comment to each of his guests, she says "the kind-hearted, polite old man might then sit down and feel that he had done his duty, and made every fair lady welcome and easy" (vol. 2, chap. 16). If he is kindhearted and polite, he is worth our love; we must learn to see how his daughter can survive the harm he has done her inadvertently and to believe that her moral survival is a beacon of hope for the social world.

Even at the beginning, when Emma is rude and patronizing to almost everyone, she is unfailingly kind to her father and his women friends. She manages not only to indulge his fussy worrying about what his guests might eat at his small parties but also to feed the guests well: "Emma allowed her father to talk—but supplied her visitors in a much more satisfactory style; and on the present evening had particular pleasure in sending them away happy" (vol. 1, chap. 3). Mr. Woodhouse, Mrs. Goddard, old Mrs. Bates, and her foolishly loquacious daughter Miss Bates—these characters are all old, weak, vulnerable, the first victims when what Thompson calls the moral economy of the agricultural village is destroyed. That they are happy, well-fed, protected, and loved is the best indication that there is something worth saving in the agricultural village. Austen's Highbury is worth saving because as a community it fosters the benevolent, self-governing possibilities in human nature, possibilities in which nineteenth-century Romantic radicals believed, possibilities scorned by the reactionaries to whom Austen paid her respects in *Mansfield Park*.

To become a heroine, Emma must fully join the community of Highbury. The process exemplifies the moral and psychological theory of the book, the radical theory at work in the self-governing village. What Emma must do is grow up, and growing up is a natural process. Here, reversing the theory of *Mansfield Park*, Austen implicitly declares that growing up is a process of accepting not of rejecting sexuality and a wide variety of other human possibilities. To grow up, Emma must conquer both the social repressiveness and snobbery of the English reactionaries and the ideas about imagination held by the shallow variety of English Romantics.

The young woman who looks down on farmers, who scorns Robert Martin as a possible husband for her young illegitimate friend, who plans to teach the Coles a lesson by refusing their invitation, is more "modern" than her neighbors in Highbury. Mr. Knightley, who is more attached to the old rural economy, is far more egalitarian than his young friend. Emma's snobbery alienates her from the social fabric of the village; she is markedly alone in making fun of Miss Bates and in refusing to visit her elderly neighbors. "She had had many a hint from Mr. Knightley and some from her own heart, as to her deficiency—but none were equal to counteract the persuasion of its being very disagreeable,—a waste of time—tiresome women—and all the horror of being in danger of falling in with the second rate and third rate of Highbury, who were calling on them forever, and therefore she seldom went near them" (vol. 2, chap. 1).

Even at the beginning, however, Emma's modernity has not totally cut her off from the older life of village women. The activity that most attaches her to the village world she does not know she loves is an activity she does without consciousness—walking. She is always on foot, either alone or with one of her chosen friends. Austen's readers would know what Emma does not, that walking is itself an act of defiance, a rejection of the kind of modern womanhood Mrs. Elton wants to bring into the village. G. M. Trevelyan writes:

Moreover "ladies" were not encouraged to exercise their bodies except in dancing. . . . The lady of this earlier period was expected to keep herself in cotton wool. When Elizabeth Bennet walked three miles in muddy weather and arrived at Netherfield with weary ankles, dirty stockings and a face glowing with warmth and exercise, Mrs. Hurst and Miss Bingley 'held her in contempt for it.' Even in the hardy North, Wordsworth in 1801 wrote a poem, as its title tells us, to console and encourage 'A Young Lady, who had been reproached for taking long walks in the country'! It was all very absurd, for in less artificial classes of society, women were walking long distances to and from their work.[9]

Emma is not a working woman, but she is still a walking woman, still linked to an older village world in ways she does not know.

Emma also is unaware of the internal conflict between instinct and modern delusion which is misleading her. She is healthier than she knows, by nature; the ideas that lead her to consider herself "an imaginist" who can concoct romances for everyone around her and to believe that as a woman she is undesirable to men are both new, and both wrong. Reliance on imagination is part of the cult of Sensibility for which Austen has no use; belief that an intelligent and powerful woman is not a woman a man would want is part of the English sexual repression of the early 1800s. Emma has bought into a new and destructive set of sexual stereotypes; her mistaken ideas lead to her harmful attachment to sweet, stupid, docile, lovely Harriet Smith as the ideal woman and adoring friend. "Warmth and tenderness of heart, with an affectionate, open manner, will beat all the clearness of head in the world, for attraction. It is tenderness of heart which makes my dear father so generally beloved—which gives Isabella all her popularity! —I have it not—but I know how to prize and respect it. Harriet is my superior in all the charm and all the felicity it gives" (vol. 2, chap. 13). Emma has lost sight of the variety Highbury has itself contained in her own intelligent mother and governess, and has become imprisoned in the new ideas of reactionary England.

Repressed and deluded, she trusts her mixed up imagination. Obsessed with the sexual romance she will not let herself feel, she almost manages to make Highbury a loveless and infertile place by interfering with true sexual relationships and inventing ones that do not exist. Having prevented Harriet from marrying the farmer Robert Martin, she mistakenly encourages her in two hopeless infatuations; in imagining first herself and then Harriet to be destined for Frank Churchill, and in imagining an illicit romance between Jane Fairfax and her friend's husband, she almost manages to destroy a second engagement.

In the moral universe of another fiction, no one could do this much harm and remain unpunished. But in Highbury, a fictional world ruled by a radical theory of human goodness, nature and fertility win, and the social life of the village will continue. Because this is a world in which repressive authority figures are unnecessary, each character can, and must, save himself. Harriet, the "natural" child without many brains, still has a conscience and stands up for Robert Martin; she has a heart wise enough to recognize Mr. Knightley as the best man she knows when Emma encourages her to look above her for a lover. She has a natural wish to live, and therefore she is able to return to her first man, Robert Martin, at the end. Jane Fairfax and Frank Churchill, too, have had better instincts than anyone has known. Jane has, in fact, been in love, although people have called her cold, and Frank has been faithful, although people have suspected him of trifling with Emma's feelings. "That she was perfectly free from any tendency to being attached to me, was as much my conviction as my wish" (vol. 3. chap. 14).

The natural processes of growth and healing that govern people in Highbury are reflected most dramatically in Emma herself, for she is both most in need of change and also most essential for the survival of the rural community. She has to change to marry Mr. Knightley, and without their marriage the principal estate of each will remain childless. Mr. Knightley encourages reform by chastising Emma on several occasions, but he is only speeding a change already occurring within her. He and her own best impulses work together. He and her heart have both reproached her for neglecting the Bateses and for discouraging Harriet's friendship with the Martins; both he and her conscience have told her she avoids Jane Fairfax because she envies Jane's accomplishments. Her heart and her friend collaborate most dramatically when he reproaches her for being wittily cruel to Miss Bates at the party at Box Hill, and thus for violating Highbury's unspoken rule that women have a duty by women. "Never had she felt so agitated, mortified, grieved, at any circumstance in her life. She was most forcibly struck. The truth of his representation there was no denying. She felt it at her heart. How could she have been so brutal, so cruel to Miss Bates" (vol. 3, chap. 7).

Both her heart and her intelligence, two natural faculties which have led her too often into arrogance and cruelty, finally exert their true power and lead her to love. Having already admitted to herself that she just might consider marrying, and that Mr. Knightley is an attractive man, she is forced into realizing that she is in love with Mr. Knightley when poor Harriet confides that she thinks Mr. Knightley loves *her*. "A few minutes were sufficient for making her acquainted with her own heart. A mind like hers, once opening to suspicion, made rapid progress" (vol. 3, chap. 11). Mind, heart, conscience—in *Emma* they all serve sexual love, and sexual love itself serves moral growth. Recognizing that she is in love sweeps the garbage out of Emma's mind so that she can blame herself for what she has done wrong: "With insufferable vanity had she believed herself in the secret of everybody's feelings; with unpardonable arrogance proposed to arrange everybody's destiny. She was proved to have been universally mistaken; and she had not quite done nothing—for she had done mischief" (vol. 3, chap. 11).

Emma's process of growth, from snobbish, self-alienated, deluded mischief-maker to loving, gracious, honest, sexual woman fully exemplifies the radical theory that governs events at Highbury. She has learned her duties; she can finally embrace her neighbors in love; and she can even accept the farmer Robert Martin as a fit husband for Harriet and as a fit friend for her husband and herself. She has learned that she lives in a fertile world and a good world and that she is deeply connected with the people who make this agricultural economy work. Mr. Knightley spells out the theory behind *Emma* so that the reader has to recognize the intellectual care and seriousness with which Austen has ordered the events of her fiction. He says that people can certainly be harmed by bad influences, that "it is a great deal more natural than one could wish, that a young man, brought up by those who are proud, luxurious, and selfish, should be proud, luxurious, and selfish too" (vol. 1, chap. 18), but he also believes that the mind has the power to correct the feelings; "as he became rational, he ought to have roused himself and shaken off all that was unworthy in their authority" (vol. 1, chap. 18). Nature and rationality are allies, not opposites. Nature does guide people toward the right, he tells Emma: "If you were as much guided by nature in your estimate of men and women, and as little under the power of fancy and whim in your dealings with them, as you are where these children are concerned, we might always think alike" (vol. 1, chap. 12). He sums up his radically hopeful view of human nature near the end of the novel, when he and Emma discuss the future of Mrs. Weston's daughter, who he says will be even more indulged than Emma was. In answer to Emma's outcry, "Poor child . . . At that rate what will become of her?" he answers, "Nothing very bad . . . The fate of thousands. She will be disagreeable in infancy, and correct herself as she grows older" (vol. 3, chap. 17). The belief that human beings *can*, by their nature, correct themselves is at the heart of the radical hopes of both the eighteenth and nineteenth centuries.

Emma certainly reflects the rational radicalism of the eighteenth century. Still, Austen makes it also part of the Romantic radicalism of the nineteenth—in her tenderness toward the weak and odd, in her celebration of the agricultural economy, in the urgency of her hope that the reader will learn what the heroine does and will come to value the threatened and precious bonds of the rural community. More than any heroine in an eighteenth-century novel, Emma must choose to take her place by her neighbors in the village. She makes a radical choice for the England of 1816: to stand by the farmers, the weak and the old, and the poor of rural England in order to resist the new economic order of people like the Eltons. Highbury can survive the Eltons, but only because it has been strengthened by a heroine who has learned to love it.

Love leads Emma to her position of the presiding woman in the rural economy; in Austen's last novel, *Persuasion*, there is nothing left for the heroine to preside over. It is impossible to say whether Austen actually thought that the economic situation of rural England had changed so much between 1816 and 1817 that she had to cast her lot, as a fiction writer, with an unexplored future; perhaps *Persuasion* is simply an intellectual experiment with the side of Romanticism that celebrates the power of the individual soul to live joyfully in virtual independence, apart from the social world.

Country life goes on in *Persuasion*—the Musgrove and Hayter families are pleasant enough. But Austen does not show us daily visits, exchanges of food, loving connections as she does in *Emma*. What we see and care about is Anne Elliot, who wanders through her world as a lovely rural landscape, feeling "the influence so sweet and sad of the autumnal months in the country," instead of presiding over the living community of an agricultural economy. We do not hear of any sensible intelligent farmers, like Robert Martin or William Larkin, in *Persuasion*; Sir Walter Elliot's tenant farmers are nameless. The only working farm belongs to the family of Charles Hayter, who is engaged to Henrietta Musgrove. The existence of all these persons is relegated to the edges of Austen's fiction.

The greatest social change in *Persuasion*, however, is the fact that the class of the country landowners has degenerated and has lost its vitality. Sir Walter Elliot, the negligent father and negligent landowner, is hardly worth Austen's attention, or ours: "Vanity was the beginning and the end of Sir Walter Elliot's character; vanity of person and of situation" (vol. 1, chap. 1). This single trait precipitates the economic catastrophe with which *Persuasion* begins. Sir Walter refuses to curtail the conspicuous expenditure—horses, dinners, servants, luxuries—he considers incumbent upon a man of his greatness, even though he cannot pay his debts. And so he decides to rent his estate, his ancestral home, Kellynch Hall, to a tenant and to move with his family to lodgings in the resort town of Bath. He is simply giving up economic power; he has never had any moral power. And

Austen gives us other evidence that his class is finished: he leaves no son; his oldest daughter, Elizabeth, remains unmarried; his daughters Mary and, eventually, Anne, marry below their class; their noble relatives, the Dalrymples and Cartarets, are entirely shallow and inconsequential; Lady Russell is a childless widow. The class is truly withering away. There is nothing in it for Anne to save, except her friendship with Lady Russell.

Anne's relationship with Lady Russell, her dead mother's friend, is at the heart of *Persuasion*; this relationship keeps the novel from being a callously cheerful vision of the death of an old order, like that in Shelley's "England in 1819." Lady Russell is old and childless; she has caused Anne great grief by persuading her not to marry the brash young sailor Frederick Wentworth, eight years earlier. Her values are essentially those of *Mansfield Park*, order and rank, quiet and propriety. She tries to persuade Anne to marry an immoral man, William Elliot; yet Anne loves her. Austen demands we share Anne's love and her grief for everything that was once good among the rural gentry and that is now dying. In this novel that goodness will die with Lady Russell; the death is a cause for sorrow. Anne cannot save the social and agricultural world Lady Russell ideally represents, but she cannot let it go lightly.

Sir Walter's class cannot be saved; in fact, the person who seems to offer Anne the opportunity to regenerate the old order is the single source of real evil in the book, William Elliot, Sir Walter's heir. Anne is tempted to marry him—tempted by his charm, by her loneliness, by the wish to return to Kellynch Hall and the old life, and by the pressure brought by Lady Russell. As a character he is as tempting as Henry Crawford, and as evil; as a part of a fictional world he is neither as interesting, nor as dangerous. In *Mansfield Park* the representative of a new, mercenary, immoral, urban class is truly threatening to the shakey remains of aristocratic life; in *Persuasion* the last scion of the aristocratic class is almost laughably powerless against the good characters. Austen does not bother to reveal him by stages, in an elegant plot. He does not seduce characters we like; we do not have to discern clues to his true nature. Austen simply allows Mrs. Smith, Anne's crippled friend, to blast his character open for Anne and for us. "Mr. Elliot is a man without heart or conscience; a designing, wary, cold-blooded being, who thinks only of himself; who, for his own interest or ease, would be guilty of any cruelty, or any treachery, that could be perpetrated without risk of his general character" (vol. 2, chap. 9). When he turns out to have been in collusion with Mrs. Clay, who is trying to seduce Sir Walter into marriage, while he is pursuing Anne, we feel only that he and Mrs. Clay deserve each other. Austen actually treats their subsequent cohabitation with amusement rather than horror; "it is now a doubtful point whether his cunning, or hers, may finally carry the day; whether, after preventing her from being the wife of Sir Walter, he may not be wheedled and caressed at last into making her the wife of Sir William" (vol. 2, chap. 12). She does not bother to punish the bad characters in *Persuasion*; they are not worth her trouble. In *Persuasion* Austen creates a new fictional world, different from that of *Mansfield Park* or that of *Emma*, where evil again exists, but has no power.

Evil does not have to be punished or purged because the characters Austen loves can escape from it. Anne, her husband, and their sailor friends can escape because they can move more freely than any of Austen's other characters. The very form of *Persuasion*—loose, sketchy, breathless, impressionistic—allows the reader to feel and share this new possibility of freedom, mystery, and change. No *place* is dominant in *Persuasion*; as readers we move with Anne from Kellynch Hall, to her sister Mary's home at Uppercross, to Lady Russell's home at Kellynch Lodge, to friends' lodgings in Lyme, back to Uppercross, and then to her father's rented home at Bath. And in spite of the traditions in the English novel that lead us to expect to know where a hero and heroine will settle when they marry, Anne's final destination, as a sailor's wife, is left unknown. The world is all before her as it has been before no earlier heroine in the English novel.

Anne's new liberty is part of Austen's new vision of humanity. *Persuasion* is not populated by fictional characters who must be on guard against corruption or who can govern themselves with a combination of kindness and rationality; the central characters in *Persuasion* live by and are protected by the human faculties celebrated by Wordsworth and Shelley—spontaneous cheerfulness, love, and joy. As a heroine Anne is not a central figure in a community; she is a free-floating priestess of joy. Her own emotions have protected her from William Elliot even before Mrs. Smith blasts him: "Mr. Elliot was rational, discreet, polished,—but he was not open. There was never any burst of feeling, any warmth of indignation or delight, at the evil or good of others. This, to Anne, was a decided imperfection.

Her early impressions were incurable. She prized the frank, the open-hearted, the eager character beyond all others. Warmth and enthusiasm did captivate her still. She felt that she could so much more depend upon the sincerity of those who sometimes looked or said a careless or a hasty thing, than of those whose presence of mind never varied, whose tongue never slipped" (vol. 2, chap. 5). Openness, frankness, warmth, enthusiasm are new values in Austen's fiction; this is a new form of Romanticism for her, a celebration of the natural impulses of the heart.

These new emotional qualities belong to all the characters in *Persuasion* to whom Austen gives England's future. They have the same basic good nature as the characters in *Emma*, but Austen shows us less of their capacity for thought and more of their playfulness, more even of their carelessness. Both Mary's son Charles and her sister-in-law Louisa are careless enough to injure themselves seriously in falls—yet they recover easily enough. The characters in *Persuasion* are free in a new way, free in their behavior, free in their actions, even free from the elegance and order of Austen's usual plots. As characters they are free to play before us. For the first time in her fiction Austen actually shows us children playing, as at the Musgroves' Christmas party. "On one side was a table, occupied by some chattering girls, cutting up silk and gold paper; and on the other were tressels and trays, bending under the weight of brawn and cold pies, where riotous boys were holding high revel" (vol. 2, chap. 2). For the first time, Austen abandons her sternness toward spoiled, noisy children and celebrates them as Wordsworth does, for their irrationality, their playfulness, their joyfulness. The young Musgrove women are playful too, more childish than the good women of Austen's earlier fiction. When Captain Wentworth is carelessly flirting with both of them they can fall carelessly in and out of love without being morally culpable. Unlike the Bertram sisters, both survive without a scar: Henrietta returns to Charles Hayter, and Louisa soon falls in love with Captain Benwick. In *Persuasion* love can be part of a world of play, not a world of danger.

The virtues of carelessness are even clearer in the sailors, the representatives of the new middle class into which Austen's heroine marries. The sailors come into the country neither to corrupt nor to join the community; the Crofts, who rent Kellynch Hall, simply replace the sterile snobbery of Sir Walter with their own vitality, their "heartiness . . . warmth . . . sincerity . . . comfort . . . freedom . . . gaiety." They cheerfully admit to Anne that they married very quickly and without the kind of self-examination Austen usually requires of her characters. "We had better not talk about it, my dear. . . . for if Miss Elliot were to hear how soon we came to an understanding, she would never be persuaded that we could be happy together" (vol. 1, chap. 10). They continue to live hopefully and carelessly, continually risking accidents. " 'My dear admiral, that post!—we shall certainly take that post.' But by coolly giving the reins a better direction herself, they happily passed the danger, and by once afterwards judiciously putting out her hand, they neither fell into a rut, nor ran foul of a dung-cart; and Anne, with some amusement at their style of driving, which she imagined no bad representation of the general guidance of their affairs, found herself safely deposited by them at the cottage" (vol. 1, chap. 10). The Crofts go gaily through the world, doing their work, meeting their friends, but always *moving*. They are true representatives of the middle classes who will gain the ascendancy in England, the class Anne will join when she leaves the country community.

The sailors' slang, like their movement, comes from a new world that offers liberty to Anne. Their slang does not indicate vulgarity, moral laxity, or inappropriate familiarity, as the slang of characters in earlier novels does. " 'Ay, a very bad business indeed.—A new sort of way this, for a young fellow to be making love, by breaking his mistress's head!—is not it, Miss Elliot? This is breaking a head and giving a plaister truly.' " Admiral Croft's manners were not quite of the tone to suit Lady Russell, but they delighted Anne. His goodness of heart and simplicity of character were irresistible" (vol. 2, chap. 1). In this novel Anne's response is right. The sailors' slang is not the degenerate, affected language of ill-bred people; it is the spontaneous, earthy, imagistic language of people who do perform honest labor. Their rough and active life has generated the kind of vital language Wordsworth attributes to rural people in his preface to the second edition of *The Lyrical Ballads*: "the essential passions of the heart find a better soil in which they can attain their maturity, are less under restraint, and speak a plainer and more emphatic language, because in that condition of life our elementary feelings co-exist in a state of greater simplicity." Austen has come to a similar theory of language in *Persuasion* and has expressed it with one of Wordsworth's key words—simplicity. The sailors offer Anne liberty of feeling, liberty of movement, and even a new liberty of speech.

Still, Anne has her own superior worth; she has her own spiritual values and remains the single true heroine of this novel. Because of the depth and strength of their love, Anne and Wentworth are superior to the other couples in the novel. Austen prevents us from categorizing them as the sort of excessive, sentimental Romantics she has always attacked in her fiction by playing them off against Louisa and Benwick. Benwick claims a love of the kind Anne and Wentworth have; he ostentatiously quotes Byron to demonstrate the depth of his grief over Fanny Harville. "He repeated, with such tremulous feeling, the various lines which imaged a broken heart, or a mind destroyed by wretchedness, and looked so entirely as if he meant to be understood, that she [Anne] ventured to hope he did not always read only poetry" (vol. 1, chap. 11). He soon reveals that he is a quite ordinary man, when he recovers quickly in the company of Louisa Musgrove. They love easily and well, but without a depth of joy.

Joy belongs to Anne and Wentworth, joy and sorrow and memory. Still grieving, still in love, still possessed by memory even after a separation of eight years, they are the first characters in the nineteenth-century novel who have mysterious, loving souls like the soul Wordsworth celebrates in *The Prelude*. Their original love was different from love in Austen's other novels, where it is made up of admiration and gratitude, shared morality and intelligence, sexual attraction and kindness. Here Austen does not try to explain or anatomize love; her narrator describes it with a new vocabulary, which resists paraphrase or analysis. "They were gradually acquainted, and when acquainted, rapidly and deeply in love. . . . A short period of exquisite felicity followed" (vol. 1, chap. 4). In no other novel does Austen ask us to value a character who falls rapidly and deeply in love; in *Persuasion* passionate, irrational love is the highest of human experiences.

The marriage between Anne and Wentworth was prevented not by flaws in their characters, but by pride on the part of Sir Walter, and by prudence on the part of Lady Russell; the reconciliation, therefore, has nothing to do with moral correction. Lady Russell, the family friend who has acted as Anne's mother, truly and honorably believes that Anne Elliot at nineteen would have been wrong to marry a man without family or fortune. Time has shown her to be wrong, but not morally wrong. And she would not have been wrong in Austen's other novels, where the good are prudent. She is wrong only because she does not share the new Romanticism of *Persuasion*, the Romanticism Anne Elliot has discovered through suffering. "How eloquent could Anne Elliot have been,—how eloquent, at least, were her wishes on the side of early warm attachment, and a cheerful confidence in futurity, against that over-anxious caution which seems to insult exertion and distrust Providence!—She had been forced into prudence in her youth, she learned romance as she grew older—the natural sequel of an unnatural beginning" (vol. 1, chap. 4). Anne thinks Lady Russell has been wrong but does not blame her and does not stop loving her; as a narrator Austen asks us, too, to forgive her. "She was a very good woman, and if her second object was to be sensible and well-judging, her first was to see Anne happy. She loved Anne better than she loved her own abilities" (vol. 2, chap. 12). In *Persuasion* the loving heart is more important than anything else.

And though we sympathize with Anne's eight years of sorrow, and share the regret she and Wentworth feel when he discovers she would have accepted him if he had returned sooner, we still marvel and rejoice in our understanding of the effect of solitude on the loving heart. Though Austen tells us Wentworth has suffered deeply, she illuminates only Anne's heart for us, and illuminates it as no English novelist had illuminated a heroine's heart before. In most earlier English novels a character as solitary as Anne would be suspect, since solitude comes from broken social bonds; Anne Elliot is different, and *Persuasion* is different. Anne's solitude and grief began long before her separation from Wentworth, as Austen tells us late in *Persuasion*; "Anne had gone unhappy to school, grieving for the loss of a mother whom she had dearly loved, feeling her separation from home, and suffering as a girl of fourteen, of strong sensibility and not high spirits, must suffer at such a time" (vol. 2, chap. 5). Though this information is unobtrusive in the narration, it is unusual; neither Austen nor earlier novelists have revealed before the secret griefs their characters felt in their youth. Grief, memory, solitude, all are the experiences given value by Romantic poetry.

Solitude has given Anne many strengths. She loves nature and loves music as a source of private pleasure, not as a means of entertaining guests. She has a rare capacity to love other women, for example, Lady Russell and Mrs. Smith, her former governess. And above all, she has gained the power to keep on loving Frederick Wentworth through the years of separation. Austen devotes most of the text of *Persuasion* to Anne's gradual discovery that her love is returned; she does not have to change her character, but has only to learn a joyful truth.

The language in which Austen reveals Anne's happiness is entirely Romantic. She concentrates on the intensity of the emotion, not on any moral or intellectual revelations to which the emotion may be attached. In earlier novels she gives only a few paragraphs to the happiness her heroines feel when they discover they are loved; here she develops Anne's happiness in subtle stages and exuberant language. First, she thinks Wentworth's apparent forgiveness when he meets her again will be a precious memory: Uppercross "stood the record of many sensations of pain, once severe, but now softened; and of some instances of relenting feeling, some breathings of friendship and reconciliation, which could never be looked for again, and which could never cease to be dear. She left it all behind her; all but the recollection that such things had been" (vol. 2, chap. 1). When she discovers Wentworth is not disturbed by Louisa's engagement, she feels something more: "No, it was not regret which made Anne's heart beat in spite of herself, and brought the colour into her cheeks when she thought of Captain Wentworth unshackled and free. She had some feelings which she was ashamed to investigate. They were too much like joy, senseless joy" (vol. 2, chap. 6).

Joy is the great new emotion of both Wordsworth and Shelley, the brief, transfiguring exaltation that transcends the rational powers of the mind. When Anne and Wentworth meet again at Bath, she has another burst of intense feeling: "it was agitation, pain, pleasure, a something between delight and misery" (vol. 2, chap. 7). At the play, when Wentworth has hinted he still loves her, she is physically transfigured, above self-consciousness. "Anne saw nothing, thought nothing of the brilliancy of the room. Her happiness was from within. Her eyes were bright, and her cheeks glowed, but she knew nothing about it" (vol. 2, chap. 8). And when they finally come to an understanding, they walk together with "smiles reined in and spirits dancing in private rapture" (vol. 2, chap. 11). These spirits are new in the novel; they are the spirits of Romantic poetry. Austen has truly created a new and Romantic heroine in Anne Elliot.

Love and joy, not order, elegance, rationality, or morality, are the final values of *Persuasion*. Anne and Wentworth are not an absolutely isolated couple, alone in their happiness; they are bound to a mobile community of friends—the Crofts and the Harvilles and the Benwicks. The only stationary friends they have are Mrs. Smith and Lady Russell. Austen has set her characters free into a world of wandering, almost like the world Shelley created for himself. In Anne Elliot, Austen has given one side of Romanticism a beautiful and moving form; Anne Elliot truly possesses the spiritual powers of imagination and memory, grief and love; she floats before our sight, a luminous individual woman, self-sufficient, almost self-creating in her loveliness.

Yet there is a price. As readers we cannot grieve to lose Sir Walter Elliot, Elizabeth, William Elliot, Mrs. Clay; but Lady Russell, the Musgroves, the Hayters remain in the country, unblest by the company of Anne and Wentworth. Anne's freedom, her radical liberation from the old bonds, is a loss both to the community of rural England and to herself. She is right to grieve that she will never be mistress of Kellynch Hall; Austen has been honest enough to admit that there is something to grieve for. The kind of protection and comfort that an agricultural village, the village ideally presented in Highbury, offers to the old and sick and silly is not available to wanderers. Anne, of course, is leaving a sterile and worthless world; but her grief reminds us of what the country community ideally was and could be. In *Emma* and *Persuasion* Austen shows us the best a woman can get from Romantic radicalism: in *Emma* the precious moral economy for which rural workers were fighting in the early nineteenth century, the economy threatened by industrial capitalism; in *Persuasion* the joyful power of the loving heart and soul, isolated and at liberty. Austen never found a way to combine them; the two roads of Romanticism remain separate. Both are radical, for both declare that human goodness does not depend on the external repression Austen the experimental reactionary praised in *Mansfield Park*, and both oppose a corrupt economic order. In *Emma* the corrupt economic power is the new world of the Eltons; in *Persuasion* it is the old world of Sir Walter.

When Anne Elliot casts her lot with what will, in fact, be the new, competitive, capitalistic middle class, she has given up economic power. Though she might keep her sailor husband company on board ship as Mrs. Croft does, she can have no economic connection with Wentworth's life. She has given up the kind of life available to women in agricultural England, a life with powers and duties like those Emma assumes in marrying Mr. Knightley. We must imagine what her world will be without her, as we imagine the abandoned village when we read Keats's "Ode on a Grecian Urn"; we must remember old Lady Russell and crippled Mrs. Smith. Realizing that the women of the centuries that follow *Persuasion* have more often chosen Anne's road than Emma's, we must also remember who has been left behind. The victims in our culture are the weak, the Miss Bateses of the world, the women who most need to know that other women, powerful women, feel a duty to them.

3. Charlotte and Emily Brontë: Masters and Mad Dogs

After almost thirty years of quiescence, Romantic radicalism reappeared in the English novels written in the isolated rural home of Charlotte and Emily Brontë. Writing in the late 1840s, when Mrs. Gaskell, Dickens, and Thackeray were beginning their distinctly Victorian careers as novelists, the Brontës—to the horror of many readers—chose the intensity, the violence, the imaginative extravagance of Romanticism for their own novels.[1] In tone, texture, and character their novels were similar—passionate, exclamatory passages, supernatural incidents, poetic language, swarthy and dangerous heroes. Yet the two sisters chose divergent Romantic paths: Charlotte followed Shelley and Austen's Anne Elliot in glorifying the individual woman's soul through love, but without their political emphasis: she turned her back on the country and its people and its past and made Romanticism a special world for her upwardly-mobile heroines. Emily turned, imaginatively, to a past more distant than one she had known; she followed Wordsworth and Austen's Emma in looking to a remoter and wilder time when human instincts were laid bare in a rural culture. Both Brontës have been admired in the twentieth century, praised for their power and vividness and intelligence, each by her own sort of admirers. Charlotte, especially as the author of *Jane Eyre*, has been the beloved Brontë fountainhead of feminism for many women critics and, simultaneously, rather harshly treated by men. Emily has appeared much less frequently in feminist criticism, but has aroused the great enthusiasm of an important male Marxist critic.

The two sisters knew they were traveling different paths, and though they spoke decorously of their disagreements, Charlotte's comments to her publisher reveal bitterness and even horror. Still keeping herself and Emily disguised as two men, Currer and Ellis Bell, she wrote: "I should much—very much—like to take that quiet view of the 'great world' you allude to, but I have as yet won no right to give myself such a treat; it must be for some future day—Ellis, I imagine, would soon turn aside from that spectacle in disgust. I do not think he admits it as his creed that 'the proper study of mankind is man'—at least not the artificial man of cities. In some points I consider Ellis somewhat of a theorist now and then he broaches Ideas which strike my sense as much more daring and original than practical; his reason may be in advance of mine, but certainly it often travels a different road."[2] Since Charlotte, who survived her sister, took charge of Emily's papers, no such direct comments from Emily remain; all we have is *Wuthering Heights*, a point-by-point attack on Charlotte's civilized, Christian Romanticism. Emily had published *Wuthering Heights* by 1847, when Charlotte began *Jane Eyre*; but Charlotte had already revealed herself in *The Professor*. The two early chose different responses to two primary subjects: the inheritance of Romanticism and their own historical situation, isolated at Haworth.

Neither as unlearned and ignorant as Jane Austen declared herself to be, nor as engaged in the intellectual life of their nation as the other Victorian novelists, the Brontës grew up on "the Border Balladists, Cowper, Burns, Byron, Scott, and the seventeenth century lyricists."[3] They were intellectually closer to the writers of the early nineteenth century, the time of Austen and the Romantic poets, than to the writers of their own time. In isolation at Halworth they were freer than other Victorian writers to live in their imaginations, as Wordsworth believed children should live. In some ways isolation and imagination canceled the thirty years between 1817 and 1847 for them; spiritually they still belonged to the time of Romanticism.

Haworth, however, was not Wordsworth's Lake Country or Austen's Steventon; the Brontës lacked both the old rural community and the new urban life of their contemporary novelists. Their home was not a place of friendly neighbors, agricultural plenty, or rural peace; it was a place of depopulation, the repression of Dissenting religion, and class war. As Terry Eagleton says,

They were, to begin with, placed at a painfully ambiguous point in the social structure, as the daughters of a clergyman with the inferior status of 'perpetual curate' who had thrust his way up from poverty; they strove as a family to maintain 'genteel' standards in a traditionally rough and ready environment. . . . and they were *educated* women, trapped in an almost intolerable deadlock between culture and economics—between imaginative aspiration and the cold truth of a society which could use them merely as 'higher' servants. They were *isolated* educated women, socially and geographically remote from a world with which they nonetheless maintained close intellectual touch, and so driven back upon themselves in solitary emotional hungering.[4]

The company of friends that Wordsworth and Austen knew was not available to the Brontës, and so it is not surprising that they did not see a culture to save in the rural community.

The two also reacted differently to the social changes in the area of Haworth. Their isolation was not a consequence of the eternal qualities of the place, but an indication of the advanced state of class struggle. Eagleton describes the situation: "The Brontës' home, Haworth, was close to the centre of the West Riding woolen area: and their lifetime there coincided with some of the fiercest class struggles in English society. The years of their childhood were years of ruination for thousands of hand-workers dispersed in hill-cottages around the region—men and women who drifted, destitute to the villages and towns. They lived, in short, through an aspect of the events which Karl Marx described in *Capital* as the most horrible tragedy of English history.[5] The Brontës were witnesses to the destruction of rural life that Wordsworth and Austen tried to fend off, with their passionately celebratory writings.

They had one more common source of information about country life, one Emily adopted and Charlotte, apparently, ignored—their old servant Tabby.

Tabby remembered the days when the wool packs were carried by pack horses with jingling bells across the moors from Lancashire; when the stone farms dotted about the hills—Elizabethan buildings most of them—were flourishing and their owners living in almost unchanged primitive conditions; a hard race submitting to no laws but their own. Tabby remembered hearing from her elders about the ministry of good Mr. Grimshaw, who had died in 1763 of the plague epidemic because he would not desert his parish; of his charity and fearful language, quite as unbridled as that of his mostly unlettered flock, but whose goodness and fervour in trying to save their souls had become legendary.[6]

Rural community, agricultural prosperity, fierce country people, and a more generous form of Christianity than Aunt Branwell's were not within the memory of the Brontës themselves, but they had access to such truths through Tabby's family memories. These two sisters had two kinds of women to choose between in Aunt Branwell and Tabby: beneath all Charlotte's fire always lurks prissy Aunt Branwell, and close to Emily's anger sits Tabby, tough and useful and a storehouse of country memories.

The strong heritage of Dissenting religion at Haworth[7] and the Brontës' private, steady source of repressive theology, their aunt, Miss Elizabeth Branwell, who came to live with them when their mother died, were oppressive influences. "Miss Branwell's influence was repressive, her religion joyless and narrow, her outlook morbid."[8] The clearest glimpse of this appears in *Wuthering Heights* in Lockwood's first dream. The unwary traveler has experienced a bit of bombastic repression in his meeting with Joseph, the puritanical old servant at Wuthering Heights, and in the memories recorded in Catherine Earnshaw's diary, which he has read before sleep. Yet what he brings to Wuthering Heights through his dreaming mind is worse than anything he has seen there. It is mid-nineteenth-century Dissenting religion at its fiercest and meanest. E. P. Thompson writes of Lockwood's dream, "Over the Industrial Revolution there brooded the figure of the Reverend Jabes Branderham (almost certainly modelled on Jabez Bunting) who appears in Lockwood's grim nightmare at the opening of *Wuthering Heights*: 'good God, what a sermon; divided into *four hundred and ninety* parts . . . and each discussing a separate sin!'" He comments further that Jabes Branderham epitomizes the "all enveloping 'Thou Shalt Not!' which permeated all religious persuasions in varying degree in these years."[9]

According to Thompson, by the middle of the nineteenth century, when the Brontës wrote their novels, the Dissenting religion they would have seen in their neighbors was perverted: "The association of feminine—or, more frequently, ambivalent—sexual imagery with Christ is more perplexing and unpleasant.

Here we are faced with layer upon layer of conflicting symbolism. Christ, the personification of 'Love' to whom the great bulk of Wesleyan hymns are addressed, is by turns maternal, Oedipal, sexual, and sado-masochistic."[10] Thompson sees Blake as the main literary enemy of this religion; Emily Brontë is in fact Blake's equal. Charlotte in large measure associated such religion with the passionate sexual relationships of her heroines; Emily rejected it entirely with a violence that is itself a power in *Wuthering Heights*.

Both Charlotte Brontë's passionate Romanticism and her prissy repressiveness are clearest in *Jane Eyre*. It is her clearest and most powerful book, more vivid that *Villette*, more decisive than *Shirley*. Jane Eyre, a lonely, suffering, motherless woman isolated as a governess in an unloving family, who finally finds ecstatic joy in the love of a man—how is she so different, as a fictional creation, from Austen's Anne Elliot? Why, as a fictional heroine, has she been both more attractive and more insideously dangerous to women? *Jane Eyre* follows *Persuasion* as a Romantic paean to sexual love, an ode to joy, a celebration of an individual woman's soul, but *Jane Eyre* is both violent and pious, full of rage and repression, radically divided between the outraged anguish of the lost child and the smug complacency of the satisfied Victorian wife. Austen sends her heroine into a new world sadly, with grief for what is gone in England, and with full knowledge that she is heralding a new economic world; Charlotte Brontë lifts her heroine out of history and places her in the realm of fairy tales, full of enemies and ogres, punishments for the wicked and bliss for the good, a world where money appears by magic in the form of inheritances and where the light of the next world glares strangely. She appeals to the emotions her readers share with her heroine as an angry child and encourages in us the same lust for pleasure and revenge.

Charlotte Brontë's Romantic rage and her capacity for radical criticism are truest when she writes straightforwardly, not surreptitiously, with the view of a child.

All John Reed's violent tyrannies, all his sisters' proud indifference, all his mother's aversion, all the servants' partiality, turned up in my disturbed mind like a dark deposit in a turbid well. Why was I always suffering, always browbeaten, always accused, forever condemned? . . .

'Unjust!—unjust!' said my reason, forced by the agonizing stimulus into precocious though transitory power; and Resolve, equally wrought up, instigated some strange expedient to achieve escape from insupportable oppression—as running away, or, if that could not be effected, never eating or drinking more, and letting myself die. (Chap. 2)

This is a brilliant illumination of the forbidden and terrifying feelings of children, a genuinely Romantic recapturing of intense, irrational emotion. And the portrait of Mr. Brocklehurst, the tyrannical Dissenting hypocrite who runs the girls' school where Jane is sent, is a genuinely Romantic protest. Brocklehurst is typical of the mid-nineteenth-century Dissenter who was quick to preach self-abnegation to the poor for the economic advantage of the rich. Reproaching a teacher who has given the girls some bread and cheese as a substitute for a burnt, inedible supper, he says, "When you put bread and cheese, instead of burnt porridge, into these children's mouths, you may indeed feed their vile bodies, but you little think how you starve their immortal souls" (chap. 7). Vile bodies—this is something different from the stern Christianity of *Mansfield Park*; it is the sexually obsessed language of Victorian Dissent.

The culmination of Jane Eyre's experiences as a child and young woman is the cry for liberty that has attracted women readers for the last 150 years. After serving dutifully at the now-reformed Lowood School for many years, apparently docile and submissive under the influence of Miss Temple, Jane Eyre once again rebels when Miss Temple leaves to be married.

My world had for some years been in Lowood: my experience had been of its rules and systems; now I remembered that the real world was wide, and that a varied field of hopes and fears, of sensations and excitements, awaited those who had courage to go forth into its expanse, to seek real knowledge of life amidst its perils.

I went to my window, opened it, and looked out. There were the two wings of the building; there was the garden; there were the skirts of Lowood; there was the hilly horizon. My eye passed all other objects to rest on those most remote and the blue peaks. It was those I longed to surmount; all within their boundary of rock and heath seemed prison-ground, exile limits. . . . I tired of the routine of eight years in one afternoon. I desired liberty; for liberty I gasped; for liberty I uttered a prayer; it seemed scattered on the wind then faintly blowing. (Chap. 10)

It sounds wonderful—but what does it mean? Liberty is one of the key words of Romanticism, but here it is detached from all political content. No French revolutions, no economically independent farmers, no rebellious laborers, not even any sexually free couples are in sight. Jane cries for liberty, but once out of Lowood she finds only what she recognizes as a new bondage, her job as a governess.

This is the point at which the Romantic radicalism of *Jane Eyre* collapses. The protests against the misjudgment and mistreatment of children are politically potent, connected with a larger vision of justice; Jane's yearning for liberty is politically empty, connected with nothing. It turns quickly into a yearning for love, and love in a particularly pernicious form. Again, the difference between the Romantic individualism of Anne Elliot's love for Wentworth and of Jane Eyre's for Rochester is revealing. Austen does not place her heroine among other female characters who must be seen as enemies. Even when Anne suspects Wentworth loves Louisa Musgrove, she does not consider Louisa an enemy, nor does Austen paint Louisa as a despicable creature; when Anne and Wentworth are finally united, they count Louisa and many other women among their friends. Though love does not anchor them in a settled community, it does tie them to a close, if scattered, group of people.

Nothing of the sort happens in *Jane Eyre*. Charlotte Brontë again surrounds her heroine with enemies, now exclusively female. Just as her aunt and cousins crushed and hurt her as a child, now Blanche Ingram and the other rich women of Rochester's social circle and monstrous, nymphomaniacal Bertha, the now legendary madwoman in Rochester's attic, are adversaries to be conquered before Jane can have her man. In *Jane Eyre*, as in *Villette* and *Shirley*, the desperation of a heroine's search for love is partly a measure of the barrenness of the novel's social world. Though some of that barrenness may reflect the life at Haworth, by the time Charlotte Brontë wrote Jane Eyre she had traveled, taught, made friends. She makes the *choice* to intensify the importance of love for her heroines by making it a refuge in a female jungle.

In *Jane Eyre* love itself is a dubious refuge. Rochester himself is half an enemy. He is the reembodiment of the Byronic heroes with whom the Brontës imaginatively spent their childhoods—swarthy, surly, unconventional, sinful but salvagable. Salvation is Jane's mission with Rochester—not mere reprimand or correction. He says he needs her purity to regenerate him after his bad life; before she can accomplish this mission they must go through an interrupted wedding, her exile and near seduction by St. John Rivers, her repentance for having made of him "an idol" who stood between her and God, his mutilation in a fire, and, of course, the gruesome death of Bertha. As an emotional experience, this great love Jane finds in her quest for liberty is all too closely connected with the kind of Dissenting religion Charlotte Brontë makes horrifying in Mr. Brocklehurst.[11] It fully deserves all the adjectives E. P. Thompson uses for mid-nineteenth-century Dissent—"maternal," "Oedipal," "sado-masochistic."

She has taken care of him like a mother yet worshipped him like a daughter; he has lied to her, teased her with Blanche Ingram, tried to seduce her into being his mistress. He finally accepts his physical punishments as just, and she ascends to a position of power over him, while still calling him her master. And all this happens in the name of a sanctified, Christian matrimony; as readers we are supposed to agree when Rochester tells his recovered Jane that he sees "the hand of God in my doom." Charlotte Brontë's heroine claims to thrive as her master's maternal, spiritual guide; the words with which she expresses her satisfaction as a wife reek of pride, of fantasy, and of a subterranean cruelty, an unspoken triumph over less fortunate women.

I have now been married ten years. I know what it is to live entirely for and with what I love best on earth. I hold myself supremely blest—blest beyond what language can express; because I am my husband's life as fully as he is mine. No woman was ever nearer to her mate than I am; ever more absolutely bone of his bone and flesh of his flesh. I know no weariness of my Edward's society: he knows none of mine, any more than we each do of the pulsation of the heart that beats in our separate bosoms; consequently, we are ever together. To be together is for us to be at once as free as in solitude, as gay as in company. We talk, I believe, all day long: to talk to each other is but a more animated and an audible thinking. (Chap. 38)

At this point the two are living in utter solitude at Ferndean, a place too damp and unhealthy for agriculture, so unhealthy Rochester had refused to house Bertha there. The only human beings they see are Jane's new-found cousins, the Rivers sisters, with whom they exchange rare visits. What they do and what they talk about are left entirely to the reader's imagination. This is a lonely woman's dream of love, a solipsistic salvation. It is liberation, all right, liberation from all the women Jane hates—her bad aunt, her mean cousins, her wicked female rivals. But it has nothing to do with what earlier Romantics called liberty.

This marriage is the harbinger of the crazily ideal marriages of which the Victorians dreamed, a transformation of religion into isolated domesticity. Jane has ceased to be the truth-telling child, the rebel, the prophet and has become a Christian exemplar, on the model of her submissive dead friend Helen Burns. The end of the book reveals the rage of the first half for what it is—not the rage of the Romantic radical who wants justice, but the rage of the outsider who just wants to get in. Jane and St. John Rivers, the man she refused as a husband, divide the Christian message of the book: she exemplifies the sacrament of marriage, and he, the heroism of chastity and missionary work. In case the reader is missing the final meaning of her novel, Charlotte Brontë gives the last words to a letter from St. John, words in which Jane rejoices: "'My Master,' he says, 'has forwarned me. Daily he announces more distinctly "Surely I come quickly!" and hourly I more eagerly respond, "Amen, even so, come, Lord Jesus"'" (chap. 38).

As readers we should not separate St. John's love for his master, for whom he is dying in India, and Jane's love for hers. The word *master* is part of a new vocabulary in both religion and love. And in portraying this Victorian religion and this Victorian love, Charlotte Brontë deliberately obscures their economic connections. St. John's missionary work in India is part of British imperialism; Rochester, as Jane's master (and her slave, too, of course) has ceased to function as the overseer of the land or as anything else. His money entails no duties. Yet *master* was a politically potent word in mid-nineteenth-century England; E. P. Thompson writes, "It is scarcely possible to write the history of popular agitations in these years unless we make at least the imaginative effort to understand how such a man as the 'Journeyman cotton spinner' read the evidence. He spoke of the 'master' not as an aggregate of individuals, but as a class. As such 'they' denied him political rights. . . . "They" conspired, not in this or that fact alone, but in the essential exploitive relationship within which all the facts were validated."[12] The economic masters of mid-nineteenth-century England, like industrialists and imperialists, are hidden from the view of Brontë's readers. The exploitiveness of economic power is secretly transformed into the supposedly spiritual power of love and religion. The little governess who emerges triumphant at the end of *Jane Eyre* claims to wield power, in her sanctified domesticity, that almost no women in Victorian England wielded economically. Love and religion have united, in the minds of the author and her heroine, to create a realm of imaginary power for women, a power that secretly supports the exploitive economic world of men.

Power is anything but imaginary in Emily Brontë's one novel, *Wuthering Heights*. It contains as much physical violence as any three ordinary Victorian novels—fist-fights, smashed windows, babies dropped over bannisters. Emily Brontë forces the physical world upon her readers, shockingly and decisively. Because of the violence, too many readers have seen *Wuthering Heights* as a crudely Gothic novel, the kind of literature both Wordsworth and Austen opposed, a distillation of everything offensive in Charlote Brontë's fiction, the cheap Romanticism of mere extreme emotion.

The truth of *Wuthering Heights* is quite different. The influential female presence is not Aunt Branwell, but Tabby; the book points not toward the individualistic Victorian future but toward a lost heroic rural past. Its Romanticism lies not in a celebration of emotion, but in an unswerving reexamination of the human instincts. It is difficult, intellectual, and radical; it demands both careful thought and a terrifying abandonment of convention from the reader.

Instead of inviting the reader to an easy identification with a heroine's loneliness and anger and need for love, as Charlotte Brontë does, Emily Brontë begins by depriving her reader of sure fictional footing, and by providing convoluted chronology and seemingly familiar, but ultimately untrustworthy, narrators. We quickly realize we are not going to feel along with the heroine, but are going to think about her. Only thought can stave off the confusion of the cut-up time scheme and the multiplicity of narrative fragments; only thought can take us beyond reaction to the violent and cruel characters of the book to recognition that what we are seeing is a glimpse of an earlier and stronger state of humanity. *Wuthering Heights* belongs with Rousseau's *Discourse on the Origin and Foundation of Inequality among Mankind* and Wordsworth's *The Lyrical Ballads* as a shattering suggestion that we must reconsider human nature itself and discover our true selves are governed by instincts very different from those taught by Christian tradition.

Emily Brontë does not give us a picture of her original man, as Rousseau does. Instead, she forces us to infer the original human qualities as we try to imagine what Heathcliff and Cathy would have been if they had not fallen into civilization. To understand the central characters of *Wuthering Heights* we must think negatively, going beyond our usual categories of critical thought, listening *through* the voices and values of the narrators who tell the story, Nelly Dean and Lockwood, and stripping away the socially created characteristics of Heathcliff and Cathy. The truth about them, finally, is shockingly simple: the two essential human feelings, which are stronger in Heathcliff and Cathy than in most civilized people, are the feelings they share with dogs. The dog is the most important animal in the book. The true human instincts are loyalty to a single loved creature and protective attachment to a single loved place.

In their true, instinctive selves, Cathy and Heathcliff are surprisingly similar. The elaborate sexual differences of most Victorian novels, seen vividly in the sinner-and-savior relationship between Jane Eyre and Rochester, dissolve here. Clearly demarcated sexual roles disappear, along with Victorian class distinctions, as we, with difficulty, imagine what true humanity might be like. *Wuthering Heights* has received little attention as a feminist novel precisely because it is too deeply radical in its reconsideration of all human beings.

Emily Brontë forces us to realize how false the accepted conception of sexual identities is through her characterizations of her two main narrators, Lockwood and Nelly Dean. Lockwood is the city man who, in his aimless travels as a tourist, rents Thrushcross Grange, the old home of the Lintons, from its new owner, Heathcliff. Nelly, who has kept house for both the Earnshaws and the Lintons, is less a country worker than a mild version of Aunt Branwell, the purveyor of proper Victorian values. They think of themselves as representatives of their sex; the more we know them, the more shallow their sexual identities seem. Their sexual identities are merely part of the tissue of clichés by which they each live.

Lockwood's clichés are, sadly, the mid-nineteenth-century remnants of one kind of Romanticism. When Lockwood meets Heathcliff, his surly and inhospitable landlord, he writes in his journal: "Possibly, some people might suspect him of a degree of under-bred pride; I have a sympathetic chord within that tells me it is nothing of the sort: I know, by instinct, his reserve springs from an aversion to showy displays of feeling—to manifestations of mutual kindliness. He'll love and hate, equally under cover, and esteem it a species of impertinence to be loved or hated again—No, I'm running on too fast—I bestow my own attributes overliberally on him" (chap. 1). These alleged attributes belong neither to Heathcliff nor to Lockwood; they belong to the Byronic hero, a Romantic type Charlotte Brontë makes her own in Rochester. That the vapid, sickly Lockwood, who imagines he has broken the heart of a woman who once smiled at him, can imagine himself to be Byron's reincarnation is vivid evidence that this once dangerous character type has become the imaginative property of the weak and foolish. This early passage also tells us we must remember, reading Lockwood's narration, that he will report everything in the deceptive language of decayed literary Romanticism. His version of Romanticism has become so weak that it is perfectly acceptable to Nelly Dean, the quintessential Victorian conformist. If it is acceptable to her, Emily Brontë asks us to see, it has lost any power it ever had.

Nelly Dean's own narration is made up of Victorian, not Romantic, words and values. She likes peace, quiet, charity, humanity, common sense, and duty; she dislikes, above all, pride and selfishness. Though we can believe she tells us the superficial truth about the events that have taken place at Wuthering Heights and Thrushcross Grange, we must not trust her interpretations. She judges everything by her own code of Victorian conformity. Commenting on the difference between Hindley Earnshaw's grief and Edgar Linton's, she says, "But, I thought in my mind, Hindley, with apparently the stronger head, has shown himself sadly the worse and the weaker man. When his ship struck, the captain abandoned his post; and the crew, instead of trying to save her, rushed into riot and confusion, leaving no hope for their luckless vessel. Linton, on the contrary, displayed the true courage of a loyal and faithful soul: he trusted God; and God comforted him. One hoped, and the other despaired; they chose their own lots, and were righteously doomed to endure them" (chap. 17). She believes that incapacitating grief must be bad since socially disruptive, that anyone who feels it is a bad person, and that every human action will incur a divine reward or punishment. She particularly advocates submissive behavior for women and believes God will punish women for transgressions. Catherine Earnshaw Linton, as a passionate woman, is utterly repugnant to her: "Well might Catherine deem that heaven would be a land of exile to her, unless, with her mortal body, she cast away her mortal character also. Her present countenance had a wild vindictiveness in its white cheek, and a bloodless lip and scintillating eye; and she retained in her closed fingers a portion of the locks she had been grasping" (chap. 15). She is not the narrator who could tell us the truth about the characters of *Wuthering Heights*.

These two conformist narrators, Nelly Dean and Lockwood, are a fictional medium through which Emily Brontë tells her readers that the Romanticism embodied in the Byronic hero has never offered any real threat to a repressive and complacent society. The image of the suffering, guilty, passionate man, hiding his tormented heart under a mask of hardness, appeals not to genuinely passionate and socially threatening characters like Heathcliff and Cathy, but to characters like Lockwood and Isabella Linton (another favorite of Nelly's), whose emotions are weak. The essence of the Byronic character is self-consciousness; built into this character type is a narcissistic fascination with one's own feelings, a conscious cultivation of guilt and passion. Although the Byronic character theatrically defies conventional morality, he is nevertheless secretly devoted to it and is always, like Rochester, on the verge of repentance and conversion. Lockwood's assumed Byronic persona, and his compatibility with Nelly Dean, creates a kind of narrative negation in the mind of the reader of *Wuthering Heights*; as we listen to these two tell their version of the story, we must realize that whatever Heathcliff is, he is not Byronic. He is not a man devoted to the seduction of women; he is not part of a world in which men and women must be entirely different from each other.

He is also not the devil he seems to the mincing, moralistic, Victorian Christians who inhabit this fictional world, characters tainted by the Dissenting religion, which brought the devil back into England in the nineteenth century to fight God for British souls. Over and over Nelly Dean and other characters use the language of Satanism to describe Heathcliff. Hindley calls him "imp of Satan"; Nelly thinks "God had forsaken the stray sheep [Catherine] there to its own wicked wanderings, and an evil beast prowled between it and the fold, waiting his time to spring and destroy" (chap. 10) and later calls him "a ghoul, a vampire"; Isabella calls him an "incarnate goblin."

Neither the Byronic drama of Lockwood's mind nor the satanic one of Nelly Dean's can account for what we glean of the facts of the story. Heathcliff has not seduced or bewitched Catherine; we must keep asking who he is, who they are, what has happened. The one thing we know quickly is that Heathcliff and Cathy Earnshaw are not self-conscious, as Charlotte Brontë's characters are; they do not understand or value themselves, as Emily Brontë demands that *we* understand and value them. We must imaginatively infer their essential being, the people they would have been if they had lived among others like themselves, if they had not descended into the world of the Victorian novel, the world of marriage and inheritance, property and Christian propriety.

The first fall is Catherine Earnshaw's. She is bitten by the Linton's dog outside Thrushcross Grange and forcibly drawn into the rich, genteel house—to return, a ruffled, proud, clean young lady, to Wuthering Heights. In moving away from the earthy agricultural class into which she was born, Catherine is following her brother Hindley, who has brought a fancy, delicate wife to Wuthering Heights and has asserted his superiority by degrading his informally adopted brother Heathcliff to the status of a farm laborer. He needs to degrade someone in order to declare himself a new, genteel farmer of the Lintons' class. As Hobsbawm says, "the very wealth of the increasingly prosperous farmers, with their piano-playing daughters, made them ever more remote, in spirit, from the pauperized labourers."[13] When she follows her brother into this new rural gentility, Catherine knows she must turn her back on Heathcliff as a husband. She knows perfectly well her motives for choosing Edgar Linton are economic and social: "And he will be rich, and I shall like to be the greatest woman of the neighborhood, and I shall be proud of having such a husband" (chap. 9). What she does not reckon with, in making this choice, is the strength of her true nature, which will draw her into self-starvation, madness, and finally, self-chosen death when Heathcliff returns, a few years later, to destroy her illusion of bourgeois respectability.

When Heathcliff returns, he too has entered the Victorian world. He had left as a gypsy, a savage, an alien, after overhearing Catherine's declaration that it would degrade her to marry him now; he returns as a gentleman with manners and money. He returns to beat Catherine and Hindley at their own economic game. The whole elaborate plot of the second half of the book is economic—Heathcliff's maniacal quest for both the Earnshaw and Linton estates, Wuthering Heights and Thrushcross Grange. He moves in with and gambles with poor drunken Hindley until he has won Wuthering Heights; he forcibly arranges a marriage between young Catherine, daughter of Cathy and Edgar Linton, and the pathetic, dying son that he has produced with Isabella Linton; he rearranges young Catherine's will and manages to make himself the heir to Thrushcross Grange as well.

Heathcliff and Cathy Earnshaw are made of the same stuff: alike as wild children, they are alike as mistaken, violent, vengeful adults who have fallen into the Victorian economic world. Only as they approach death do they begin to recognize what they have done to themselves; we know more than they do of what they might have been, what kind of man, what kind of woman, free and equal in a different culure. Some of the right words for that culture appear in the text of *Wuthering Heights* and in at least one contemporary review. Nelly tells Lockwood that as children Heathcliff and Cathy "promised fair to grow up as rude as savages"; Catherine, dying, corroborates this with, "I wish I were out of doors—I wish I were a girl again, half savage, and hardy, and free" (chap. 12). In a famous, scathing review, Lady Eastlake picked up this idea of savagery and turned it into a term of damnation. Comparing *Jane Eyre* and *Wuthering Heights*, she said, "For though there is a decided family resemblance between the two, yet the aspect of the Jane and Rochester animals in their native state, as Catherine and Heathcliff, is too odiously and abominably pagan to be palatable even to the most vitiated class of English readers."[14] Savages, pagans, animals—to Christians like Lady Eastlake, these are damned souls.

To the inclusive impulse of Romantic radicalism, however—in Wordsworth, in Coleridge, in Blake—pagans and animals are living creatures, just like Christians in their deepest being. Words like *pagan* and *animal* had changed meaning by 1847, when capitalists were defensively justifying the enclosure of common lands, the kind of free land on which Cathy and Heathcliff had spent their youth. E. P. Thompson's analysis of the new fear of wild people on common land is again relevant: "The commons . . . were now seen as a dangerous center of indiscipline . . . a breeding ground for 'barbarians', 'nursing up a mischievous race of people!', . . . 'a race of people as wild as the fen'."[15] So much for Wordsworth and the wild-eyed women of *The Lyrical Ballads*. By the time Emily Brontë wrote *Wuthering Heights*, wildness, in political terms, had returned to blackness.

Words like *pagan, savage, animal,* and the wild action of the book all draw Heathcliff and Cathy into the dimly remembered past, a past thrust before us on the first page, when we see Wuthering Heights through the eyes of Lockwood. Over the door is the date 1500; the dishes are not modern copper and tin but ancient silver and pewter; the house has no proper ceiling. "The roof . . . had never been under-drawn: its entire anatomy lay bare to an inquiring eye, except where a frame of wood laden with oat-cakes and clusters of legs of beef, mutton, and ham concealed it" (chap. 1). This is the house of a farmer who is also a serious hunter, a hunter for food, not elegant sport. "Above the chimney were sundry villainous old guns, and a couple of horse-pistols. . . . In an arch under the dresser reposed a huge, liver-coloured bitch pointer surrounded by a swarm of squealing puppies, and other dogs haunted other recesses" (chap. 1). This is the house of the kind of farmer Tabby remembered, whose life was unchanged from that of his Elizabethan ancestors.

Later on Lockwood sleeps in Cathy's old bed, the likes of which he has never seen: "a large oak case, with squares cut out near the top, resembling coach windows . . . a singular sort of old-fashioned couch, very conveniently designed to obviate the necessity for every member of the family having a room to himself" (chap. 3). This unfamiliar bed is exactly like the one Pierre-Jakez Helias describes in *The Horse of Pride* as the special property of peasant culture: "I . . . was born in a box bed, and when I'm sometimes asked whether I would still sleep in one, the answer is no, not on your life. Unless my youth could be given back to me, along with the complete world I was brought up in, and which time has destroyed."[16] Characters in other nineteenth-century novels do not sleep in such beds; the box bed is a potent, silent emblem of the ancient life into which the ignorant Lockwood stumbles in his misguided search for rural relaxation.

The rural past to which the bed, the house, the guns belong is not where we stop, however, in searching out the true identities of Heathcliff and Cathy; it is only a fictional signpost, an arrow telling us which way to look. The culture that belongs to this part of rural England is gone; there are only glimpses of it, in the ballads Nelly sings, in the country dialect the grumbling old servant Joseph speaks. In this novel there is no rural community left to save, no rightful human home for a man like Heathcliff and a woman like Cathy. The Earnshaw family is isolated; the country now belongs to enticingly polished, comfortable bourgeois people like the Lintons and to travelers like Lockwood. Catherine Earnshaw can be a redeeming heroine, a beacon of new life, only by disrupting the culture into which she has been born. There is nothing left for her to save.

Yet she and Heathcliff, the gypsy foundling whose adoption begins the destruction of the Earnshaw family, are not simply marauders. They *are* savage, pagan, and animal, but savages, pagans, and animals have their own cultures—though such cultures did not satisfy good Victorian ladies like Lady Eastlake who had rejected everything radical in Romanticism. In *Wuthering Heights* Emily Brontë brings Romanticism back to life, with its radical inclusions of previously despised kinds of life and thought—those of children and animals, idiots and madwomen, illiterate people and paupers.

Heathcliff and Cathy, violent and vengeful as they are, might have been perfectly acceptable members of a pagan culture—the kind of culture still silently alive in rural England a few generations before the Brontës suffered through their isolated lives. Emily Brontë's own life reveals an affinity with pagan culture—she named her hawk, Hero;[17] her friend Ellen Nussey recollected that "Emily, half-reclining on a slab of stone, played like a young child with the tadpoles in the water, making them swim about, and then fell to moralizing on the strong and the weak, the brave and the cowardly, as she chased them with her hand."[18] It is not pure destructiveness, but these pagan, heroic values Emily Brontë re-creates in the hero and heroine of *Wuthering Heights*.

The pagan strength of the hero and heroine of *Wuthering Heights* lies in the power of their two deepest instincts, absolute love for each other and for their home. Emily Brontë guides us to the recognition that these two attachments are instincts, not individual eccentricities, by showing us they exist in other characters as well, though in attenuated form. Hindley Earnshaw shocks Nelly Dean by being so attached to his wife that he falls apart after her death; Joseph, the unpleasant old servant, is unalterably faithful to the Earnshaw family and to Wuthering Heights as a place. He is grief-stricken when the younger Catherine and Hareton Earnshaw dig up part of his garden: "Aw *hed* aimed tuh dee wheare Aw'd sarved fur sixty year. . . . Bud nah, shoo's taan my garden frough me, un' by th' heart, Maister, Aw cannot stand it" (chap. 33). Loyalty is also very strong in Hareton Earnshaw, the boy Heathcliff has unintentionally strengthened with rough treatment; he defends Heathcliff to young Catherine. "If he were the devil, it didn't signify; he would stand by him; and he'd rather she would abuse himself, as she used to, than begin on Mr. Heathcliff" (chap. 33). Even Nelly Dean, who repeatedly says Heathcliff and Cathy are revolting to her, shares their instincts, for she is irrevocably attached to her own childhood friend, Hindley. Coming to a guidepost where they had played as children, she is overwhelmed with unexpected memories:

> I gazed long at the weather-worn block; and, stooping down, perceived a hole near the bottom still full of snail-shells and pebbles, which we were fond of storing there with more perishable things; and, as fresh as reality, it appeared that I beheld my early playmate seated on the withered turf, his dark, square head bent forward, and his little hand scooping out the earth with a piece of slate.
> "Poor Hindley!" I exclaimed, involuntarily.
> I started—my bodily eye was cheated into a momentary belief that the child lifted its face and stared straight into mine! It vanished in a twinkling; but, immediately, I felt an irresistible yearning to be at the Heights. (Chap. 11)

People like Nelly try to forget their childhood attachments in order to grow up and become responsible adults in the nineteenth-century social world, but the deep, instinctive attachments prevail, in spite of their efforts.

The instincts are purest not in human beings, but in the dogs in *Wuthering Heights*. Lockwood is immediately startled by the number of dogs at Wuthering Heights and at their fierce protectiveness; Catherine Earnshaw is drawn into Thrushcross Grange by the attack of a guard dog. Isabella Linton, when she runs away from Heathcliff, is "accompanied by Fanny, who yelped wild with joy at recovering her mistress" (chap. 17). Isabella has also been touched by the fidelity of another dog she had known when it was a puppy: "An unexpected aid presently appeared in the shape of Throttler, whom I now recognized as a son of our old Skulker; it had spent its whelphood at the Grange, and was given by my father to Mr. Hindley. I fancy it knew me: it pushed its nose against mine by way of salute" (chap. 13). Heathcliff is welcomed by a dog when he comes to see Cathy on the day she dies; Nelly recalls, "As I spoke, I observed a large dog lying on the sunny grass beneath, raise its ears as if about to bark, and then smoothing them back, announce by a wag of the tail that someone approached whom it did not consider a stranger" (chap. 15).

To understand the importance of the dogs in *Wuthering Heights* we must remember that they are not wild animals, but have evolved along with human beings, as loving companions. Dogs are a part and a product of an early human culture; the dog that waits twenty years for Odysseus in Homer's *Odyssey*, and dies only after he has welcomed his returning master home, is the same kind of creature as the dogs in *Wuthering Heights*. And dogs are not very different, in the end, from the human beings in *Wuthering Heights*. Emily Brontë, in the French essays she wrote in Brussels, stated unequivocally her opinion of the relative value of the two species: "Man . . . cannot stand up to comparison with the dog; for the dog is infinitely too good."[19] The reason Heathcliff and Cathy Earnshaw tower over the human world of Emily Brontë's novel is that they retain more of their doglike instincts than the other characters do; it is those instincts that form the basis of a potentially better and stronger human culture.

The characters of her fiction compare Heathcliff to a dog, intending to insult him. Isabella, mocking his attachment to Cathy, suggests, "If I were you, I'd go stretch myself over her grave and die like a faithful dog" (chap. 17). And Nelly describes her horror in watching Heathcliff embrace Cathy before she dies: "He flung himself into the nearest seat, and on my approaching hurriedly to ascertain if she had fainted, he gnashed at me, and foamed like a mad dog, and gathered her to him with greedy jealousy. I did not feel as if I were in the company of a creature of my own species" (chap. 15). She is in fact too civilized, too Victorian, to recognize her own species in its true form. What looks like a mad dog to Nelly Dean is, in *Wuthering Heights*, a sign of human possibilities. Through Heathcliff and Cathy, Emily Brontë offers her readers a way back into a life of nearly forgotten power, a life where men and women can live in fierce equality.

Through the wreck Heathcliff and Cathy make of themselves and the people around them, we can still glimpse what human life might be like for those who have not grown to adulthood in a Christian world dominated by the abstract virtues so dear to Nelly Dean and so dominant in her distorting narrative voice—pity, charity, peace, duty. This system of generalities and abstractions is antithetical to the absolute uniqueness of people and places that lie at the heart of *Wuthering Heights*; we must cut through the language, the abstractions, that dominate our minds and recognize that though Heathcliff and Cathy are destructive in the world of the Victorian novel, they represent a genuine human culture. They live by the heroic code of the warriors in the *Iliad* or *Beowulf,* a code of loyalty and honor, vengeance and fealty. Cathy explains the code to Isabella: "I never say to him, 'Let this or that enemy alone because it would be ungenerous or cruel to harm them'; I say, 'Let them alone because *I* should hate them to be wronged'" (chap. 10). Once we realize that Heathcliff and Cathy, hero and heroine, live by such a code, we can further realize that they are not the asocial creatures the horrified critics of *Wuthering Heights* imagined they were. Epic heroes are violent, but when they are not fighting they go home to their farms and their families, bound to both by love and loyalty instead of by Victorian duty and virtue.

Heathcliff and Cathy gain their pagan strength as much from their attachment to their home as from their attachment to each other, an attachment sacrificed by both in their wrong-headed pursuits of Victorian respectability and upward mobility. When Cathy explains to Nelly why she is going to marry Edgar, she knows she is turning her back on two immutable passions, not one—Heathcliff and her home. Though she does not know she will die in the attempt to become civilized, she knows even as a young woman that her deepest tie is to Wuthering Heights. For her a Christian heaven is the subject of a nightmare, not a dream: "Heaven did not seem to be my home: and I broke my heart with weeping to come back to earth; and the angels were so angry that they flung me out, into the middle of the heath on the top of Wuthering Heights; where I woke sobbing for joy" (chap. 9).

The only heaven for this pagan heroine is her home. She and Heathcliff love the house and the land around it because they know these places, know them with a clarity and precision that cannot be described by any narrator in this fiction. Emily Brontë merely suggests and illuminates the kind of knowledge Heathcliff and Cathy have when Cathy is murmuring over the feathers she has pulled from her pillow in her last illness. "'That's a turkey's,' she murmured to herself; 'and this is a wild-duck's; and this is a pigeon's. Ah, they put pigeons' feathers in the pillows—no wonder I couldn't die! Let me take care to throw it on the floor when I lie down. And here is a moor-cock's; and this—I should know it among a thousand—it's a lapwing's. Bonny bird; wheeling over our heads in the middle of the moor. It wanted to get to its nest, for the clouds touched the swells, and it felt rain coming'" (chap. 2). She possesses the intimate and absolute knowledge of the natural world that hunter-gatherers have and that most civilized people lose.

Cathy and Heathcliff, as pagans, have even gone back beyond the meanings Romantic poets attach to nature; they do not feel a Spirit rolling through it, but see exactly what is there. They are connected to their home as Wordsworth's Michael is connected to his; it is a place that furnishes life, not pleasure. Emily Brontë herself, according to Ellen Nussey, knew nature in this way: "Emily knew every height and hollow, every expanse of pasture, every clump of bilberry, every jutting rock, as landmarks in an otherwise trackless ocean of bracken and heather. She knew and loved the creatures nesting in the heather, and brought the injured ones home in her hands, as the servants remembered; she had no fear of any of them."[20] Even Charlotte, who was unsympathetic to Emily in many ways, recognized that to be at home was the deepest passion of her sister's life. She recognized that Emily would die if she stayed at school: "Her nature proved here too strong for her fortitude. Every morning when she woke, the vision of home and the moors rushed on her, and darkened and saddened the day that lay before her. . . . I felt in my heart she would die, if she did not go home, and with this conviction obtained her recall."[21]

Nature proves too strong for fortitude in the heroine of *Wuthering Heights* as well. In creating a character like Catherine Earnshaw, Emily Brontë defies all that the nineteenth and twentieth centuries have called civilization and progress. People cannot "advance themselves" or move upward in class or grow richer than their parents or "broaden their horizons" without moving. Mere physical mobility is an essential link between Austen's Anne Elliot and Charlotte Brontë's Jane Eyre—these women are "on their way." Attachment to home links Austen's Emma and Emily Brontë's Cathy, and links them, in turn, to the Romantic radicalism that defies economic and industrial "progress" for the sake of the independent economy of rural England. Cathy dies in her attempt to be a modern woman; through this character Emily Brontë asks her readers to consider what they might gain by turning away from mobility. She asks us to imagine what we might be if we regained the attachment to place that belongs to the kinds of people despised by advocates of progress.

The simplicity of the two great, pagan passions that dominate the heroine of *Wuthering Heights* is shocking, as simplicity is shocking in other Romantic manifestos—Wordsworth's *Lyrical Ballads*, Rousseau's *Discourse on the Origin of Inequality*, Thoreau's *Walden*, Kropotkin's *Mutual Aid*. *Wuthering Heights* does more than shock and offer us a spectacle of destruction; it also offers hope. The obvious, believable, but relatively mild hope lies in the marriage of Hareton Earnshaw, Hindley's son, and Catherine Linton, Cathy and Edgar's daughter, for they seem to combine paganism and civilization. Catherine comes to Wuthering Heights as a sweet little ladylike Linton; living there with Heathcliff and Hareton she becomes hotter tempered, more forceful—more like her mother. She even picks up bits of the old country language. "I should like to be climbing up there—Oh! I'm tired—I'm *stalled*, Hareton" (chap. 31). Hareton, whom Heathcliff has vengefully turned into an illiterate country laborer, has actually profited from the intended abuse and has become rough and surly, but also strong and loyal, the kind of person who might have inhabited rural England in an earlier century. He becomes more civilized under Catherine's influence, gentler and literate. When they marry we know life will go on, that the cycle of destruction has ended.

This marriage, however, is not the fictional equivalent of the destruction we have seen, and we need a wilder hope. Emily Brontë gives us this hope in several ways. The still-deluded Lockwood gives us a sign of change at the end which he cannot understand. "My walk home was lengthened by a diversion in the direction of the Kirk. When beneath its walls, I perceived decay had made progress, even in seven months; many a window showed black gaps deprived of glass; and slates jutted off, here and there, beyond the right line of the roof, to be gradually worked off in coming autumn storms" (chap. 34). The old Christian order is dying so the English rural paganism can be reborn.

The final fictional declaration of hope in *Wuthering Heights* is that Heathcliff and Cathy return to their true, pagan, heroic selves when they return to earth as ghosts. Love, finally, rather than vengeance rules them. Before Heathcliff dies he simply gives up his elaborate plans against young Catherine and Hareton, not because he repents but because, as he says, "I have lost the faculty of enjoying their destruction" (chap. 33). He has seen Cathy's eyes in both Catherine and Hareton, and almost in spite of himself stops seeking revenge. And then, Emily Brontë asks us to believe, he gets what he wants—Cathy's ghostly presence. Nelly says, "Now, I perceived he was not looking at the wall, for when I regarded him alone, it seemed exactly that he gazed at something within two yards distance. And, whatever it was, it communicated, apparently, both pleasure and pain, in exquisite extremes" (chap. 34).

Emily Brontë breaks the realistic conventions of the English novel by asking us to believe in ghosts. She makes sure we can choose to disbelieve, by dismissing whichever narrator is reporting them; she also makes sure we will want to believe, and to understand the meaning of the ghosts in this particular novel. We get our first hint that Cathy may be a haunting presence when Lockwood, sleeping in her old bed, dreams that she begs him to let her in; if we want to dismiss this, we can, since Heathcliff has already mockingly suggested that "her spirit has taken the post of ministering angel." We can also dismiss what Heathcliff thinks he sees when he stares in front of him, and the tales Nelly tells Lockwood at the end, after Heathcliff dies.

But the country folks, if you asked them, would swear on their Bible that he *walks*. There are those who speak to having met him near the church and on the moor, and even within this house. Idle tales, you'll say, and so say I. Yet that old man by the kitchen fire affirms he has seen two on 'em looking out of his chamber window, on every rainy night, since his death—and an odd thing happened to me about a month ago.

I was going to the Grange one evening—a dark evening—threatening thunder—and just at the turn of the Heights, I encountered a little boy with a sheep and two lambs before him; he was crying terribly, and I supposed the lambs were skittish, and would not be guided.

"What is the matter, my little man?" I asked.

"They's Heathcliff and a woman, yonder, under t'Nab," he blubbered, "Un Aw darnut pass 'em."

I saw nothing; but neither the sheep nor he would go on, so I bid him take the road lower down. (Chap. 34)

We can dismiss the ghosts, but we do not want to, for *Wuthering Heights* has drawn us beyond the customary social world of the novel into a pagan rural world. These ghosts do not push the novel into the realm of the Gothic, the extreme, the unbelievable; they push the audience back into the rural world of folklore that progressives in the nineteenth century were trying to destroy. Heathcliff and Cathy, we finally believe, are part of the pagan world that once inhabited rural

England; why should they not escape from Christianity's heaven and rejoin a pagan supernatural world? Even Nelly, after all, still sings ballads left over from this pagan world she hates: "It was far in the night, and the bairnies grat,/The mither beneath the mools heard that." (chap. 9). The dead mother hears her children crying even though she is buried; she loves them too much to leave them, as Heathcliff and Cathy love their home too much to leave it.

The pagan hero and heroine of *Wuthering Heights* are not part of a self-conscious classicism in Emily Brontë; they are not the re-creation of other literary texts. Emily Brontë re-creates a heroic, pagan world in Heathcliff and Cathy because she rediscovers this world, in herself, in her animals, in her country home, in the glimpse of a lost rural culture that Tabby bequeathed her. The country world of *Wuthering Heights* is not the same country world Austen and Wordsworth ask their readers to understand, and value, and save; it is older, wilder, and more lost. It is lost, in the nineteenth century, as a pagan culture that actually inhabits the Elizabethan farmhouses of rural England; it can be reborn because it is essentially more human and stronger than the quiet Christian culture of the nineteenth century, the pleasant respectability of the Lintons and Nelly Dean—of Charlotte Brontë and her blustering, conformist heroines. In Catherine Earnshaw, Emily Brontë offers the women of Victorian England the genuine possibility of power—if they can resist Catherine Earnshaw's mistakes, and choose their own true, pagan, instinctual selves instead of the false selves the Nelly Deans and Charlotte Brontës of the world are trying to foist upon them. Although Cathy and Heathcliff are disruptive aliens in the rapidly changing, increasingly bourgeois culture of nineteenth-century England, they are not harbingers of the isolated couples of the Victorian future; they are alone in a Christian, false world, but they are both reminders and prophets of a rural pagan culture in which they would not be lonely aliens. Through these fictional characters Emily Brontë asks her readers to remember a rural world still barely within the memory of the living and to envision the possibility of re-creating it by giving up their misbegotten quests for social respectability in Victorian England.

4. Nathaniel Hawthorne: Public Men and Private Views

Nathaniel Hawthorne's name occurs rarely in feminist books on the nineteenth-century novel. He is, after all, a man, and an American man at that. Nevertheless, he belongs with Austen and Emily Brontë as a Romantic, a radical, and a champion of women; no novelist before Hardy saw more clearly that the increasingly unjust economy of the nineteenth century was depriving the poor of land and destroying women. Hawthorne's most famous woman victim, the adulteress Hester Prynne, is placed, fictionally, in the Puritan seventeenth century; his most powerful woman character—though a less noticed one—is Hepzibah Pyncheon, who belongs to the nineteenth.

The politics of the nineteenth-century present are more vivid in *The House of the Seven Gables* than in any of Hawthorne's other fiction. Here he combines his clearest sense of political and economic wrong, his angriest and most straightforward narrative voice, and his most daringly radical heroine. Hepzibah Pyncheon is remarkable, as a fictional character, in the profundity of her vision, the depth of her suffering, and the power of her voice; like an Old Testament prophet, she can cry out against the sins of her people. Her anger is different from the much-heralded "feminist" rage of Charlotte Brontë's Jane Eyre because it is neither self-justifying nor self-serving; Hepzibah's rage is radically directed at all incarnations of worldly power in mid-nineteenth-century America.

Hawthorne's politics, notoriously difficult to define,[1] are the result of a unique combination of beliefs: the sweeping anarchism of Shelley and a tragic, deeply individualistic Christianity. He does not address specific abuses as clearly as some of his American contemporaries do; nothing he wrote is politically radical in exactly the same way as Thoreau's "Civil Disobedience" or Melville's "Tartarus of Maids" or Margaret Fuller's *Woman in the Nineteenth Century*. A disillusioned member of the utopian community at Brook Farm, friend of conservative president Franklin Pierce, and creator of fictional reformers whose obsessions quickly turn to evil, Hawthorne has often been glibly dismissed as a conservative. But beneath and beyond the superficial conservatism is a sweeping Romantic radicalism that relates his vision of American wrongs to the horrors of two thousand years of Western culture.

Unlike his contemporaries in Romantic America, whose intellectual affinities were with Coleridge, Goethe, Carlyle, and Mill, Hawthorne chose Shelley. He states his preference openly in his fantastic tale "Earth's Holocaust," a description of cosmic bonfire in which all cultural artifacts are consumed. "Methought Shelley's poetry emitted a purer light than almost any other production of his day, contrasting beautifully with the fitful and lurid gleams and gushes of black vapour that flashed and eddied from the volumes of Lord Byron." Hawthorne does not mention Wordsworth in this story for an obvious reason: the rural community Wordsworth wanted to save as a bulwark against the economic injustices of industrial capitalism—ancient rights, common laws, traditions of mutual aid—did not exist in America. Though Hawthorne does speak, briefly, for American rural life in *The House of the Seven Gables*, he has no ancient villages, no characters like Michael in his barely three-hundred-year-old country in which he could find a source of radical strength.

The truly ancient life available to Hawthorne's imagination was something unique to America, and disruptive of all the premises of what is called Western civilization. Hawthorne had glimpses not of agricultural villagers, but of the hunting and gathering tribes native to America. Not only did he find native American artifacts in his garden, as he says in "The Old Manse," but he also saw native

Americans walking the streets. This constant, forced acknowledgment of the tribal peoples white Americans had displaced gives Hawthorne a view of history different from that of any nineteenth-century English novelist. Though the English could see a kind of tribal life, occasionally, the Gypsies, they did not have to remember that the Gypsies were the rightful owners of England. Meditating on the location of his Old Manse near a famous battlefield of the Revolutionary War, Hawthorne, the historical romancer, startlingly disavows any interest in history:

> Many strangers come in the summer time to view the battleground. For my own part, I have never found my imagination much excited by this or any other scene of historic celebrity; nor would the placid margin of the river have lost any of its charm for me had men never fought and died there. There is a wilder interest in the tract of land—perhaps a hundred yards in breadth—which extends between the battle-field and the northern face of our Old Manse, with its contiguous avenue and orchard. Here, in some unknown age, before the white man came, stood an Indian village, convenient to the river, whence its inhabitants must have drawn so large a part of their subsistence. The site is identified by the spear and arrowheads, the chisels, and other implements of war, labor, and the chase, which the plough turns up from the soil. ("The Old Manse")

The history Hawthorne disclaims belongs to white *men*. The life that fascinates him belongs to the nonwhite people, men and women, who have been lost to what white men call history. The life he imaginatively reconstructs for the native Americans includes women and children and the activity of *play*, which the still puritanical descendants of the early white Americans have tried to forget.

> There is an exquisite delight, too, in picking up for one's self an arrowhead that was dropped centuries ago and has never been handled since, and which we thus receive directly from the hand of the red hunter, who purposed to shoot it at his game or at an enemy. Such an incident builds up again the Indian village and its encircling forest, and recalls to life the painted chiefs and warriors, the squaws at their houshold toil, and the children sporting among the wigwams, while the little wind-rocked papoose swings from the branch of the tree. It can hardly be told whether it is a joy or a pain, after such a momentary vision, to gaze around in the broad daylight of reality and see stone fences, potato fields, and men doggedly hoeing in their shirtsleeves and homespun pantaloons.

Hawthorne contrasts native Americans, with women and children, at hunting, fighting, and play, to a culture in which only men are visible, and in which those men have fenced off their property, have planted the vegetables of the poor, and must work constantly. His own culture has degraded men and made women invisible. The glimpse of the native American culture gives him a possible basis for a radical feminism. (His final disclaimer, that he has been talking nonsense, does not cancel his radical meaning.)

The tempting possibility of a life lost to Western culture draws Hawthorne to Shelley. He shares Shelley's anarchism but not his sexual self-indulgence or his self-congratulatory maunderings on the wonders of the soul. Shelley's "Witch of Atlas" celebrates the life of play, sex, and imagination that exists at the beginning of human life, before "Error and Truth had hunted from the Earth/All those bright natures which adorned its prime." Witches, hunter-gatherers, native peoples—all have been seen as enemies by white man's culture, Western civilization. Play, magic, sexual abundance: all have been associated with women and primitive peoples, and all have been repressed in the names of order, progress, error and truth, civilization, history. Both witches and native Americans were extirpated as agents of evil in the American seventeenth century, the beginning of the culture Hawthorne believes is still living in the nineteenth.

Hawthorne's radical criticism of his own culture and his radical sympathy with the forbidden life of pleasure are given the clearest historical form in *The House of the Seven Gables.* Here the victims of white man's culture have more dignity and power than they do in his other fiction; his representatives of hope have more solidity; and above all, his villain has more historical specificity. The power of Hawthorne's dissenting and damaged characters in *The House of the Seven Gables*, especially his prophetess and heroine, Hepzibah Pyncheon, grows from the clarity of their enemy, Judge Jaffrey Pyncheon. In this novel, unlike Hawthorne's others, the villain is not a timeless *type*, the evil meddler in human souls, a Chillingworth, a Westervelt. This villain is a politically and economically powerful man who belongs to both a type—the grasping American Puritan—and a time, mid-nineteenth-century America. Hawthorne creates his strongest voice of women's resistance here because he portrays so clearly what she must resist.

History and the conventions of realism that most novels presuppose seem to be at odds in the modest, playful preface, where Hawthorne calls *The House of the Seven Gables* a "Romance" instead of a novel. His first reason for this generic definition is that he allows himself to include what he calls the "Marvellous." The second is that he is making historical connections between his present and a distant past: "The point of view in which this Tale comes under the Romantic definition, lies in the attempt to connect a by-gone time with the very Present that is flitting away from us. It is a Legend, prolonging itself, from an epoch now gray in the distance, down into our own broad daylight, and bringing along with it some of its legendary mist, which the Reader, according to his pleasure, may either disregard, or allow to float almost imperceptibly about the characters and events, for the sake of a picturesque effect." This sounds humble enough, as if the historical connections in the book were a mere literary decoration. In fact, in this historical romance, the connection between the Pyncheons and Maules of seventeenth-century Salem and their nineteenth-century descendants is a radical filter through which Hawthorne can lay bare the deepest and cruelest tendencies of white man's civilization.

It is the bareness with which Hawthorne displays his villains and the class war they have waged that separate *The House of the Seven Gables* from contemporary English Victorian novels. By the middle of the nineteenth century, England and the United States shared many political and economic problems—forms of progress, for those who were profiting—increasingly urban, industrial, capitalistic, and monopolistic. One great difference is that the Americans were more unconstrained, less inhibited by custom, by the past, by the kind of rural culture in which Wordsworth placed his faith. The dream of boundless land (encumbered only by a few unfortunate nonwhite people) and boundless wealth allowed the spirit of what is called free enterprise to bloom a little more quickly, freely, and unabashedly in the New World than it had in the Old. Nineteenth-century Americans did not need an English Carlyle to scream "Work!" at them, for they inherited the spirit of hard-won conquest from their seventeenth-century Puritan ancestors. The historical romance of *The House of the Seven Gables* lays bare the exploitive basis of the economy that was, in one way or another, driving both nineteenth-century England and nineteenth-century America.

The narrative voice through which Hawthorne removes the religious veil from the Puritan past American children have been taught to revere is quite different from the tentative and gentle voice of his preface. He says outright, in his first chapter, that the witch trials were not merely an unfortunate outbreak of excessive religious zeal; they were a cover for class war. When powerful Colonel Pyncheon, "characterized by an iron energy of purpose," covets the homestead of powerless Matthew Maule, now that it has become a desirable piece of town real estate rather than a solitary farm, a charge of witchcraft serves his purpose well.

> Old Matthew Maule, in a word, was executed for the crime of witchcraft. He was one of the martyrs to that terrible delusion which should teach us, among its other morals, that the influential classes, and those who take upon themselves to be leaders of the people, are fully liable to all the passionate error that has ever characterized the maddest mob. . . . But, in after days, when the frenzy of that hideous epoch had subsided, it was remembered how loudly Colonel Pyncheon had joined in the general cry, to purge the land from witchcraft; nor did it fail to be whispered, that there was an invidious acrimony in the zeal with which he had sought the condemnation of Matthew Maule. It was well known, that the victim had recognized the bitterness of personal enmity in his persecutor's conduct towards him, and that he declared himself hunted to death for his spoil. (Chap. 1)

This is the story of Wordsworth's "Michael," recast in fury. Hawthorne's victim is not a noble patriarch, only a poor farmer; his destroyer is not a promissory note, but a villain. Already, in the seventeenth century, the American rich were using whatever they needed—politics, religion—to acquire the property of the poor. So much for Jefferson's dream of a country of small farmers: America was on its way to being a country of rich and poor, oppressors and oppressed, capitalists and propertyless laborers—just like England.

As a type, the first Pyncheon is distinctly and terrifyingly male, the kind of man who is born to seize political and economic power in an unjust world. He victimizes his less fortunate, less aggressive, less manipulative neighbors of both sexes and, Hawthorne's narrator says explicitly, his women. "The Puritan, again, an autocrat in his own household, had worn out three wives, and, merely by the remorseless weight and hardness of his character in the conjugal relation, had sent them, one after another, broken hearted to their graves" (chap. 8). This is hardly the new sexual equality Tocqueville thought he saw in America;[2] it is a more violent and absolute domination than the mere repression of women's spiritual creativity about which Margaret Fuller complained.[3] Because Colonel Pyncheon is more than an individual—he is a type of white man who has been leading our economic and political life—Hawthorne is implicitly making a sweeping and startling charge: sexual tyranny and even sexual sadism against women have been built into the dominant culture of America.

The character traits of this Puritan ancestor are reincarnated in Jaffrey Pyncheon, the embodiment of power in the nineteenth century. And to his inherited lust for power and cruelty to the weak Hawthorne has added the particularly nineteenth-century vices of unctuous sociability and hypocrisy. Like his ancestor, Jaffrey has misused the law to acquire property; thirty years before *The House of the Seven Gables* opens, he has contrived to inherit the Pyncheon property by implicating his pathetic cousin Clifford in the (actually natural) death of their uncle, a man so quixotic that he had intended to return the property to the Maules. Now, having arranged for Clifford to be released from prison so that he can extract from him the hiding place of what he imagines is the deed to a huge property in Maine, he reenacts the role of witch hunter in nineteenth-century form. As he explains to Hepzibah, Clifford's sister and protector:

Since your brother's return, I have taken the precaution (a highly proper one in the near kinsman and natural guardian of an individual so situated) to have his deportment and habits constantly and carefully overlooked. Your neighbors have been eye-witnesses to whatever has passed in the garden. . . . From all this testimony, I am led to apprehend—reluctantly, and with deep grief— that Clifford's misfortunes have so affected his intellect, never very strong, that he cannot safely remain at large. The alternative, you must be aware—and its adoption will depend entirely on the decision which I am now about to make—the alternative is his confinement, probably for the remainder of his life, in a public asylum for persons in his unfortunate state of mind. (Chap. 15)

This passage precedes by nine years John Stuart Mill's exraordinary note in "On Liberty":

There is something both contemptible and frightful in the sort of evidence on which, of late years, any person can be judicially declared unfit for the management of his affairs; and after his death, his disposal of the property can be set aside. . . . All the minute details of his daily life are pried into, and whatever is found which, seen through the medium of the perceiving and describing faculties of the lowest of the low, bears an appearance unlike absolute commonplace, is laid before the jury as evidence of insanity, and often with success.[4]

The power mongers of the nineteenth century create a class of utterly victimized people, just as the witch hunters of the seventeenth century did. And though in both centuries the victims can be women and weak men alike, the victimizers, as a class, are men.

Jaffrey Pyncheon has abused women personally, both as a profligate youth and as the domineering husband whose wife could survive only a few years with him. "There was a fable . . . that the lady got her death-blow in the honey-moon, and never smiled again, because her husband compelled her to serve him with coffee, every morning, at his bedside, in token of fealty to her liege-lord and master" (chap. 8). Serving coffee is a mild form of servitude, admittedly; the important words are those that indicate the symbolic psychological meaning of the act—"compelled," "serve," "fealty," "liege-lord and master." Hawthorne leads us to believe that this Pyncheon granted his wife no mercy, and that she too is one of the victims of the Pyncheon spirit, the spirit of American male power.

Jaffrey Pyncheon is a unique villain in nineteenth-century fiction because of Hawthorne's determination to make us see him as the type of powerful man who has run the Western world for centuries, not as a perverted exception. He does not behave like other Victorian villains because he has no excesses, no self-destructive quirks, no telltale eccentricities that indirectly offer a reader hope that not all powerful men are like this one. Hawthorne suggests, relentlessly, that they are. In the last chapter, "Governor Pyncheon," Hawthorne tells us how entirely Jaffrey is wedded to the fabric of American culture: he has "railroad, bank, and insurance shares, United States stock"; he is a bank director; he owns a country estate for which he is about to buy rare fruit trees; and if he had not died of the ancestral apoplexy, he would have met his political friends for dinner, and become governor. He is the kind of man other men like and trust.

These gentlemen . . . have assembled, not without purpose, from every quarter of the State. They are practised politicians, every man of them, and skilled to adjust those preliminary measures, which steal from the people, without its knowledge, the power of choosing its own rulers. The popular voice, at the next gubernatorial election, though loud as thunder, will be really but an echo of what these gentlemen shall speak, under their breath, at your friend's festive board. They meet to decide upon their candidate. This little knot of subtle schemers will control the Convention, and, through it, dictate to the party. And what worthier candidate—more wise and learned, more noted for philanthropic liberality, truer to safe principles, tried oftener by public trusts, more spotless in private character, with a larger stake in the common welfare, and deeper grounded, by hereditary descent, in the faith and practice of the Puritans—what man can be presented for the suffrage of the people, so eminently combining all these claims to chief-rulership, as Judge Pyncheon here before us? (Chap. 18)

The male culture that rules the nineteenth-century world, socially, politically, economically, even religiously, is as corrupt as Judge Pyncheon, in Hawthorne's radical view. He is no worse than his fellows; they *all* deprive the poor of their power, even if the poor do not know it.

These men, commonly called "pillars of society," are the persons without whom society cannot stand. Hawthorne makes the connection between Jaffrey's *type* and the institutions requiring massive architecture, the kind of architecture that uses pillars.

They are ordinarily men to whom forms are of paramount importance. Their field of action lies among the external phenomena of life. They possess vast ability in grasping and arranging, and appropriating to themselves, the big, heavy, solid unrealities such as gold, landed estate, offices of trust and emolument, and public honors. With these materials, and with deeds of goodly aspect, done in the public eye, an individual of this class builds up, as it were, a tall and stately edifice, which, in the view of other people, and ultimately in his own view, is no other than the man's character, or the man himself. Behold, therefore, a palace! (Chap. 15)

Power resides in palaces, mansions, banks, office buildings. Of course the building necessitated by all these others is the prison, which Hawthorne's narrator, in the first chapter of *The Scarlet Letter*, calls "the black flower of civilized society." The prison is always the unseen presence in *The House of the Seven Gables*, the building from which poor Clifford has just emerged. The prison is the architectural reminder that the power of public men in civilized society rests on a class of victims. Hawthorne's insistence that we understand Jaffrey as an emblem of this totality of male power forces us to imagine a total and radical alternative, or a set of alternatives, ways of living that would not give power to unscrupulous men, and would not need an underclass of victims in the odd, the weak, and women.

In *The House of the Seven Gables*, Hawthorne never lets his readers forget that a culture run by men like Jaffrey—as all Western cultures are—ruins women. Besides the swiftly deceased wives of Jaffrey and his ancestor, other victims appear, nameless figures or vivid characters. One of the first customers in the little shop Hepzibah Pyncheon opens to earn enough money to take care of her brother is "a pale, care-wrinkled woman, not old, but haggard and already with streaks of gray among her hair, like silver ribbons; one of those women, naturally delicate, whom you at once recognize as worn to death by a brute—probably, a drunken brute—of a husband, and at least nine children" (chap. 3). This is the sort of woman whom less radical novelists—both men and women—leave invisible. Hawthorne reminds us that men of the working classes are not exempt from the cruelties of the Pyncheons; abuse unites women of all classes in *The House of the Seven Gables*.

The men who observe Hepzibah's sad attempts to set up a shop deride her; even the boys of the town have lost any kindness of heart. When Hepzibah fears that her brother is lost, she imagines him "To be the sport of boys, who, when old enough to run about the streets, have no more reverence for what is beautiful and holy, nor pity for what is sad—no more sense of sacred misery, sanctifying the human shape in which it embodies itself—than if Satan were the father of them all" (chap. 16). Satan is not their father, but as a spiritual influence the witch hunter Colonel Pyncheon is.

Although the men running the American world of *The House of the Seven Gables* are bad, and have no intention of giving up their power, Hawthorne has filled his fiction with strange, secret hopes. The world that seems so solid to men like Jaffrey Pyncheon, and so solidly under control, is susceptible to other influences. Although there is no hope of revolution here, subversion and resistance are at work, creating fissures, chasms, potential earthquakes in the social and economic edifices in which the Jaffrey Pyncheons of the world embody themselves. In this unusually inactive fiction, almost plotless, the mere presence of three pairs of characters—three men and three women—radiates power and generates hope. Phoebe Pyncheon and Holgrave, the last of the Maules, offer the most conventional hope for a better life on earth; Clifford and Hepzibah Pyncheon, Jaffrey's two saddest victims, together offer wilder hopes and, more important, a heroic resistance; the ghost of Alice Pyncheon and Uncle Venner, Hepzibah's ancient and peculiar friend, the strangest and most evanescent pair, offer hope both supernatural and natural. The three couples work on our imaginations as the three couples— young Cathy and Hareton, doomed Cathy and Heathcliff, and ghostly Cathy and Heathcliff—do in *Wuthering Heights*; they offer sensible comfort, heart-wrenching sorrow, and a final, utopian hope that a bad world may be broken open. Though women have no power in the world of Jaffrey Pyncheon; in these hidden forces of regeneration they find their secret strength.

Holgrave and Phoebe—young, attractive, marriageable—seem to be the stuff of which ordinary novels are made, yet the golden, housewifely, singing girl and the young man, recognizable to Hawthorne's audience as one of the New England reformers Emerson viewed with both affection and skepticism, carry seeds of subversion. As historically specific characters, they have more political meaning than the superficially similar characters in Hawthorne's other fiction. Though they look like his meddlesome reformer and his sweet conventional woman, they are fictionally unique, and daring, and powerful.

Holgrave is related to Hawthorne's usual villains, his mad scientists and meddling utopians, but more complicated and more capable of change than the others. He is economically identified; his family, the Maules, represent the class of propertyless wage earners in America, for they have never recovered the land of which Colonel Pyncheon deprived their ancestor. "They were generally poverty-stricken; always plebian and obscure; working with unsuccessful diligence at handicrafts; laboring on the wharves, or following the sea, as sailors before the mast; living here and there about the town, in hired tenements, and coming finally to the alms house, as the natural home of their old age" (chap. 1). Yet economic deprivation has become economic liberty for Holgrave himself; as a most modern artist—a daguerreotypist—and reformer, short-story writer and peddler, traveler and dentist, he is a version of a favorite character in nineteenth-century Romantic literature, the many-sided man who Goethe, Emerson, Thoreau, and the young Marx of *The German Ideology* all hoped would replace the stunted specimens of humanity they saw around them, victims of the division of labor.

Yet Holgrave is more subversive than these other many-sided men. Hawthorne says outright that he is a potential victim of another witchcraft scare. Even his friend and landlady Hepzibah "had reason to believe that he practiced animal magnetism, and, if such things were in fashion now-a-days, should be apt to suspect him of studying the Black Art, up there in his lonesome chamber" (chap. 5). He is as dangerous as a witch because he can speak some of Hawthorne's most subversive thoughts, specifically against architecture, the symbol of wicked earthly power.

But we shall live to see the day, I trust . . . when no man shall build his house for posterity. . . . If each generation were allowed and expected to build its own houses, that single change, comparatively unimportant in itself, would imply almost every reform which society is now suffering for. I doubt whether even our public edifices—our capitols, state-houses, court-houses, city-halls, and churches—ought to be built of such permanent materials as stone or brick. It were better that they should crumble to ruin, once in twenty years, or thereabouts, as a hint to the people to examine into and reform the institutions which they symbolize. (Chap. 12)

When we meet him, he wants to take on the world; given a chance, he might disintegrate into one of Hawthorne's obsessive, failed utopians.

Holgrave does not have the chance because he falls in love with Phoebe Pyncheon. We feel pleasure and loss when he changes; we rejoice that he resists the temptation to hypnotize her, as his ancestor had hypnotized Alice Pyncheon and destroyed her; and we share his surprise and regret at the ease with which he becomes "conservative" and looks forward to living in a stone house. He is acknowledging that he himself is no longer ill at ease, and he is ready to settle down and keep the population going. On the other hand, he remains committed to the belief that the world *has* an onward impulse—"The world owes all its onward impulse to men ill at ease" (chap. 20). He has played his part in it; now it will be the turn of other young men.

Marrying, planting trees, all the domestic activities Hawthorne associates with Holgrave's wife-to-be, Phoebe Pyncheon, could be the activities of the spiritually dead. After all, Jaffrey Pyncheon plants trees to demonstrate his respectability. But, in *The House of the Seven Gables*, the rural, agricultural life Phoebe represents has its own subversive meaning. This wholesome young woman, who brings butter from her country home, and cuts flowers, feeds chickens, and bakes cakes is a conventional Victorian heroine who redeems her man through love and also a woman of forbidden power. She practices "homely witchcraft." This phrase, in this fiction, is potent. Witchcraft is dangerous business in Hawthorne's New England! And Phoebe is secretly allied with the other condemned men and women who have been the victims of men like Jaffrey. She is part of the modest, rural agricultural economy that Matthew Maule wanted, and that men like Jaffrey have tried to stamp out of existence. Phoebe is poor not rich, generous not greedy; she is less a Victorian heroine than a Jeffersonian ideal. She is "the example of feminine grace and availability combined, in a state of society, if there were any such, where ladies did not exist" (chap. 5).

The powerful, rich Pyncheons are distinctly urban; Colonel Pyncheon did not even want Matthew Maule's land until it became valuable. So agricultural Phoebe brings a political and economic alternative into the fictional world of *The House of the Seven Gables*. When Jaffrey Pyncheon dies of apoplexy as his ancestors had, Phoebe and Holgrave preside over the transplantation of their little clan to Jaffrey's country home "for the present" (chap. 21). The Maules are getting back a farm the Pyncheons took away from them two hundred years before. "For the present" this new beginning of Jeffersonian, agricultural, egalitarian America is what sweet, dependable Phoebe Pyncheon offers. In this novel, where urban architecture looms so oppressively and evilly, Phoebe is indeed a radical heroine. She offers a clear hope for social regeneration and a more just life.

Yet Phoebe, for all her brightness, is a smaller, paler figure than Jaffrey Pyncheon's victims, Clifford and Hepzibah. She and Holgrave alone cannot outweigh Jaffrey's power in the fiction. Hepzibah and Clifford are the suffering, vital, figures who grab the reader's imagination as Heathcliff and Cathy do in *Wuthering Heights*. Both couples force upon us the tragic knowledge of the power of the wrong; both resist wrong, in different ways; and both combine what are commonly considered men's and women's qualities in a way that forces us to reconsider the roles into which people have been cast. Part of the tyrannical power of men like Jaffrey Pyncheon and his ancestor the Colonel is the rigidly separate and unequal roles they assign to themselves and the women of their families. Part of the hope poor ruined Clifford and Hepzibah offer is the possibility of sexual individuality.

Clifford's feminine characteristics, his gentleness, his sensuality, his beauty, his aesthetic love of pleasure, all make him a born victim in a world where manhood is defined by Jaffrey Pyncheon. As Hepzibah says, "They persecuted his mother in him! He never was a Pyncheon" (chap. 4). And in contrast, Hepzibah's moral force, her ferocious wisdom, her articulate and defiant voice all make her a forbidden woman in the Victorian middle of the nineteenth century. Introducing Clifford, a wreck after thirty years of unjust imprisonment, Hawthorne defines both him and his sister as types not bound by sex. Even if Clifford had been free, he would never have won approval in the social, civilized, Christian world.

Beauty would be his life; his aspirations would all tend towards it; and, allowing his frame and physical organs to be in consonance, his own developments would likewise be beautiful. Such a man should have nothing to do with sorrow; nothing with strife; nothing with the martyrdom which, in an infinite variety of shapes, awaits those who have the heart, and will, and conscience, to fight a battle with the world. To these heroic tempers, such martyrdom is the richest meed in the world's gift. To the individual before us, it could only be a grief, intense in due proportion with the severity of the infliction. He had no right to be a martyr; and, beholding him so fit to be happy, and so feeble for all other purposes, a generous, strong, and noble spirit would, methinks, have been ready to sacrifice what little enjoyment it might have planned for itself—it would have flung down the hopes, so paltry in its regard—if thereby the wintry blasts of our rude sphere might come tempered to such a man. (Chap. 7)

Clifford, born for beauty and pleasure, is a remnant of an earlier world when good and evil did not exist.

In describing the pleasure-seeker and the martyr, Hawthorne plays with the double meanings of the word *world*, suggesting both that Clifford is always doomed on this earth and that in a less *worldly* culture, a culture not dominated by men like Jaffrey, he might, indeed, be his happy self. The world a martyr fights is not the earth but the realm of political and economic power; what is more worth fighting for than a freer and more peaceful and pleasure-loving earth? Clifford needs a culture radically different from the one he is doomed by; the modest agricultural alternative offered by Phoebe Pyncheon is not free enough for him. He dreams of an even more utopian future than the young Holgrave does, a world without any architecture, police, or prisons. In his brief fling at freedom, riding a train, Clifford imagines that the future will be a refined version of the most ancient human past, a nomadic state like that of the native Americans who fascinated Hawthorne.

My impression is, that our wonderfully increased, and still increasing, facilities of locomotion are destined to bring us around again to the nomadic state. ... The past is but a coarse and sensual prophecy of the present and the future. ... In the early epochs of our race, men dwelt in temporary huts, or bowers of branches, as easily constructed as a bird's nest, and which they built—if it should be called building, when such sweet homes of a summer-solstice rather grew, than were made with hands—which Nature, we will say, assisted them to rear, where fruit abounded, where fish and game were plentiful, or, most especially, where the sense of beauty was to be gratified by a lovelier shade than elsewhere, and a more exquisite arrangement of lake, wood, and hill. This life possessed a charm, which, ever since man quitted it, has vanished from existence. (Chap. 17)

Clifford, who is unjustly held in an architectural monument, the prison, because Jaffrey desired to possess another monument, the family mansion, understands very well the utopian implications of a world without architecture: "Just imagine, for a moment, how much of human evil will crumble away, with this one change! What we call real estate—the solid ground to build a house on—is the broad foundation on which nearly all the guilt of this world rests. A man will commit almost any wrong—he will heap up an immense pile of wickedness, as hard as granite, and which will weigh as heavily upon his soul, to eternal ages—only to build a great, gloomy, dark-chambered mansion, for himself to die in, and for his posterity to be miserable in" (chap. 17). The world of guilt is not the earth; it is the civilized world where, as Clifford says, "bank-robbers . . . are about as honest as nine people in ten, except that they disregard certain formalities, and prefer to transact business at midnight, rather than 'Change-hours" (chap. 17). The world in which a feminine, sensuous, indolent man like Clifford is doomed is not eternal; it is, in utopian dreams, eradicable, replaceable by a new version of the old world of hunter-gatherers.

These most radical of all Romantic dreams are no maunderings of an insane man, even though placed in the mouth of a character whose irrationality will allow the skeptical reader to dismiss them. They are the insights of an anthropologically intuitive author. The radically utopian possibilities of a hunting-and-gathering life have been supported by recent anthropology; in *Human Scale* Kirkpatrick Sale corroborates Clifford's dream of the one culture where he might be happy.

Once upon a time the greater part of the world's population lived in conditions that, as we view them from our contemporary perspective, could only be considered opulent. They spent their time—all of them, regardless of birth or beauty—in the closest thing to indolence, working only a few hours a day, sitting around and sleeping and making love for hours at a time, literally living off the fat of the land and gorging themselves when food came along with little thought of saving for the morrow. They surrounded themselves with beautiful objects, participated in elaborate useless rituals, devoted resources to nothing more substantial than jewelry and wall paintings. They ate well, with balanced diets, got plenty of regular exercise, were spared most serious diseases, and lived to relatively ripe old ages. They were for the most part free of poverty, privation, pollution, crime, and war.[5]

The hope Clifford offers the reader in *The House of the Seven Gables* is the wildest dream of nineteenth-century Romantic radicalism, a utopian anarchism. Yet it is not a hope that has not been or could never be true. It has been true, and it could be again. But it needs people stronger than Clifford to bring it into being.

Hepzibah offers the strength necessary for a martyr's fight against the world. She, a poor, old spinster, is the radical warrior of this book. Too proud to take any of Jaffrey's money, she has chosen poverty and loneliness—and has gained a terrible, radical wisdom about Jaffrey and his world. Like Phoebe and Holgrave, she has a secret affinity with the witches the men of America have been fearing and oppressing for centuries; as one of her nasty neighbors says, "She's a real old vixen, take my word of it. She says little, to be sure;—but if you could only see the mischief in her eye" (chap. 4). She offers us not utopian hope but radical, angry vision and grim, tragic resistance. She is the sort of hero who must prepare the way for the better world she cannot see. Only Hepzibah dares see Jaffrey for what he is and to stand up to him. She has the power to defy and perhaps even to destroy him, for he dies of apoplexy immediately after she has finally expressed her heroic rage. Hawthorne tells us early in the book that Hepzibah's wrath is part of a prophetic vision that can subvert an evil male power.

So also, as regards the Judge Pyncheon of to-day, neither clergyman, nor legal critic, nor inscriber of tombstones, nor historian of general or local politics, would venture a word against this eminent person's sincerity as a christian or respectability as a man, or integrity as a judge, or courage and faithfulness as the often-tried representative of his political party. But, besides these cold, formal, and empty words of the chisel that inscribes, the voice that speaks, and the pen that writes for the public eye and for distant time—and which inevitably lose much of their truth and freedom by the fatal consciousness of so doing—there were traditions about the ancestor, and private diurnal gossip about the Judge, remarkably accordant in their testimony. It is often instructive to take the woman's, the private and domestic view, of a public man; nor can anything be more curious than the vast discrepancy between the portraits intended for engraving, and the pencil-sketches that pass from hand to hand, behind the original's back. (Chap. 8)

Jaffrey is in collusion with other men to preserve their power in the public world, the world of architecture, politics, and law; yet for Hawthorne women, the silent, oppressed victims, possess secret, subversive radical power simply by being able to see the truth. Their own traditions exist out of public view; what they pass hand to hand is radical vision, the power to turn the world upside down.

Hawthorne puts more fire into Hepzibah's words than into any-one else's; even the fiery narrator pales beside this prophetic old spinster. She can accuse Jaffrey to his face: "In God's name, whom you insult—and whose power I could almost question, since He hears you utter so many false words, without palsying your tongue—give over, I beseech you, this loathsome pretence of affection for your victim! You hate him! Say so, like a man" (chap. 15). Her thoughts go even further in condemning the structures of power that support Jaffrey. Imagining what would happen if she called to her neighbors for help against Jaffrey, she realizes, "How wild, how almost laugh-able the fatality, and yet how continually it comes to pass . . . in this dull delirium of a world—that whosoever, and with however kindly a purpose, should come to help, they would be sure to help the strongest side! Might and wrong combined, like iron magnetized, are endowed with irresistible attraction" (chap. 16). This is not merely unfeminine. Through Hepzibah, Hawthorne attacks the deepest, wrongest, and most powerful assumption of what we call civiliza-tion, the assumption that political and economic power should be respected. In giving such vision and such power to an outcast woman, the kind of woman most other writers would treat with disdain, Hawthorne has participated in Hepzibah's Romantic radicalism; as an author, he has created a more heroic heroine than any woman in the nineteenth century ever did. He has given Hepzibah the heroic wrath against wrong that is the other side of all Romantic hope for joy.

The final couple of the book, the strangest of all, give the reader a final vision of hope. The last lines of *The House of the Seven Gables* belong to Uncle Venner, Hepzibah's old friend, and to Alice Pyn-cheon, the ghost who has haunted the house and suffered ever since Holgrave's ancestor hypnotized her. "Just before the family is about to leave for the country, Uncle Venner gives us one last look at the ancestral house. "And wise Uncle Venner, passing slowly from the ruinous porch, seemed to hear a strain of music, and fancied that sweet Alice Pyncheon—after witnessing these deeds, this by-gone woe, and this present happiness, of her kindred mortals—had given one farewell touch of a spirit's joy upon her harpsichord, as she floated heavenward from THE HOUSE OF THE SEVEN GABLES" (chap. 21). These two apparently minor characters, a long-dead woman, another tragic victim, and an utterly contented man with none of Jaffrey's aggressively male qualities, tip this fiction toward radical hope. And they rescue both the family and the fiction from the bourgeois respectability threatening to envelop the new Pyncheon-Maule family in their country seat. They are going to take Uncle Venner the visionary along, and the one thing he will never be is respectable. An ancient man, once considered the town idiot, he has discovered for himself something very like the nomadic life Clifford imagines as part of the distant human past and the ideal human future. He lives cheerfully, without the encumbrances of property or social pride. He runs errands, splits wood, digs gardens, shovels snow for his neighbors. "Within that circle, he claimed the same sort of privilege, and probably felt as much warmth of interest, as a clergyman does in the range of his parishioners. Not that he laid claim to the tithe pig; but, as an analogous mode of reverence, he went his rounds, every morning, to gather up the crumbs of the table and overflowings of the dinner-pot, as food for a pig of his own" (chap. 4). He is a little like Hawthorne's friend Thoreau, the natural-born anarchist, without any hint of bitterness. He is unembarrassed at the thought of ending up at the almshouse, which he cheerfully calls his "farm"; he does not have to look into a utopian future to hope, as Clifford does, for a life of idleness and pleasure. "What can be pleasanter than to spend a whole day, on the sunny side of a barn or a wood-pile, chatting with somebody as old as one's self; or perhaps idling away the time with a natural-born simpleton, who knows how to be idle, because even our busy Yankees have never found out how to put him to any use?" (chap. 4).

Uncle Venner, whom Holgrave calls another Fourier, is as much a discord in the male world of Jaffrey Pyncheon and the busy Yankees as Clifford is. A man who has violated the laws of white man's civilization without pain or struggle, he is the natural ally of the women in *The House of The Seven Gables* in their more conscious struggle against Jaffrey. Women, sensualists, anarchists, idlers—they are all enemies, not merely victims, of male power.

Uncle Venner is Hawthorne's chosen visionary, the one character who can hear Alice Pyncheon's ghostly music and see that she is finally at peace. She is the last heroine of *The House of the Seven Gables*, the last victim, and the last witch. As Holgrave re-creates this long-dead woman, she possesses the rare beauty that belongs also to Clifford: "At an open window of a room in the second story, hanging over some pots of beautiful and delicate flowers-exotics, but which had never known a more genial sunshine than that of the New England autumn—was the figure of a young lady, an exotic, like the flowers, and beautiful and delicate as they. Her presence imparted an indescribable grace and faint witchery to the whole edifice." (chap. 13). Both Alice and Clifford remind us of the depth of Hawthorne's Romantic radicalism in *The House of the Seven Gables*: the life of ease and pleasure and beauty to which they belong is as deep a threat to white man's civilization as witchcraft. Alice has been the victim of the Pyncheons and the Maules: her father, in his search for the lost Pyncheon lands, effectually sold her to young Matthew Maule as a hypnotic medium; Maule kept her in a posthypnotic state of thrall-dom. Maule sought revenge because she dared look at him with sexual desire, admiring his "comeliness, strength, and energy"; such desire is a natural part of the ancient life of pleasure to which Alice belongs, and is anathema to white male culture, the culture to which Pyncheons and Maules, property owners and workers, both belong. Alice's sexuality is a genuine pleasure, an open desire, not a form of oppression like the sexual brutality with which the Pyncheons have worn out their wives. We only glimpse her; she reminds us that Clifford is not the only person who was born for beauty, that all such people are victimized by the structure of power of civilization.

At the end of *The House of the Seven Gables*, Alice is free at last, a ghostly, beautiful heroine, an emblem of the radical, utopian streak in this unique novel, the only novel in the nineteenth century in which Shelley's sweeping anarchism is given fictional form. Haw-thorne's utopian hopes remain mysterious; we cannot know whether the new nomadic life of pleasure will ever come to the earth. We can see that the flowers Alice once flung onto the roof of her house are blooming on earth, "flaunting in rich beauty and full bloom, . . . a mystic expression that something within the house was consum-mated" (chap. 19). Expressions of utopian hope must be mystic in *The House of the Seven Gables*, for they point to a future that subverts nineteenth-century culture. Feminine, ruined Clifford and young, radical Holgrave can dream of this future; disreputable Uncle Venner can prefigure it in his present life. And three good witches, Phoebe, Hepzibah, and Alice, three interconnected forms of Roman-tic radicalism, can begin to bring it into the world. Hawthorne offers women a vision of revolution by subversion, a glimpse of the possibility that in their private lives they might undermine the public edifices men like Jaffrey Pyncheon have labeled Western civilization. No other novelist in the nineteenth century, man or woman, dreamed of such power for his heroines. *The House of the Seven Gables* is a wildly utopian culmination of the first phase of Romantic radicalism in the nineteenth-century novel.

Part 2
Reactions

5. Mary Shelley: Fiends and Families

When Hawthorne gave Romantic radicalism three extraordinary heroines in 1850, the literary reaction to Romantic politics was already well established. Reaction had been virtually simultaneous with the revolutionary impulse of the late eighteenth century in England; literary radicals were never unopposed.[1] Austen's *Mansfield Park* is a somber, rational, fictional defense of hierarchical and authoritarian order in England; Mary Shelley's virtually contemporary *Frankenstein*, published in 1818, is a reactionary novel of a different sort—one that points the way to worst of the Victorian future. In *Mansfield Park* men and women possess the same natures, have the same moral duties, and face the same dangers; in *Frankenstein* men and women are very different. Men make revolutionary mischief, and women stand guard—pitiful, helpless, and saintly—over the family.

Mary Shelley's girlish, awkward reactionary novel has held our imaginations for most of two centuries because her reaction against Romantic radicalism has the power of heartbroken experience behind it. Mary Shelley did not have Hawthorne's freedom to pick the best from Shelley's radical ideas; as a daughter and wife she was trapped in one of the most revolutionary families in England with the most radical pedigree possible, as the daughter of the theoretical anarchist William Godwin and the free-living feminist Mary Wollstonecraft. Wollstonecraft died a month after Mary was born and left as part of the family evidence of her own unconventional life—Fanny Imlay, her daughter by a man she had known before she married Godwin. When Godwin later married Mrs. Clairemont, Mary Godwin gained another set of siblings to whom she was not related in the usual way. She could not have been ignorant for a moment in her life, as a girl or a woman, that her family was not like other English families.

Mary Godwin did not even have the one reliable protection available to the unconventional—wealth. Though she escaped from the poverty of her father's household when she eloped with the aristocratic and potentially wealthy Shelley, she simply changed one debtor for another. And besides debt, she acquired the real meaning of free love in her relationship with her husband. Unlike some other apostles of liberty, Shelley practiced what he preached—or, to be cynical, he chose to preach as celestial freedom what he and other men have practiced as promiscuity. The seventeen-year-old Mary took up with him while he was still married to his first wife, Harriet; after Harriet committed suicide, Mary married him and had to live through his subsequent, repeated infatuations with other women. She had no settled home, but traveled with Shelley and various companions—her sister Claire Clairemont, Leigh Hunt, Lord Byron—from place to place. She knew the true, lived meaning of a life detached from the old institutions her mother, father, and husband considered spiritually imprisoning.

The Romantic radicalism of *The Lyrical Ballads* and "Michael" and *Emma*, that defended the moral economy of agricultural England against the exploitation of urban industrial capitalism, was something this wandering woman never knew. Her family was on the other side of Romantic radicalism, apostles of individual liberation, free minds, free love. Mary Shelley had this side of Romanticism thrust upon her, and so, without knowledge of other radical possibilities, turned her back on the whole complex of ideas, in the name of the family. *Frankenstein* could hardly be called a feminist novel, since it confers neither power nor dignity upon women, but it is absolutely a female novel, expressing in mythically powerful ways a hurt woman's sense of wrong. It is the first important fictional declaration in the nineteenth century that Romantic radicalism is not just bad—it is especially bad for women. *Frankenstein* is a wail of pain, a young woman's protest that Romantic radicalism has too great a price, and that the people who pay are women and children.

Even Shelley himself knew, in the decade of the 1810s, that Romantic radicalism needed defense. Like Wordsworth and Blake before him, he had to rewrite the French Revolution in poetry in order to redeem it from terror and from the final tyranny of Napoleon. His "Prometheus Unbound" and Mary's *Frankenstein* (or, *The Modern Prometheus*) amount to a literary argument, an argument about whether the mythic figure of Prometheus, the archetype of all revolutionaries, could be redeemed. Because Shelley wrote his revolutionary poem the year after Mary published her reactionary novel, her version of the myth cannot exactly be called a reaction to his. But because the ideas of "Prometheus Unbound" are not new to Shelley, largely borrowed from his father-in-law Godwin's *Enquiry Concerning Political Justice* (1793), her *Frankenstein* can legitimately be seen as a reaction to the revolutionary hopes of the early nineteenth century, of which "Prometheus Unbound" is a part.

"Prometheus Unbound" is the most hopeful re-vision of the French Revolution in English Romantic poetry. Like Wordsworth in *The Prelude*, Shelley locates the source of revolutionary wrong in the incompletely changed hearts and minds of those who make revolution; the great difference between *The Prelude* and "Prometheus Unbound" is Shelley's continuing belief that changed hearts and changed minds will bring political change. In his difficult, demanding poem he carries his reader through a double repentance and a double transformation; first we share the spirit of Prometheus, the chained revolutionary Titan, the male mind, the spirit of Greek liberty that has revived briefly and incompletely in Christ and the French Revolution. In the second act we imaginatively follow Asia, Prometheus' wife, a more ancient culture, the feminine spirit, the incarnation of Love. They are both corrupted, at the start, by hatred and a wish for revenge on the tyrant Jupiter; they are both potentially redeemable parts of all human beings. In "Prometheus Unbound" men and women are irrevocably connected in revolutionary struggle.

The length, the difficulty, the historical and poetic complexity of Shelley's poem make it persuasive. The idea that hearts and minds must be purged of hatred before they can make a good revolution sounds simple enough, but readers struggling through a poem full of cosmic characters, some recognizable, some not—Prometheus, Asia, Furies, Jupiter, Demogorgon, a singing Earth and Moon—feel and experience the mental and emotional difficulty of the transformation that must precede revolution. Both Prometheus and Asia must stop defining themselves as Enemies, even though they must oppose a tyrant; they must give up their wish to curse; they must escape despair; they must recover hope and faith in spite of their failures. When both have changed, the tyrant Jupiter falls easily, without the bloodbath conservatives predict every time a revolution is about to succeed. "Prometheus Unbound" is certainly not a sure-fire program for revolution, but it is a true vision of the necessary transformation of the revolutionary mind. More recent history has shown not only that tyrannies can fall as easily as Shelley's Jupiter, but that the revolutionary victors are very likely to imitate their former oppressors. Shelley's hope remains alive, but his lesson remains unlearned.

In *Frankenstein* Mary Shelley refuses to give the myth of Prometheus a happy ending. She denies redemption to the monster and to his revolutionary maker. The book is a call to retreat, to hunker down in the home, to beware of men who meddle with dreams of revolutionary benevolence. Although Mary Shelley always spoke of her radical parents and radical husband with the utmost reverence— "[Shelley was] a superior being among men, a bright planetary spirit enshrined in an earthly temple"[2]—the book speaks for itself. It is a fictional rejection of everything her radical family believed in.

The political content of *Frankenstein* is barely disguised as science; *disguise* is not even the right word, since science and politics were often inseparable in the minds of nineteenth-century revolutionaries. The three men who dominate this fiction—Walton, Victor Frankenstein, and Frankenstein's created monster—mirror both the benign hopes and the destructive lives of three other men— Shelley, Godwin, and Rousseau. This nineteenth-century myth of mad scientists, a myth that has dominated the popular culture of the last two centuries, is a parable about revolutionary hope itself, a warning that any attempt to change the human world will bring untold trouble. It has gripped our imaginations because it is a myth for our time: these male scientists and their monster transcend their Christian predecessors, the Faustuses who have broken the laws of God, into the potential reality of political and scientific revolution. What brings together revolution and science, the goddess Reason of the French Revolution and the theory of animal magnetism, the Aryan Superman and the dream of spliced genes in our own century, is the idea that human nature can be made new. Not born again, but made again, not born by women, but made by men.

Walton, Mary Shelley's first narrator in *Frankenstein*, and Victor Frankenstein, like Percy Shelley and like Hawthorne's Holgrave, all combine science and politics in their hopeful dreams. Walton, the explorer, wants to discover the secrets of magnetism; he is willing to sacrifice his life "for the dominion I should acquire and transmit over the elemental foes of our race" (letter 3). The presence of Walton reminds the reader that Victor Frankenstein is only one of many men who are enthralled by the utopian possibilities of science, and of scientific politics. Both men, we are supposed to believe, are entirely benevolent in their intentions. Through the portrait of Frankenstein Mary Shelley gives the reader a barely concealed double message about her own mad scientist, her sainted husband: both a madman and a saint, a genius and a destroyer. Walton's initial description of the pathetic creature he had rescued near the North Pole sounds very much like the Shelley his contemporaries described: "I never saw a more interesting creature: his eyes have generally an expression of wildness, and even madness; but there are moments when, if any one performs an act of kindness towards him, or does him any the most trifling service, his whole countenance is lighted up, as it were, with a beam of benevolence and sweetness that I never saw equalled. But he is generally melancholy and despairing; and sometimes he gnashes his teeth, as if impatient of the weight of woes that oppresses him" (letter 4). Other clues connecting Frankenstein to Shelley are hardly even subtle. When Frankenstein tells his story to Walton, he regularly echoes Shelley's poetry. He borrows a description of Mont Blanc from Shelley's poem, uses Shelley's favorite self-pitying metaphor, the wounded deer, to describe himself, and even quotes a whole stanza from Shelley's "Mutability."

The important meaning of the biographical connection is that the secret presence of Shelley reveals more than the text itself about the true target of Mary Shelley's rage. The biographical connection amplifies the political meaning of the kinds of science the two characters, one real and one fictional, share. For both, science has assumed the transfiguring power of magic; like Romantic poetry, it is a form of natural supernaturalism. Frankenstein tells Walton about his childhood fascination with alchemists, electricity, necromancy, in words that are virtually a paraphrase of the description of the youthful Shelley in the biography written by his friend Thomas Jefferson Hogg.[3] "Under the guidance of my new preceptors, I entered with the greatest diligence into the search of the philosopher's stone and the elixir of life; but the latter soon obtained my undivided attention. . . . What glory would attend the discovery, if I could banish disease from the human frame, and render man invulnerable to any but a violent death" (chap. 2). For Frankenstein and for Shelley the university provides a connection between the magic of their youth and the new possibilities of science. Frankenstein studies at Ingolstadt, the home of the eighteenth-century secret revolutionary society of the Illuminati, which fascinated Shelley;[4] there his chemistry professor casts the fatal spell over him by telling him the powers of the new scientific philosophers. "They ascend into the heavens: they have discovered how the blood circulates, and the nature of the air we breathe. They have acquired new and almost unlimited powers; they can command the thunders of heaven, mimic the earthquake, and even mock the invisible world with its own shadows" (chap. 3). These words inspire Frankenstein to dream of a new, better race of men: "Life and death appeared to me ideal bounds, which I should first break through, and pour a torrent of light into our dark world. A new species would bless me as its creator and source; many happy and excellent natures would owe their being to me" (chap. 4).

Shelley, fascinated by the scientific enterprise of exploration, also made the easy leap to a utopian transformation of human beings in his years at Oxford. He even speculated that if Africa were explored, "the shadow of the first balloon, which a vertical sun would project precisely underneath it, as it glided over that hitherto unhappy country, would virtually emancipate every slave, and would annihilate slavery forever.[5] Reason, the new deity of the French Revolution, could hardly have spawned two more devoted sons than the radical poet and his fictional shadow, for whom science leads inevitably to utopian political hopes.

With the postrevolutionary hindsight of 1816, Mary Shelley corrects such dreamers in *Frankenstein*, and she does her correcting in a unique, narrow way. She does not attribute malevolence, confusion, unpurged hatred, historical ignorance to her revolutionary scientist as the Romantic poets Shelley and Wordsworth do to theirs. In her fiction Frankenstein and his double Walton have good minds, pure hearts, benevolent motives; why need their dreams go bad? Mary Shelley's answer is simple: they are men, unguided by women. It is true that explorers, scientists, and revolutionaries have often been lonely men; loneliness itself is a deadly sin in *Frankenstein*. The hopeful revolutionary scientist is doomed from the moment he begins his deadly venture, the creation of a new form of life, for the very process isolates him from both nature and love. Shelley's revolutionary, Prometheus, is in this state after the Tyrant Jupiter betrays him, not at the beginning of his attempt to aid man, and he can eventually recover his ability to love; Mary Shelley's revolutionary loses love forever when he begins to dream of scientific transformation of humanity.

Frankenstein's creation, the new man, the monster who has captured our imaginations in a way that his fey creator has not, is the final clue to horror's source in the minds of men. In our imaginations the *name* Frankenstein has been transferred to the monster, for it is mysteriously resonant; it sounds like *Francophile*, a word almost synonymous with *devil worshiper* in the Napoleon-hating England of 1816. The monster is not specifically Napoleon; he is the whole complex of French ideas that led to Napoleon by way of the French Revolution.

The monster owes his fictional character to one French man more than any other—Rousseau, the father of the French Revolution. The original character of the monster and his subsequent development come directly and unmistakably from Rousseau's first revolutionary essay, *The Discourse on the Origins and Foundations of Inequality among Mankind*. Before he begins his story, the monster compares himself to both Adam and Satan, the characters of Christian myth to whom Rousseau gives new meaning—the true original man, and the true cause of his fall. As an original man, the monster follows precisely the path Rousseau posited: discovery of the elements of the natural world, discovery of fire, emotional and intellectual growth through attachment to a family. At first he has only Rousseau's two newly invented instincts—self-preservation and pity; having settled secretly by a family's hut, the monster first takes their food for himself, but when he recognizes their suffering, he stops stealing and he gathers firewood for them. He goes beyond his two instincts by learning affection and language from them.

Mary Shelley compresses into a few months of the monster's life what took many centuries in Rousseau's imagined history of man. The monster advances to a knowledge of social structures beyond the family by listening to readings from Volney's *Ruins of Empires*, another clue to his origins in nineteenth-century radicalism. "Unlike William Godwin's *Political Justice* (1793), whose influence was confined to a small and highly literate circle, Volney's *Ruins* was published in cheap pocket-book form and remained in the libraries of many artisans in the 19th century. Its fifteenth chapter, the vision of a 'New Age,' was frequently circulated as a tract."[6] The innocent monster's first reaction to historical atrocity is "disgust and loathing." And having learned to read, he discovers true social virtues in Plutarch and admires the same "peaceable law-givers, Numa, Solon, and Lycurgus" whom Rousseau most admires in *The Social Contract.*

The extensive similarities between Frankenstein's monster and Rousseau's imagined man enlarge the meaning of Frankenstein himself. In personality he is like Shelley; as a type of Romantic revolutionary he is also like William Godwin and like Rousseau himself. Mary Shelley emphasizes the connection between Frankenstein and Rousseau by setting the beginning of her story in Geneva, Rousseau's birthplace. As she says in a famous letter, "Here a small obelisk is erected to the glory of Rousseau, and here . . . the magistrates, the successors of those who exiled him from his native country, were shot by the populace during that revolution which his writings mainly contributed to mature, and which, notwithstanding the temporary bloodshed and injustice with which it was polluted, has produced enduring benefits to mankind, which not all the chicanery of statesmen, nor even the greatest conspiracy of kings, can entirely render vain" (1 June 1816). Mary Shelley's final clue to the interrelationship between the monster, his maker, and the French Revolution is that the first language the monster learns, from the de Lacey family, is French.

The fictional, metaphoric view of the French Revolution, Rousseau's child, in *Frankenstein* is much harsher than the view expressed in the letter by Shelley's loyal wife. In her fiction "temporary bloodshed and injustice" predominate; the monster's "Reign of Terror" produces no enduring benefits whatsoever. Through the history of the monster, who begins as Rousseau's innocent original man, and matures into the violent creature spawned by Rousseau's revolutionary ideas, Mary Shelley suggests that no matter how well intentioned the makers of revolutionary dreams are, these ideas will create only horror when they are put into practice. The monster is still innocent when he tries to become part of the human world; when he carefully approaches the blind father of the de Lacey family, who will not recoil from his ugliness, he is interrupted by the son, Felix, who beats him in self-protective terror. The family abandons their home, and the benevolently conceived, innocently disposed monster becomes a destroyer. "My protectors had departed, and had broken the only link that held me to the world. For the first time the feelings of revenge and hatred filled my bosom, and I did not strive to control them; but, allowing myself to be borne away by the stream, I bent my mind towards injury and death" (chap. 16).

The monster's creator, Victor Frankenstein, almost brings a version of this violence to England; the fictional, emblematic representation of the revolution so dreaded by the English at the beginning of the nineteenth century is just barely averted. Moved by the monster's plea that he would reform if he were not alone, Frankenstein goes to England to construct a mate for him; he breaks off only when he realizes that he would have no guarantee of the monster's good faith. "Even if they were to leave Europe, and inhabit the deserts of the new world, yet one of the first results of those sympathies for which the Daemon thirsted would be children, and a race of devils would be propagated upon the earth who might make the very existence of the species of man a condition precarious and full of terror" (chap. 20). Nothing will ever be able to tame the destructive force that he has loosed upon the world, in all utopian, Romantic, radical, good faith.

The blank spots in the political allegory of *Frankenstein* must be filled in by Mary Shelley's barely disguised messages about men and women, politics and families. Just as she forces us to relate Victor Frankenstein and his science to historical Romantic radicals and their politics to understand the metaphorical meaning of his monster, she forces us to fill in a connection between the politics the monster represents and the reaction he causes in people. Shelley and Wordsworth try to explain the failure of revolution in terms of incomplete spiritual change in both the revolutionaries and the people they would benefit; Mary Shelley shows us only the raw melodrama of a hideous eight-foot-high man with yellow skin and watery eyes who, understandably, strikes terror in everyone who sees him. He turns bad because he is rejected, and he is rejected because he is ugly, as he himself recognizes. "I had sagacity enough to discover that the unnatural hideousness of my person was the chief object of horror with those who had formerly beheld me" (chap. 15). Presumably if he had looked like a normal human being he would have been accepted, and would have remained virtuous. We have to ask questions. Why didn't Victor Frankenstein notice that the creature he was constructing was turning out ugly? Why should people react to an ugly face more than to a good heart? What is the connection between the physical ugliness that evokes fear and the flaw in radical theory and practice that generates terror?

Against rational questions stands the mythic power of Mary Shelley's story. As readers we all understand why people react to the monster as they do. We may be ashamed, but we all shudder at the sight of deformity. Ugliness is one staple of horror fictions and horror films; we react because we cannot help it. The people who reject the would-be benevolent monster are otherwise good; Mary Shelley implicitly suggests a theory of the intractable nature of our instincts to explain why people scream in horror. To pursue her political allegory, we arrive at what has become a maxim of reactionary rhetoric, that people are not "ready" for radical change, no matter how noble that change may be. In *Frankenstein*, the daughter and wife of nineteenth-century radicals grants benevolence and intelligence in the creator of the monster, grants the original benevolence of the creation—and still takes her stand, irrevocably, against them. She denies the deepest assumption of radical thought—that wrongs can be eradicated, that people can change. In *Frankenstein* instinct wins—not good instincts, but bad ones, not pity and mutual aid or attachment to home or capacity for joy, instincts radical writers defend against the falseness of bourgeois culture, but fear, cruelty, blindness. Mary Shelley returns, in this fiction, to the heart of all the repressive ideologies her father, mother, and husband fought against, the idea that human nature is essentially unchangeable and cruel.

Mary Shelley appeals to our emotions, as readers, in presenting this fictional case for reaction by making us understand and sympathize with the monster as well as with the people who fear and hate him. He is the most moving and eloquent creature in the book, both political emblem and neglected child. This poor creature, abandoned by his male creator as soon as he comes to life, is the saddest progeny in nineteenth-century fiction. Monster that he is, he can still break our hearts. He saves a child from drowning and is promptly shot. "I had saved a human being from destruction, and, as a recompense, I now writhed under the miserable pain of a wound, which shattered the flesh and bone. . . . For some weeks I led a miserable life in the woods, endeavouring to cure the wound which I had received. The ball had entered by shoulder, and I knew not whether it had remained there or passed through; at any rate I had no means of extracting it. My sufferings were augmented also by the oppressive sense of the injustice and ingratitude of their infliction" (chap. 16). He is a neglected child precisely because he is a political emblem; he is an alien because he is the product of male revolutionary thought, not part of a family. Not belonging to a family of his own, he becomes a destroyer of other families. Through this monster Mary Shelley begins what has become another battle cry of conservative politicians for the last two centuries—the real danger in radical change is that it will destroy the nuclear family, father, mother, and children.

Those the monster murders are themselves identified more as family members than as individuals. The monster takes revenge on Frankenstein, his creator, by murdering his family and close friends. He strangles William, the beloved baby of the family; plots the execution of Justine, a servant who has joined the family, by implicating her in the murder; strangles Frankenstein's closest friend, Clerval; strangles Elizabeth, Frankenstein's adopted sister and bride; drives Frankenstein's old father into death from grief. The monster's innocence, his ugliness, his anger, his destructiveness are inseparable; all of his multiple characteristics point back to one idea: his damned, doomed existence is a violation of the laws of the family because he was made, not born. The conection between revolutionary thought and the destruction of the family is neither logically nor historically necessary, but the experience of Mary Shelley's life conspired to bring these ideas together in her fiction. In the years when she was writing *Frankenstein* she had to endure three deaths: her first—illegitimate—baby died suddenly in 1815, and, in 1816, both Fanny Imlay, her illegitimate half sister, and Harriet Shelley, her lover's wife, committed suicide. What young woman could help feeling guilt and rage over the deaths of her child, her sister, her rival, all touched by illicit, revolutionary love? The absence of a mother, the presence of a revolutionary father, two inescapable facts of Mary Shelley's life, now converge with the absence of a marriage, the presence of a revolutionary lover, and a new series of deaths.

The two epigraphs with which Mary Shelley begins *Frankenstein* suggest that a father, for her, is not a source of family love. She dedicates the book to Godwin with words that make him sound like an adored stranger: "To William Godwin, Author of *Political Justice, Caleb Williams*, etc. These volumes are respectfully inscribed by The Author." She adds the words of the fallen Adam to God in *Paradise Lost*: "Did I request thee, Maker, from my clay to mould me man? Did I solicit thee From darkness to promote me?" The words clearly apply to the monster's feelings toward his creator, Frankenstein; it is easy to believe that the trapped, hurt woman feels the same way toward hers, as she wanders through Europe forlorn, in debt.

In other nineteenth-century families the death of a mother might have been less disastrous. For Mary Shelley the death of her mother is compounded by the absences of an extended family, neighbors, a settled home. She is the victim of three men—Rousseau, Godwin, Shelley. They took Romantic radicalism out of the rural community, away from labor, away from the ancient traditions of mutual aid, away from the moral economy of agricultural England, and tried to find the road to revolution through personal liberty and liberated love. In feeling she is as abandoned as her fictional monster, or as the children Rousseau cheerfully left at the foundling home.

The loneliness, misery, and rage that create a mad scientist and a murderous monster also conjure up in *Frankenstein* a fictional heaven, a family, and a new kind of saintly heroine. In a book full of untransmuted pain, it is not surprising that the author could secretly identify with both the saintly heroines and the monster; forbidden rage generates its opposite. As a political emblem the monster is mad, bad, male; as a lonely child he is also poor female Mary Shelley, his creator. Yet this angry fiction also demands some unalloyed innocence with which the creator and the reader can side; the women of *Frankenstein* embody that innocence. They are the forerunners of the angels who inhabit the houses of Victorian fiction. They preside over the family, loving and guarding it; if they fail it is the fault of the many misguided men who are working, unwittingly, against them.

Beneath the one, huge, lumbering revolutionary emblem who murders families are the smaller male villains of *Frankenstein*. Woman's family after woman's family is wrecked by a man, usually a man attempting to right a political wrong. The pattern of the book is consistent; angelic women are hurt by men, and need to be rescued by other, better men. Frankenstein's saintly mother, drawn into isolation and poverty by her economically imprudent father is rescued, married, and protected by Frankenstein's father, who knows how to treat a woman right. "Everything was made to yield to her wishes and her convenience. He strove to shelter her, as a fair exotic is sheltered by the gardener, from every rougher wind, and to surround her with all that could tend to excite pleasurable emotion in her soft and benevolent mind" (chap. 1). She, in turn, protects their children. "I was their plaything and their idol, and something better—their child, the innocent and helpless creature bestowed upon them by Heaven" (chap. 1). This fantastic family lives by emotions alone. In the fictional fabric of *Frankenstein* are no words about work, friends, neighbors, food, clothing, shelter. We know nothing about the material conditions or social relationships of this family; it is the true fictional precursor of the Victorian nuclear family.

The other angelic women of the book—Justine, Agatha de Lacey, Saphie, and Elizabeth Lavenza—are all cut from the same cloth, and need the same protection. Elizabeth is an orphan because her father was a patriot, imprisoned for his role in an abortive Italian revolution, "one of those Italians nursed in the memory of the antique glory of Italy—one among the *schiavi ognor fermenti*, who exerted himself to obtain the liberty of his country. He became the victim of its weakness. Whether he had died, or still lingered in the dungeons of Austria, was not known. His property was confiscated, his child became an orphan and a beggar" (chap. 1). The orphan child, another victim of misplaced political fervor, is a heavenly being irresistible to Frankenstein's family: "Her brow was clear and ample, her blue eyes cloudless, and her lips and the moulding of her face so expressive of sensibility and sweetness, that none could behold her without looking on her as of a distinct species, a being heaven-sent, and bearing a celestial stamp in all her features" (chap. 1). Her character is essentially the same when she reaches a sexually desirable adolescence; she remains, for Frankenstein, "the living spirit of love to soften and attract" (chap. 2). These women of the Frankenstein family are "spirits of love" like Shelley's Asia, but they need no spiritual redemption and have no power. Elizabeth cannot affect Frankenstein, the Prometheus of this fiction, once he leaves the domestic circle.

Saphie, Felix de Lacey's sweetheart, and Agatha de Lacey are also powerless angels in need of protection. They are protected in exile by the men of their family, but they are in exile in the first place because Felix—like Frankenstein, Walton, and Elizabeth's father—tried to do some active good outside the family. Saphie's father, a Turk, had been unjustly tried and condemned to death in Paris; Felix plots his escape only to be betrayed by him and then condemned by the French government. Mary Shelley does not cover up the fact that governments and legal systems, like the one that condemns Justine to death, are unjust; she simply suggests, in *Frankenstein,* that it is hopeless to try to change them. Every man who tries makes victims of the women in his own family, frail, beautiful, helpless angels.

The angelic helplessness of the women in *Frankenstein* lies behind the final lesson that the dying, repentant Victor Frankenstein bestows on Walton (who quickly repents and returns to his sister).

A human being in perfection ought always to preserve a calm and peaceful mind, and never to allow passion or a transitory desire to disturb his tranquillity. I do not think that the pursuit of knowledge is an exception to this rule. If the study to which you apply yourself has a tendency to weaken your affections, and to destroy your taste for those simple pleasures in which no alloy can possibly mix, then that study is certainly unlawful, that is to say, not befitting the human mind. If this rule were always observed; if no man allowed any pursuit whatsoever to interfere with the tranquillity of his domestic affections, Greece had not been enslaved; Caesar would have spared his country; America would have been discovered more gradually; and the empires of Mexico and Peru would not have been destroyed. (chap. 4)

The betrayal of domestic affections is not merely the result of revolutionary activity; it is also the cause of all political disaster. The transformation of Greece and Rome into empires, and the destruction of the native peoples of the Western hemisphere, political developments that have never been attributed to anyone's radical, benevolent dreams, are here joined with the specter of revolution. They are all the result of men's ambition. The world collapses in violence when men leave home. Women cannot join them and make political work better, nor can they even keep the home safe. Detached, isolated, liberated from land and community, the women and families of *Frankenstein* are precious, fragile, and impotent.

When Frankenstein tells Walton, "How much happier that man is who believes his native town to be the world, than he who aspires to become greater than his nature will allow" (chap. 4), we have to remember that these are false alternatives, thrust on Mary Shelley by her unusual life. The life of the "native town" she never knew and could not even imagine for her wandering fictional characers. It is the other possibility of Romantic radicalism, the life Wordsworth wanted to protect, a solidly economic and social laboring life. And though such a life may indeed be incompatible with the scientific knowledge or radical activity that seafaring wanderers and itinerant freedom fighters seek, it is not incompatible with the ambitious poetry, philosophy, science that has been produced by settled men— Wordsworth, Kant, Newton.

Mary Shelley's father and husband created this false opposition for her. They were the Romantic radicals who associated political revolution with sexual liberty, the end of political oppression with the end of marriage. The family does indeed survive better in a native town than on the run—particularly if a debt collector is hot on its trail. It is for the sake of a new, fragile, detached uprooted family and helpless women that Mary Shelley cries anathema on science, on revolution, on all men who do anything but protect their wives. These families are the only source of goodness in the dangerous world *Frankenstein* projects.

Yet if Mary Shelley had been entirely wrong, if no one but the daughter of Godwin and Wollstonecraft and the wife of Shelley could feel so endangered, *Frankenstein* would not have become a mythic part of our popular culture. Fragile, endangered families, and a new ideal of the saintly, frail, loving, housebound woman abound in politically conservative Victorian fiction, the novels that followed *Frankenstein* by thirty years and more. Mary Shelley was not alone in her vision. Historically, it was not male-created revolution but a new economic order that changed the social life of England, wreaking havoc with native towns. There is a reason, though, why Mary Shelley's horrified reaction to Romantic radicalism, in a novel devoid of economic and social reality, should be the forerunner of Victorian images of the home and women. The form of Romantic radicalism Mary Shelley, as a human being, was victim to, shares several deep antipathies with the industrial capitalism that was the new economic power of England. They share antipathy to agricultural life, disdain for the ideals of justice rooted in common law and traditions of mutual aid, and contempt for the productive work once done by women. The radicalism of Godwin and Shelley can fit right in with an economic ethos valuing the "progress" and "development" of the lucky individual over the moral economy of the community. Shelley's form of Romantic radicalism, cut off from a genuine economic base, was easily adopted and transformed by a capitalist culture. Men could use it to evade their responsibilities to women; women, in turn, could use it to evade their responsibilities to their children, their neighbors, and other women. Mary Shelley's frail, pure, victimized angels, the bourgeois saints of the Victorian novel, and Mary Daly's neo-witches are sisters under the skin; all are self-enclosed, ultimately narcissistic; all owe their identity to Percy Shelley's individualistic form of Romantic radicalism.

6. William Makepeace Thackeray and Charles Dickens: Angels and Asylums

Both Dickens and Thackeray, the two male Victorian novelists whose heroines come very close to being angels in their bourgeois houses, agree with the sad lesson of *Frankenstein*: good women and Romantic radicalism are eternal enemies. The novels of both are full of parodic figures of Romantics and radicals. Blanche Amory of *Pendennis* weeps endlessly over her own nonexistent suffering; Mr. Skimpole of *Bleak House* uses a pose of Romantic aestheticism as a way of bilking his friends; Mathilda Crawley of *Vanity Fair*, a selfish old hypocrite, declares herself to be a sympathizer with all things fiery and French. The collection of feminists and other female reformers in *Bleak House* are fools all, but the most loathesome of the lot is Mrs. Skewton in *Dombey and Son*; ancient, withered yet painted and dressed like a girl, grasping, avaricious, she claims to be the advocate of "heart," "Arcadian simplicity," and "cows." Not one of this group of characters in the works of Thackeray and Dickens have ever come near a cow. These Romantic and radical frauds are all part of urban, Victorian England; they are all cut off from the radical possibilities of rural life. They are the fictional creations of authors for whom Wordsworth has no political meaning, who lump "cows" together with maudlin Byronism as literary fraud and folly.

Yet the ideas of Romanticism take many forms, and in giving a socially realistic embodiment to the saintly, ideal women conjured up by reactionary fantasy, both Thackeray and Dickens indirectly give Romanticism itself a strange new life. These two male authors have bestowed on English fiction a panoply of heroines who have set contemporary feminists' teeth on edge, from Little Nell to Lady Castlewood, as Thackeray writes in *Pendennis*, all "women in whose angelic natures there is something awful, as well as beautiful to contemplate: at whose feet the wildest and fiercest of us must fall down and humble ourselves in admiration of that adorable purity which never seems to do or think wrong" (chap. 2). These heroines, certainly not the conscious, direct product of anyone's Romantic or radical thought, are nevertheless a mutant product of the side of Romanticism that values sensitive souls and loving hearts more than rational minds. In their domestic isolation,their separation from agriculture, nature, and community, they are the products of Shelley's vision of ideal life. Behind Dickens's and Thackeray's heroines, behind Mary Shelley's fragile saints, behind Jane Eyre and Rochester lies the ghost of Percy Shelley's "Epipsychidion," the dream of perpetual, cosmic bliss on an island, bliss created by love alone.

In detaching the ideal of sensibility and the image of isolated love from any larger radical context, the Victorian creators of these new heroines bring a form of Romanticism into the bourgeois family. Their heroines are not free spirits wandering over Europe in the company of Lord Byron. The angels of Victorian fiction are fictionally fleshed out characters, existing in a social world, ministering to their erring husbands. It is the realistic fabric of Victorian fiction that makes this set of female characters so potent as a social myth in England. Real women, walking the English earth, had to live with these fictional heroines as a cultural ideal they were supposed to emulate.

As heroines, these angels are deadly, an ideal that tortures through its sheer impossibility. In the two most psychologically developed of their angelic heroines—Florence Dombey of *Dombey and Son*, and Amelia Sedley of *Vanity Fair*—Dickens and Thackeray expose the ideal for what it is—a demand that women go mad in the service of men. In presenting these heroines as deluded and masochistic, detached from reality and still good, both authors transform still another Romantic idea that began as something radical—respect for mad people. Walt Whitman exhorted his American readers: stand up for the stupid and crazy. Wordsworth shocked his by asking that they love his Idiot Boy and his mad Martha Ray. To ask readers to love, respect, cherish the mad is a radical demand, a radical assertion of human equality. Florence Dombey and Amelia Sedley are the sad daughters of this humane and equalizing impulse in Romanticism. But Dickens and Thackeray do not ask their readers to stand up for their crazy heroines; they come close to suggesting that male readers need not worry about being good, since crazy women—angels—will stand up for them.

The two heroines are similar, in their sweetness and their madness; but their function, as characters in created, fictional worlds, is quite different. *Vanity Fair* and *Dombey and Son* are overwhelmingly urban novels about the powerful capitalists who dominate the economic life of Victorian London. Dickens and Thackeray make different connections between their heroines and this economic world, as narrators and plot makers. In *Vanity Fair* the heroine serves as a deadly illumination of a wicked world; her madness and the corrupt material conditions of her life are inseparable. In *Dombey and Son* both plot and narration separate Florence from her economic world, and lift the angel-in-the-house out of the material world into an eternal, ideal, mythic state. Thackeray's Amelia Sedley is part of a historically particular radical vision; Dickens's Florence Dombey is a pawn in a fictional defense of the rich businessmen of nineteenth-century London.

In Florence the remnant of Romanticism is worse than cheap and sentimental; it is destructive. And it is powerful. This Victorian ideal of womanhood permeated a culture; it is this ideal, this perverted version of Romanticism, that most feminists of both the late nineteenth and twentieth centuries have addressed as if it were an eternal enemy, the product of the dark power of patriarchy. In fact these fictional angels are the products of a historically specific culture. They belong to the city and not the country, to men who produce money and not food, to nuclear, not extended, families. They have lived on, given new life in film and fiction and advertising because the underlying economic facts of our world go back to the great changes that took place in nineteenth-century urban England.

Hobsbawm describes the new life of urban England as Victorian *men* experienced it:

The ideal of an individualist society, a private family unit supplying all its material and moral needs on the basis of a private business, suited them, because they were men who no longer needed traditions. Their efforts had raised them out of the rut. They were in a sense their own reward, the content of life, and if that was not enough, there was always the money, the comfortable house increasingly removed from the smoke of mill and counting-house, the devoted and modest wife, the family circle, the enjoyment of travel, art, science, and literature. . . . Only the nightmare shadow of bankruptcy or debt sometimes lay over their lives, and we can still recognize it in the novels of the period.[1]

As Walter Houghton suggests, this new life for men necessitated a new image for women: in a world where men are at each other's throats, they need angels to take care of them. In Houghton's view, failure is more than a shadow,—"In this environment failure is the worst fate one can imagine. 'What is it,' asks Carlyle, 'that the modern English soul does, in very truth, dread infinitely and contemplate with entire despair? What *is* his Hell?. . . With hesitation and astonishment, I pronounce it to be: The terror of "Not succeeding."' 'Terror' is scarcely too strong a word. To be left behind in the race of life was not only to be defeated, it was to be exposed to the same kind of scorn and humiliation visited upon poverty (itself a symbol of failure)."[2]

This is a more vicious economic world than the countryside of Wordsworth's "Michael," where everyone is poor, or the village of Highbury in Austen's *Emma*, where even the failures are loved. In the new urban world, where women no longer have the work that belonged to them in an agricultural economy, they have been given a formidable new job—taking care of their perpetually endangered men. As Houghton says, the Victorian home "Was both a shelter *from* the anxieties of modern life, a place of peace where the longings of the soul might be realized (if not in fact, in imagination), and a shelter *for* these moral and spiritual values which the commercial spirit and the critical spirit were threatening to destroy, and therefore also a sacred place, a temple. . . . A more important factor, working to the same end, was the impact of modern business. In the recoil from the City, the home was irradiated by the light of a pastoral imagination."[3] He sees the angel-in-the-house as a necessary antidote to nineteenth-century capitalism, rather as Dickens and Thackeray do. "The angel in the house serves, or should serve, to preserve and quicken the moral idealism so badly needed in an age of selfish greed and fierce competition."[4] Male historians, unlike many modern feminist literary critics, have been able to identify the historical source of the angel-in-the-house—not in eternal patriarchy, but in nineteenth-century capitalism.

More recent feminist historians have brought to light what this image meant to women. Victorian psychiatry was in the control of men, and it played its part in creating these necessary angels. Though psychiatrists condemned the kind of violent, antisocial insanity that Charlotte Brontë makes loathesome in Bertha Rochester,[5] they actually fostered another kind of insanity—the passive, self-deluding, irrational behavior that Dickens and Thackeray embody in their angelic heroines, Florence Dombey and Amelia Sedley. For example, excessive "sensibility" was condemned in male patients, encouraged in female patients.[6] According to Elaine Showalter, the Victorian lunatic asylum was becoming more and more like a middle-class urban home for women. "Even to middle class women the asylum could be an acceptable environment; for as the Victorian asylum became more overtly benign, protective, and custodial, it also became an environment grotesquely like the one in which women normally functioned. Such factors of asylum life as strict chaperonage, restriction of movement, limited occupation, enforced sexlessness, and constant subjugation to authority were closer to the 'normal' lives of women than of men. The theory of asylum management was, according to one progressive spokesman, to treat inmates 'as children under a perpetual personal guardianship.'"[7] This is the environment in which household angels flourish. Protection and imprisonment are hard to distinguish.

The other side of what Showalter says is what Dickens and Thackeray reveal in their fiction, with different degrees of consciousness: that middle-class homes were becoming more and more like lunatic asylums. The rural freedom of the heroines of earlier novels is thrown into sharp relief by the new urban imprisonment Thackeray describes in *Vanity Fair*.

It was an awful existence. She had to get up of black winter's mornings to make breakfast for her scowling old father, who would have turned the whole house out of doors if his tea had not been ready at half-past eight. She remained silent opposite to him, listening to the urn hissing, and sitting in tremor while the parent read his paper, and consumed his accustomed portion of muffins and tea. At half-past nine he rose and went to the City, and she was almost free till dinner-time, to make visitations in the kitchen and to scold the servants: to drive abroad and descend upon the tradesmen, who were prodigiously respectful: to leave her cards and her papa's at the great glum respectable houses of their City friends; or to sit alone in the large drawing-room, expecting visitors; and working at a huge piece of worsted by the fire, on the sofa, hard by the great Iphigenia clock, which ticked and tolled with mournful loudness in the dreary room. The great glass over the mantelpiece, faced by the other great console-glass at the opposite end of the room, increased and multiplied between them the brown holland bag in which the chandelier hung; until you saw these brown holland bags fading away in endless perspectives, and this apartment of Miss Osborne's seemed the centre of a system of drawing rooms. (Chap. 42)

It *is* the center of a system of drawing rooms. Jane Osborne lives the typical life of a rich woman in the city, where the families of successful businessmen reside in separate, capitalistic dignity, without neighbors, rich and poor, whom rural families had to know, without gardens, without turkeys, without pigs.

The most astonishing of Showalter's historical revelations, and the revelation that most clearly illuminates both *Dombey and Son* and *Vanity Fair*, is that insane women were particularly recommended as good Victorian wives. "The primary occupational risk of the 'certified' woman was marriage. And Thomas Bakewell suggested that a term in an asylum could even be an attraction in a prospective wife, for 'humility is a quality which men wish for in a wife. This complaint [insanity] cannot so properly be said to teach humility, as to implant it in the very nature.'"[8] Humility itself is not a new quality for men to want in their wives, humility engendered by a mental illness so severe it requires a term in a benighted and cruel asylum—that is a Victorian innovation.

Madness has its own history, as Foucault has shown.[9] The most remarkable fact about Florence Dombey and Amelia Sedley is that though they share the mental characteristics of heroines earlier authors call mad, their creators, Dickens and Thackeray, call them only good. Male authors have never lifted mad heroines to the terrifying grandeur of mad heroes; they have bestowed a special tenderness on those heroines whose madness keeps them sweet and pure in an immoral world. Shakespeare's Ophelia, who remains a ministering angel in rotten Denmark, and Sterne's Maria, who calls forth compassion in a country community, lose their minds instead of their tempers with the men who have wronged them. To remain loving, even if mad, is to retain the essential humanity that claims our sympathy. We do not lose sight of the fact that men have wronged them, nor do we ever forget that in their detachment from the world around them they are helpless and pathetic. Madness and goodness coexist in earlier heroines, but they are not identified as the same thing.

The great change wrought by Dickens and Thackeray in *Dombey and Son* and *Vanity Fair* is to blur the idea of woman's madness until it becomes inseparable from woman's goodness. The passivity, irrationality, and excessive sensibility earlier authors called madness now have no special name. These novels are in effect part of a propaganda campaign in Victorian England to create a new kind of woman who would play her angelic part in the home of an urban man. These heroines, late descendents of Romantic "sensibility," do not inherit Romanticism's resistance to the developing system of exploitive industrial capitalism; as created fictional beings they are part of that system. The isolated nuclear family, a rural woman's Romantic fantasy in *Jane Eyre*, is now an urban social reality; the woman's special mission to save a man's soul has become an impossible and oppressive social duty. Both Thackeray and Dickens use all of their art, as novelists, in this transformation of madwomen into angels. Powerful, ever-present, narrative commentary, huge casts of characters, and intricate plots all contribute to the creation of a deadly Victorian myth about women.

The myth is powerful in *Vanity Fair*, but so are Thackeray's revelations of its deadliness. The narrative voice that dominates *Vanity Fair* pulls the reader two ways at once, toward weary, half-humorous cynicism and toward the kind of prophetic rage the Romantics felt forty years earlier. At his most wrathful, Thackeray is also most radical; he inherits the radical Christianity of Coleridge, the angry vision of a world dominated by Mammon and not Christ. From his title page to his final page he keeps both his cynical voice and his furious voice before us, so neither Victorian, worldly humor nor radical, Romantic prophecy can ever engage us completely. Nevertheless, as this long novel, covering more than twelve years, progresses, the passages of fiery Christian morality become more and more frequent as more and more characters grow sick, mad, old, and finally die.

In the end the narrator brings us to a view of the world like that of *Anna Karenina;* he condemns the sinful life of worldly people and demands that we choose Christian virtue rather than earthly pleasure. The narrator drops humor, drops cynicism when he finally asks his reader to meditate on the death of poor, bankrupt John Sedley:

Suppose you are particularly rich and well-do-to, and say on that last day, "I am very rich; I am tolerably well known; I have lived all my life in the best society, and, thank Heaven, come of a most respectable family. I have served my King and country with honour. I was in Parliament for several years, where, I may say, my speeches were listened to and pretty well received. . . . I bequeath my plate and furniture, my house in Baker Street, with a handsome jointure, to my widow for her life; and my landed property, besides money in the Funds, and my cellar of well-selected wine in Baker Street, to my son. I leave twenty pound a year to my valet, and I defy any man after I am gone to find anything against my character." Or suppose, on the other hand, your swan sings quite a different sort of dirge, and you say, "I am a poor, blighted, disappointed old fellow, and have made an utter failure through life. I was not endowed either with brains or with good fortune: and confess that I have committed a hundred mistakes and blunders. I own to having forgotten my duty many a time. I can't pay what I owe. On my last bed I lie utterly helpless and humble: and I pray forgiveness for my weakness, and throw myself with a contrite heart at the feet of the Divine Mercy." Which of these two speeches, think you, would be the best oration for your own funeral? Old Sedley made the last; and in that humble frame of mind, and holding by the hand of his daughter, life and disappointment and vanity sank away from under him. (Chap. 61)

The choice is God or Mammon, virtue or Vanity Fair. The power of this narrative voice plays a large part in determining our response to the characters. Gentleness and kindness, self-sacrifice and humility will bring a woman much closer to this absolute standard of Christian virtue than will strength, charm, wit, rationality. Thackeray shares with Hawthorne a profound insight into the corrupting power of nineteenth-century capitalism, but he does not suggest that the economic system can be corrected or subverted. His complex vision of capitalism is at the heart of his double tone: he sees it with a clarity and fury that would draw him toward radicals and Romantics, but he chooses a Christianity of withdrawal and resignation and humility, a Christianity that transforms a woman's weakness into a form of goodness. Amelia Sedley, his heroine, is the kind of woman his narrative voice ultimately validates.

The plot too draws us toward Amelia Sedley. The usual values associated with characters in the novel—wit, exuberance, strength, activity—all dissipate by the end of *Vanity Fair*. At first the novel seems to present a lively, bustling world like that of *Tom Jones*, a world of adventure, variety, excitement, the world readers expect in a long picaresque novel. By the end, however, we see not variety but a terrifying simplicity. This is a world where the ruthless structure of nineteenth-century capitalism rules all. We must judge Amelia Sedley, the angel of this novel, as she exists in this fallen world, run by businessmen, a world without heroes or villains, a world dominated by three words—*fortune, victim,* and *victimizer*. These three words contain Thackeray's double view of his fiction: *fortune* points back through Christian literature to Chaucer and Boethius, back to the conviction that all earthly goods but virtue are ultimately worthless, since they are subject to fortune and her wheel. The plot of *Vanity Fair* can be reduced to something like this fatalistic medieval simplicity; in an unstable economic world some people rise and others fall. The Osbornes replace the Sedleys in prosperity, and then Jos Sedley rises again. Becky Sharp begins as a poor orphan and governess, when Amelia Sedley is happy and comfortable; later, when Becky is married, glittering in London society, Amelia is a poor widow. And when Becky goes off to Europe, disgraced and separated from her husband, Amelia is on her way back up. Fortune rules a world of helpless, hapless mortals, a world that invites only resignation from the reader.

The other simplicity of *Vanity Fair*, the idea that the world is made of victims and victimizers, is a simplicity of fury. If we read Thackeray's fiction in these terms, we are compelled to believe that a woman like Amelia, a born victim, is morally preferable to the people who victimize her. And we must see that Amelia's character as a victim is a result not of an eternal, God-given scheme, but of a specific historical situation. Amelia is a victim in the corrupt, predominantly male world of business just as Ophelia is a victim in the corrupt, male Danish court of *Hamlet*. Most women in *Vanity Fair* are economically helpless, and the men part of an economic system in which the success of some depends on the failure of others, in which failure is dreaded by all because it comes to the good and the bad alike. It is a system from which no one can escape. The fact that John Sedley, bankrupt after making unlucky investments, must go through the final humiliation of seeing his house and possessions auctioned off does not prevent his son Jos from purchasing his own household possessions at just such an auction a few years later.

"Scape, ruined, honest, and broken-hearted at sixty-five years of age, went out to Calcutta to wind up the affairs of the house. Walter Scape was withdrawn from Eton, and put into a merchant's house. Florence Scape, Fanny Scape, and their mother, faded away to Boulogne, and will be heard of no more. To be brief, Jos stepped in and bought their carpets and sideboards, and admired himself in the mirrors which had reflected their kind handsome faces"(chap. 60). No individual man, neither victimizer or victim, is a villain; but the economic system as Thackeray presents it in *Vanity Fair* is villainous. If a woman like Amelia can exist in the midst of such a system without becoming hardened, she is precious.

The system leaves no one untouched. As the narrator tells us, England provides no place of refuge. The country is now run by the likes of Sir Pitt Crawley, who lives by law suits and stock investments, the new economy of the market, not the old economy of agriculture that Austen defends in *Emma*. As Raymond Williams says, "It was characteristic of rural England, before and during the Industrial Revolution, that it was exposed to increasing penetration by capitalist social relations and the dominance of the market, just because these had been powerfully evolving within its own structures."[10] The home, in Thackeray's view, no more than the country is a haven. As readers we are pushed into longing for a heroine like Amelia Sedley by the repeated realization that the family is as full of cruelty and exploitiveness as the business world of *Vanity Fair*. Thackeray shows us competition and viciousness within the Osborne, Steyne, and Crawley families, and he draws his readers into his cruel circle, refusing to allow us to imagine that we are different from his corrupt characters. "Perhaps in Vanity Fair there are no better satires than letters. Take a bundle of your dear friend's of ten years back—your dear friend whom you hate now. Look at a file of your sister's; how you clung to each other till you quarrelled about the twenty-pound legacy! Get down the round-hand scrawls of your son who has half broken your heart with selfish undutifulness since; or a parcel of your own, breathing endless ardour and love eternal, which were sent back by your mistress when she married the nabob—your mistress for whom you now care no more than for Queen Elizabeth." (chap. 19). The middle-class, leisured readers of Thackeray's novel are presumed to be in the camp of the victimizers, along with the majority of his characters.

The single clearest, cleverest, and most captivating victimizer is Becky Sharp. Too often assumed to be the true heroine of *Vanity Fair*, because of her wit and energy, she is in fact the single character who is most obviously intended to make us realize that Amelia Sedley, the victim, represents the only available form of virtue in a corrupt world. Up to a point, she can succeed in this world because she is clever enough to avoid the failure so dreaded by men. No one has the heroic power to do good in Thackeray's fiction, but those who know how to be ruthless can wield a great deal of worldly power. Most of the successful businessmen in *Vanity Fair* are, of course men— Osborne, Steyne, Tufto; Becky Sharp knows how to play their game. Since neither she nor her husband, Rawdon Crawley, has any money, she has to get money from the men who do have it, in the form of checks, jewels, and, most important, credit. The tradesmen who see the carriage of her rich male victims, like Steyne and Pitt Crawley, at her door, assume she will eventually pay them for their goods; the illusion that money is available enables Becky and Rawdon to "live well on nothing a year." Though the narrator keeps reminding the reader that Becky begins as an economic victim—an orphan, a poor woman who must hunt for her own husband because she has no manipulating mother to hunt for her, a governess who has to struggle for money—he finally insists that this gifted victimizer had a choice. "It may perhaps have struck her that to have been honest and humble, to have done her duty and to have marched straightforward on her way, would have brought her as near happiness as that path by which she was striking to attain it. But—just as the children at Queen's Crawley went round the room, where the body of their father lay;—if ever Becky had those thoughts, she was accustomed to walk round them, and not look in. She eluded them, and despised them—or at least she was committed to the other path from which retreat was now impossible" (chap. 41). In passages like this, where irony and cynicism are set aside, Thackeray declares his Christian conviction that in spite of an economic system that taints everything, a person can still try to be good.

Amelia Sedley is one of the small group of characters in *Vanity Fair* who has chosen goodness. Lady Jane Crawley, Miss Briggs, Raggles, even ridiculous Peggy O'Dowd, all have chosen virtue; as a group of characters they make us uncomfortable because, in *Vanity Fair*, goodness bestows not power, not success, not even dignity.

Virtue and failure are almost inseparable in this world of economic victims and victimizers. The structure of the new social world drives a sweet woman like Amelia Sedley into a state of helpless, guilt-ridden submission. The angelic heroine and the other women like her in *Vanity Fair* are good, but they are neither happy nor powerful.

When we meet Amelia, she is the ideal product of Miss Pinkerton's boarding school for elegant young ladies. Her prosperous, urban, bourgeois parents have paid the school to turn their daughter into a marriageable young woman—in Victorian England, a docile, submissive, well-behaved eternal child. Such a school is a social institution ultimately serving the businessmen of London by producing the women they desire, trained to be angels in their houses. Because of her natural sensibility, Amelia is born for the role. Thackeray's narrator treats her with both love and contempt, calling her "a poor little white-robed angel" and also a "silly little thing [who] would cry over a dead canary bird" (chap. 1). We know from the very beginning of *Vanity Fair* that the angel in this fictional house is going to be a difficult heroine to accept and love.

Once Amelia leaves the school, she is plunged into a terrible world. As a sensitive creature destined to be an angel, she is also destined to be in a state of war with other women. In *Vanity Fair* Thackeray exposes a dramatic shift in English social relations: the competitive enmity among women, which Austen condemns and Charlotte Brontë expresses in an unconscious way, is now a deeply rooted part of the social world. Detached from the kind of community where, Austen insists, women have duties to each other, each woman in *Vanity Fair* is struggling against the others to establish herself as the mistress of a rich man's house, the mother of a nuclear family. Other women, less angelic, can spot Amelia as the kind of woman men will prize, and sneer at her gentleness, her silence, her sweetness. The new social world that demands angelic sweetness from wives, and sets wives off in separate urban houses, has deprived women of something very precious—each other's friendship.

Without other women, Amelia is entirely alone in the misery of her love for George Osborne. The two families planned the match years before, when it looked like a mutually profitable alliance for two rich business families; Amelia, without such calculation, has given George her whole heart. We never doubt that George is, as Becky finally says, a "selfish humbug, that low-bred Cockney dandy,

that padded booby, who had neither wit, nor manners, nor heart"
(chap. 67), and so we cannot share Amelia's grief when he neglects
her, but feel only pity. Having been taught to stake her life on a man's
love, since only marriage will give her a place in the society of
London, she cannot extricate herself from the love of a rotten man.
Everything she has been taught at home and at school has deprived
her of the ability to make rational judgments. Even before she is
married, she is doomed to be a man's slave: when the cult of isolated
love, so enthralling to Percy Shelley and Charlotte Brontë, becomes a
social reality, it does nothing but harm to women.

Amelia's slavish weakness is compounded when her father becomes bankrupt and she loses her small stake in the economic world.
As a woman with only love to offer, she is at any man's mercy.
Because the most vicious person in the economic murder of John
Sedley has been George Osborne's father, her love is compounded by
guilt; in an economy where the families of competing businessmen
are natural enemies, a woman is almost forced into betraying her own
family by loving a man who belongs to another. Amelia goes beyond
sensibility into a state that earlier writers would call madness; she
retreats into listless, depressive, passivity. To Thackeray, she is the
type of Victorian womanhood. "She did not dare to own that the man
she loved was her inferior; or to feel that she had given her heart away
too soon. Given once, the pure bashful maiden was too modest, too
tender, too trustful, too weak, too much woman to recall it. We are
Turks with the affections of our women; and have made them sub-
scribe to our doctrine too. We let their bodies go abroad liberally
enough, with smiles and ringlets and pink bonnets to disguise them,
instead of veils and yakmaks. But their souls must be seen by only
one man, and they obey not unwillingly, and consent to remain at
home as our slaves—ministering to us and doing drudgery for us"
(chap. 18). Reading this passage, we have to assume that weakness is
good, like tenderness and modesty. We have already been given
ample evidence that the strength of women like Becky Sharp leads to
cruelty and exploitiveness.

Yet this weakness is not simply women's natural state. Thackeray also attacks men—himself, his characters, his readers—for
having reduced women to this state. "Turks," "slaves,"—these are
strong words. They suggest that women are weak because men have
become tyrannical. George Osborne knows exactly what he is doing

to Amelia when he finally decides to marry her: "he saw a slave before him in that simple yielding faithful creature, and his soul within him thrilled secretly at the knowledge of his power" (chap. 20). In this new social world, where men battle each other economically and each man is locked into a house with his wife, men grow crueler and women more slavish. As Thackeray's narrator says, "I know few things more affecting than that timorous debasement and self-humiliation of a woman. How she owns that it is she and not the man who is guilty; how she takes all the faults on her side; how she courts in a manner punishment for the wrongs which she has not committed, and persists in shielding the real culprit! It is those who injure women who get the most kindness from them" (chap. 50). Women who are trained to be angels are also trained to be masochistic, deluded, and guilty—and no one calls them mad.

Marriage and widowhood exacerbate Amelia's mental state. She feels inadequacy and guilt rather than anger when George flirts with Becky; the shock of his death at Waterloo drives her into a state other people must recognize as madness—even in the nineteenth century. "The poor girl's thoughts were not here at all since her catastrophe, and, stupified under the pressure of her sorrow, good and evil were alike indifferent to her" (chap. 35). Trained to be an angel, she has been stripped of the strength that might have enabled her to withstand shock. This extreme state is only temporary in Amelia, but it is nevertheless a revelation of where her normal life is going.

As a widow, in an economy where women do not own land or businesses, Amelia has nowhere to go with her baby but back to her bankrupt parents. And it is in this family that Thackeray most shockingly exposes the madness built ino the Victorian urban family. As Peter Gay has said of the sexual tensions endemic in such families, "The nineteenth-century middle-class family, more intimate, more informal, more *concentrated* than ever, gave these universal human entanglements exceptional scope and complex configurations."[11] Dead George Osborn becomes Amelia's "saint in heaven," still resented by her parents; young Georgy becomes the living object of adoration, envy, and competition. Amelia adores him even more blindly than she did her husband; her parents resent him as the scion of their enemies and the object of Amelia's care, and they also enslave themselves to him as the one person in the family who can return to the world of wealth and ease.

These jealous hostilities explode when Amelia discovers her mother giving Georgy a medicine of which she does not approve.

"I will *not* have baby poisoned, mamma," cried Emmy, rocking the infant about violently with both her arms round him, and turning with flashing eyes at her mother.

"Poisoned, Amelia!" said the old lady; "this language to me?"

"He shall not have any medicine but that which Mr. Pestler sends for him. He told me that Daffy's Elixir was poison."

"Very good; you think I'm a murderess then," replied Mrs. Sedley. "This is the language you use to your mother. I have met with misfortunes: I have sunk low in life: I have kept my carriage, and now walk on foot: but I did not know I was a murderess before, and thank you for the *news.*"

"Mamma," said the poor girl, who was always ready for tears—"you shouldn't be hard upon me. I—I didn't mean—I mean, I did not wish to say you would do any wrong to this dear child: only—"

"Oh, no, my love—only that I was a murderess; in which case I had better go to the Old Bailey. Though I didn't poison *you,* when you were a child; but gave you the best of education, and the most expensive masters money could procure. Yes; I've nursed five children, and buried three: and the one I loved the best of all, and tended through croup, and teething, and measles, and whooping-cough, and brought up with foreign masters, regardless of expense, and with accomplishments at Minerva House—which I never had when I was a girl—when I was too glad to honour my father and mother, that I might live long in the land, and to be useful, and not to mope all day in my room and act the fine lady—says I'm a murderess. Ah, Mrs. Osborne! may *you* never nourish a viper in your bosom, that's *my* prayer." (Chap. 38)

The Romantic ideal of "Epipsychidion" and *Jane Eyre*, the self-enclosed family that lives on emotion alone, has born terrible fruit in *Vanity Fair.*

Yet as readers we must go beyond this terrible revelation. Mrs. Sedley is not wicked; she is not an enemy from whom Amelia can escape. Mrs. Sedley is cruel, but she is also old, weak, dying. Though the family produces misery, it is the source of the only love that exists in *Vanity Fair.* We cannot wish that Amelia would turn her back on her old parents as we do wish she could turn her back on George Osborne. Faced with poverty, sickness and death, a woman truly needs to be an angel. When Amelia has finally given Georgy up to his grandfather Osborne in return for an allowance that will give her enough to feed herself and her parents, she is no longer a silly little woman yielding to a pompous husband, but the true Christian that both the action of the book and the narrative voice have demanded that we learn to value.

However, when Amelia is most truly an angel, and when the narrator praises her most lovingly, she is also most clearly part of a large-scale social madness.

In the midst of all these solitary resignations and unseen sacrifices, she did not respect herself any more than the world respected her; but I believe thought in her heart that she was a poor-spirited, despicable little creature whose luck in life was only too good for her merits. O you poor women! O you poor secret martyrs and victims whose life is a torture, who are stretched on racks in your bedrooms, and who lay your heads down on the block daily at the drawing-room table; every man who watches your pains or peers into those dark places where the torture is administered to you, must pity you—and—thank God that he has a beard. I recollect seeing, years ago, at the prison for idiots and madmen at Bicêtre, near Paris, a poor wretch bent down under the bondage of his imprisonment and his personal infirmity, to whom one of our party gave a halfpennyworth of snuff in a *cornet* or "screw" of paper. The kindness was too much for the poor epileptic creature. He cried out in an anguish of delight and gratitude: if anybody gave you and me a thousand a year, or saved our lives, we could not be so affected. And too, if you properly tyrannize over a woman, you will find a halfp'orth of kindness act upon her, and bring tears into her eyes, as though you were an angel benefitting her. (Chap. 57)

This is one of those radical passages in which both the conformist standards of behavior and the Christian resignation which dominate much of *Vanity Fair* are blown apart. What Thackeray's narrator says is terrifying: the confinement of the mad in prison is like the imprisonment of women in the home; women and madmen have both been so oppressed that they are irrationally grateful for the smallest favors—even favors bestowed by their oppressors. The impersonal *you* of the last sentence is addressed to Thackeray's male readers in England. They have treated women so terribly by imprisoning them as if they were mad that they have in fact made women mad—for their own benefit. Only madwomen would behave kindly to the cruel and oppressive men of nineteenth-century urban England. The world of victims and victimizers has here become a world of madmen and jailers—and most of the madmen are women.

In *Vanity Fair* Thackeray promulgates the myth of the angel-in-the-house but also exposes the horror that necessitates such a myth. In exposing the horror, he returns to the Romantic and radical sympathy for the mad; in promulgating the myth he acquiesces to the hideous distortion of Romanticism by Victorian culture. Though Thackeray finally rescues Amelia from her misery and lets her marry faithful Dobbin, the one person *she* has been able to victimize, he does not allow us to forget. He has not offered a solution to the problem of who should care for aging parents, or suggested that the economic system of urban England could be overthrown or undermined. He leaves his heroine with a double image, as angel and madwoman, and his reader with a double response—Christian acquiescence and radical, Romantic rage.

Though *Dombey and Son* is also full of rage, Dickens, in order to liberate his mythic angel from the madness of the world in which she lives, guides us away from the material conditions that oppress Florence Dombey. Dombey is not intended, as a character, to have Amelia Sedley's power to expose a world demanding female angels. Within Dickens's fiction she exists to serve men—her brother, her father, her husband—without illuminating the reader. As a moral exemplar produced by fiction, she is a gift from a male author to a male audience. The Victorians loved Dickens's saintly female characters; by continuing to produce them in novel after novel he did his part in creating an image of women that served the Victorian economic system.

Whereas Thackeray uses his narrative voice and the gradual revelation that a deadly economic system governs both his plot and his characters in order to force us to believe that Amelia, flawed as she is, possesses the only kind of goodness available in *Vanity Fair*, Dickens uses his narrative voice, his complicated plot, and his enormous cast of characters to make us believe that Florence has not been harmed by her suffering and that the one person most responsible for that suffering, her father, should be forgiven by us as he is forgiven by her. Paul Dombey is the economic king of Dickens's London: to forgive him is to accept the economic system over which he and other men preside—the system that demands women like Florence.

Dickens's narrative voice in *Dombey and Son* does not contain the deep ambiguity of Thackeray's in *Vanity Fair*. Though it is varied—sometimes angry, sometimes humorous, sometimes loving—it gives us only one view of the world as a place of high Christian drama, where good and bad individuals can play their significant parts. The other side of this Christian drama is an air of economic unreality. In *Vanity Fair*, when Becky and Rawdon Crawley live well on nothing a year, Thackeray lets us know that they are exploiting the labor and the goods of many people; though Dickens includes characters from a lower, poorer class than Thackeray does, and so can claim a gritty economic reality in his fiction, he also includes a number of people who float innocently through London, supported by their mysterious, unnamed, inheritances and investments. Sweet, feeble-minded Toots has an inheritance; the retired sailor Captain Cuttle still has an income of some sort; most important, the instrument maker without a customer, Sol Gills, ultimately becomes rich from "investments."

Sol Gills, an old-fashioned artisan, keeps lamenting that the times have passed him by: he is, in fact, exactly the sort of worker most clearly victimized by the large-scale, imperialistic, industrial capitalism that looms so large in *Dombey and Son*. E. P. Thompson says of his class: "From this culture of the craftsman and the self-taught there came scores of inventors, journalists, and political theorists of impressive quality. It is easy enough to say that this culture was backward-looking or conservative. True enough, one direction of the great agitations of the artisans and outworkers, continued over fifty years, was to *resist* being turned into a proletariat. When they knew that this cause was lost, yet they reached out again, in the Thirties and Forties and sought to achieve new and only imagined forms of social control."[12] To turn Sol Gills into a sweet sentimental figure in 1848, a figure economically and spiritually unhurt by large concentrations of capital, is a profoundly emblematic falsehood in *Dombey and Son*. It is part of the fictional fabric that supports Florence as an angelic heroine instead of a poor child damaged by a harmful economic system.

Even though for a time we believe Sol Gills is going to repeat the archetypal economic tragedy of nineteenth-century literature, Dickens makes all come out well. Like Wordsworth's Michael, Sol Gills needs money because he has countersigned a promissory note; Dombey lends him the money, but sends his nephew, Walter Gay, on a perilous voyage. It looks as if Sol Gills has been forced to give up a child in economic desperation, as Michael does, as Amelia Sedley does, but in *Dombey and Son* he finally gets to have his money and his nephew too, when long-lost Walter finally turns up safe. In spite of himself, the big capitalist Paul Dombey has put his money to good use. Against all economic likelihood, Sol Gills has prospered; his prosperity is one of Dickens's fictional tricks to exonerate Paul Dombey in the opinion of the reader; it is one of the tricks to help elevate Florence, Paul Dombey's primary victim.

The entire fictional fabric of *Dombey and Son* asks us to forget that Paul Dombey, the head of a large London trading company, is a powerful man of the type who does harm—economic harm to men like Sol Gills, and psychological harm to women like his first pathetic wife, his female servants, and his hurt, angelic daughter. He is similar to Thackeray's Mr. Osborne—rough, greedy, cold, abusive to women, entirely involved in the success of his financial life. But Thackeray makes Osborne part of a system, and Dickens makes Dombey a character in a melodrama so extraordinary that we forget how typical he is. When we watch him descend first into new cruelty, and then into the disgrace of bankruptcy, and finally emerge into a redeemed life, we can forget he is only one of many men of his type in London. Dickens has to keep us from judging Paul Dombey too harshly, or from seeing him too economically, if he is to lure us into believing the myth that a woman like Florence is a redeeming angel on earth and not the creation of an economic system.

Dickens asks us to believe that Dombey is himself a victim. Although he is economically powerful and psychologically imperious, he turns out to have been manipulated by his assistant, James Carker, a willfully malign figure of the type Thackeray excludes from his fiction. Unctuous, toothy, hypocritical, James Carker debauches women, rejects his own brother and sister, destroys his employer, and attempts to seduce his employer's wife, apparently for the mere evil fun of it. Carker has been manipulating the books of Dombey's trading house to make the house look greater than it is in the eyes of its arrogant head, to undermine the solidity of the house in the eyes of the rest of the world, and to finally bring about its collapse. Having heard of the wrong Carker is doing to Dombey, we readers are supposed to put aside our historical knowledge of the harm men like Dombey are doing to men like Sol Gills and women like Florence.

Dickens turns Dombey's eventual bankruptcy into a tragedy, the result of Carker's villainy, not a misfortune built into an economic system requiring that some fall so that others can prosper. Dombey's household sale is an event of special horror, not the everyday occurrence that such sales are in *Vanity Fair*. "Herds of shabby vampires, Jew and Christian, overrun the house, ... striking discordant octaves on the grand piano, drawing wet forefingers over the pictures, breathing on the blades of the best dinner–knives, punching the squabs of chairs and sofas with their dirty fists" (chap. 59). And with a final twist of his plot, Dickens avoids either having to find a new occupation for the ruined capitalist or having to show him suffering in poverty. Dombey gets what amounts to an allowance from Harriet and John Carker, who inherit their evil brother's money when he commits suicide. Since James Carker stole Dombey's money in the first place, Dombey in effect gets to keep a nice chunk of his own money. Even though Dickens includes shocking images of poverty in *Dombey and Son*, like the slums of Staggs Garden and the prostitute Alice Brown, nevertheless as a whole the fiction is an economic fairyland, a denial that money is power in nineteenth-century England, a refusal to acknowledge the suffering capitalism causes.

The fictional transformation of Paul Dombey from an economic master to a tragic victim is supported by the narrator's ever-present vision of his secret sufferings. Dickens instructed his readers to believe in Dombey's psychological reality, not in the psychological reality of his angelic daughter. He says in his preface: "Mr. Dombey undergoes no violent change, either in this book, or in real life. A sense of his injustice is within him all along. The more he represses it, the more unjust he necessarily is. Internal shame and external circumstances may bring the contest to a close in a week or a day; but it has been a contest for years, and is only fought out after a long balance of victory." By making Dombey forgivable and redeemable, Dickens empowers the myth Victorian businessmen wanted: if women were angelic and kind enough to them, they would eventually change for the better. This myth has an appeal for women too since it offers them a vision of their own power, but while they are attempting to work their spiritual magic, they must remain under men's thumbs.

Dombey, only one of many oppressive, abusive parents in Dickens's novels, alone among them has the power to undergo a full redemption. He gets special fictional treatment because, unlike Mrs. Joe, Miss Havisham, Mrs. Jellyby, he is a man. Cruel mothers are not redeemed by saintly sons, nor cruel wives by saintly husbands, in Victorian mythology. Cruelty is the privilege of men, and saintliness the duty of women. In *Dombey and Son* itself Dickens includes two particularly hideous, unforgivable mothers in order to make Dombey look good by comparison. Mrs. Skewton, the fraudulent Romantic, and Mrs. Brown, the petty criminal, have both turned their beautiful daughters, Edith and Alice, into prostitutes. Mrs. Skewton sells her daughter to rich husbands; Mrs. Brown sells hers to anyone. These two mothers, like Carker, are wicked individuals from whom we need not conclude anything about the economic structure of all nineteenth-century marriages, from whom we are indirectly supposed to glean sympathy for Dombey. The two prostituted daughters also indirectly suggest that Dombey could have been worse. These two women are sexually depraved, mad for revenge, possessed by their passions; because Dombey's abused daughter turns out to be an angel rather than a devil, we are led to conclude that he could not have been as bad as the mothers who have created Edith and Alice.

The narrator of *Dombey and Son* never lets us forget about the feelings of the cruel man who is being redeemed by an angelic woman. His feelings, after all, are the validation of her power. At the beginning he is merely indifferent to Florence as a child not worth considering: "But what was a girl to Dombey and Son! In the capital of the House's name and dignity, such a child was merely a piece of base coin that couldn't be invested—a bad boy—nothing more" (chap. 1). In nineteenth-century London, as Dickens reveals, fathers have a new reason to prefer sons; in the business world daughters and wives have lost the dignity of agricultural and domestic work, and with it the human dignity—if not equality—that was still available in the rural England Wordsworth and Austen wanted to save. Dickens's narrator's explanation of Dombey's original antipathy to Florence sets up his eventual redemption: he has to learn that businessmen cannot live by business alone—they need household angels to keep them human. The message to women is also clear—abusive business-men are not wicked, only mistaken.

Dickens paints a vivid, terrifying picture of parental hatred in Paul Dombey, yet at every step he gives an explanation that encourages us to forgive him. Dombey's indifference turns to hatred when his wife dies in bearing his son, and Florence loves the baby as a mother would. Dickens has genuine insight into hatred, calling it the frustrated inability to love and jealousy of those who *can* love: "The last time he had seen his slighted child, there had been that in the sad embrace between her and her dying mother which was at once a revelation and a reproach to him. Let him be absorbed as he would in the Son on whom he built such high hopes, he could not forget that closing scene. He could not forget that he had had no part in it" (chap. 3). This hatred intensifies in four subsequent stages: first, Florence and her brother become devoted to each other; second, young Paul dies and leaves Florence alive and unwanted; third, Dombey's second wife, Edith, loves Florence rather than him; and fourth, Edith runs away with Carker, again reminding Dombey that he is not loved. His hatred reaches its violent climax when Florence attempts to comfort him after Edith leaves. "In his frenzy, he lifted up his cruel arm and struck her, crosswise, with that heaviness, that she tottered on the marble floor; and as he dealt the blow, he told her what Edith was, and bade her follow her, since they had always been in league" (chap. 47). Even here Dickens's narrator asks us to see Dombey as a sinner who can repent. He repeatedly calls Dombey's hatred part of his "cold armor of pride"; knowing that pride goeth before a fall, we expect his fall, and expect to pity him.

Florence's sacrifice would be mere suffering if it had no object, to save Dombey. The narrative fabric and structure of plot in *Dombey and Son* push us into seeing Florence not as a damaged child, but as a perfect Victorian woman. Dickens does not treat her with the narrative ambivalence with which Thackeray treats Amelia Sedley; never does she look like a simpering fool. From the beginning of *Dombey and Son* to the end, as a child and as a woman, Florence is possessed by her unrequited love for her father, just as he is possessed by jealous hatred of her. Abuse has only made her sweeter, more loving, and more lovable in the eyes of everyone else who knows her.

This angelic child, however, also has such a bizarrely imaginative temperament that another author might call her insane. Dickens provides us with an unusually detailed description of her obsessive delusions. Both Florence and her brother Paul are the products of the Romantic belief that a child's imagination bestows precious insights into the truths of love and nature; but truth is hardly what their imaginations bestow. In this Victorian novel the Romantic faculty of imagination simply prevents the oppressed from recognizing their oppression. Delusion is highly desirable in abused children. Paul sees mysterious animals in the wallpaper, and after he dies Florence becomes increasingly absorbed in more extreme fantasies. Utterly isolated, she watches the family in the next house, four girls and their loving father; she imagines them to be the family, friends, neighbors she does not have. Solitude is an essential part of her life, as it is of

Amelia Sedley's in Thackeray's fiction; both are victims of the new social conditions of London, in which, Houghton says, "because density of population intensifies the struggle for existence, economic isolation is increased. Carlyle on his first visit to London in 1831 said to himself: 'Miserable is the scandal mongery and evil speaking of the country population: more frightful still the total ignorance and mutual heedlessness of those poor souls in populous city pent. . . . Each must button himself together, and take no thought (not even for evil) of his neighbor.'"[13]

In both *Vanity Fair* and *Dombey and Son* isolation is the necessary condition for the creation of angels. Guilt and magical redemptive power can flourish best in women who are cut off from each other, and from what other people consider reality. Social reality is exactly what Dickens asks us to put aside when we think of Florence. As she grows more solitary, more imaginative, and more loving, Dickens uses a new set of metaphors to describe her experience— magic, enchantment, fairy tales.

> Florence lived alone in the great dreary house, and day succeeded day, and still she lived alone; and the blank walls looked down upon her with a vacant stare, as if they had a Gorgon-like mind to stare her youth and beauty into stone.
> No magic dwelling-place in magic story, shut up in the heart of a thick wood, was ever more solitary and deserted to the fancy than was her father's mansion in its grim reality, as it stood lowering on the street: always by night when lights were shining from neighborhood windows, a blot upon its scanty brightness; always by day, a frown upon its never-smiling face.
> There were not two dragon sentries keeping ward before the gate of this abode, as in the magic legend are usually found on duty over the wronged innocence imprisoned; but besides a glowering visage, with its thin lips parted wickedly, that surveyed all comers from above the archway of the door, there was a monstrous fantasy of rusty iron, curling and twisting like a petrifaction of an arbour over the threshhold, budding in spikes and corkscrew points, and bearing, one on either side, two ominous extinguishers that seemed to say, "Who enter here, leave light behind!" (Chap. 23)

This imagery of fantasy in the voice of the narrator keeps us from thinking of words like *abused child* or *schizophrenia*; it lifts Florence into a magical world where we have learned to expect happy endings. The imagery also leads us into Florence's own mind, where reality and fantasy become more and more confused. "Shadowy company attended Florence up and down the echoing house, and sat with her in the dismantled rooms. As if her life were an enchanted vision, there arose out of her solitude ministering thoughts that made it fanciful and unreal" (chap. 23). Dickens's narrator asks us to feel a melancholy sympathy for the pathetic little girl without suggesting, as Thackeray's narrator does, that a person who lives in fantasy rather than in reality will sooner or later pay a price.

Dickens acknowledges the dark side of Florence's fantasies and her deep unhappiness, but he does not allow his narrator to express either sorrow or outrage on her behalf. The narrator does not even protest when Dickens acknowledges that she always chooses guilt instead of anger. When she visits the Skettles family and sees other children who are loved by their father, she concludes that it must be her own fault that her father does not love her. She can remember her mother did love her, but she begins to tremble and cry, "as she pictured to herself her mother living on, and coming also to dislike her, because of her wanting the unknown grace that should conciliate that father naturally, and had never done so from her cradle" (chap. 24). From childhood to womanhood, she never changes. Adulthood never brings her the ability to see that she is innocent and her father guilty. Dickens manages his fiction so that we are led to believe that abuse and suffering have not harmed her, that deluded guilt is a fine basis for a sweet woman's life.

Though Florence runs away from her father after he hits her, taking refuge with Captain Cuttle in Sol Gills's shop, she cannot run away from what he has done to her. When she marries her childhood friend Walter Gay, the self-abnegation she has learned in her childhood becomes ideal wifely love. "[I am] nothing Walter. Nothing but your wife. . . . I am nothing any more that is not you. I have no earthly hope any more that is not you. I have nothing dear to me any more that is not you" (chap. 56). Her new family brings her total joy and peace; Dickens creates a fantastic family like those in *Jane Eyre* and *Frankenstein*, a perfect haven that could exist only in a hurt imagination. Florence's family haven is almost identified with the heaven of the next world: "The voices in the waves are always whispering to Florence, in their ceaseless murmuring, of love—of love eternal and illimitable, not bounded by the confines of this world, or by the end of time, but ranging still beyond the sea, beyond the sky, to the invisible country far away" (chap. 57). Though in other novels—*Great Expectations, Our Mutual Friend*—Dickens explores the ways in which love itself can be destructive and insane, here the self-abnegating love of an angelic woman for the men in her family is sanctified, utterly right, beyond the reader's scrutiny.

At the very end of the novel this supernaturally strong love redeems Paul Dombey and brings him back into Florence's family. His fatal pride has gone: he has been injured, has lost his wife and his money. We are asked to believe that this suffering has purified him and that he can now love Florence and accept her redeeming love. The idea of humility and a reconciliation with Florence is certainly not incredible, yet the nature of the reconciliation Dickens creates is astonishing.

> "Papa! Dearest Papa! Pardon me, forgive me! I have come back to ask forgiveness on my knees. I can never be happy more without it."
>
> Unchanged still. Of all the world, unchanged. Raising the same face to him as on that miserable night. Asking *his* forgiveness.
>
> "Dear Papa, oh don't look strangely on me! I never meant to leave you.... I am penitent. I know my fault. I know my duty better now. Papa, don't cast me off, or I shall die." (Chap. 59)

As Dickens presents Florence's guilt, it is not the terrible madness imposed on women in a ruthless economic world, like Amelia Sedley's obsessive guilt in *Vanity Fair*, but the essence of perfect Victorian womanhood.

Percy Shelley's Romanticism has borne bad fruit in angels like Florence Dombey. Such characters do not appear in Wordsworth's poetry or in the fiction built around what E. P. Thompson calls the moral economy of agricultural England. They float down from Shelley's empyrean sphere, first to the isolated home of Jane and Rochester and then to the urban homes of Victorian businessmen in the fictions of Thackeray and Dickens. In the process of descent, sensibility and love and imagination become masochism and madness—and all the better for men who look for their wives in schools like Miss Pinkerton's or the mental hospitals where they would have learned humility. These heroines in whom Romanticism has become so twisted are not the eternal victims of eternal patriarchy; they are the myth that the urban nuclear families of Victorian England needed. They have their source in Romanticism, but they serve what the Romantic poets saw as their enemy—the economic processes of industrial capitalism.

7. George Eliot: Women and World History

Epigraphs from Wordsworth and Blake, allusions to Byron, references to Shelley—a reader quickly recognizes that George Eliot considers herself a friend of both Romanticism and radicalism. Yet just as Dickens and Thackeray could not keep Romanticism out of their novels, even though they consciously opposed it, so George Eliot includes much that seems irrevocably and unfortunately Victorian, particularly in her treatment of female characters who break social or sexual rules. Eliot knew the price of breaking the rules in Victorian England: as an Evangelical Christian, then as an apostate from Christianity, and then as the unmarried companion of George Lewes, she knew what estrangement from family and community really meant. Her fiction, like the work of other Victorian writers, Arnold, Carlyle, Mill, Tennyson, contains two deep impulses difficult to reconcile: rebellious individuality and conformity to community. Eliot the double impulse built into Victorian social theory is poignantly personal, and in her fiction it is focused most sharply and painfully on women. Eliot lived her adult life as the mistress of a very liberal man in a social world in which men like Dickens and Thackeray had defined the ideal, angelic wife: it was the worst of times, in many ways, for an unusual woman.

A Victorian by historical fact, if not by spiritual choice, Eliot creates in her fiction a strangely twisted version of Romantic radical-ism. Loosely associating her close-knit rural communities with Wordsworth and her rebellious radicals with Shelley, she transforms the ideas of both in ways that deny their historical immediacy and their true radicalism. Filtering Romantic radical ideas through Victo-rian experience, Eliot creates a complicated, surprisingly coherent historical scheme in her fiction, a scheme by which she can combine her version of Wordsworth and her version of Shelley. It is also a scheme by which she can use a false radicalism to turn her back on rural England, on contemporary historical fact, and on women.

Eliot's intellectual concerns and her intelligent artistry are con-centrated in *Middlemarch*, her greatest novel. *Middlemarch* is also the novel in which she most clearly withdraws from the political and economic welfare of rural England. Set in the years just before the Reform Bill of 1832, it is the last of her consciously historical fictions. The one novel that follows it, *Daniel Deronda*, is set in an English present of the 1870s, a present more terrible than the present of the 1840s Dickens portrays in *Dombey and Son*. The crucial question for a novelist who claims, as Eliot does, to be concerned with history, science, Romanticism, radicalism, and the lot of women is how the hopeful, politically active England of 1832 could have turned into the decayed, fragmented England of 1876, a culture particularly horrible for women. Yet, this is the question that Eliot, for all her intellectual pretensions, will not address. The evasion of this question vitiates the apparent Romantic radicalism of *Middlemarch*.

In spite of differences in tone and narrative voice, Eliot's fiction before *Middlemarch* adds up to a coherent historial scheme. Eliot is not merely torn between individualism and community, rebellion and conformity, as other Victorians are; she makes these two im-pulses part of an ongoing historical dialectic. Two of her fictions are set in the Renaissance—*Romola*, in Renaissance Florence, and *The Spanish Gypsy*, a dramatic poem, in fifteenth-century Spain. The rest are set in the relatively recent English past, in English villages at the end of the eighteenth century in "Mr. Gilfil's Love Story" and *Adam Bede*; in a village about 1810 in *Silas Marner*; in English towns of about 1830 in "Janet's Repentance," "The Sad Fortunes of the Rev-erend Amos Barton," *The Mill on the Floss*, and *Felix Holt the Radical*; and in both an English town and English villages of 1832 in *Middlemarch*. Three different forms of social organization are present: the entirely conformist, heroic tribe, the Gypsies; the relatively coherent and benevolent community of the village; and the conformist, gossipy, trivial, cruel community of the town, both that of nineteenth-century England and Renaissance Florence. In praising the heroic dignity of the tribe and the protective warmth of the village, as opposed to the degraded nastiness of the town, Eliot borrows from and fuses an enormous variety of historical theories, from Rousseau, Carlyle, to German Romantics like Schiller, Riehl, and Goethe. Dispraise of the vulgar commercial present of the English town was a common stance of both English and European writers of Eliot's time.

Eliot's theory of historical decay, however, is unique in some ways—particularly unusual are her combination of biological pessimism and spiritual optimism, and her pervasive antifeminism. Eliot begins with a more scientific and more contemptuous assumption about the nature of the human species than other writers do: the human community in any historical stage tends to reveal certain unpleasant characteristics because human beings are still members of the animal kingdom and will therefore exhibit conformist traits like those of any other species. Even before *Middlemarch*, Eliot's most flashily intellectual novel, she uses animal images and scientific language to remind us that we are not really a species set apart, but are just as constrained by instinct and habit as our fellow animals. Although people of different historical stages may talk, dress, and work differently, they all have what Eliot considers the fundamental human qualities: ignorance, self-congratulatory pride in belonging to a place, distrust of everything new. In Florence and Milby, in Raveloe and Middlemarch, men and women are superstitious, gossipy, intrusive, difficult to change. Even though Eliot bathes the late eighteenth-century villagers of *Adam Bede* in a warm golden light, and gushes over the beauty of the countryside, the richness of the land, and the quaintness of the speech, the people are just as narrow and conformist as those who inhabit her fictional towns of a later historical time.

The most pernicious twist Eliot gives to this theory that human conformity is biological, instinctive, essentially ineradicable, is that from her first fiction to her last, she views this conformity as a quality that becomes worse, more vicious, with historical progress from village to town, and views the agents of this degeneration as women,

women like the Dodson sisters and "The World's Wife," who destroy Maggie Tulliver in *The Mill on the Floss*. Eliot may have felt the ostracism of women more than that of men in her own nonconformist Victorian life: she projects the Victorian experience backward and expands it into a historical verity. In doing so she falsifies the history of earlier nineteenth-century England, her ostensible subject. Though Eliot repeatedly claims, through epigraph and allusion, to share Wordsworth's love of rural life and his belief that it is a worthy subject of literature, she gives little thought to the historical processes that threaten it, attributing its decay rather to the pernicious influence of women. And in *Middlemarch* she finally turns her back on English rural life altogether—in favor of the other side of her historical dialectic.

There is a reason to hope in Eliot's historical scheme, a source of spiritual progress. Eliot shares with Hegel, Shelley, and Carlyle a belief in the world-historical character who causes the upheaval necessary for human progress. One of the greatest differences between Eliot and all other nineteenth-century English novelists is that she usually includes in her fiction at least one character who is by nature spiritually ahead of the others; these characters cause the cataclysms she believes are as much a part of human nature as of geological nature. Ironically describing the present torpor of the town of St. Ogg's in *The Mill on the Floss*, she says, "And the present time was like the level plain where men lose their belief in volcanoes and earthquakes, thinking tomorrow will be as yesterday and the giant forces that used to shake the earth are forever laid to sleep. The days were gone when people could be greatly wrought upon by their faith" (bk. 1, chap. 12). Men may lose their belief in earthquakes, volcanoes, and spiritual conflict, but all will wake again. The human cataclysm will be set in motion by the advanced, unique individual, driven by the ardent impulse to seek a better life, an impulse than can be embodied in any number of spiritual forms.

Predictably, just as Eliot believes that conformist degeneration is the special product of women, so world-historical inspiration usually belongs to men. If women have any spiritual energy at all, it brings them sacrifice and suffering rather than power. Janet Dempster, Dinah Morris, and Romola all imbibe their spiritual energy from the great men they follow, and they go on to suffer various forms of deprivation—unhappy marriage, loss of the right to preach, widowhood. Poor Maggie Tulliver, genetically marked as different from the other women of St. Ogg's, suffers most of all. Her first, childish attempt to be a world-historical character, the queen of the Gypsies, ends in terror and mortification; as an adult she succeeds only in becoming an outlaw, loving first the son of her father's enemy, then the fiancé of her cousin. Though she loses the love of her family and her community, she refuses to leave St. Ogg's, and finally dies trying to rescue her brother in a flood. Eliot creates a story of stubborn, self-willed unhappiness for her intelligent, unusual heroine, and nevertheless asks us to believe that Maggie the martyr has played her part in world history. "The suffering, whether of martyr or victim, which belongs to every historical advance of mankind is represented in this way in every town and by hundreds of obscure hearths" (bk. 4, chap. 1). A world-historical woman is going to be a martyr; only a world-historical man is going to be a true savior, a true source of spiritual advancement in the torpid world of women's conformity.

In the novel most clearly dominated by a world-historical man, *Daniel Deronda,* Eliot reveals with shocking clarity the desired end of her historical scheme. In the future ideal state of Israel, the next stage of progress in the spiritual history of the world, women will be forever kept in their place. The state will be founded by men like Deronda and his personal prophet Mordecai; women will not have the power to rebel, as Deronda's mother rebelled, as Gwendolen Harleth rebelled, or the power to exert their collective degenerative power as the women of Eliot's bourgeois fictions do. They will be firmly under the control of Jewish antifeminist law, a law in which Eliot, the author of *Daniel Deronda,* rejoices. The women of Israel will be like Mordecai's sister Mirah, Deronda's wife, who contentedly accepts the separation of women in the synagogue, the sacrifice of her own modest career as a singing teacher, her endless duty to her criminal father, the sexual roles described by Mordecai's protector, Mr. Cohen. "A man is bound to thank God, as we do every Sabbath, that he was not made a woman; but a woman has to thank God that He has made her according to His will. And we all know what He has made her—a child-bearing, tender-hearted thing is the woman of our people" (bk. 6, chap. 46). We are to consider the Jewish family and the ideal Jewish state exemplary; the narrator supports Mr. Cohen, explaining that in a time of revolutionary struggle in Europe, women still have their place. "What in the midst of that mighty drama are girls and their blind visions? They are the Yea or Nay of that good for which men are enduring and fighting. In these delicate vessels is borne onward through the ages the treasure of human affections" (bk. 2, chap. 11). The angel-in-the-house has returned, the proper role for the wife of even a world-historical man like Daniel Deronda.

The pressure of the fictional English present, in *Daniel Deronda* a world of divorce, sadism, lost children, absent fathers, massive bankruptcies, large-scale economic speculations, is meant to make us believe that it is better for women to be oppressed in a reborn tribal culture, the new Jewish state, than to be free to destroy themselves. Every free woman in the novel does destroy herself—Mrs. Davilow and her daughter Gwendolen Harleth both marry sadists; Daniel Deronda's mother gives up her child and suffers forever; Lydia Glasher leaves her husband for the sadistic Grandcourt and spends the rest of her life in agony. The fiction asks us to believe that the wills of women have brought a state of total decay to England; we are meant to long for the new era of men.

The seeds of this Hegelian destiny lie beneath the humor, the tightness, the brilliance, the historical detail, the scientific commentary of *Middlemarch*. Even when Eliot tries her hardest to convince us, as readers, that we are getting a scrupulously, scientifically accurate portrait of both the social surface of English life and the deep historical forces impelling it, she is in fact weighting the scales. Though she keeps both Wordsworth, the poet of rural England, and Shelley, the poet of the world-spirit, in our minds through quotation and allusion, she keeps subtly shifting our attention from economic causes to supposedly spiritual ones, and so denies Wordsworth his radicalism and hands the victory to Shelley. *Middlemarch* is the book in which Eliot gives up even pretending to care about the people of rural England: as the crucial book in her historical scheme, set at a crucial time of English history, it reveals the falseness of her legendary attachment to Wordsworth and the determination of her Victorian denial that progress, the great god of Hegel and Shelley, could be fought. In denying that fight, Eliot denies both the working people of agricultural England and women their due, and hands them over to their historical victimizers.

From the first clause of the first sentence of *Middlemarch*, Eliot lets her readers know that this is to be no ordinary novel, but an embodiment of grandiose historical theory. "Who that cares much to know the history of man, and how the mysterious mixture behaves under the varying experiments of Time, has not dwelt, at least briefly, on the life of Saint Theresa, has not smiled with some gentleness at the thought of the little girl walking forth one morning hand-in-hand with her still smaller brother, to go and seek martyrdom in the country of the Moors?" With such a beginning, Eliot should not have been surprised that *Middlemarch* was not as beloved as *Adam Bede*; the ordinary readers of England had no desire to know "the history of man" and probably had never given Saint Theresa a thought. The image of history as a series of chemical experiments on "the mysterious mixture" of human types initiates the repeated scientific images with which this most unusual narrator regales the reader and, subtly, removes the moral intensity that informs the narrative voice of most other Victorian novelists.

The scientific images implicitly support a theory of history, a Victorian faith shared by authors as different as Tennyson and Carlyle, that the world was, indeed progressing, and that history was not a process subject to the control of ordinary human beings. The absence of human control is exactly the part of Victorian historical theory E. P. Thompson finds most pernicious, especially in connection with the events of the period Eliot claims to be analyzing in *Middlemarch*, the time when the working people of rural England were losing their battle.

We are so accustomed to the notion that it was both inevitable and "progressive" that trade should have been freed in the early 19th century from "restrictive practices" that it requires an effort of imagination to understand that the "free" factory-owner or large hosier or cotton–manufacturer who built his fortune by these means, was regarded not only with jealousy but as a man engaging in *immoral* and *illegal* practices. The tradition of the just price and the fair wage lived longer among "the lower orders" than is sometimes supposed. They saw *laissez faire*, not as freedom, but as "foul Imposition." They could see no "natural law" by which one man, or a few men, could engage in practices which brought manifest injury to their fellows.[1]

Just as Dickens uses one distorted version of Romanticism—the myth of the angel-in-the-house—to disguise Dombey's urban economic power, so Eliot uses another—the Victorian reincarnation of Shelley's spiritual history—to disguise the economic destruction of rural England in 1832, and to shift the blame for social decay from the economic power of men to the spiritual torpor of women.

The narrative comments themselves, so full of knowledge and

wisdom, present a historical theory of simultaneous intellectual advancement and social decay, but never reveal the causes of social decay in the economic world. Intellectual progress is easy enough for this narrator to demonstrate; the narrator constantly thrusts evidence of her knowledge before us, with elaborate images and analogies, references to microscopes, amoebae, batteries, the Rosetta stone, all the paraphernalia of modern science, about which the poor inhabitants of Middlemarch in 1832 knew little or nothing. She attributes much of the intellectual advance to Romanticism: "Romanticism, which has helped to fill some dull blanks with love and knowledge, had not yet penetrated the time with its leaven and entered into everybody's food: it was fermenting still as a distinguishable vigorous enthusiasm in certain long-haired German artists at Rome, and the youth of other nations who idled near them were sometimes caught in the spreading movement" (bk. 2, chap. 19). Now, in the 1870s, Eliot suggests, the mind of England and Europe is less dull because of the "leaven" of Romanticism than it was in 1832; she detaches Romanticism from political hope, which she admits was greater in 1832. "Will became an ardent public man, working well in those times when reforms were begun with a young hopefulness of immediate good which has been much checked in our days" (bk. 8, finale). What Eliot calls Romanticism seems to be allied only with intellectual and artistic progress, not with social and political justice.

The narrator's comments suggest that social life in England has been getting worse, by some unnameable process. Her one passage of true nostalgia is for Fielding's eighteenth century, "when days were longer (for time, like money, is measured by our needs) when summer afternoons were spacious, and the clock ticked slowly in the winter evenings" (bk. 2, chap. 15). She condemns the present by calling Dorothea's inheritance ample in those days when prominent families were "innocent of future gold-fields, and of that gorgeous plutocracy which has so nobly exalted the necessities of genteel life" (bk. 1, chap. 1). That gorgeous plutocracy, the present, is the social world of *Daniel Deronda.* Eliot's narrator has suggested a three-stage degeneration in England's social life, from the leisurely eighteenth century, to the conformist time of 1832, to the plutocracy of the present, without daring to mention a cause. That refusal colors her study of rural England in *Middlemarch.*

Eliot turns history into sentiment, and treats leisure as if it were a literary myth instead of a valuable part of a rural economy. E. P. Thompson takes the loss of leisure very seriously and connects it unmistakably with the rich taking traditional land and traditional work from the poor. There "was a conscious resistance to the passing of an old way of life, and it was frequently associated with political Radicalism. As important in this passing as the simple physical loss of commons and 'playgrounds' was the loss of leisure in which to play and the repression of playful impulses."[12] Eliot will not look at rural life this clearly.

Three elements of her general historical theory are simultaneously present in *Middlemarch*: village, town, and the large, world-historical element of spirit, here embodied in the characters who represent science, art, or religious ardor. Eliot weaves these elements together brilliantly in a seamless, convincing narration; she does a masterful job of creating a fictional structure that supports the narrator's historical evasion. Ultimately, the fictional structure falsifies the history of both rural working people and women. In portraying all three historical possibilities—village, town, and spirit—Eliot denies working people and women a useful role to play; in doing so, she denies the validity of Wordsworth's rural radicalism and hands the book over to Shelley and to progressive, educated men.

The village characters in whom earlier novelists placed their trusts—the landowners and the clergy—are in *Middlemarch* at best personally upright, charming, and politically ineffectual. At worst they are scheming, nasty, and politically malign. The Chettams, the Cadwalladers, the Farebrothers (by birth and class villagers, though they have been engulfed by the town), and Mr. Brooke, in his nonpolitical life, are among the pleasanter, wittier, more intelligent characters in Eliot's fiction. Mr. Farebrother even achieves a personal moral nobility in sacrificing his own happiness to his duty when he helps his parishioner Fred Vincy stay straight enough to win Mary Garth. This is, however, an isolated act, not a socially meaningful one. Farebrother is not one of the Christian characters of Eliot's fiction whose ardent desire for justice on earth brings him into the sacred ranks of the world-historical characters. In *Middlemarch* even the best of the traditional inhabitants of the village are relegated to historical meaninglessness.

Other villagers like grasping old Peter Featherstone, are worse than historically meaningless. The two through whom Eliot sends her most important historical message are Edward Casaubon and Mr. Brooke: both pretend to be intellectual, and Brooke, to be liberal; both, in Eliot's opinion, are doing more harm than good. Casaubon is an ungenerous Christian and a worthless scholar, concocting a Key to All Mythologies in the long-outdated mode of the seventeenth century, ignorant of the advancements in biblical scholarship made by progressive intellectuals on the Continent. Mr. Brooke is a dilettante, incapable of sustained thought or action, a declared liberal who hypocritically neglects his own tenants. Through these two men Eliot leads us to believe that the English village cannot foster intellectual or political activity of any worth; what happens there is useless, retrograde, foolish. It is Brooke, rather than a genuine radical, whom Eliot associates with Wordsworth; the first words we hear from him are, "Sir Humphrey Davy? . . . Well now, Sir Humphrey Davy; I dined with him years ago at Cartwrights, and Wordsworth was there too—the poet Wordsworth, you know" (bk. 1, chap. 2). In *Middlemarch* Wordsworth is assigned to the amiable and idle class whose charm does not keep them from heading for political and intellectual oblivion. It is an oblivion Eliot treats lightly; she gives neither outrage nor sorrow to this class of village people who have stopped trying to protect the agricultural economy.

The village women are the idlest and most useless of all. Eliot does not show any of the high-born country women doing so much as tending a flower garden. The only woman among them who does not placidly enjoy her life of ease is Dorothea Brooke; through Dorothea, Eliot tries to persuade her readers that a woman who wants to make the world better has to get out of rural England. Dorothea begins as a potential world-historical character, through whose genetically inherited ardor the slothful world might be moved forward. "In Mr. Brooke the hereditary strain of Puritan energy was clearly in abeyance; but in his niece Dorothea it glowed alike through faults and virtues" (bk. 1, chap. 1). She has inherited the tendency to make revolution, to be a Romantic and a radical; Eliot weaves a plot that leads us to believe these tendencies will only rot in the country.

Eliot interweaves two different kinds of development in Dorothea—religious and political—so subtly and skillfully that we must stand back from the fiction in order to realize that the two need not be connected. Dorothea begins as a self-sacrificing, otherworldly, masochistic Christian who is driven into a hellish marriage with Casaubon because she imagines she can find both learning and suffering with this Miltonic man. The life of a rich woman in the village of 1832, Eliot suggests, can offer neither intellectual challenge nor spiritual work; so we must understand why Dorothea is foolish enough to imagine that her mind and her soul will thrive with this old fraud. In the torments of her marriage Dorothea becomes less otherworldly, discovering the true, human meaning of words like *duty* and *sacrifice*. When Casaubon dies, leaving her emotionally free but economically bound by his will, which cuts her off from his estate if she marries Will Ladislaw, she happily shocks her neighbors even more than she did by marrying Casaubon, by leaving the money for the young, radical, sexy man. This part of her development is moving, convincing, joyful; Eliot finally allows a heroine some happiness.

However, the other part of Dorothea's development is by no means necessary, or necessarily connected with the change from masochistic Dissenter to happy, humanistic wife. Dorothea also changes from a woman with a personal political conscience and a devotion to the people of rural England to a passive adjunct of the world-spirit, as it is manifested in her new husband. At the beginning she wants to correct her uncle's negligence toward his tenant farmers and to plan habitable cottages for them. According to G. M. Trevelyan writing in 1942, the improvement of cottages was one of the genuine advances in rural life in the years after 1832: "In the 'fifties and 'sixties, while agriculture still flourished, good brick cottages with slate roofs and two or even three bedrooms apiece were being built by landlords as 'estate cottages.' . . . The bad cottages were the old ones."[3] With the hindsight of the 1870s, Eliot could well have made this venture of Dorothea's successful; she might have given her heroine a productive place in English agricultural life. Instead, she gives Dorothea a more grandiose scheme for an industrial colony something like those of Robert Owen—and then makes her quickly abandon it, claiming to have been persuaded by her brother-in-law that it would be too expensive. Eliot then is free to move her heroine into marriage with Ladislaw, out of the countryside, out of political action. This move also takes her out of the existing economic life and social fabric of England and into Eliot's third historical category, that of pure spirit, the realm dominated in this fiction by Will Ladislaw.

To be a radical heroine in *Middlemarch*, Dorothea must enter a realm that does not exist in rural England.

Eliot gives the English village a male-dominated family of saviors, that of Caleb Garth and his redeemed son-in-law Fred Vincy, but they do not save the village by having any respect for its inhabitants. This family descends into the village from the middle class, the town: Caleb has started his economic life over, after a business "failure" which, predictably, alienated him from the other businessmen of the area. In character and person he is similar to Eliot's earlier village hero, Adam Bede: the upright workman, the strong, muscular old Englishman who speaks in half-biblical phrases, who represents both the best in an ancient English rural tradition and the possibility of a true improvement in rural culture. In some ways Caleb Garth is genuinely and admirably radical; witnessing what Eliot's narrator calls the "Christian carnivora" waiting to hear Peter Featherstone's will, he shocks his neighbors into calling him "un-Christian" by saying he wished there was no such thing as a will. To challenge the laws of inheritance was radical in both 1832, the time of the novel, and 1870, the time of Eliot's present. As a man who believes in productive work, not inherited money, Caleb Garth does indeed look like the kind of man who could save rural England.

When Caleb Garth becomes the overseer of the Brooke and Chettam estates, we are led to believe he will bring the English village new life. However, Eliot gives this character, like Dorothea, a twist that negates his alliance with those Romantics and radicals who wanted to protect the working people of rural England. She describes, in language almost like Whitman's, his love of work:

Caleb Garth often shook his head in meditation on the value, the indispensable might, of that myriad-headed, myriad-handed labour by which the social body is fed, clothed, and housed. It had laid hold of his imagination in boyhood. The echoes of the great hammer where roof or keel were a-making, the signal-shouts of the workmen, the roar of the furnace, the thunder and plash of the engine, were a sublime music to him; the felling and lading of timber, and the huge trunk vibrating star-like in the distance along the highway, the crane at work on the wharf, the piled-up produce in warehouses, the precision and variety of muscular effort wherever exact work had to be turned out,—all these sights of his youth had acted on him as poetry without the aid of poets . . . a religion without the aid of theology. (Bk. 3, chap. 24)

These inspiring images are those of industrial, not agricultural labor.

Furnaces and engines belong to the factory owners who were turning small farmers and artisans into a proletariat.

Eliot leaves no doubt about Garth's ultimate alliance when he castigates the village workers who are trying to stop the new railway: "Now, my lads, you can't hinder the railroad: it will be made whether you like it or not. And if you go fighting against it, you'll get yourselves into trouble. The law gives those men leave to come here on the land" (bk. 6, chap. 56). We are virtually forbidden to consider the possibility that these poor working men might be right, and might be their own best defenders. Eliot makes both the men fighting the railroad and Mr. Brooke's irate tenant, Dagley, into ignorant, despicable characters, entirely unworthy of our respect. Both narrative comment and uncouth, stupid language in the mouths of these characters turn us against the workers who are receiving Garth's reprimand. "In the absence of any precise idea as to what railways were, public opinion in Frick was against them; for the human mind in that grassy corner had not the proverbial tendency to admire the unknown, holding rather that it was likely to be against the poor man, and that suspicion was the only wise attitude with regard to it" (bk. 6, chap. 56). When Caleb tries to explain that the railway will be good for them, Eliot puts contemptible words into the mouth of Timothy Cooper: "I'n seen lots o' things turn up sin' I war a young un—the war an' the peace, and the canells, an' the oald King George, an' the Regen'. . . . an' it's been all aloike to the poor mon. What's the canells been t' him? They 'n brought him neyther me-at nor be-acon, nor wage to lay by, if he didn't save it wi' clemmin his own inside. Times ha' got wusser for him sin' I war a young un. An' so it'll be wi' the railroads. They'll on'y leave the poor mon furder behind. . . . This is the big folks's world, this is. But yo're for the big folks, Muster Garth, yo are" (bk. 6, chap. 56). We are supposed to be offended by his bad grammar, bad pronunciation, other signs of ignorance, but historically he is right. Caleb Garth's industrial progress has been for the big folks and against the poor men. Eliot chooses to give her agricultural laborers unattractive voices instead of the eloquent, almost biblical voices of the poor that ring through *The Making of the English Working Class*. She degrades their voice to degrade their cause, and to blind us to the historical fact that in the battles of 1832 they had both a just cause and many intelligent spokesmen. She lowers them in order to raise Caleb Garth, the progressive industrialist, as the savior of the village.

Through the elevation of Caleb Garth Eliot also subtly denigrates another class of women. Just as she denies the village gentry any of their traditional work, she denies Mrs. Garth and Mary any connection with other country women. They possess Caleb's virtues, but neither his ardor nor the psychological complexity of characters like Lydgate and Bulstrode; they remain Caleb's shadows, firmly and unalterably separated from companionship with the class of rural women.

[Mrs. Garth] had never poured any pathetic confidences into the ears of her feminine neighbours concerning Mr. Garth's want of prudence and the sums he might have had if he had been like other men. Hence these fair neighbours thought her either proud or eccentric, and sometimes spoke of her to their husbands as "your fine Mrs. Garth." She was not without her criticism of them in return, being more accurately instructed than most matrons in Middlemarch, and—where is the blameless woman?—apt to be a little severe towards her own sex, which in her opinion was framed to be entirely subordinate. On the other hand, she was disproportionately indulgent towards the failings of men, and was often heard to say that these were natural. (Bk. 3, chap. 24)

In this last quality she resembles her female creator. Her combination of domestic skills and education makes her not an ideal for Eliot's rural women, but a woman set apart. She is proud of being able to teach her pupils and work in the kitchen at the same time, and hopes they will see "she might possess 'education' and other good things ending in 'tion' and worthy to be pronounced emphatically, without being a useless doll" (bk. 3, chap. 24). The useless dolls are presumably other rural women.

What Eliot does to Mrs. Garth as a fictional character is parallel to what she does to the rural laborers. She takes a figure who is a natural representative of the radical rural history of 1832 and transforms her into a shadow of her progressive husband. In fact women's arts like the ones Mrs. Garth excels in were being destroyed, and women as a class were being degraded, according to E. P. Thompson. "The Radicalism of northern working women was compounded of nostalgia for lost status and the assertion of new-found rights. According to conventions which were deeply felt, the woman's status turned upon her success as a housewife in the family economy, in domestic management and forethought, baking and brewing, cleanliness and child-care. . . . Each stage in industrial differentiation and specialisation struck also at the family economy, disturbing customary relations between man and wife, parents and children, and differentiating more sharply between 'work' and 'life' ".[4] By separating Mrs. Garth so decisively from her rural neighbors, and by making her a complacent prophet of women's inferiority to men, Eliot cuts her off from the history of women's radicalism of which she seems a natural part.

Her daughter Mary is cut in her mold: an excellent seamstress, a hardworking nurse to Peter Featherstone, a loving and patronizing wife to Fred Vincy. Fred, by refusing to become a minister, in spite of his university education, and by joining Caleb Garth in productive labor, rejects his family's wish to see him rise in class; as his wife, Mary can stay close to her father, and away from women, just as her mother has done. She (and her creator) rejoice that she gives birth only to sons; the great accomplishment of her life is a children's book *Stories of Great Men, Taken from Plutarch.* The possibility that the regenerators of the English village of 1832 could include either women or agricultural laborers is shunted aside in Eliot's fiction. Both women and workers must bow out when the prophets of progress appear. Wordsworth's villagers lose to Shelley's world-spirit even in the village.

The village itself exists only at the periphery of the fictional web of *Middlemarch.* At the center is the more advanced, and more decayed, social organization of the town. Eliot is at her most savage when describing the women of the town; they are truly malevolent, as a group, an active hindrance to all who would try to advance spirit. Not that the men of the town are admirable—we see them in groups, bankers and coroners, businessmen and doctors, auctioneers and politicians, at funerals, parties, meetings. And they combine the ignorance and conformity of Eliot's villagers in earlier fiction with the new pettiness that belongs to the town. They speak from habit, without love, without wit, without reason. Yet they are perfect innocents compared with the women. They are less involved than the men in large, semipublic gatherings, and spend more time in private visiting, without the kindness and charm and charity of the poor villagers of Eliot's earlier fiction or the intelligence and warmth of the village gentry in *Middlemarch.* At best, they gossip. "Now Mrs.

Bulstrode had a long-standing intimacy with Mrs. Plymdale. They had nearly the same preferences in silks, patterns for underclothing, china-ware, and clergymen; they confided their little troubles of health and household management to each other" (bk. 3, chap. 31). At worst, they destroy.

In Middlemarch a wife could not long remain ignorant that the town held a bad opinion of her husband. No feminine intimate might carry her friendship so far as to make a plain statement to the wife of the unpleasant fact known or believed about her husband; but when a woman with her thoughts much at leisure got them suddenly employed on something grievously disadvantageous to her neighbours, various moral impulses were called into play which tended to stimulate utterance. Candour was one. . . . Then, again, there was the love of truth—a wide phrase, but meaning in this relation a lively objection to seeing a wife look happier than her husband's character warranted, or manifest too much satisfaction in her lot: the poor thing should have some hint given her that if she knew the truth she would have less complacency in her bonnet, and in light dishes for a supper-party. Stronger than all, there was the regard for a friend's moral improvement, sometimes called her soul, which was likely to be benefited by remarks tending to gloom, uttered with the accompaniment of a pensive staring at the furniture in a manner implying that the speaker would not tell what was on her mind, from regard to the feelings of the hearer. On the whole, one might say that an ardent charity was at work setting the virtuous mind to make a neighbour unhappy for her good. (Bk. 8, chap. 74)

It is impossible to judge the historical accuracy of such a slashing portrait of a class of women, but it is not impossible to see that the special traits Eliot most loathes in these women are historically specific, not universal. It is then possible to connect their historical specificity with discernible causes, causes that Eliot, as narrator and author, chooses to hide. The particular kind of moral judgment exercised by these women is not that of Shakespeare or Milton or Austen; it is the kind of judgment generated when too many women are trying to be angels in their husbands' houses. After all, how better to show what a good job one is doing in monitoring one's own husband than by making other women feel they are doing a slipshod job? These are not eternal women but Victorian women, projected back a few years before the queen's coronation. In Middlemarch women we see the "new morality" of the nineteenth century, a compound of Evangelical influences and the new conventions of the urban household, which are encroaching on the customs of rural England. These women make their own use of the feminine ideal Dickens and

Thackeray helped propagate; a woman, as well as a man, can *use* the ideal of the angel-in-the-house as an instrument of domineering power.

Eliot, however, asks us, in reading *Middlemarch*, to believe that these women invented this role and wield genuine power, something more than psychological power, in the town. Eliot implicitly asks us to forget that the men of Middlemarch have the economic power, and that one of the reasons the women are so busy in their moral watchfulness is that they have been deprived of their own kinds of work, the work Mrs. Garth still does. By giving these women power, instead of exploring the historical forces that influenced them, Eliot makes them the true villain of *Middlemarch*, a class of people without a redeemer, a class without any remnants of Wordsworth's virtues, a class untouched by Shelley's spirit of progress. The texture of Eliot's fiction suggests that this group of bourgeois women, not their husbands or the more powerful men in London, is responsible for the spiritual deadness of the general population of England.

The town's drama is centered on three characters—Lydgate, Bulstrode, and Rosamond Vincy; again the fiction asks us to believe that the woman is the true villain, the true source of deadening power in bourgeois culture. Rosamond has none of the Evangelical solemnity of her aunts and older neighbors, but she has all of their petty worldliness, plus a more modern element—the social aspirations engendered by her education at a fancy finishing school. Even though she lives in what has recently been the country, she is a member of the world Thackeray calls Vanity Fair. As Eliot portrays her, she becomes a creature of almost demonic power, the malign goddess of a cruel town, the enemy of the small bit of Romantic radicalism trying to survive there.

Rosamond, like Thackeray's Amelia Sedley, is the product of a finishing school. She is another young woman whose parents have paid to have her turned into a desirable property for a Victorian man. "She was admitted to be the flower of Mrs Lemon's school, the chief school in the county, where the teaching included all that was demanded in the accomplished female—even to extras, such as the getting in and out of a carriage" (bk. 1, chap. 11). Rosamond, however, like the other women of the town, has figured out how to use the image men want for her own purposes. She knows how to look and act like an angel—always decorous, polite, agreeable, pleasant—and how to convince men she would be the perfect wife. The image becomes a commodity in the marriage market. A conniving, selfish woman like Rosamond can use what was serious, though deadly, in the ideal women of Dickens and Thackeray as a mere disguise in pursuit of a husband. As a character, she is powerful, gripping, for she is determined in her narcissism, relentless in her materialism, winning in her fraudulence. There is no reason for us to doubt that the newly bourgeois countryside of the 1830s might not have contained characters like her.

The possible realism of her individual character, however, is not enough to validate the cosmic role Eliot gives her. Almost single-handedly she destroys the one person who would like to regenerate the town with radicalism—the new doctor, Tertius Lydgate. It is one thing to show that a selfish woman can gain a measure of sexual power by masquerading as an angel; it is another to blame such a woman, as a type, for a culture's faults. Women like Rosamond are the products of a materialistic culture, not the producers of it. But in the way Eliot tells the sad story of Lydgate, we are led to see Rosamond as the obstacle to his progressive influence as a scientist and a doctor.

Eliot does admit, as an author, that Lydgate is responsible—and blamable—for his initial choice of Rosamond, the woman all other men want, the town beauty, the mayor's daughter. Like the least progressive of his Victorian brothers, he wants a woman who will make his home a place for "reclining in a paradise with sweet laughs for bird-notes, and blue eyes for a heaven" (bk. 1, chap. 11). Nevertheless, as the book moves on and we watch him marry Rosamond, spend more than his income providing for her (and himself too) an elegant home and furnishings, and as we watch him gradually crumble under the pressure of anxiety and debt, Eliot pushes us into shifting our anger to Rosamond. She becomes "the irresistible woman for the doomed man of that date" (bk. 3, chap. 27); his idea that with her he can lead a life of solitary scientific work becomes an idea as "blind and unconcerned as a jelly-fish which gets melted without knowing it" (bk. 3, chap. 27). By the end, Rosamond has driven him to opium, driven him away from the progressive scientific research and progressive medical practice he wanted, and driven him to borrow money from her Uncle Bulstrode, fatally, just before scandal strikes. He loses his science, his radicalism, his integrity; all he gains is the realization that the woman he has got is not the one he wanted. "How far he had travelled from his old dreamland, in which Rosamond Vincy appeared to be that perfect piece of womanhood who would reverence her husband's mind after the fashion of an accomplished mermaid, using her comb and looking-glass and singing her song for the relaxation of his adored wisdom alone" (bk. 6, chap. 58). We hear echoes of Victorian demonology here, and know he was mistaken in ever thinking mermaids to be prettily subhuman. We remember Becky Sharp is called a mermaid too—and that mermaids heartlessly kill their men. At this point Eliot as narrator and creator of fictions does not deserve our trust. The responsibility for Lydgate's failure to bring science and progress to a provincial town should not lie with women—either the collective matrons or the single mermaid.

The third member of the town's drama, Nicholas Bulstrode, Rosamond's uncle by marriage, is the kind of man who possessed true power in the provincial towns of England in 1832. Though Eliot portrays him vividly and weaves the strands of his waiting doom with great subtlety, she emphasizes those points of his character and his story that will direct our attention away from his economic power. For only by casting his power, and the power of other rich men in the town, into shadow can she arrange to show Rosamond and the gossiping matrons as the true enemies of progress. Bulstrode, like Dorothea, is the heir of Puritanism, but instead of growing into humanistic, progressive religion, he demonstrates the soul-withering, self-deceiving qualities into which Puritanism has dwindled.

Bulstrode begins as the self-righteous moralist whom the complacent materialists of the town regard with self-protective suspicion; he becomes a terrified, guilty man whose ancient crime—preventing his dying wife from learning that her daughter is still alive, and so securing her money for himself—is hideously exposed, and compounded by his willful negligence in the death of his blackmailer. The intricacies of his semitheological rationalizations and the agonies of his guilt tell us that Dissenting religion has fallen on evil days. In a man like Bulstrode, who has kept the self-righteous pride of Dissent while joining the established church, and attempting to join the community of Middlemarch, what was once a radical religion has become a mode of hypocrisy.

Yet Eliot transforms him again, into a tragic figure, a man more sinned against than sinning, and so completes the screen that the fiction places before our eyes, keeping us from seeing who calls the shots in nineteenth-century England. Bulstrode is condemned by the town—publicly by the men, privately and even more viciously by the women—and driven into exile. Sick, broken, tormented, he is punished more than his crimes deserve, for he has done little that others have not done with impunity. His manipulation of his first wife's will was not much different from the tricks Featherstone played with his, or the cruelty Casaubon's grandparents committed through theirs, in disinheriting his Aunt Julia. And the fatal medical treatment of Raffles's delirium tremens, which violated Lydgate's orders, was exactly what any other doctor in Middlemarch would have prescribed. The injustice of Bulstrode's destruction turns our rage back on the town that destroys him, and reminds us he has, after all, been right in accusing his accusers of being worldly, selfish, materialists.

In all this high moral drama we tend to lose sight of who Bulstrode has been. Economically he has been no victim, but a center of power. A rich banker who has turned the profits from his first wife's pawnbroking and fencing operation into financial and social respectability, he is a controlling force in the town. "Mr. Bulstrode's power was not due simply to his being a country banker, who knew the financial secrets of most traders in the town and could touch the springs of their credit; it was fortified by a beneficence that was at once ready and severe—ready to confer obligations, and severe in watching the result. He had gathered, as an industrious man always at his post, a chief share in administering the town charities, and his private charities were both minute and abundant" (bk. 2, chap. 16). Though he claims to want power only for the glory of God, his neighbors are not impressed. "They had a strong suspicion that since Mr. Bulstrode could not enjoy life in their fashion, eating and drinking so little as he did, and worrying himself about everything, he must have a sort of vampire's feast in the sense of mastery" (bk. 2, chap. 16). Eliot alienates our sympathies so entirely from the townspeople that we cannot hear the truth of Mr. Vincy's accusation against Bulstrode, as we cannot hear the truth of what Timothy Cooper says about the railroad. "If you mean to hinder everybody from having money but saints and evangelists, you must give up some very profitable partnerships, that's all I can say. . . . It may be for the glory of God, but it is not for the glory of the Middlemarch trade, that Plymdale's house uses those blue and green dyes it gets from the Brassing manufactory; they rot the silk, that's all I know about it" (bk. 2, chap. 13). The fiction invites us to forget this, so that Eliot can suppress male economic power and elevate women to the status of powerful cultural villains.

Men like Bulstrode were very powerful in 1832. E. P. Thompson's analysis of the role of Noncomformist religion in manufacturing towns supports Vincy's accusation, and reminds us that men like Bulstrode had many victims in rural England. The melodrama of Bulstrode and Raffles diverts our attention from the dyes that rot the silk—and from the people who make them. "If . . . the treatment of childhood and of povety are the two 'touchstones' which reveal the character of a social philosophy, then it is the liberal and Noncon-formist tradition which suffers most severely in 1830, from this test. . . . The years between 1790 and 1830 see an appalling declension in the social conscience of Dissent."[5] Bulstrode's special brand of self-abasing Christianity is just what the industrialists ordered: "The younger leaders of Methodism were not only guilty of complicity in the fact of child labour by default, they weakened the poor from within, by adding to them the active ingredient of submission; and they fostered within the Methodist Church those elements most suited to make up the psychic component of the work discipline of which the manufacturers stood most in need."[6] Eliot turns Bulstrode, a true example of economic power in 1832, into another victim of the town, almost another Lydgate, and she never lets us forget that in her view the town is ruled by women. *Middlemarch* implicitly suggests a social theory in which women of the middle classes are responsible for social stasis and the repression of all progressive, radical change; we forget all about the power of Noncomformist manufacturers.

At the head of Eliot's demonic legions at the end of the book stands Rosamond Vincy; she triumphs when her uncle and her husband are forced into exile. She gets to go to London, and fun and fashion, her lifetime ambition; in going, she takes from the town its only hope for radical change, her husband. For Eliot, the town is consigned to damnation, in the form of the rule of the bourgeois matrons. Though Caleb Garth remains to regenerate the village, the town is beyond hope. It belongs to women.

The prime area of hope in *Middlemarch* is entirely removed from both town and village. The place for Romantic radicals is the city. Eliot gives us glimpses of Romantic art in the young Germans who have studios in Rome, and mentions, through Will Ladislaw, the Germans' progressive scholarship in mythology, scholarship that is radical in a Christian culture. But she gives the greatest fictional emphasis to the radicalism of Will Ladislaw and Dorothea, who escape from the country to London, bearing with them the energy of their world-historical destinies.

Ladislaw is a compound of many forms of Romanticism. Like Hawthorne's Holgrave he is the many-sided man of whom the German Romantics dreamed—a radical, an artist, a journalist. Mr. Brooke, his patron, connects him with English Romanticism, labeling him "a kind of Shelley, you know" (bk. 4, chap. 37). And through him Eliot irrevocably tilts her fiction away from Wordsworth, away from the country, away from working people, away from rural woman, and toward the ineffable realm of disembodied spiritual progress. Both economics and genetics have made Ladislaw what he is. His Romantic, radical nature is partly the product of disinheritance: he is cut off from the corruption of inherited wealth not once, but twice. His paternal grandmother, Mr. Casaubon's Aunt Julia, was disinherited when she married a Polish patriot, "a bright fellow—could speak many languages—musical—got his bread by teaching all sorts of things" (bk. 4, chap. 37). And the money that should have come to him from his maternal grandmother, Mrs. Dunkirk, was intercepted by her second husband, Bulstrode. When Bulstrode finds out from Raffles, his blackmailer, that the grandson he defrauded is at hand, in Middlemarch, he tries to assuage his conscience by offering Will money; Will, unlike poor Lydgate, turns down the tainted money and keeps his spiritual liberty. Ladislaw's very name, Will, reminds us of the economic system from which he has been shut out; without inherited money, he is tied to no class, and no class interest. Disinherited, he is free, free to be a radical in the realm of the world-spirit.

Ladislaw does, however, have a genealogical inheritance. Eliot never contradicts what the good neighbors of Middlemarch whisper viciously—that the Evangelical pawnbrokers, the Dunkirks, were converted Jews. By the end of the book Will's ancestry is about as bad as it can get: "The Casaubon cuttle-fish fluid to begin with, and then a rebellious Polish fiddler or dancing-master, was it? and then an old clo—" (bk. 8, chap. 84) says Mrs. Cadwallader. Yet in Eliot's own genetic theory, both the radical Polish patriot and the Jews have done their part in making Will what he is. Like Dorothea, and the later hero Daniel Deronda, he genetically inherits his wish to be a radical, to move the world from its torpid sloth.

Eliot asks us to take Will's radicalism, and its efficacy, virtually on faith. In love with Dorothea, he leaves behind his dabbling in various forms of art in order to devote himself to the political life that will please her. His attempts to bring radicalism to the countryside, through his association with Mr. Brooke, fail; he leaves Middlemarch with his bride for London and national politics, a career in Parliament. Eliot tells us no more, but expects us to believe that Will's Romantic radicalism has done its part in "The growing good of the world." He becomes part of the spirit of progress Eliot inherits not from Wordsworth, but from Hegel and Shelley.

Dorothea, Eliot's heroine, is mysteriously included in this sweeping spiritual destiny. The phrase so dear to Victorian progressives, "the growing good of the world," occurs in the narrator's description of Dorothea's life as Will's wife. "The effect of her being on those around her was incalculably diffusive: for the growing good of the world is partly dependent on unhistoric acts; and that things are not so ill with you and me as they might have been, is half owing to the number who lived faithfully a hidden life, and rest in unvisited tombs" (bk. 8, finale). This is a pleasant sentiment, but it requires even more faith on the part of the readers than Will's political career does. Dorothea has actually failed at everything she tried in the country—building cottages, founding a school of industry, restoring Lydgate's ruined reputation.

Eliot wishes us to see Dorothea as a heroine, however; she puts an exalted vision of her into the mind of Lydgate, a vision we as readers are supposed to accept. "This young creature has a heart large enough for the Virgin Mary. She evidently thinks nothing of her own future, and would pledge half her income at once, as if she wanted nothing for herself but a chair to sit in from which she can look down with those clear eyes at the poor mortals who pray to her. She seems to have what I never saw in any woman before—a fountain of friendship towards men—a man can make a friend of her" (bk. 8, chap. 76). The Virgin Mary is a rather strange image for a woman who begins as the inheritor of revolutionary Puritan blood! And yet it is the true image, the true meaning of the heroine of *Middlemarch*. She begins as a would-be radical, reformer, Romantic and ends as the woman alone of all her sex. The image of the Virgin Mary takes us back to Saint Theresa of the prelude, and to Eliot's biologically deterministic metaphor for her modern counterparts: "Here and there a cygnet is reared uneasily among the ducklings in the brown pond, and never finds the living stream in fellowship with its own oary-footed kind."

A woman cannot choose her genetic inheritance, cannot choose to be a madonna or a swan among the ducks. These images reveal that even though Dorothea is Eliot's most cheerful and secular heroine, and the heroine who seems, at first, most radical, she is, by the end, one more weapon in Eliot's war against women. Her reward for her spiritual, genetic affinity with the world-spirit is that she escapes from her family, her home, the countryside, and, most important, from the society of women. She remains friendly with her sister, but all those gossiping rural matrons are left behind. Like the Garth women, she associates exclusively with men. And she, like Mary, is rewarded with male children, in contrast to Rosamond, who has daughters.

Nothing in Eliot's fiction suggests that Lydgate's image of Dorothea should be corrected. He admires her fountain of friendship for men—never thinking, apparently, that she might find room in her heart for women as well. Her supposedly benevolent gesture toward Rosamond, in the short period when she believes that Will and Rosamond are having an affair, hardly constitutes what most people would consider kindness. Lecturing an imagined rival on the duties of marriage is not exactly a selfless act. And it is virtually the only contact Dorothea has with women outside her family in all of *Middlemarch*. Within this intricately woven, richly textured novel of many characters, this alleged portrait of a whole rural community, lies the same kind of ideal marriage—isolated and complacent—that Charlotte Brontë celebrates in *Jane Eyre*.

In *Middlemarch*, however, Eliot has made the separation of her heroine from other women open, explicit, and a matter of principle. Dorothea is separate for more than merely psychological reasons; she must choose the exclusive society of men because Eliot has invented a unique theory of history in which bourgeois women are the active agents of historical decay, and radical men are the agents of spiritual progress, which is in perpetual battle against social stagnation.

Within this historical scheme, Dorothea's destiny is logical and in-evitable. The scheme itself is wrong.

Eliot's superficially radical theory of history casts aside the known and knowable truths of nineteenth-century history in favor of blind faith in spiritual progress. It ignores the wrongs and oppressions Wordsworth saw perpetrated in the English agricultural world and allies itself with Shelley's disembodied spiritual hopes. It justifies and hardens the separation of most women and most men, which is one of the most pernicious aspects of Victorian sexual ideology. And in the name of an ahistorical, imaginary radicalism, it separates woman from woman. A few good women are allied with men and progress, and many rotten women are virtual conspirators against all that is radical. It is less pernicious that Dorothea, in the end, turns into another angel in Ladislaw's house than that Eliot consigns Rosa-mond and the legions of matrons to the realm of rural darkness.

George Eliot, brilliant, learned, acquainted with the wide world, could have made another choice. Information was at hand with which she could have created a radical heroine who remains active while she is married, and who allies herself with the causes at hand, instead of with the ineffable Shelleyan mysteries of spirit, who turns her back on neither men nor women. Frances Wright, the Grimké sisters, the Blackwell sisters, and others whose names have almost perished, were all around her in England and in America. For exam-ple, the radical publisher Carlile is similar to the one-time radical publisher Ladislaw; instead of going to Parliament he went to jail, and finally triumphed, and returned to publishing in his freedom; women were at his side. "Banishment apart, Carlile could not be silenced, unless he were to be beheaded, or, more possibly, placed in solitary confinement. But there are two reasons why the Government did not proceed to extreme measures. First, already by 1821 it seemed to them less *necessary*, for the increased stamp duties were taking effect. Second, it was apparent after the first encounters that if Carlile were to be silenced, half a dozen new Carliles would step into his place. The first two who did so *were* in fact Carliles: his wife and sister."[7] Not wife or sister alone: wife and sister together, unafraid of associating with other women in a radical cause. In George Eliot's fiction, no such thing ever happens. The radicalism she sprinkles on the surface of her fiction works not for women, but against them.

8. Bram Stoker: Semidemons and Secretaries

In the first great horror novel of the nineteenth century, Mary Shelley had portrayed women as the helpless, pure, and innocent victims of men's Romantic radicalism, in the guise of a misguided scientist and his lumbering creation. In one of the last, Bram Stoker makes the danger to women more terrifying by making it seductive. In *Dracula* he suggests that the innocent, playfully liberated young women of the late nineteenth-century England might become the satanic accomplices of recently reborn Romantic radicalism in the guise of an elegant, aristocratic vampire from eastern Europe. Unlike *Frankenstein*, mythically lifted into a world where the historical texture of nineteenth-century life can be gleaned only by analogy and inference, *Dracula* is a brilliant amalgam of mythic, ahistoric horror, implied political analogy, and vivid social detail—zoos, mental hospitals, telegraphs, shorthand, the SPCA and the Aerated Bread Company, clerks and secretaries. In spite of his departure from the novel's usual "realism" in creating a tale of a vampire, Stoker makes the daily life of London as present to the reader as Dickens and Thackeray do. The demonic threat of Count Dracula's domination, the latest incarnation of Romantic radicalism, is specifically directed at the young women of 1897, young women who believed they had the right to freedom. Stoker teaches them a fictional lesson, bringing one phase of Romantic radicalism in the novel to a chilling close. Mary Shelley, Dickens, Thackeray, Eliot, and now Stoker have all, in one way or another, consciously or unconsciously, made Romantic radicalism the enemy of women: it will strangle them, drive them mad, cast them into rural oblivion—and make them devils.

In all of these novels Romantic radicalism is detached from its origins in agricultural England. In none does the country offer a woman a productive life. In *Middlemarch* it condemns women to a stifled life; finally, in *Dracula*, the city becomes the one place of defense against the demonic dangers that lurk in the country, the temporary home of the evil count. To be safe, Stoker suggests, women need the life London offers them—not the life of radicalism George Eliot hoped her heroine would find there, but a life of proper, angelic womanhood.

The London of the 1890s, Stoker's setting for *Dracula*, was the center of a new wave of radicalism and the home for a new kind of radical individual, not English, but living in England. Hobsbawm says, "Socialism reappeared in the 1880's and recruited an elite of active and able workers who in turn created and transformed the broader-based labor movements."[1] This socialism was largely inspired and led by foreigners like those James W. Hulse describes in *Revolutionists in London*: "In addition to the advantage of proximity and tolerance, Britain offered its visitors a cosmopolitan audience on which to test their various ideas. The hub of the Victorian empire, London, had assembled representatives from scores of principalities and provinces beyond the seas, and it Anglicized non-Britishers by the thousands, enabling them to share ideas and impressions more readily than in any other place in the world."[2] The radical foreigners who came to London all through the second half of the nineteenth century were of many types. Marx and Engels, who invented the phrase "the idiocy of rural life," were spiritual allies of Shelley and Hegel in their hopes for worldwide change; the anarchist prince Kropotkin shared Wordsworth's belief in the preciousness of rural life.

They were all closer to Shelley than to Wordsworth, however. All were interested in science. Marx and Engels referred to their socialism not as "utopian" but as "scientific"; Kropotkin, the revolutionary most prominent in London when Stoker wrote *Dracula*, had done extensive research in geography. "Kropotkin brought to England substantial scientific training as well as revolutionary zeal. He was one of the better educated of Russia's aristocratic young men and one of his country's most promising scholars. . . . In his early twenties, he had explored Siberia and Manchuria with military and scientific expeditions and had produced a new—and correct—thesis about the geographical structure of northern Asia. His fertile imagination and his study of Arctic Ocean currents enabled him to speculate on the existence of the Franz Joseph Islands north of the heartland of Russia several years before they were discovered."[3] The anarchist prince Kropotkin virtually invites another invention of another mad scientist as a purveyor of revolutionary horror; he is ready-made for the creator of *Dracula*.

Although foreign radicals were officially welcomed and tolerated in England, they engendered an undercurrent of fear, fear that Stoker taps in *Dracula* as Mary Shelley taps the English fears of the French Revolution in *Frankenstein*. As early as 1851 Engels wrote to Marx, "To judge by *The Times* things must be terrible in London now that the Tartars, French, Russians, and other barbarians are said to have taken total possession of it" (Manchester, 1 May 1851).[4] And in 1894 in one of the most virulent attacks on the insidious power of late nineteenth-century radicalism, Ralph Derechef translated into English Felix Dubois's *The Anarchist Peril*. The first line, about Bakunin in Germany, also sounds the warning theme about Kropotkin in London: "About the year 1841 a young Russian aristocrat arrived at Berlin."[5] The book provides details about the philosophy of anarchism, its advocates, and the character of persons most likely to be converted, in terms that make this radical political philosophy sound like the deadliest of taints. It provides several clues to the political meanings of the plot of *Dracula*, in which another eastern European aristocrat arrives to spread poison in London. The translator of *The Anarchist Peril*, who adds a chapter on anarchism in England, tries to scoff at the influence of anarchists on the stalwart English, but ends, edgily: "More has been heard of the anarchists, and the number of them, at least in London, has increased, but the men connected with the movement have been for the most part foreigners."[6] Foreigners may start it, but the worry is always present that the English may not resist forever.

The Anarchist Peril also presents a vivid form of another political danger on which Stoker capitalizes in *Dracula*—a surge of feminism.

After being told to be angels for half a century, the women of England, and of London especially, were now rebelling. And a woman anarchist was, of course, the very worst of her sex. "A word may be said of the female champions of the cause, though it is true the temptation is great to class them with the Furies rather than the Graces."[7] Along with their political perversion came sexual license; quoting extensively from sexual poems said to be composed by female anarchists, the author of *The Anarchist Peril* spares the reader the unmentionable: "the idea indicated in these lines is developed in the remainder of the poem with some force, but also with considerable crudeness of expression."[8]

Female anarchists were few, but New Women were many. Outright feminism was in a new phase; no longer was an occasional Mary Wollstonecraft or John Stuart Mill a voice in the wilderness. The Married Woman Property Act was passed in 1882; a magazine, The Adult, published between 1897 and 1899, openly advocated free love; and the women's suffrage movement was gathering steam in just the years before Stoker wrote *Dracula*.

Liberal women began to take a more active interest in female suffrage. Initially, they ran up against some opposition from the established suffrage society, which—like many moderate feminist groups—felt that it was important to preserve its own political neutrality, even if most of its members belonged to one particular part of the political spectrum. In 1888 those suffragists who believed in admitting Liberal women's groups seceded from Becker's [Lydia Becker] society and formed the central National Society for Women's Suffrage. 1889 saw the foundation of the Women's Franchise League, which was closely connected with the Liberal Party. . . . These developments culminated in 1897 with the union of all the various female suffrage societies in the National Union of Women's Suffrage Societies.[9]

Many of the women who were demanding the right to vote had already claimed the right to work. They had already entered the urban work force in new numbers, not merely as domestic servants and governesses, or even as nurses and teachers. When Beatrice Webb, in 1896, protested that women factory workers needed the protection of regulatory legislation, she took it for granted that women had fully entered the economic life of England: "We are so accustomed, in the middle-class, to see men and women engaged in identical work, as teachers, journalists, authors, painters, sculptors, comedians, singers, musicians, medical practitioners, clerks, or what not, that we almost inevitably assume the same state of things to exist in manual labor and manufacturing industry. But this is very far from being the case."[10] English women were out in the world in 1897, out of their houses, out from under the protection of their fathers and husbands, potentially susceptible to any number of bad influences. *Dracula* is a warning to the women of England that those dangerous influences might be worse than anyone dreamed in the cheerfully imperialistic, secular London of 1897.

Stoker brings two social and political fears together in *Dracula*—fear of foreign political agitation and fear that women, newly free, were also newly corruptible. *Dracula* is the final escalation, in the nineteenth-century novel, of the battle between good women and their bad sisters that Charlotte Brontë begins in *Jane Eyre* and that Dickens, Thackeray, and George Eliot continue. It is the final warning that if women do not protect themselves in order to remain as angelic as Dickens and Thackeray could have wished them to be, they are in danger of becoming devils, the very worst women in the nineteenth-century novel.

Though most of the "bad" women in nineteenth-century novels from whom the good must separate themselves are flirtatious, manipulative, and exploitive, no novelist but Charlotte Brontë dares make them overtly, physically sexual. The unabashed appetite of a whole horde of earlier literary subjects—from the Wife of Bath and Shakespeare's Cleopatra to the women Fielding treats with such humanity and generosity in *Tom Jones*, Molly Seagrim, Mrs. Waters, even Lady Bellaston—has been banished from the nineteenth-century novel, relegated to the realm of pornography, the domain of the Other Victorians. Hidden, forbidden, suppressed, hated, women of great sexual appetite become demons when they do appear in the novel—first in poor Bertha Rochester, and then in the vampire women of *Dracula*. Charlotte Brontë actually anticipates Stoker in Jane's vision of Bertha: "The lips were swelled and dark; the brow furrowed, the black eyebrows widely raised over the bloodshot eyes. Shall I tell you of what it reminded me? Of the foul German spectre—the vampire" (chap. 25). Rochester tells Jane that he needs her to cure him of the taint the nymphomaniac has left with him, the mark of the vampire that must be eradicated with holiness. The love Jane feels for him is that of the household saint, not of the lustful woman. She marries him both purified and mutilated, missing the sight of one eye and a hand; she has removed the taint with a vengeance.

In *Dracula* women like Bertha Rochester abound, in the supernatural form of the Undead, women who have been transformed by the demonic sexual potency of the Count. And these are not poor mad Creoles who can be locked in the attic; they are superhuman creatures who can live forever, on human blood, if they are not forcibly destroyed. Through the eyes of Jonathan Harker, the first narrator, trapped in Dracula's castle in Transylvania, Stoker gives us our first glimpse of what women can become. Three vampire women materialize and are about to attack him:

Two were dark, and had high aquiline noses, like the Count, and great dark, piercing eyes, that seemed to be almost red when contrasted with the pale yellow moon. The other was fair, as fair as can be, with great wavy masses of golden hair and eyes like pale sapphires. I seemed somehow to know her face, and to know it in connection with some dreamy fear, but I could not recollect at the moment how or where. All three had brilliant white teeth that shone like pearls against the ruby of their voluptuous lips. There was something about them that made me uneasy, some longing and at the same time some deadly fear. I felt in my heart a wicked, burning desire that they would kiss me with those red lips. (Chap. 3, Jonathan Harker's journal, Later: The morning of 16 May)

Jonathan knows that he both recognizes and fears them because they are the women whose existence no virtuous Victorian man or woman is supposed to recognize. "I am alone in the castle with those awful women. Fough! Mina is a woman, and there is nought in common. They are devils of the Pit" (chap. 4, Jonathan Harker's journal). And Harker dreads that they are what Dracula, his client, will make of the sweet women of England. "This was the being I was helping to transfer to London, where, perhaps, for centuries to come he might, amongst its teeming millions, satiate his lust for blood and create a new and ever-widening circle of semi-demons to batten on the helpless" (chap. 4, Jonathan Harker's journal, 30 June, morning).

Stoker shows us the process of transformation when Dracula comes to England and attacks first Lucy Westenra and then Mina Harker. He takes two cheerful, wholesome, desirable young Victorian women and turns them into sexual monsters (he does not quite succeed with Mina, but not for want of trying). Stoker portrays a process of gradual transformation; Lucy's battle against evil sexual possession is terrifying to watch. Even before Dracula arrives in England, he has exerted a kind of mental power over Lucy. She repeatedly sleepwalks, escaping from the protective care of her mother and Mina; she is, without her own knowledge, ready to meet Dracula in the graveyard when he arrives. Once infected, Lucy changes in apparently opposite ways simultaneously. She becomes both more restless and more sensual, more listless and more beautiful. "She has more colour in her cheeks than usual, and looks, oh so sweet" (chap. 8, Mina Murray's journal). The double transformation accelerates in London, until Lucy is entirely weak, debilitated, and depressed by day, and, even before her apparent death, a sexual monster by night, voluptuous, enticing, and deadly.

In her weak, but still human state, she dreads and fears Dracula; in her vampire state, she welcomes him, and subverts the attempts of her friends to protect her. These measures have been heroic; the combined force of her fiancé, Arthur Holmwood, Lord Godalming, her other two suitors, Quincy Morris and John Seward, and Dr. Van Helsing, the old Dutchman who knows what their enemy is, cannot save her. Blood transfusions, night watches, protective garlic, crucifixes—all are subverted, either by Lucy's transformed will or by the careless actions of her mother or her maids. Stoker shows us the true danger he believes is waiting for the women of England when Lucy becomes a vampire, after her apparent death. We must be educated by Dr. Van Helsing along with Lucy's friends, who cannot believe that the mysterious lady enticing children and leaving them with small wounds in their necks is Lucy, and that she must die a second death. Van Helsing finally takes the men to Lucy's grave, in order to convince them that they must conquer their revulsion and help decapitate her and drive a stake through her heart; the sight of her convinces them. "My own heart grew cold as ice, and I could hear the gasp of Arthur, as we recognized the features of Lucy Westenra. Lucy Westenra, but yet how changed. The sweetness was turned to adamantine, heartless cruelty, and the purity to voluptuous wantonness. . . . By the concentrated light that fell on Lucy's face, we could see that the lips were crimson with fresh blood, and that the stream had trickled over her chin and stained the purity of her lawn death-robe" (chap. 16, Dr. Seward's diary). She is now a sexual monster, the demon the Victorians most wanted to suppress, in both their lives and their novels.

Only a gruesome ceremony can bring a woman who has become a vampire back to humanity: first a stake must be driven through her heart, and then she must be beheaded and stuffed with garlic. The result is a deadly orgasm that will end all orgasms and all danger. "The Thing in the coffin writhed; and a hideous, blood-curdling screech came from the opened red lips. The body shook and quivered and twisted in wild contortions; the sharp white teeth champed together till the lips were cut, and the mouth was smeared with a crimson foam. But Arthur never trembled. He looked like a figure of Thor as his untrembling arm rose and fell, driving deeper and deeper the mercy-bearing stake" (chap. 16, Dr. Seward's diary).

The Victorians were in fact ready to resort to other violent methods to restore women whose sexuality was socially unacceptable: clitoridectomies were not infrequent in late Victorian England.[11] Though the principal proponent of the operation as a cure for insanity, Isaac Baker Brown, was expelled in 1867 from the obstetrical society of London, the practice continued. Brown believed the symptoms of insanity were loss of appetite, depression, and a wish to work outside the home; Lucy exhibits the first two as soon as she meets Dracula, and the third was characteristic of the New Women, who gave women like Lucy a measure of social freedom. In no case, Brown claimed, was he so certain of a cure as with acute nymphomania, for he had "never seen a recurrence of the disease after surgery."[12] The midnight ceremony at Lucy Westenra's grave is closer to Victorian social and medical reality than it first appears. Sexual satanism is the ultimate woman's evil, to be destroyed by any means. The evil women of *Dracula* are the ultimate villainnesses of both the Victorian novel and Victorian society.

As vampires, the bad women of *Dracula* are part of the ahistorical realm of myth and romance; as women, they are part of the late nineteenth century. Their historical meaning is connected with the multiple political meanings of the vampire count who transforms them from women to vampires; he too is a mythic figure who also belongs to the history of nineteenth-century England. He has his origins in Transylvanian myth and folk tale, but as Stoker presents him, he is one of the dangerous aristocratic foreigners who have arrived in London to corrupt the English; he is a late nineteenth-century demonic version of Romantic radicalism. By making Count Dracula the men all other men fear, the man who can seduce any woman and transform her into a nymphomaniac, Stoker makes Dracula the ultimate home-wrecker. His most terrifying power is his

ability to rip the veil from Victorian England's biggest secret—
women's sexuality.

The Romantic radicalism Stoker embodies in Count Dracula is
three generations older than that Mary Shelley embodied in Victor
Frankenstein and his poor monster; a whole new set of Romantic
political writers have played their part in defining the Count from
Transylvania. He contains both some of the enduring ideas of
Romanticism, ideas that can be traced back to Blake and Words-
worth, and some of the new ideas of the Victorian inheritors of
Romanticism—Carlyle, Marx, George Eliot, Nietzsche, Kropotkin.
The simplest and clearest link between the fictional figure of Count
Dracula and the original sources of Romanticism is his closeness to
the natural world. He can command wolves, rats, fogs, winds, in-
sects; he is himself partly akin to the animal world, with his sharp
teeth, eyes that glow red in the dark, and ability to turn into a bat.
This is very far from the spiritual connection between human beings
and the spirit that rolls through all things in "Tintern Abbey," but it
is not too many steps away from Emily Brontë's recognition of the
vital instincts shared by people and dogs. The big difference is that
the power to be one with nature belongs to evil, not to good, in
Dracula.

Stoker also assigns to the realm of evil Dracula's affinity with
tribal people, the kind of people whose natural vigor Romantics from
Emerson to George Eliot admired. Stoker shows us these people not
in England but in eastern Europe; through the journal of Jonathan
Harker we discover that Gypsies are powerful and are in the pay of the
Count. "These Szgany are gypsies: I have notes of them in my book.
They are peculiar to this part of the world, though allied to the
ordinary gypsies the world over. There are thousands of them in
Hungary and Transylvania, who are almost outside all law. They
attach themselves as a rule to some great noble or *boyar,* and call
themselves by his name. They are fearless and without religion, save
superstition, and they talk only in their own varieties of the Romany
tongue" (chap. 4, Jonathan Harker's journal, 28 May). These Gypsies,
in whom the modern young Englishman takes the anthropological
interest of a tourist, soon turn out to be anything but harmless. They
intercept his letters and give them to Dracula, and later try to protect
Dracula, coming home in his coffin, from his band of fearless English

enemies. The illiterate, non-Christian tribal peoples of the world whom Romantics admired are thrust back, not merely into the realm of the unsaved, but into the realm of active, demonic evil. By reversing the Romantic meaning of affinity with tribal people and the natural world, Stoker is denying the deepest radical premise of Romanticism, that the white, educated, Christian readers of literature could believe themselves to be part of a larger human and natural world supporting their goodness. Stoker is redividing the saved from the damned, the educated from the tribal, the human from the natural.

In Count Dracula, Stoker is also embodying the later Romantic political theories of Victorian writers from Carlyle to George Eliot to Nietzsche: the vampire count is a dramatic example of the Romantic hero who was supposed to counteract the world's growing tendency toward gray, dull mediocrity. The world-historical figures in whom George Eliot places her trust, the aliens who can disrupt a dying culture and change it for the better, are the fictional forerunners of this particularly ambitious, intruding alien. The heroes of Carlyle, Eliot, and Nietzsche, however, all depart from their Romantic sources in an essential and terrible way: they are assumed to exist in a world of inferior creatures who can do nothing better than follow their leader. Some of the key words of Romanticism are transformed in Victorian descriptions of the hero: "He is the living light-fountain, which it is good and pleasant to be near . . . a flowing light-fountain . . . of native original insight, of manhood and heroic nobleness."[13] These heroes have the affinity with the wilder parts of nature Stoker picks up in his demonic count: Carlyle's first heroes are born in "a wild land of barrenness and lava; swallowed many months of every year in black tempests, yet with a wild gleaming beauty in the summertime; towering up their, stern and grim, in the North Ocean; with its snow jokuls, roaring geysers, sulphur-pools and horrid volcanic chasms, like the waste chaotic battle-field of Frost and Fire."[14] This new Romantic tradition of the Victorian hero finds its sinister culmination in Nietzsche's supermen, and his resurrection of Napoleon as a hero a few years before Stoker wrote *Dracula*: "Like a last signpost to an *alternative* route Napoleon appeared, most isolated and anachronistic of men, the embodiment of the noble ideal. It might be well to ponder what exactly Napoleon, that synthesis of the brutish with the more than human, did represent."[15]

Napoleon was safely dead in 1897, but Stoker imaginatively combines the literary heroes of Carlyle, Nietzsche, and even Eliot with the charismatic alien radicals living in London in 1897, to create a politically resonant villain in Count Dracula. He is the hero, the alien, the leader of slavish multitudes who promises a better material life on earth, disdaining the promise of a Christian heaven. As readers, we feel nothing like the confused pity that misguided Victor Frankenstein and his monstrous neglected child evoke; Dracula demands, instead, a fearful admiration. He is not a misguided revolutionary, but a terrifyingly powerful, manipulative demon who can transform others into mindlessly satanic followers. Strong, handsome, intelligent, courtly, he was in the past a true human hero exactly like those admired by Carlyle and Nietzsche:

We Szekelys have a right to be proud, for in our veins flows the blood of many brave races who fought as the lion fights, for lordship. Here, in the whirlpool of European races, the Ugric tribe bore down from Iceland the fighting spirit which Thor and Wodin gave them, which their Berserkers displayed to such fell intent on the seaboards of Europe. . . . Was it not this Dracula, indeed, who inspired the other of his race who in a later age again and again brought his forces over the great river into Turkey-land; who, when he was beaten back, came again, and again, and again, though he had to come alone from the bloody field where his troups were being slaughtered, since he knew that he alone could ultimately triumph! They said that he thought only of himself. Bah! What good are peasants without a leader? (Chap. 3, Jonathan Harker's journal, midnight)

Van Helsing substantiates everything Dracula claims for himself, leaving no doubt in the reader's mind that he is indeed a genuine military hero; Van Helsing also adds qualities that link Dracula to both his fictional ancestor Victor Frankenstein and his contemporary prototype, Kropotkin. He is a hero and a scientist: "Soldier, statesman, and alchemist—which latter was the highest development of the science-knowledge of his time. He had a mighty brain, a learning beyond compare, and a heart that knew no fear and no remorse. He dared even to attend the Scholomance, and there was no branch of the knowledge of his time that he did not essay" (chap. 23, Dr. Seward's diary, 30 October). He has tapped the physical powers of the earth—using geological knowledge like Kropotkin's—for his superhuman strength: "With this one, all the forces of nature that are occult and deep and strong must have worked together in some wondrous way. The very place, where he have been alive, Un-Dead for all these centuries, is full of strangeness of the geologic and chemical world. There are deep caverns and fissures that reach none know whither. There have been volcanoes, some of whose openings still send out waters of strange properties, and gases that kill or make to vivify. Doubtless, there is something magnetic or electric in some of these combinations of occult forces which work for physical life in strange ways" (chap. 24, Mina Harker's journal, 5 October, 5 P.M.). And so the elegant aristocratic scientist is also akin to Frankenstein's lumbering monster; both are superhuman men, created from what should have been dead, by the physical forces being investigated by nineteenth century scientists. Dracula is both experimenter and experiment, Frankenstein and his monster, mad scientist and bad creation.

What Dracula offers to his slaves and victims is no mean thing: eternal life on earth. Like Frankenstein, like other nineteenth-century revolutionaries, he "would be . . . the father or furtherer of a new order of beings" (chap. 23, Dr. Seward's diary, 30 October). And these beings retain intelligence, strength, sexually enticing good looks, and extraordinary sexual power; within limits, they can pass for human beings and can infiltrate the human world with ease. In fact, their behavior is very like that of the insidious, infiltrating anarchists of *The Anarchist Peril*, who seduce their victims and transform them instead of attacking them. Stoker acknowledges the depth of our desire for eternal life through the character of Renfield, a patient in Dr. Seward's modern mental hospital. Diagnosed as "zoophagous," Renfield feeds flies to spiders, spiders to birds, and then eats the birds (since he cannot acquire a cat, the next step); he pushes to a comic, grisly extreme the primitive idea that a person assumes the characteristics of what he eats. By eating enough living animals, Renfield figures, he will acquire infinite life. In a lucid moment he explains, "I used to fancy that life was a positive and perpetual entity, and that by consuming a multitude of live things, no matter how low in the scale of creation, one might indefinitely prolong life" (chap. 18, Dr. Seward's diary, 30 September). Renfield is a ready victim for Dracula; he helps illuminate the meaning of vampirism in Stoker's novel as the ultimate materialistic philosophy, the final, radical rejection of hope for a life in heaven in favor of hope for life on earth.

Renfield is a clue to the most compelling question *Dracula* demands of us: what social conditions make England in 1897 so receptive to evil aliens, demonic foreigners who will infect women with nymphomania? The social life of the characters is easy, relaxed, pleasant before Dracula arrives; we are not given the smallest glimpse of poverty, bankruptcies, crimes, drunkenness, class conflict, bad marriages—the stuff of which other novels are made. Only Renfield is clearly a character in trouble; only he is an obvious clue to the weak spot in English culture. The rest are all cheerfully modern, some of the first representatives in the English novel of a new class of people blissfully detached from either the rural economy or the real sources of money in the urban economy. Lord Godalming is presumably part of the old rural aristocracy, but Stoker shows us nothing of his social role; Seward is a modern young psychiatrist; Quincy Morris is a rich young Texan; Jonathan Harker has just graduated, by passing an examination, from being a solicitor's clerk to being a solicitor. Mina is an assistant schoolmistress before her marriage, and her husband's assistant, a stenographer, after. Lucy, somewhat younger, lives in London with her mother. The presence of Lord Godalming does nothing to disrupt the contentedly middle-class, urban air that surrounds these characters. They belong to institutions, bureaucracies, offices; together they suggest the cleanest and most efficient city life imaginable.

Stoker does more than ignore the country in *Dracula*; he suggests that it is a more dangerous place than the city. Though the life of the main characters seems safe and secure enough, they are surrounded by a world of wildness and danger. Transylvania is full of the kind of peasants that once inhabited the English countryside, and even the English countryside itself, of which Stoker shows us little, has its menace. Lucy, a newly made vampire, is buried not in the city, but in Hampstead, where she becomes the "bloofer lady" who attacks children; when her band of warriors goes to her grave to redeem her, Dr. Seward finds comfort and salvation in the vision of the distant city. "How humanizing [it was] to see the red lighting of the sky beyond the hill, and to hear far away the muffled roar that marks the life of a great city" (chap. 16, Dr. Seward's diary). The political implication of this meditation on the safety of the city is illuminated by *The Anarchist Peril*: Dubois warns that peasants are particularly susceptible to anarchism[16] and that anarchists prefer to go into the country and work on women and children, even giving pamphlets "to children in the street, telling them to take them home to their parents."[17] In the minds of people who feared anarchist aliens, the ignorance of country people makes them vulnerable, and the education and sophistication of the middle classes of the city make them relatively immune to the lure of radical philosophy.

Yet the city and its modern inhabitants are demonstrably not protected against Dracula; Stoker makes some clever and supersubtle distinctions so that he can both point out how the qualities of modern urban life allow Dracula to enter England *and* how that life is the best protection against him. He manages to chastise his city and to praise it by finally dividing its inhabitants along sexual lines. Poor mad Renfield is the only vulnerable man; even the healthiest and happiest of London's women will succumb. The full transformation of Lucy Westenra into a vampire, and the partial transformation of Mina Harker, amounts to a pointed fictional warning that the free and easy young women of London had better be kept in line. Men, brave strong men, must mobilize to protect them, for they most certainly cannot protect themselves from the evils incarnate in Dracula.

Stoker gives us the details of Dracula's entrance into England in a way that illuminates the social life of London and demonstrates that the men of the late nineteenth century have stopped doing their necessary job of protecting their women. The Count does not enter the world of an earlier English novel, where people worried when they met a stranger; he comes to a city of strangers, where no one expects to know his neighbors, where everyone acts with professional detachment. By the time the young solicitor Jonathan Harker realizes who his client is, the real estate contracts have already been signed, the professional machinery has been set in motion, and nothing on earth can stop the Count. The owners of the ship do not ask questions when a nobleman from Transylvania has fifty huge boxes of dirt (in which he can rest in his periods of hibernation) shipped to himself; when the ship arrives, in the strangest possible way—the dead captain alone, chained to the rudder by his own crucifix—the English become obsessed with the technicalities of the law. "The fact that a coastguard was the first on board may save some complications, later on, in the Admiralty Court; for coastguards cannot claim the salvage which is the right of the first civilian entering on a derelict. Already, however, the legal tongues are wagging, and one young law student is loudly asserting that the rights of the owner are already completely sacrificed, his property being held in contravention of the statues of mortmain, since the tiller as emblemship, if not proof, of delegated possession, is held in a *dead hand*" (chap. 7, cuttings from the "Dailygraph"). The polite, professional English of 1897 are also benevolent in the most modern way. According to the newspaper, "a good deal of interest was abroad concerning the dog which landed when the ship struck, and more than a few of the members of the S.P.C.A., which is very strong in Whitby, have tried to befriend the animal" (chap. 7, cuttings from the "Dailygraph"). The "animal" is of course Dracula in one of his animal forms.

All of this propriety, professionalism, benevolence works to Dracula's advantage. What he wants is entrance to England and access to women; he finds a world without suspicion, without defenses against evil. Stoker especially emphasizes the freedom of the women themselves. They are protected neither by men nor by their own fears. Mina jokes easily about the possibility that soon "The New Woman . . . will do the proposing herself" instead of waiting for a man (chap. 8, Mina Murray's journal), never imagining that women might be in any real danger. Lucy, more flirtatious and openly sexual, writes to Mina about receiving three proposals in one day and complains, "Why can't they let a girl marry three men, or as many as want her, and save all this trouble? But this is heresy, and I must not say it" (chap. 5, letter from Lucy Westenra to Mina Murray). She can play with the idea that she is sexually capable of satisfying three men, unaware that she is courting the deadliest of dangers.

Lucy is the more vulnerable of the two modern young women because of what Mina calls her great sensitivity. "Lucy is so sweet and sensitive that she feels influences more acutely than other people do" (chap. 7, Mina Murray's journal, 10 August). She has exactly the qualities *The Anarchist Peril* ascribes to persons most susceptible to the influences of evil alien radicals. In her sensitivity she displays "a warm affection for . . . fellow creatures, a highly developed moral sensibility"; in her rebellion against the constraints of marriage, she shows a glimmer of "the spirit of revolt."[18] She fits perfectly into the modern urban culture Stoker sketches in *Dracula*, a pleasant life of freedom and ease; she is part of a culture that has let down its guard.

Stoker presents in three oddly disparate forms the solution to the evil the unsuspicious English invite: men and women must rediscover the reality of radical, satanic evil; men must employ the devices of both religion and modern science to combat it; and the one remaining woman, Mina, must give up most of her modernity, and all of her freedom. The women, after all, have been the ones Dracula has transformed into nymphomaniacal devils; they are the ones who must change the most. Even mad Renfield died struggling against the master he first welcomed. Men, in Stoker's fiction, have a built-in capacity to protect themselves from the satanic alien which women do not.

The first step toward safety is the recognition that evil still exists. Jonathan Harker, in Transylvania, must recognize that the fear of his host is based on fact, not mere peasant superstition; in England, Van Helsing must convince his skeptical, modern, trusting friends that their enemy is the kind of satanic creature in whom liberal late-nineteenth-century English Christians had ceased to believe. When charity displaces vigilance, and hope for heaven displaces fear of hell, Christians are inviting doom. The liberal, perfunctory Christianity of the new urban middle class in *Dracula* has left the door open to a satanic embodiment of sexuality, atheism, materialism, radicalism.

The cure for this newly discovered evil is not, however, a return to the kind of culture the urban middle class has abandoned. Stoker never suggests that these people would be safer in a rural community where people protect their neighbors. Instead, the band of awakened warriors arm themselves with the paraphernalia of the religion they had forgotten—crosses and holy wafers—and with primitive weapons—knives and stakes. This is a superficial return to religion, but hardly a return to a Christian life. The emblems of religion fit perfectly well here with the methods of modernity. When the men want to get into one of Dracula's houses to sterilize his coffin-home, they take advantage of the anonymity of London, just as he has done: "My friend Jonathan, you go take the lock off a hundred empty house in this your London, or of any city in the world; and if you do it as such things are rightly done, and at the time such things are rightly done, no one will interfere" (chap. 22, Jonathan Harker's journal, 3 October). They also use new scientific techniques and methods of thought. Van Helsing and Mina use studies in the psychology of criminals to predict Dracula's actions: "The Count is a criminal, and of criminal type. Nordau and Lombroso would so classify him, and *quà* criminal he is of imperfectly formed mind. Thus, in a difficulty he has to seek resource in habit" (chap. 25, Dr. Seward's diary, 28 October). Having figured out, scientifically, that Dracula has returned to Transylvania, they follow him there. In this modern chivalric quest, the band of warriors also makes use of another relatively recent discovery, hypnotism. Van Helsing makes "passes in front of her [Mina], from over the top of her head downward, with each hand in turn" (chap. 23, Jonathan Harker's journal, 4 October, morning) until she goes into a trance, and becomes a medium through which the mind of Dracula, her possessor, can be read.

Mina's passivity in her hypnotized state is the end of her redeeming spiritual journey. At the beginning Stoker makes her an intelligent, educated, active, fearless woman; to be saved she must leave most of her modernity and all of her independence behind, and be reborn as a good Victorian angel-in-the-house. She begins as a woman who can live alone, without a family's protection; when she marries Jonathan she is a virtual equal. But her liberty is her undoing, for Dracula gets to her when she is unprotected. From then on she becomes weaker, more passive, more listless—more a conventional Victorian woman. Lucy Westenra could not be saved from her liberty by anything but death and decapitation; Mina is saved alive, by a return to a life her earlier self would have disdained. She must retreat to the role Van Helsing describes: "We are men and able to bear; but you must be our star and our hope, and we shall act the more free that you are not in the danger, such as we are" (chap. 18, Mina Harker's journal).

As Mina grows weaker physically, she also becomes more aware that she is spiritually weak, in need of men's strength: "Oh, thank God for good, brave, men" (chap. 23, Jonathan Harker's journal). Knowing she may become a vampire, she asks her band of knights to kill her if they must: "It is men's duty towards those whom they love, in such time of sore trial" (chap. 25, Dr. Seward's diary). Weak, depressed, passive, Mina ascends to a final height of angelic womanhood when she actually intercedes on Dracula's behalf. The men approach him with pure hatred, but she pleads, "The poor soul who has wrought all this misery is the saddest case of all. Just think what will be his joy when he, too, is destroyed in his worser part that his better part may have spiritual immortality. You must be pitiful to him, too, though it may not hold your hands from his destruction" (chap. 23, Dr. Seward's diary 30 October). No female character in the

Victorian novel can top this act of angelic generosity! As an interces-
sor and an angel, Mina is never again alone: male protection will
forever be part of her life, even after her saviors have destroyed
Dracula in Transylvania. A woman alone, in Stoker's fictional world,
is simply too easy a mark for the alien evils of the satanic men who
are invading England.

Mina is, however, not without an activity of her own, something
the purely domestic angels of earlier Victorian urban novels did not
possess. We never see Mina cooking, sewing, taking care of a house or
children (though at the very end we learn that she has had a child); her
skills are those of the stenographer and secretary. She keeps a record
of activities while the men rest: "I feel so grateful to the man who
invented the 'Traveller's' typewriter, and to Mr. Morris for getting
this one for me. I should have felt quite astray doing the work if I had
to write with a pen" (chap. 26, Mina Harker's journal, 30 October,
evening). She also produces a "memorandum" on Dracula's probable
escape route; she is the best of executive secretaries.

The transformation of Mina, in her battle against Dracula, leads
her both backward into the role of Victorian angel and, curiously,
forward into the role of high-class urban factotum. And so, at the end
of this Gothic fiction, social reality again predominates. Mina's
transformation into a minion of men truly predicts the social fate of
many women in late nineteenth-century urban England. Being a
secretary, in Stoker's view, is compatible with being a household
angel. In both roles a woman will be safely under the protection—or
the thumb—of a man. In both roles she will be protected from the
liberty that might lead her astray and make her susceptible to the
satanic doctrines of alien radical men. In both roles she is safe from
the infection of radicalism and from her own sexuality; in both roles
she can play a cheerful supporting part in the new urban bureaucracy
of England.

As a creator of a fictional heroine, Stoker follows Mary Shelley,
Dickens, Thackeray, and George Eliot; all separate their heroines
from the life of agricultural England, and all agree that women and
Romantic radicalism should be (or, in the case of Eliot, *are*) separate.
The fictions of all contain the ideas of Romantic radicalism, but all
consider only the form of radicalism that descended from Shelley and
left agriculture and the rural community behind. All rightly see,
though in different ways, that such radicalism was indeed the enemy

of women. They go wrong in mistaking this form of Romantic radicalism for the whole, and the city as the true location of a good life. Shelley and the city are spiritually and politically compatible; so are Shelley and the isolated family in which false forms of Romanticism can flourish. Women and Romantic radicalism are not reconciled in nineteenth-century fiction until another group of writers reconsiders the radicalism that descends from Wordsworth, and the possibility that women could lead brave and radical lives in rural and in urban England.

Part 3
Returns

9. Anthony Trollope: Fortune Hunters and Friends

In 1914 the anarchist prince Kropotkin, Bram Stoker's radical demon, wrote, "Communal institutions having persisted as late as that [c. 1895] a great number of mutual aid habits and customs would undoubtedly be discovered in English villages if the writers of this country only paid attention to village life."[1] Kropotkin had clearly never read Trollope's Barsetshire chronicles. In them he would have found exactly what he was looking for: a fictional portrait of a surviving rural life in England that is based on mutual aid. The characters with whom Trollope peoples his fictive villages are direct literary descendants of the characters in *The Lyrical Ballads* and *Emma*. They are not the creations of nostalgia and reminiscence like those of George Eliot's *Adam Bede*, for they bear a message of desperate and radical hope, an image of resistance to the new and destructive economic life of the city. Trollope saw in cities much of what Dickens and Thackeray did, but instead of centering hope in saintly women and bourgeois households, he looked back to the still-living rural traditions and found a life that offered both men and women duties and liberties, obligations and integrity.

The Last Chronicle of Barset (1866) is roughly contemporaneous with Eliot's *Middlemarch*; the rural communities Eliot portrays as hopelessly moribund, in need of correction by advanced and theoretical Shelleyan radicals, are for Trollope threatened but still vital, and a source of the rural radicalism that can be traced to Wordsworth. Though no ultimate argument about the truthfulness of a fiction is possible, the political power of Trollope's vision would be vitiated if it could be demonstrated that his Barsetshire was entirely a sentimental dream, and Eliot's Middlemarch a harsh reality. It is worth remembering that Eliot wrote her rural fictions from her nest among the literati of London, and that in the years before he wrote the Barsetshire chronicles, in his travels to reorganize the postal services of the southwest of England, Trollope had gained a view of rural England possessed by few other Victorian novelists. Trollope described those years as "two of the happiest years of my life";[2] he "visited every house in the large district assigned to him, riding over the country and carefully measuring the distances which the letter-carriers were instructed to cover."[3] This sense of known space and known people, in the territory Kropotkin thought was unknown, becomes the fabric of the fictional world of Barsetshire.

The other territory even recently considered uncharted, but in fact radically illuminated by the Barsetshire chronicles, is the complicated and close relationships among rural women. Carroll Smith-Rosenberg begins her now famous essay, "The Female World of Love and Ritual: Relationships between Women in Nineteenth Century America," by saying, "The female friendship of the nineteenth century, the long-lived, intimate, loving friendship between two women, in an excellent example of the type of historical phenomena which most historians know something about, which few have thought much about, and which virtually no one has written about."[4] Trollope wrote about exactly these relationships, in nineteenth-century rural England. Within his portrait of a rural social structure based on mutual aid are portraits of an astonishing range of strong women: there is not a single household angel to be found in Barsetshire! Without trumpeting feminism as an abstract cause, Trollope dismisses the predominant Victorian ideal of the saintly wife trapped in a bourgeois home and creates not one other kind of woman, but many other kinds, who gain their power and their individuality from the social structure of Barsetshire. The radical idea that the rural, agricultural communities threatened by urban capitalism can give human beings free, strong lives begins in Wordsworth and Austen; Trollope picks this idea up and gives it new and unique life.

Trollope's radicalism is clearest in the last two of the Barsetshire chronicles, *The Small House at Allington* and *The Last Chronicle of Barset*. The first four—*The Warden, Barchester Towers, Doctor Thorne,* and *Framley Parsonage*—are tentative and exploratory, lacking the fully developed social network of the last two. Still, the radicalism of the last two develops from elements of the first four; some of these elements belong to Trollope's particular way of creating fictions, and some are part of his subject, the life of rural England, a subject with which novelists had hardly dealt for a generation.

The first radical element is the chronicle form itself. The six novels of the Barsetshire series and the six of the Palliser series virtually span Trollope's life as a novelist, from 1855 to 1880; he put them aside to write other novels, but always returned. The two sets of novels are themselves connected by character and place, since Plantagenet Palliser represents part of Barsetshire in Parliament. In attaching himself, for life, to this form, Trollope demonstrates the seriousness with which he insists on defying a reader's expectation that all will be wrapped up in one nice ending, usually involving a marriage between two healthy, active, fertile young people. With such narrative comments as, "The end of a novel, like the end of a children's dinner party, must be made up of sweet-meats and sugar plums" (*Barchester Towers*, chap. 53), Trollope forces his readers to recognize his uneasiness with the artificial, happy neatness of the traditional comic ending. Marriage is less important than friendship, endurance, and integrity, and these take longer to prove themselves. The open-endedness of Trollope's chronicle form both defies the tradition of the happy ending that reinforces the predominance of the nuclear family, and allows Trollope to do fictional justice to extended families, to intricately interwoven communities, and to the social structures that are the basis of his political message.

The other predominant quality of Trollope's fiction, which ultimately becomes part of the radical treatment of women in *The Small House at Allington* and *The Last Chronicle of Barset*, is his tenderness toward his characters, both as a creating author and a commenting narrator. Trollope makes us aware that his characters will not always do what he wants; he makes us aware how much other novelists arrange the lives of their characters to fulfill their own fictional plans and create their own meanings. Quietly, by implication, Trollope asks whether novels should be so much more perfectly arranged than life. He comes closest to explaining his intention in *The Small House at Allington*, describing the widow Mary Dale: "The life which Mrs. Dale led was not altogether an easy life,—was not devoid of much painful effort on her part. The theory of her life one may say was this—that she should bury herself in order that her daughters might live well above ground. And in order to carry out this theory, it was necessary that she should abstain from all complaint or show of uneasiness before her girls. . . . I think that Mrs. Dale was wrong. She would have joined that party on the croquet ground, instead of remaining among the pea-sticks in her sun-bonnet, had she done as I would have counselled her" (chap. 3). People obey their own laws, not the wishes of their creator, in Trollope's novels.

This characteristic of Trollope's fiction becomes the basis of the individuality and nonconformity possible in the rural communities of Barsetshire. The continuity between the tenderness of the narrator and the tenderness of the characters toward each other invites the reader into a coherent fictional world, and into a belief that the human world need not operate on the hostile principles that prevail in the nineteenth-century London of other Victorian novelists. Trollope acknowledges, and brings to his reader's consciousness, this pervading spirit of Barsetshire in his final farewell:

And now, if the reader will allow me to seize him affectionately by the arm, we will together take our last farewell of Barset and of the towers of Barchester. . . . I may not boast that any beside myself have so realized the place, and the people, and the facts, as to make such reminiscences possible as those which I should attempt to evoke by an appeal to perfect fellowship. But to me Barset has been a real county, its city a real city, and the spires and towers have been before my eyes, and the voices of the people are known to my ears, and the pavements of the city ways are familiar to my footsteps. To them all I now say farewell. That I have been induced to wander among them too long by my love of old friendships, and by the sweetness of old faces, is a fault for which I may perhaps be more readily forgiven, when I repeat, with some solemnity of assurance, the promise made in my title, that this shall be the last chronicle of Barset. (Conclusion)

This web of friendships, among narrator, characters, and readers, because of the gentleness, the tenderness, the emphasis on the long duration of the connection, is different from Fielding's genial fellowship.

There are two fictionally re-created historical facts to which Trollope connects the unique sense of connection in Barsetshire—

agriculture and architecture. The great cathedrals and rich fields were there for other Victorian novelists as well, but they chose not to represent them in their fiction, as they chose not to look at the village people of England. Trollope chooses to see, and makes his characters inseparable from both an ancient economic life and an ancient cultural and religious life. The characters of the Barsetshire chronicles are not holding out against Victorian London by sheer will; they are half created by the places and the work to which they are rooted.

According to Trevelyan, English agriculture and the English agricultural village, so noticeably absent in most Victorian novels, were in fact still quite healthy in the 1860s. They were threatened, but they still could have been saved: "With locomotion constantly diminishing the distance between the village and the city, with the spread of science and machinery even in the processes of agriculture, in a small island with a dense urban population that had now lost all traditions of country life, it was only a question of time before urban ways of thought and action would penetrate and absorb the old rural world, obliterating its distinctive features and local variations. But the time was not yet. In the 'sixties two things were still lacking before the change could be complete—the economic ruin of British agriculture and a town-made system of universal education."[5] Agriculture is particularly important in the last two Barsetshire novels; food forms a medium of communication here, as it does in *Emma*. But in the long chronicles of Trollope we see a complicated network of food-producing places, not just one village. The rich Luftons send gifts of food to the poverty-stricken Crawleys; Mrs. Dale picks and eats her own peas; the great Lord de Guest, usually seen covered with mud, breeds prize cattle and is nearly killed by his beloved bull when Johnny Eames rescues him. Lily Dale exclaims with outrage that her urban fiancé Adolphus Crosbie says she cannot keep pigs in London. The good food produced by the good earth of England is never far from us in the Barsetshire chronicles.

The elemental reality of the agricultural life is nowhere clearer than in the conclusion of *The Small House at Allington*: a complicated family quarrel is ended by a pact about manure, the true basis of a healthy self-sustaining agriculture, free from petroleum-based fertilizers. Hopkins, Squire Dale's gardener at the Great House at Allington, has mended a quarrel between the squire and his sister-in-law, Mary Dale of the Small House, over whether the squire should have any influence in choosing husbands for her daughters. Only Hopkins is eloquent enough to persuade Mary Dale not to leave, telling her the squire will die like an old apple tree without her: "Ah, ma'am, you don't know him,—as I knows him;—all the ins and outs and crinks and crannies of him. I knows him as I does the old apple-trees that I've been a-handling for forty year. There's a deal of bad wood about them old cankered trees, and some folk say they ain't worth the ground they stand on; but I know where the sap runs, and when the fruit-blossom shows itself I know where the fruit will be the sweetest. It don't take much to kill one of them old trees,—but there's life in 'm yet if they be well handled" (chap. 53). In Barsetshire one favor begets another. When Hopkins himself falls out with the squire because the bailiff thinks he is taking too much manure from the farmyard for his own garden, Lily Dale comes to his rescue: "Uncle, you must forgive poor Hopkins." Apple trees and manure inform the language and the feelings and the thoughts of these characters; apple trees and manure are what make Trollope's Barsetshire live.

The other important physical presence in the Barsetshire novels is architecture, something other novelists rarely spend much time describing. Trollope gives us long, loving looks at old houses and old churches; Constable's painting of Salisbury Cathedral could be used to illustrate any Barsetshire novel. The great houses and great churches are cut of the same stone and embody the same meaning. They stand, in these novels, for an ancient self-governing life that lets the villages live in virtual freedom from the authorities of the nineteenth-century state. The life of mutual aid depends on a sense of tradition and duty, what E. P. Thompson calls the moral economy; for Trollope the physical presence of old buildings encourages these human qualities.

The very location of the buildings carries moral and political meaning. The Great House at Allington, for example, is not an elegant modern mansion in a park out of sight of the village and the church. The Dales still live in the old house, near the road; "to be near the village, so as in some way to afford comfort, protection, and patronage, and perhaps also with some view to the pleasantness of neighborhood for its own inmates, seemed to be the object of a gentleman when building his house in the old days" (*The Small House at Allington*, chap. 1). And the physical nature of the Gothic architecture itself carries meaning:

It [Plumstead Episcopi] is cruciform, though the transepts are irregular, one being larger than the other; and the tower is much too high in proportion to the church. But the colour of the building is perfect; it is that rich yellow grey which one finds nowhere but in the south and west of England, and which is so strong a characteristic of most of our old houses of Tudor architecture. The stone work also is beautiful; the mullions of the windows and the thick tracery of the Gothic workmanship is as rich as fancy can desire; and though in gazing on such a structure one knows by rule that the old priests who built it, built it wrong, one cannot bring oneself to wish that they should have made it other than it is. (*The Warden*, chap. 12)

Trollope's contemporary, Ruskin, expresses and elaborates on the potential political meaning of the imperfect beauty of the Gothic:

The Greek gave to the lower workman no subject which he could not perfectly execute. The Assyrian gave him subjects which he could execute imperfectly, but fixed a legal standard for his imperfection. The workman was, in both systems, a slave.

But in the medieval, or especially Christian, system of ornament, this slavery is done away with altogether; Christianity having recognized, in small things as well as great, the individual value of every soul. But it not only recognizes its value; it confesses its imperfection, only bestowing dignity on the confession of unworthiness.[6]

For both Trollope and Ruskin, Gothic architecture embodies the supreme value of individuality, the human quality Trollope believes communities like those of Barsetshire foster.

The recognition that Gothic architecture, the object of destruction in revolutionary France, might serve English radicalism has been continued by William Morris, Ruskin's more clearheaded radical follower, and by E. P. Thompson, Morris's admiring biographer. Thompson discusses Morris's participation in the "Anti-scrape" movement against the restoration of old buildings, and quotes his eloquent statement that in a more just future society, the English people as a whole will be inspired by "the little grey weather-beaten building, built by ignorant men, torn by violent ones, patched by blunderers, that has outlived so many hopes and fears of mankind, and yet looks friendly and familiar to them."[7] This is an English radicalism of which Trollope is a part, the antithesis of French theoretical radicalism; it is a radicalism that can use the hidden traditions of the working people of rural England as a beacon and a hope for the future.

Trollope suggests that the Gothic churches and homes of Barsetshire can accommodate change and keep comforting people. Old country homes do not have to stay in old country families; they can house new people, new money, and can bless both their new inhabitants and their old neighbors. These buildings, in Trollope's Barsetshire, are part of a flexible economic structure like that of Austen's *Emma*, where people from the city can join people of the country. When Doctor Thorne and his rich wife Martha Dunstable, whose money comes from the city, buy an old country home that belonged to a rotten aristocrat, Trollope asks us to understand the snobbery of some of his favorite characters, "dear old Lady Lufton" and "Miss Monica Thorne of Ullathorne, a lady of the very old school," and still asks us to join him in welcoming the Thornes to Barsetshire: "Mrs. Grantly gave way, and having once given way, found that Dr. Thorne, and Mrs. Thorne, and Emily Dunstable, and Chaldicote House together, were very charming" (*The Last Chronicle of Barset*, chap. 2). As long as people come to the country in order to join the community, and not to exploit it, Trollope gives them his blessing.

The old buildings of Trollope's Barsetshire not only cheer and shelter the living; they comfort the dying. A reticent and mysterious Christianity pervades Barsetshire, a religion that has more to do with ceremony and community than with sin and despair. The community connected to agriculture and architecture robs death of some of its sting in Barsetshire. Old Septimus Harding, the hero of *The Warden*, contemplates his coming death in *The Last Chronicle of Barset* and illuminates the best nature of this rural community. "Had not the world and all in it been good to him; had he not children who loved him, who had done him honour, who had been to him always a crown of glory . . . had not his lines fallen to him in very pleasant places; was it not his happy fate to go and leave it all amidst the good words and kind loving cares of devoted friends" (*The Last Chronicle of Barset*, chap. 49). The extended families of Barsetshire are not the isolated, imprisoning institutions of the novels set in London, like *Dombey and Son* and *Vanity Fair*; families and friends blend easily into a culture of mutual aid. Trollope's Barsetshire is a good place for the dying, and a good place for the living to bury their dead. The nature of the fictional community that he has built up through six volumes and three generations enables Trollope to enter sacred ground that is almost forbidden to other novelists; he can write eloquently about a funeral, without irony and without bitterness.

They buried him in the cathedral which he had loved so well, and in which nearly all the work of his life had been done; and all Barchester was there to see him laid in his grave within the cloisters. . . . The bell had been tolling sadly all the morning, and the nave and the aisles and the transepts, close up to the door leading from the transept into the cloister, were crowded with those who had known the name and the figure and the voice of Mr. Harding as long as they had known anything. Up to this day no one would have said specially that Mr. Harding was a favourite in the town. He had never been forward enough in anything to become the acknowledged possessor of popularity. But, now that he was gone, men and women told each other how good he had been. They remembered the sweetness of his smile, and talked of loving little words which he had spoken to them,—either years ago or the other day, for his words had always been loving. (Chap. 81)

Nothing could be more different from the unloving rapaciousness of Peter Featherstone's funeral in *Middlemarch*, one of the events through which Eliot seeks to demonstrate that the country is beyond hope.

Rural England is still alive in Trollope's Barsetshire, able to offer England the radical hope that the new culture of Victorian London need not conquer the earth. Trollope acknowledges, however, that the culture of Barsetshire is gravely threatened. The first novels of the Barsetshire chronicles are all about the dangers that exist in Barsetshire itself, primarily the intrusive arrival of the low-church Proudies and their cohorts, whose self-righteous, moralistic ways tear the delicate social bonds of the country community, a fabric already torn by the death of Bishop Grantly and the retirement of Septimus Harding from a place of public trust. In the last two novels, where Trollope most fully develops the culture of mutual aid that is home to a remarkable collection of strong-minded women, he also gives fullest expression to the larger, national threat to the country community, the growing economic and cultural power of London.

Just as George Eliot attaches Wordsworth to the bumbling Mr. Brooke in order to write him off as an intellectual and radical power, Trollope attaches Shelley and Byron to the bedraggled inhabitants of his dreary London in order to separate the Romantic tradition that lives in the country from the Romantic tradition that has become the property of lovelorn urban wretches. This form of Romanticism is nothing threatening or dangerous in Trollope; it is pathetic. It is part of the degraded life of the married couples with whom Trollope peoples his fictional version of the city. The dream of the Romantic isolated couple has fit in all too well with the reality of the lonely, trapped, urban family.

Trollope's London does not contain the drama that Thackeray's or Dickens's London does. Its horror is slow, gray degradation for both men and women. The men occupy the same economic stations as the bourgeois heroes of *Dracula* do; they are clerks, lawyers, government workers, part of the vast new bureaucracy that the economic life of the city demands. The fictional versions of London in *The Small House at Allington* and *The Last Chronicle of Barset* are virtually identical in character, but they play different roles in the two novels. In *The Small House at Allington* London sends a new kind of intruder, Adolphus Crosbie, into the country to demonstrate for Trollope's readers the damage that London's code of personal relations does to women; in *The Last Chronicle of Barset* London serves primarily as a negative standard by which the better code of the country can be judged.

Armies of clerks, lawyers, speculators, moneylenders, Raffle Buffle, Mr. Kissing, Cradell, Crosbie, Mortimer Gazebee, Musselboro, Dobbs Broughton—a scurvy lot—embody Trollope's version of the widespread Victorian fear that people were losing their strength, dignity, individuality, honor—all the qualities that once constituted heroism. These urban characters exemplify and validate Wordsworth's prediction in the preface to the *Lyrical Ballads* that what England had most to fear was "the increasing accumulation of men in cities, where the uniformity of their occupations creates a craving for extraordinary incident." Stuck in their offices, their boarding houses, or their cheap new semisuburban homes like the one Adolphus Crosbie buys for his bride, Alexandrina de Courcy, in Princess Royal Crescent, these men become disconcertingly similar to each other: emotionally shallow, bored, always on the lookout for money. This is most definitely *not* a culture of mutual aid; when Cradell or Adolphus Crosbie or Dobbs Broughton needs money, he has to wheedle it from an acquaintance—for none of them have any friends—or go to an ever-more-exploitive moneylender. When someone finally sinks economically, as Dobbs Broughton does, no one is about to extend a saving hand, or even a hand of comfort as John Sedley's clerks do in *Vanity Fair.* In Trollope's London economic ruin precipitates a suicide that lacks all dignity or tragedy, for it is merely a way to escape demanding creditors.

The effect of city life on a man's character is clearest in the case of Johnny Eames, with whom we travel between the city and the country. He has been forced into the city by his father's bankruptcy, a symptom of the economic hard times of English agriculture. "He had been a man of many misfortunes, having begun the world almost with affluence, and having ended it in poverty. He had lived all his days in Guestwick, having at one time occupied a large tract of land, and lost much money in experimental farming; and late in life he had taken a small house on the outskirts of the town, and there had died, some two years previously to the commencement of this story" (*The Small House at Allington*, chap. 4). Without his father's farm or another job in the country, Johnny is forced into the urban bureaucracy. Nevertheless, when he is at home he is still a country man, the friend of the eccentric Earl de Guest, the devoted admirer of Lily Dale; in the city he is the acquaintance of worthless, whining men like Joseph Cradell and the other unctuous bureaucrats who work with him in the Income Tax Office, and the dispirited suitor of desperate, pathetic women like Amelia Roper and Madalina Demolines.

It is in the female characters of London, even more than the male, that Trollope demonstrates the perils of urban life, and of the Romanticism that the bored middle class has inherited from Shelley and Byron. Respectable London matrons like the two married de Courcy sisters simply have nothing to do; the poorer and more desperate ones, like Mrs. Dobbs Broughton, play at their foolish Romanticism, concocting imaginary love affairs to stir their listless souls. "She would sacrifice her own feelings, and do all in her power to bring Conway Dalrymple and Clara Van Siever together. If, after that, some poet did not immortalize her friendship in Byronic verse, she certainly would not get her due. Perhaps Conway Dalrymple would himself become a poet in order that this might be done properly. For it must be understood that, though she expected Conway Dalrymple to marry, she expected also that he should be Byronically wretched after his marriage on account of his love for herself" (*The Last Chronicle of Barset*, chap. 51). This is a kind of Romanticism, but it certainly has no connection whatsoever with radicalism.

The bored wretchedness of the married women of Trollope's London does not discourage the desperate efforts of the unmarried to change their state. Amelia Roper and Madalina Demolines are two objects of cynical amusement to Johnny Eames in his character as an urban bachelor; each of them, however, fights for him in earnest. They are old maids, stuck with their mothers, one in a boarding house, one in a moneylender's establishment, friendless and jobless. They too assume the stance and adopt the language of Byronic and Shelleyan Romanticism: "You will perhaps have discovered that a woman may be as changeable as the moon, and yet as true as the sun;—that she may flit from flower to flower, quite unheeding while no passion exists, but that a passion fixes her at once" (*The Last Chronicle of Barset,* chap. 80). This language and its object—a bourgeois urban marriage—are inseparable, in spite of the pathetic tawdriness of the situation. These women are, finally, the sad heiresses of "Epipsychidion" and *Jane Eyre,* trapped in the delusive language of Romantic love and the fact of the isolated nuclear family. These women have to be fortune hunters because London offers them no choice, no haven, no help. Although they will move only from the trap of a mother's house to the trap of a husband's, they still prefer the second trap, for marriage is the only route to economic dignity and power in the competitive world of London.

Things are different in the country, for Trollope. Because the agricultural communities of *The Small House at Allington* and *The Last Chronicle of Barset* still operate on the principle of mutual aid, despair does not lead to suicide, and possible spinsterhood does not lead to predatory fortune hunting. The chronicle form, the loving narrative voice, the ever-present facts of agriculture and architecture are all part of Trollope's fictional creation of a unique group of characters whose very existence is inseparable from their precious, threatened social structure. Characters who are almost absent in other novels flourish in Trollope's Barsetshire: strange, silent, tragic, even heroic, men, and intelligent, articulate, outspoken, active, loving women, both married and single. Quietly and radically, Trollope destroys the repressive Victorian image of women by turning to the territory almost unexplored since Wordsworth and Austen, England's surviving village culture.

As a creator of fiction, Trollope breaks down barriers of both sex and class in Barsetshire. His men and women are more similar to each other than men and women are in most other Victorian novels; they both exist in a community where rich and poor (Earl de Guest and

Mrs. Eames), aristocrat and worker (Squire Dale and Hopkins), scholar and rowdy (Francis Arabin and the brickmakers of Hogglestock) are economically and socially connected. These characters are all part of a true community, ruled not by the abstract justice bestowed by the modern state, but by the ancient rules of mutual aid. All are not equal, certainly, but all are still cared for.

The power of the rural community itself, the power Eliot so loathes in *Middlemarch*, is what Trollope most values in Barsetshire. By the end of the six chronicles of Barset, we believe that the great Gothic houses and churches shelter people who are worthy of them. We watch people marry, have children, grow old, and die; we watch families quarrel and make up; above all, we watch friends take care of each other. Barsetshire is full of unmarried and widowed people; unlike the single people in most other novels, they remain important members of extended families and of the community as a whole. We hear about an intricate web of relationships: the Earl de Guest is the uncle of Bernard Dale; Mr. Toogood, the London lawyer, is related to Josiah Crawley's wife; Septimus Harding is the maternal grandfather of worldly Lady Dumbello; Eleanor Arabin, who holds the clue to Josiah Crawley's innocence, is the aunt of Henry Grantly, who wants to marry Mr. Crawley's daughter. In this intricate web, quarrelsome, cantankerous people like Christopher Dale and Lady Julia de Guest can also show themselves to be loyal and loving. Barsetshire could not survive without the kind of characters other novelists cast aside.

Trollope's characters are bound together by more than economic and family ties; they are connected by silent, inward experiences. The lifelong relationships the chronicle form allows him to portray are bound by memory, a faculty almost absent in the characters of most other novels. One of the most touching moments in *The Small House at Allington* comes when Squire Dale and Earl de Guest try to figure out a way to mend Lily Dale's life after Adolphus Crosbie has jilted her:

"But it's too late now, De Guest."

"No, no; that's just where it is. It mustn't be too late! That child is not to lose her whole life because a villain has played her false. Of course she'll suffer. Just at present it wouldn't do, I suppose, to talk to her about a new sweetheart. But, Dale, the time will come; the time will come;—the time always does come.

"It has never come to you and me," said the squire, with the slightest possible smile on his dry cheeks. The story of their lives had been so far the same; each had loved, and each had been disappointed, and then each had remained single through life.

"Yes, it has," said the earl, with no slight touch of feeling and even of romance in what he said. "We have retricked our beams in our own ways, and our lives have not been desolate." (Chap. 33)

This inwardness, this presence of shared memories, is what gives the mutual aid culture of Trollope's Barsetshire its special tenderness, a melancholy sweetness different from anything in Austen's Highbury.

The idea that rural rich and rural poor could be bound together by both an agricultural economy and silent, emotional ties is not simply a nostalgic or reactionary fantasy of Trollope's, concocted to justify the poverty of the poor. The laborers of Barsetshire, who at least have their gardens as a source of food, are better off than their counterparts in London. And as recently as 1962 rural laborers in England have testified to the reality of the emotional bonds Trollope describes. In *Akenfield* Ronald Blythe quotes a poor man—not only a poor man, but a socialist—describing a rich woman who assumed (as Lady Lufton would) that all her servants voted Tory: "Like so many people of her type in East Anglia, I suppose that she simply believed that anybody who was nice just couldn't vote Labour. And these people were nice. They had worked for the lady for years and they were all fond of each other. This is a common situation in Suffolk—loving feudalism is what I call it. There is plenty of it about."[8] In Trollope's Barsetshire the loving feudalism is more loving than feudal; it is truly mutual aid that crosses class boundaries.

In *The Small House at Allington*, however, this rural culture is not enough to protect the community from disaster. When Adolphus Crosbie comes to Allington as the guest of Bernard Dale, entices Lily Dale into an engagement, and then quickly jilts her for Lady Alexandrina de Courcy, he demonstrates how little power the rules of the country have over someone who wants to break them. Lily Dale, the wronged young woman, is in a new cultural situation, as part of a surviving rural culture that is threatened by the new code of the city. She is a radically new character in the English novel, a jilted woman who neither retires tragically nor learns a lesson that enables her to marry the right man in the end, but instead declares herself an old maid and sticks to her declaration with dignity.

Lily is nineteen, and behaves like a nineteen-year-old in *The Small House at Allington*. Not endowed with the extraordinary wisdom that enables the young heroines of other novels to pick the right man, she is won by the good looks, superficial charm, and spurious affection of a bad man. Crosbie has the charm and style he has picked up in London. We know part of his power comes from the simple fact that there are so few eligible young men in the country because they are being economically forced into the city; their absence helps Crosbie look good. Trollope calls our attention to the fact that Lily is a country girl in love with a city man. At one point they meet at a place called Gruddock Gate, and as a narrator Trollope emphasizes the meaning of the name: "It is thus that the game is carried on among unsophisticated people who really live in the country. The farmyard gate at Farmer Gruddock's has not a fitting sound as a trysting-place in romance, but for people who are in earnest it does as well as any oak in the middle glade of a forest" (chap. 7). Because Lily *really* lives in the country, she cannot see that she is being deceived by a man with an unsavory character, as the other characters, the narrator, and the reader see. Knowing that Lily is being deceived, we have to learn that intelligence and goodness are not enough to protect a passionate young woman from mistaken love. Her passion and her innocence and her loyalty are all part of the sincerity the village culture encourages. Lily is one of the characters who cannot recover from a broken heart in Trollope's novels; everyone in Allington knows that "the Dales are always constant." Trollope asks us, as readers, to put aside our desire to punish Crosbie and provide Lily with a happy ending; we have to learn to sympathize with her, and believe, as the narrator does, that "love does not follow worth, and is not given to excellence;—nor is it destroyed by ill-usage, nor killed by blows and mutilation" (chap. 31). This is not the praiseworthy self-sacrifice of the angelic women of other Victorian novelists; Lily's continuing, painful love is part of the earnest stalwartness of Trollope's country culture.

Crosbie, however, is entirely part of the culture that is the subject of other Victorian novels, the urban culture of *Vanity Fair*, the culture that lives by the new code that is still ours today. The "flight from commitment"[9] Barbara Ehrenreich thinks is new to American men of our generation can be traced straight back to Crosbie's London. Trollope's narrator, commenting on the beginnings of Crosbie's wish to escape from his engagement, says that at least he did not convince himself Lily was unworthy: "Nor as yet, at any rate, had he had recourse to that practice so common with men who wish to free themselves from the bonds with which they have permitted themselves to be bound" (chap. 16). Only one of the pair who met at Gruddock Gate was in earnest; the other does not know what earnestness is.

Escape Crosbie eventually does, back into London, and all the mutual aid of the country cannot stop him. The country people grow in our estimation as they react to him, however. Hopkins says succinctly that he wants to punch Crosbie's head, even before Crosbie jilts Lily; cross old Lady Julia de Guest becomes a heroine when she confronts Crosbie at Courcy castle, where he is courting Lady Alexandrina. When he tells her he does not understand why she is inquiring into his affairs, she answers bravely, "Yes, sir, you do know; you know very well. That poor young lady who has no father and no brother, is my neighbour, and her friends are my friends. She is a friend of my own, and being an old woman, I have a right to speak for her. If this is true, Mr. Crosbie, you are treating her like a villain" (chap. 24). Lily's Uncle Christopher, another difficult, dry, melancholy character, also becomes morally grand in response to Crosbie; he tracks Crosbie to his club in London, where Crosbie escapes through the back door. Shocked, Christopher Dale exclaims, "On my honour, Bernard, I can hardly yet bring myself to believe it. It is so new to me. it makes me feel that the world is changed, and that it is no longer worth a man's while to live in it" (chap. 27). Squire Dale is absolutely right; the world has changed. Crosbie's escape through the back door of his club is truly an image of what the new "liberty" of London means; his escape tells us clearly what the new code of Romantic personal relationships detached from community will actually mean for women.

Though we eventually have the satisfaction of watching Johnny Eames do what everyone in Allington would have liked to do, when he beats up Crosbie in a railway station, and of knowing that Lady Alexandrina proves a very bad bargain, Trollope's message remains clear. Nothing can heal Lily; the rural culture is vulnerable. What Londoners call freedom is nothing but pain for Trollope's rural heroine. The code of Romantic love has become the snare of careless love.

The jilting of Lily Dale is Trollope's saddest warning about the vulnerability of the country code; with a beautifully balanced double plot he reaffirms the power of the rural culture of mutual aid in *The Last Chronicle of Barset* and also sets a subtle limit to the community's power over the heart of an individual. The rural community, here primarily a community of heroic women, is at its best in saving Josiah Crawley and his family from an unjust conviction for theft, from poverty, and even from madness; the same community must learn to refrain from interfering in the mysterious inner life of Lily Dale. Women predominate in both plots. In the rural culture of Barsetshire, women are anything but tremulous and angelic; they are intelligent, strong-minded, inventive, and powerful. Patriarchy is hardly the rule in Trollope's Barsetshire, no matter what the laws of inheritance are; something more like matriarchy and sorority holds the culture together. The many, varied women of the country—quiet, beautiful, radical Bell Dale, elegant reactionary Monica Thorne, energetic Tory Lady Lufton, reticent scholar Grace Crawley, strong-minded spinster Lily Dale—all are part of Trollope's radical defiance of Victorian sexual conventions. All are part of his declaration that an agricultural community run by mutual aid gives women the freedom and power they will not find in the city.

The accusation of theft against Josiah Crawley is a severe test. He is the kind of character only Trollope could create and love—and only Trollope's Barsetshire could accept and protect. Brilliant, learned, morally spotless, he has become so embittered by poverty and obscurity that he has become surly, self-pitying, and even, at his worst, mad. "He was a man who when seen could hardly be forgotten. The deep angry remonstrant eyes, the shaggy eyebrows, telling tales of frequent anger,—of anger frequent but generally silent,—the repressed indignation of the habitual frown, the long nose and large powerful mouth, the deep furrows on the cheek, and the general look of thought and suffering, all combined to make the appearance of the man remarkable, and to describe to the beholders at once his true character. No one ever on seeing Mr. Crawley took him to be a happy man, or a weak man, or an ignorant man, or a wise man" (chap. 18). His depressions, his moodiness, his despair, his anger, his pride all make him hard to love, even for his wife and children and old friends. He is hard to love, but love him we must, for he is worth loving, even noble, in both his personal integrity and his actions on behalf of others. He has made his daughters as well educated as himself, even teaching them Greek (an accomplishment a reader of *Middlemarch* would assume no country woman could possibly have), and he has labored stubbornly for his parishioners, the brickmakers of Hogglestock, the poorest laborers in Barsetshire.

When he is accused of having stolen the check with which he paid his nagging butcher, a check drawn by Lord Lufton and lost by his man of business Mr. Soames, Mr. Crawley behaves like a hero—an eccentric, stubborn, perverse, self-destructive hero, but still a hero. He defends himself as well as he can, first saying, mistakenly, that Soames gave him the money, and then declaring that the money came in a charitable packet from his old friend Dean Arabin. When Arabin, not knowing that his wife had added the check to a packet for the Crawleys, denies that it came from him, Crawley simply insists that he cannot explain how he got the check but that he knows he did not steal it. Though he first defies the bishop and his meddling wife, who want him to resign before his trial, he finally realizes that he must be judged either a thief or a madman (before the mystery is solved) and takes his judgment upon himself, deciding to resign for the honor of the church. The honor and the tragedy Victorian writers feared were leaving the earth come back to life in this unlikely hero. He is tragic, not merely muddled, because he can judge himself so clearly, even when he must break the heart of everyone who loves him. " 'The truth is, that there are times when I am not—sane. I am not a thief,—not before God; but I am—mad at times.' These last words he spoke very slowly, in a whisper,—without any excitement,—indeed with a composure which was horrible to witness. And what he said was the more terrible because she was so well convinced of the truth of his words. . . . 'My spirit is broken, and my mind has not been able to keep its even tenour amidst the ruins. But I will strive. I will strive. I will strive still. And if God helps me, I will prevail' " (chap. 19). When the truth finally is revealed, that the Dean had in fact given the Crawleys the check, and that Mr. Crawley had trusted his old friend more than his own memory, Henry Grantly says simply, "I call that man a hero" (chap. 74). In making a hero out of a melancholy, mad Greek scholar Trollope breaks the comic conventions of the novel—and again enlightens his readers about the capacity of the rural community to encourage variety and strength of character. Perhaps, he implicitly suggests, the Victorian writers who bemoan the absence of heroism in their world are looking in the wrong place; perhaps the neglected villages of rural England are more likely homes for great characters than London is.

Trollope's Barsetshire does more than recognize Mr. Crawley's heroism. His neighbors, even those who do not like him, will not turn him over to either the ecclesiastical or secular legal authorities; without any concerted plan they work together to save him. Part of their motivation is their collective memory of the past goodness of Mr. Crawley, his moral rescues of Dean Arabin and Mark Robarts long before, and his continuing goodness to the "lawless, drunken, terribly rough lot of humanity" who are his present parishioners. Both rich men and poor men help him: Mark Robarts and Henry Grantly are his bondsman, and Giles Hoggett the brickmaker gives him stamina simply by saying, in his own country language, "It's dogged as does it" (chap. 61). In the meantime Johnny Eames, still spiritually part of Barsetshire, has followed Eleanor Arabin to Europe and discovered how the check got to the Crawleys; Mr. Toogood, a cousin of Mrs. Crawley's who is now in league with Johnny, picks up the search and finds the true thief. And some of the unnamed, poorer male citizens of Barsetshire play their part in this scheme of mutual aid by giving the thief a rough exit from Barsetshire. The final act comes from Septimus Harding, who asks, on his deathbed, that his living be given to Mr. Crawley, so that he can be relieved from his terrible poverty. At the end of this complicated network of acts all motivated by the principle of mutual aid, the old friendship between Mr. Crawley and Dean Arabin is restored, along with Mr. Crawley's sanity and sense of humor: "Verily the news came in time, Arabin . . . but it was a narrow pinch,—a narrow pinch" (chap. 78).

Good as the men of Barsetshire are, the women are far better. Lily Dale speaks for them all: when her mother says a jury will not understand that poor Mr. Crawley could not have stolen the check consciously, she says, "A jury of men will not. I wish they could put you and me on it, mamma" (chap. 31). The women know the legal system is controlled by men, but they do everything they can for the family. They give as much food and hospitality as the family will accept, and they give indirect aid by encouraging Henry Grantly to be loyal to Grace Crawley. Henry, the son of worldly, proud Archdeacon Grantly, would have trouble making poverty-stricken Grace welcome in his family even without a legal disgrace; the temptation to slip out of his relationship, to adopt the code of Adolphus Crosbie, is great, especially since they are not actually engaged, and she refuses to see him after her father is accused. But this time the community of women has its way, and protects a woman in love as it could not protect Lily Dale. Lily and her mother shelter Grace; the Miss Prettymans, at whose school Grace teaches, give her clothes, money, and love. And above all, the great matriarch Lady Lufton, the "presiding genius" of Framley Court, remembers that Mr. Crawley helped her son and shows her continuing gratitude by offering to take the whole family in and by working for Grace's marriage. Though she cannot utter all her own thoughts to Mrs. Crawley, we hear them, and hear the best spirit of Barsetshire. "Let us be women together;—women bound by humanity, and not separated by rank, and let us open our hearts freely. Let us see how we may be of comfort to each other" (chap. 50).

Lady Lufton is also the one person who can soften Archdeacon Grantly's heart toward Grace. Only after she has asked Grace to stay with her does she discover from her old friend that his son wants to marry Grace, and that he himself is miserable. Lady Lufton understands them both, sympathizes with them both, loves them both, remembering that she had once wanted to prevent her own son from marrying Lucy Robarts because she was not rich. "Since that she had learned to think that young people might perhaps be right, and that old people might perhaps be wrong. This trouble of her friend the archdeacon's was very like her own old trouble. . . . The more she thought of the similarity of the stories, the stronger were her sympathies on the side of poor Grace. Nevertheless, she would comfort her old friend if she knew how; and of course she could not but admit to herself that the match was one which must be a cause of real sorrow to him" (chap. 56). In passages like this Trollope tells his reader that the mutual aid of the rural community is no mere primitive instinct; it is made of the subtlest kinds of sensitivity and intelligence. Lady Lufton senses she should let the archdeacon speak to Grace, whom he has never met; one meeting gives the women their conquest, when Grace swears she would never marry Henry as long as her father is in disgrace. "It was not the archdeacon who had taught her that it would not be her duty to bring disgrace into the house of the man she loved. As he looked down upon her face two tears formed themselves in his eyes, and gradually trickled down his old nose. 'My dear,' he said, 'if this cloud passes away from you, you shall come to us and be my daughter'" (chap. 57). Time and the influence of women have improved both the archdeacon and his son. By the end of the Barsetshire chronicles Henry Grantly has gained the nobility and integrity of the old men of Barsetshire; he offers Trollope's readers hope that rural England has a future. The whole community has helped clear Mr. Crawley and helped make sure his daughter marries; the marriage of Grace Crawley and Henry Grantly joins them to that community, instead of separating them into a nuclear family and bourgeois, isolated household. The bonds of loyalty and honor and aid—everything the footloose urban man Adolphus Crosbie did not know—have proved their worth. Trollope's Barsetshire, like Austen's Highbury, is a place where the community allows strong women to be strong, and keeps weak women from being destroyed. The rules of aid and duty work for women, protecting them against the spurious liberty that will only make them the prey of unscrupulous men.

Yet Trollope also asserts radical individuality in Barsetshire, setting a limit to the rights of the community. In the other country story, that of Lily Dale, the community must learn when to be quiet. Trollope knows that friendships among country neighbors can be oppressive, but does not call the oppression unforgivable and cruel, as Eliot does in her angry fictions about town life. He makes his feelings clear near the beginning of *The Last Chronicle of Barset*, in a subtle conversation between Lily Dale and Grace Crawley, who asks why she "dislikes" an old neighbor, Mrs. Boyce.

"I don't dislike her. I like her very well," said Lily Dale. "But don't you feel that there are people whom one knows very intimately, who are really friends,—for whom if they were dying one would grieve, whom if they were in misfortune one would go far to help, but with whom for all that one can have no sympathy. And yet they are so near to one that they know all the events of one's life, and are justified by unquestioned friendship in talking about things which should never be mentioned except where sympathy exists."

"Yes; I understand that."

"Everybody understands it who has been unhappy. That woman sometimes says things to me that make me wish,—wish they'll make him bishop of Patagonia. And yet she does it all in friendship, and mamma says that she is quite right." (Chap. 16)

The neighbors and the readers must learn what Trollope's narrator knows—to deny themselves the novel's traditional happy ending, a wedding for Lily Dale, and to stop meddling with the mysterious individual soul. Trollope's nineteenth-century readers behaved just like the people of Barsetshire and implored him to make Lily marry Johnny Eames, but he refused them all, knowing that Lily could not be bent to follow the rules of novels, for those are not the rules of Barsetshire. At its best Barsetshire is subtler, sadder, and more protective of women's individuality than the traditional comic novel.

In *The Last Chronicle of Barset,* four years after Crosbie jilted her, Lily is still living with her mother, still being courted by Johnny Eames, and still being encouraged by her friends and family to marry him. But Trollope has allowed her character, as a fictional creation, to grow; she has become wise and articulate. She values her community more seriously and more consciously than before and knows how to resist it with new eloquence and new self-assurance. She has always valued her friends—her one quarrel with Crosbie was over his demand that she stop seeing Johnny Eames and his family; now she has a real place in the community, treasuring the friendship with people as different as old Mrs. Hearn and Grace Crawley, Johnny Eames and Hopkins. The most striking change in Lily Dale at the beginning of *The Last Chronicle of Barset* is that she speaks critically, rather than flippantly, about men. Through her, Trollope expresses the deepest truths about love in Barsetshire, truths sometimes too bold for his gentle narrator. What she tells Grace about her Uncle Christopher reveals that she has thought seriously about love, and that she has discovered the value of the kind of character she finds in the country. "His heart, and mind, and general disposition, as they come out in experience and days of trial, are so much better than the samples of them which he puts out on the counter for men and women to judge by. He wears well, and he washes well. . . . The Apollos of the world,—I don't mean in outward looks,— . . . but the Apollos in heart, the men—and the women too, —who are so full of feeling, so soft-natured, so kind, who never say a cross word, who never get out of bed on the wrong side in the morning,—it so often turns out that they won't wash" (chap. 16). Lily Dale's understanding of her cantankerous old uncle and of Adolphus Crosbie, whom she once called an Apollo, has been expanded into a theory of human nature. The country community fosters relationships that last so long that a person can discover who stands up by the tests of experience and times of trial; in the city, where a man can escape through the back door of his club, people can get away with the superficial pleasantness that can win them short-term reputations as Apollos. Like Austen's Emma, Lily has become a worthy heroine by learning the true goodness of the threatened country community in which she lives.

Trollope, however, couples with love a more forthright condemnation of the superficial life that nineteenth-century culture allows men.

Now, with women, it is supposed that they can amuse themselves or live without amusement. Once or twice in a year, perhaps something is done for them. There is an arrow-shooting party, or a ball, or a picnic. But the catering for men's sport is never ending, and is always paramount to everything else. And yet the pet game of the day never goes off properly. In partridge time, the partridges are wild, and won't come to be killed. In hunting time the foxes won't run straight,—the wretches. They show no spirit, and will take to ground to save their brushes. Then comes a nipping frost, and skating is proclaimed; but the ice is always rough, and the woodcocks have deserted the country. And as for salmon,—when the summer comes round I do really believe that they suffer a great deal about the salmon. I'm sure they never catch any. So they go back to their clubs and their cards, and their billiards, and abuse their cooks and blackball their friends. (Chap. 9)

This astonishing passage about the shallow, exploitive life allowed to wealthy men is attributed to a young female character by a male novelist; Trollope has allowed one of his created women to attack the sexual and social mores of Victorian England more radically than Charlotte Brontë or George Eliot ever does, as narrator or creator of character. Lily recognizes that she has been the object of sport, just like the hunted animals, and that Crosbie has acted not as an individual dastard, but as a socially programmed man.

The sexual radicalism of Lily's new vision goes beyond Victorian culture. Though the country culture of mutual aid is better than the city culture of shallowness and mutual exploitation, the deep unfairness of sexual relations exists everywhere: "A man may assure himself that he will find for himself a wife who shall be learned, or beautiful, or six feet high, if he wishes it, or who has red hair, or red eyes, or red cheeks,—just what he pleases; and he may go about till he finds it, as you can go about and match your worsteds. You are a fool if you buy a colour you don't want. But we can never match our worsteds for that other piece of work, but are obliged to take any colour that comes, and therefore it is that we make such a jumble of it!" (chap. 31). Neither Trollope, as a narrator, nor any of his out-spoken women characters suggests a cure for this "jumble"; but Lily Dale's mother, reflecting on her daughter's sorrow, implicitly asks that we at least alleviate a woman's suffering by refraining from adding our judgment to her loneliness. Meditating on Grace Craw-ley's good luck in pleasing a good man like Henry Grantly, she asks some profound questions: "But her daughter, her Lily, had come across a man who was a scoundrel, and, as the consequence of that meeting, all her life was marred! Could any credit be given to Grace for her success, or any blame attached to Lily for her failure. Surely not the latter! How was her girl to have guarded herself from a love so unfortunate, or have avoided the rock on which her vessel had been shipwrecked?" (chap. 28). These two women of the Dale family radically criticize one of the cruelest axioms of a culture based on the nuclear family, an axiom reinforced by the form of the traditional comic novel—the idea that a woman's marital status reflects her worth. Marriage has more to do with luck than with justice in Trollope's Barsetshire, and the women of Barsetshire go beyond their culture in recognizing this fact.

As he develops the character of Lily Dale in *The Last Chronicle of Barset*, Trollope offers his readers a heroine who combines passion and strength, sorrow and gaiety, intelligence and integrity; she is the best possible antidote to the ideal of the angel-in-the-house. She does not condemn herself for having loved passionately or warn other women against love, but encourages Grace to adore Henry; she wants to believe, in spite of her own experience, that "there is something of the poetry and nobleness of love left" (chap. 28). In the course of the book she must grow into her own true strength, into absolute accept-ance of what she tells Grace early, that her neighbors consider her an old maid, and that she must assert her independence from the com-munity she loves so well.

Lily Dale is forced into thought when Crosbie, now a widower, writes to her mother and asks to see Lily again. Her first decision is to refuse to see him, even though she still loves him, for "he would condemn me because I had borne what he had done to me, and had still loved him—loved him through it all. He would feel and know the weakness;—and there is weakness. I have been weak in not being able to rid myself of him altogether" (chap. 23). She has escaped from the false, deadly polarities of other Victorian novels; she is neither suffering angel nor hard-boiled exploiter, neither Amelia nor Becky, neither Florence nor Edith. Trollope has created a heroine who can have a broken heart and still be a strong-minded woman. She goes beyond the bitterness of feeling that "things have gone wrong with me" when she is shocked by two accidental meetings with Crosbie in London. "To tell the truth, the vision of the man had disenchanted her. When last she had seen him he had been as it were a god to her; and though, since that day, his conduct to her had been as ungodlike as it well might be, still the memory of the outward signs of his divinity had remained with her. It is difficult to explain how it had come to pass that the glimpse which she had had of him should have altered so much within her mind. . . . I think it was chiefly that she herself was older, and could no longer see a god in such a man" (chap. 53). Trollope's reticent, respectful narrator will not analyze Lily's inarticulated feelings for the curious reader; he will not intrude, will not meddle with the mystery of personality. He respects her self-knowledge and her sorrow.

All that remains in Lily's development as a heroine after she ceases to love Crosbie is her battle with Johnny Eames and with the community that wants her to marry him. In speaking to Johnny himself, refusing him still again, she reveals the depth of her sorrow with a haunting metaphor: "If you take a young tree and split it, it still lives, perhaps. But it isn't a tree. It is only a fragment. . . . I will not have myself planted out in the middle, for people to look at. What there is left would die soon" (chap. 77). In *The Small House at Allington*, four years earlier, Lily heard Hopkins say her Uncle Christopher was like an old apple tree that would die if it was hurt; now she too picks up this country metaphor and recognizes that she has the heart of a Dale and cannot change or mend herself any more than a tree can. The integrity Trollope celebrates in the rural community of Barsetshire can be an integrity of sorrow.

In public, however, Lily declares her decision to remain single with jaunty dignity. Everyone she knows has tried, and continues to try, to convince her to marry Johnny Eames; Mrs. Arabin gives her the final push into defiant wisdom by asking her to marry Johnny to "reward" him for his goodness to the Crawleys. Good, kind Eleanor Arabin does not yet understand why Lily will not play by the conventions of the novel, will not please an audience with a happy ending, will not bow to the wishes of this close community. Lily is soon ashamed of her first answer to Mrs. Arabin, that she must stay with her mother: "as soon as these words were out of her mouth, she hated herself for having spoken them. There was a maudlin, missish, namby-pamby sentimentality about them which disgusted her" (chap. 76). It is neither love for Crosbie nor loyalty to her mother that prevents her from marrying Johnny and pleasing the community; it is her refusal to violate her own deepest emotions. Lily Dale has developed the honor and integrity of the older inhabitants of Barsetshire; she has become a true heroine of the rural community, the kind of person Victorian writers like Mill and Carlyle feared was vanishing from the earth. She is as much a heroine, in her defiant, sad strength, as Josiah Crawley is a hero.

She speaks her defiant pride when she says, soon after her conversation with Mrs. Arabin. "I know in what college I'll take my degree, and I wish they'd let me write the letters after my name as the men do. . . . O. M., for Old Maid. I don't see why it shouldn't be as good as B. A. for Bachelor of Arts. It would mean a great deal more" (chap. 76). It is daring for Lily to suggest, in mid-Victorian England, that she might get a college degree; it is shocking for her to claim that the words *old maid* might connote independence and learning, as the word *bachelor* does, and that a single woman deserves the same respect as a single man. Her declaration that she intends to remain single indicates the completion of her education as clearly as a college diploma would. An old maid, the most socially despised kind of woman in conventional novels, has here become the bearer of Trollope's radical hope that women might live as strong individual souls.

Having educated herself, Lily Dale becomes capable of educating the community of Barsetshire. Without wavering in her love for her family and friends, she demands that they learn to understand and respect her. When Emily Dunstable reminds her that she has gone against the wishes of all her friends in refusing Johnny, she answers, "That is true; and yet I have settled it rightly and I would not for worlds have it unsettled again. There are matters on which friends should not have wishes, or at any rate should not express them" (chap. 77). Marriage is the business of the community when people like Grace Crawley and Henry Grantly want to be married and must overcome difficulties, but the community has no right to interfere, or even to comment, when someone has chosen not to be married. At the end we understand that Lily will have her way, for "in these days she could assume a manner, and express herself with her eyes as well as with her voice, after a fashion, which was apt to silence unwelcome questioners, even though they were as intimate with her as was her cousin Bernard" (chap. 77).

In the villages of the Barsetshire chronicles such women and the men like them are not outcasts or misfits; they are members of extended families and feel the bonds of friendship. As Lily tells Johnny, "Old maids have friends." Unmarried people often have more love to give to their friends than married people do; in Barsetshire they often provide the strongest links among families. In defying the community, Lily is actually bringing it to its own best self; she knows, as the readers do, that the special blessing of Trollope's Barsetshire is to embrace and protect the people who have been neglected in the Victorian novel—people who are old, or lonely, or silent, or stubborn, or unmarried. The endangered, precious rural community Trollope has created in Barsetshire can combine the ancient traditions of mutual aid and a respect for eccentric, outspoken, even radically modern, people. It is, after all, a community made of eccentric individuals, and as an author Trollope is satisfied to see Lily become a woman like her mother or Lady Lufton or Monica Thorne. Not since Austen created the village of Highbury, where people understood their duty to women like Miss Bates, has any English novelist made the moral worth of the ancient agricultural community so vivid.

To make lonely or eccentric people the heart of a series of novels is a radical act on Trollope's part. He has rescued his women characters, in particular, from the stultifying role of household saint. The Barsetshire chronicles are more than radical acts of fictional creation; they are radical acts of historical observation, and constitute a demand that the bourgeois readers of Victorian England reconsider the direction of their political economy. If places like Barsetshire, the agricultural villages that educated and progressive people despise and ignore, can produce strong women and heroic men as well as the good food that keeps England alive, then they are worth saving. At the end of the chronicles Barsetshire is reviving, beginning to flourish again; Trollope has subtly lifted his series of novels into the realm of radical hope. It is a hope he inherits from Wordsworth's Romanticism.

10. Thomas Hardy: Modern Men and Milkmaids

After listing the intellectual and political controversies of the years after Trollope finished the Barsetshire chronicles—Darwinism, the women's movement, democracy—G. M. Trevelyan writes, "But the greatest single event of the 'seventies, fraught with immeasurable consequences for the future, was the sudden collapse of British agriculture."[1] That collapse, and the further degradation of life in the rural villages that Trollope found so good, took place at the beginning of Thomas Hardy's career as a novelist. In 1891, when he wrote *Tess of the D'Urbervilles*, the collapse of agriculture had ceased to be a peripheral theme in Hardy's fiction; it became the deepest source of tragedy. Tess Durbeyfield and her three women friends, all agricultural laborers, are doomed but dignified; as part of a threatened class they rise to the stature of heroines. As heroines they defy Victorian stereotypes and, at the same time, offer hope to Hardy's readers, hope that women do not need to be as weak and tremulous and essentially selfish as those in the bourgeois domesticity of Dickens and Thackeray.

Like Emily Brontë in *Wuthering Heights*, Hardy, in *Tess of the D'Urbervilles*, forces his readers to cut through the voices and the mentalities of educated, modern characters—including himself, as narrator—to reach the transcendently different mind of his heroine.

Tess Durbeyfield is not a familiar character in the nineteenth-century novel because she is part of a class virtually invisible in earlier literature, the laborers of the English agricultural village. Trollope gives us glimpses of them; Hardy makes this class central and heroic. In doing so he makes a radical political statement, and he returns to the beginning of English Romanticism, Wordsworth's *Lyrical Ballads*. Both attempt to open the eyes of their urban readers to the truer and better human selves possessed by England's forgotten people; the great difference is that Hardy chooses the nobility of rural women as his tragic theme, instead of the nobility of rural men like Michael.

Over and over in *Tess of the D'Urbervilles* Hardy offers us evidence—evidence transformed into fiction, but evidence nevertheless—of the human consequences of the agricultural collapse. As Trevelyan says, because the doctrine of free trade opened the English market to the cheaper, machine-produced grain of the American Midwest, and to cheaper meat from Australia, New Zealand, and South America, the English people and the English land began to deteriorate. "Both the Liberal and the Conservative intelligentsia of the 'seventies and 'eighties were saturated with the Free Trade Doctrine: they believed that if one industry, agriculture for instance, went under in free competition, so other industries would gain proportionately and would take its place—and so all would be well. But all was not well. For political economy does not cover the whole field of human welfare. The men of theory failed to perceive that agriculture is not merely one industry among many, but is a way of life, unique and irreplaceable in its human and spiritual value."[2] E. P. Thompson offers another, complementary view of this period; he points out that the late nineteenth century was the last stand of one of the cultural bonds of rural England, the fair, a time when "drink and meat were more plentiful, luxuries like apples and ribbons were bought for the children, dancing, courtship, convivial visiting and sports took place. Until late in the 19th century, there was still a network of fairs held throughout the country (many of which authority tried in vain to limit or proscribe) at which a fraternity of pedlars, card-sharpers, real or pretended gipsies, ballad-mongers and hawkers were in attendance."[3] The fairs were dying at the end of the century, along with English agriculture.

This terrible moment of change in rural England gives *Tess of the*

D'Urbervilles its tragic urgency. The book itself reenacts the larger historical process, as Tess travels northward in space and forward in time, from Marlott to Flintcomb-Ash; even at the beginning Hardy fills his fiction with information about the harm that has already come to rural England. We do not know how many generations of rural laborers have been as ignorant as the Durbeyfields, who talk about "Oliver Grumble" and "King Norman" as historical figures, and try to divine the future from *The Compleat Fortune-teller*, or how many generations have taken solace, as John Durbeyfield does, at the Pure Drop Inn. But Hardy lets us know that the rural England of this novel is not a static entity, surviving from time immemorial; it is a culture that is being systematically attacked from without, by economic forces that are large and nameless. The narrator says of the workers at Trantridge, for example, that they spend "Sunday in sleeping off the dyspeptic effects of the curious compounds sold to them as beer by the monopolizers of the once independent inns" (chap. 10). Almost every word in the sentence carries political meaning. The workers are drinking too much; the production of food—beer, in this case—has been taken out of local hands; the product is no longer wholesome; monopolists are destroying the cultural autonomy of communities by taking over central economic and social institutions, like the town inn.

The silent presence of buildings too keeps the social, political, and economic history of rural England before our eyes. The landscape of *Tess of the D'Urbervilles* is dominated not by Gothic churches and houses like those of Trollope's Barsetshire, but by ruined or empty mansions—the dilapidated farmhouse that is now Alec D'Urberville's chicken house, the empty mansion, once a home of the true D'Urbervilles, where Tess and Angel spend what is supposed to be their honeymoon, the empty mansion in which Tess and Angel take final, brief, refuge. "Towards evening, turning the corner of a lane, they perceived behind an ornamental gate a large board on which was painted in white letters: 'This desirable Mansion to be Let Furnished'; particulars following, with directions to apply to some London agents" (chap. 57). The fictional history of Tess and her two men is also an economic and social history; Hardy makes sure we are prepared to understand that it is only a part of a large and terrible story.

The most striking feature of Hardy's narrative commentary on the history he represents in *Tess of the D'Urbervilles* is the intellectual, philosophical radicalism of his voice. Unlike Trollope, whose radicalism exists in subtle transformations of form and character and in wholehearted affirmation of a culture of mutual aid, Hardy trumpets his radicalism with ongoing commentary through which we must read his story, a story about characters unintellectual and unphilosophical. As a narrator he demands that his readers acknowledge and learn to share both his learning and his iconoclastic view of his culture. Like Eliot's narrator in *Middlemarch*, he demonstrates wide-ranging knowledge: the poetry of Wordsworth, Browning, Whitman, Tennyson, Shakespeare, Aeschylus; the paintings of the Renaissance; astronomy; both recent history and what is called prehistory; and even anthropology, in references to natives of Polynesia and the Malay Peninsula. The sum of the narrator's learning leads to a radical cultural relativism: artists do not agree; Englishmen do not know all; Western civilization is not eternal; earth is not the center of the universe. This relativism leads to a head-on attack against the received dogmas of Christianity and the laws and customs governing sex—the subject of most of Hardy's earlier fiction.

This radicalism links Hardy to the sexual rebels of nineteenth-century English poetry, Browning and Shelley. The texture of the narrative voice contains a subtle battle between Wordsworth and Shelley, as the narrative voice of *Middlemarch* does; in *Tess of the D'Urbervilles*, however, though Shelley prevails in the superficial battle, the deeper victory, that of the heroine, belongs to Wordsworth. The struggle with Shelley is reflected even in Hardy's struggle to find a title; he changed it from *The Body and Soul of Sue* to a phrase from "Epipsychidion," "Too Late, Beloved," and then finally to *Tess of the D'Urbervilles*.[4] The narrative commentary, though, is still a strong link both to Shelley and to Hardy's earlier fiction, his almost obsessive concern with the irrationalities and unfairness of marriage law. The depths of the book belong to Wordsworth and to Hardy's later concern with the fate of agricultural England.

As a narrator Hardy uses Wordsworth and Shelley to define a philosophy of nature, a coherent set of ideas with which his readers can rationally attack Victorian sexual and religious dogma. The opening shot is fired at Wordsworth:

If the heads of the Durbeyfield household chose to sail into difficulty, disaster, starvation, disease, degradation, death, thither were these half-dozen little captives under hatches compelled to sail with them—six helpless creatures, who had never been asked if they wished for life on any terms, much less if they wished for it on such hard conditions as were involved in being of the shiftless house of Durbeyfield. Some people would like to know whence the poet whose philosophy is in these days deemed as profound and trustworthy as his song is sweet and pure, gets his authority for speaking of "Nature's holy plan." (Chap. 3)

Yet the Wordsworth whom Hardy is going after is not really the Wordsworth of the subtle, tentative, suggestive "Lines Written in Early Spring":

> The budding twigs spread out their fan
> To catch the breezy air;
> And I must think, do all I can
> That there was pleasure there.
>
> If this belief from heaven be sent,
> If such be Nature's holy plan,
> Have I not reason to lament
> What man has made of man?

The Wordsworth who is the object of Hardy's scorn is the old poet who had become a conservative Victorian sage, whose words were being used by those who wanted to forbid the use of birth control as "unnatural."

The Wordsworth of the original poem in *The Lyrical Ballads*, who suggests only that both the human and natural worlds are infused with the capacity for pleasure, is entirely compatible with the narrator of *Tess of the D'Urbervilles*, who says of Tess, "Her hopes mingled with the sunshine in an ideal photosphere which surrounded her as she bounded along against the soft south wind. She heard a pleasant voice in every breeze, and in every bird's note seemed to lurk a joy. . . . The irresistible, universal, automatic tendency to find enjoyment, which pervades all life, from the meanest to the highest, had at length mastered her, no longer counteracted by external pressures" (chap. 16). There is no logical disjunction between this and the more obviously radical use of nature as a point of reference from which the narrator can judge the falseness of human customs. Speaking of Tess when she is most possessed by guilt over her illegitimate pregnancy, the narrator says, "Walking among the sleeping birds in the hedges, watching the skipping rabbits on a moonlit warren, or standing under a pheasant-laden bough, she looked upon herself as a figure of Guilt intruding into the haunts of Innocence. But all the while she was making a distinction where there was no difference. Feeling herself in antagonism, she was quite in accord. She had been made to break an accepted social law, but no law known to the enrivonment in which she fancied herself such an anomaly" (chap. 13). Such thoughts are not derived from Wordsworth, certainly; if Hardy has a source for this idea, it is the Shelley of "Mont Blanc," where nature has a voice that does not give positive messages, but serves as a check on false ideas: "Thou hast a voice, great Mountain, to repeal/Large codes of fraud and woe" (lines 80–81). The nature surrounding Tess does not give her rules for living, but it does, by its very existence, expose the falseness of the sexual codes that human beings have mistakenly invented for themselves. Nature does not provide a holy plan of morality, but only the basic fact of pleasure, and evidence that men's holy plans are wrong.

Even the narrative comments that are most cynical and dissonant in tone are logically consistent with these ideas. For example, Hardy's narrator slips into an oddly old-fashioned and apparently sexist personification of nature when he says of Tess, on the morning after she confesses her unchastity to her husband, "Nature, in her fantastic trickery, had set such a seal of girlishness upon Tess's countenance that he gazed at her with a stupified air" (chap. 36); a little later, after Tess is startled by Angel's reminder that if they lived together they would probably have children, the narrator says, "Such is the vulpine slyness of Dame Nature that, till now, Tess had been hoodwinked by her love for Clare into forgetting it might result in vitalizations that would inflict upon others what she had bewailed as a misfortune to herself" (chap. 36). The tone is different, but the meaning holds true: nature is dominated by a principle of sex and pleasure, and that principle is strong enough to take over the minds and bodies of human beings, encouraging them to have sex, even against what they consider their better judgment. Words like "trickery" and "vulpine slyness" ironically incorporate a bit of that supposed better judgment. In fact only those who do not see nature as a principle of both truth and sex would call her tricky. The real tricks are those that deluded human beings have played on themselves, in imagining, as the saying goes, that they could fool Mother Nature.

The final element in the narrator's philosophy of nature belongs neither to Shelley nor Wordsworth, but to Hardy alone. The narrator suggests that women—rural women, at least—are tied more closely to the natural world than men are. "A field-man is a personality afield; a field-woman is a portion of the field; she has somehow lost her own margin, imbibed the essence of her surrounding and assimilated herself with it" (chap. 14). "Women, whose chief companions are the forms and forces of outdoor Nature, retain in their souls far more of the Pagan instincts of their remoter forefathers than of the systematized religions taught their race at a later date" (chap. 16). Spoken by another narrator of another novel, these sentiments could suggest inferiority in women, a need for, at best, guidance, and at worst, repression. Spoken by this narrator, in this novel, they are part of a theory that prepares the reader to value Tess and her three friends as something more than individuals—as embodiments of a last remnant of a better, more natural humanity. Relatively untouched by modern culture, these female agricultural laborers retain more of their instinctive selves than the people around them; like Emily Brontë's Heathcliff and Cathy, they offer Hardy's educated readers a glimpse of their own buried, better selves. Through these women, Hardy continues the radical and rural tradition of Wordsworth.

Though the radical theory of *Tess of the D'Urbervilles* returns to Wordsworth, in 1891 the forces of destruction had changed from what they were in 1800. Both Wordsworth and Shelley had been appropriated, in one way or another, by the forces of destruction, and had been misused and misinterpreted to serve Victorian urban culture. In forcing his readers to cut through and react against his own learned, Victorian narrative voice, a voice that includes both Wordsworth and Shelley, and to cut through and react against the relatively learned and sophisticated male characters between whom Tess is caught, Hardy is reenacting, with the historical facts of 1891, Emily Brontë's radical fiction of 1847; he is rescuing a true and shocking Romanticism from the false and destructive forms into which it has degenerated.

Destruction awaits Tess and her class at every turn. In the starkly simple, pared-down drama that lies beneath the intricate subtleties and philosophical ironies of the narrative voice, the two most visible incarnations of destruction are the two distinctly modern men, Alec D'Urberville and Angel Clare. The swarthy, swashbuckling, brutish, nouveau-riche phoney aristocrat and the delicate, rebellious, skepti-

cal, even squeamish Dissenting minister's son turned radical farmer
are two halves of the Victorian culture that dooms Tess. Both are
intruders in the world of agricultural labor, and both are the products
of the seventy years of English life that have followed Romanticism.
The falseness of their characters is shown by their instability; both
can quickly turn into an apparent opposite. Alec can turn from rake
to Evangelical convert in minutes under the influence of Angel's
strict, Pauline father; Angel can turn from philosophical radical into
Victorian sexual prude in an equally short time. For both, Victorian
values, Victorian misapprehensions about women, are the deepest
sources of action; in both, these values are secretly dominant and
deeply buried. Each believes he is playing a part inherited from
Romanticism; each is, actually, a quintessentially modern, late
Victorian man. Hardy gives his readers a final specific clue about the
very Victorian nature of these two; they both quote the poet laureate
Tennyson, the only poet who could rival Wordsworth as a figure of
cultural importance.

Alec is the more familiar figure to readers of English novels. He is
a descendant of the aristocratic rakes who wreak havoc among country girls—Richardson's Lovelace, Austen's Wickham, Eliot's Arthur
Donnithorne, Trollope's Adolphus Crosbie—but he belongs particularly to the England of 1891, both economically and culturally. The
old gentry had lost so much power that Alec's father, Mr. Stoke the
moneylender, a fictional descendant of Eliot's Bulstrode, could pass
himself off as a D'Urberville without the slightest trouble. "He
decided to settle as a country man in the south of England, out of hail
of his business district, and in doing this he felt the necessity of
recommencing with a name that would not too readily identify him
with the smart tradesman of the north, and that would be less commonplace than the original bold stark words" (chap. 5). Alec can enter
the village of Trantridge with his father's money and set himself up as
a new kind of country squire, with a new kind of country house. "It
was not a manorial home in the ordinary sense, with fields and
pastures, and a grumbling farmer, out of which a living had to be
dragged by the owner and his family by hook or crook. It was more, far
more, a country house, built for enjoyment pure and simple, with not
an acre of troublesome land attached to it beyond what was required
for residential purposes, and a little fancy farm kept in hand by the
owner, and tended by a bailiff" (chap. 5). The D'Urbervilles want land

because it signifies class status; they have no intention of being part of a village community or taking care of England's agriculture. Alec wields almost unlimited sexual power over the women who do agricultural labor—the many women like Tess—because he has economic power that is absolutely unconstrained by the kinds of social bonds Trollope could still write about twenty years before. In the quickly decaying agricultural village of the late nineteenth century that Hardy portrays, the power of the rich over the poor—especially of rich men over poor women—has increased dramatically and tragically.

Alec's abusive and exploitive sexuality is more than the product of economic power; it is also a strange product of both Romantic and Victorian poetry. Rather than professing the cheerful lust of an eighteenth-century rake, he combines the self-tormenting, grandiose lust of Byron with the prudishness of Tennyson, whom he ostentatiously quotes. Hardy lets us know that Alec has read his Tennyson when he sneers at Tess, "The old order changeth," to remind her that her once noble family has now descended to the economic depths. These four famous words reveal Alec's imprisonment in the Victorian sexual myths that his rakish behavior appears to defy. He is playing out both the Byronic role of the man who has gained almost mythic power through his wicked sexuality and the Victorian role of the sexual villain in Tennyson's *Idylls of the King*. He brags about his own wickedness, making himself worse than he would have been if he had lived by simple lust: "I suppose I am a bad fellow—a damn bad fellow. I was born bad, and I have lived bad, and I shall die bad in all probability" (chap. 12). The lust of earlier exploiters, like that of Tess's own aristocratic ancestors, whom Hardy reminds us about in various narrative comments, did not contain this destructive late nineteenth-century mythology. The image of the angel-in-the-house generates its necessary opposite, the image of male-as-lustful-brute, in men like Alec, to the detriment of women like Tess.

Hardy tells us how very Victorian Alec has always been; when we meet him again, after Tess's luckless marriage, he has recently been converted by Angel's father. "The lip-shapes that had meant seductiveness were now made to express divine supplication; the glow on the cheek that yesterday could be translated as riotousness was evangelized to-day into the splendor of pious enthusiasm; animalism had become fanaticism; Paganism, Paulinism; the bold, rolling eye that had flashed upon her shrinking form in the old time with such gross mastery now beamed with the rude energy of a theolatry that was almost ferocious" (chap. 45). He too has always been seeking his opposite, valuing Tess "on account of your intrinsic purity in spite of all" (chap. 46). And now, briefly, he assumes such purity as a mask for himself. He has turned lust and sexual and economic exploitation into high sexual melodrama; he has, indirectly, used both Romantic and Victorian poetry, both Byron and Tennyson, as weapons against women.

In 1891 Wordsworth too has been perverted, and has become a weapon in the hands of Tess's precious husband, Angel Clare. Angel combines Wordsworth and Tennyson, and even a bit of Shelley. He too is Tennyson's prisoner, even as he imagines himself to be a follower of rural Wordsworth and Greece-loving Shelley. He is one of the characters in Victorian fiction who has stripped Romanticism of its radicalism and turned it into a pathetic appendage of Victorian culture. In cultural awareness and self-knowledge Angel is several steps below the radical, skeptical philosophical narrator of the novel, yet there is a disconcerting affinity between the two. Both are "modern," both are "intellectual," both are "advanced," and neither belongs to the English village. The difference is that Hardy's narrator expresses genuine knowledge of his great difference from Tess and her people, while Angel is self-deluding, sentimental, unaware of his cultural imprisonment.

Angel first intrudes upon rural England as a seeker of Wordsworthian rural beauties. He and his prissy brothers are seeing the sights of the English countryside, passing through Tess's village for the sake of a little relaxation, when he stops to dance at the women's spring festival. At the end of the century England is full of such travelers, as Hardy's narrator tells us: "the village of Marlott lay amid the northeastern undulations of the beautiful Vale of Blakemore or Blackmoor aforesaid, an engirdled and secluded region for the most part untrodden as yet by tourist or landscape-painter, though within a four hours' journey from London" (chap. 2). The Clare brothers are among the travelers who have made Romanticism into a leisure-time activity.

Angel's second intrusion is more serious, though in some ways it is more admirable. His apprenticeship at Richard Crick's dairy farm is a genuine though unsuccessful attempt to leave behind both

Christian dogma and middle-class status, and to join the rural working class Wordsworth praised. His father has refused to give him the money to attend the university as his brothers have done, because Angel has declared that he cannot believe in the orthodox technicalities of Christianity, and therefore cannot follow the family tradition in becoming a minister. So he goes to work as an apprentice farmer. This one step away from conformity and below what he considers his class dazzles Angel; he imagines himself a new man, liberated, a lover of the soil and the poor, an enlightened farmer. He professes to love farm workers and to hate old families, to prefer Greek culture to Christian; he is another fraudulent Romantic radical in the tradition of Emily Brontë's Lockwood. Imagining himself a Romantic and a friend of the poor, he deludes himself; he deludes Tess; he does not delude us. His language is a compendium of literary phrases that repeatedly reveal his misconceptions about the rural world he thinks he wants to join. He imaginatively elevates the dairymaids with poetic imagery; to him Tess is a "fresh and virgin daughter of nature," a "dew-fresh daughter of the soil," "Artemis, Demeter." Demeter is a mother, though not one of the sexier Greek goddesses; all the other phrases imply virginity. Clare is a sentimental fool, and above all a Victorian fool, who has mixed up the new myth of woman's saintliness and purity with the older, radical rural vision of Wordsworth. Over and over he reveals the falseness of his supposed change of class, his great love for England's working people. He is ecstatically excited by the news that Tess is really a D'Urberville: "Society is hopelessly snobbish, and this fact of your extraction may make an appreciable difference to its acceptance of you as my wife, after I have made you the well-read woman that I mean to make you. My mother too, poor soul, will think so much better of you on account of it" (chap. 30). Mother, alas, still knows best. Tess is not a real working woman to Angel, but virgin soil on which he can plant his own ideas. He likes his plans for her, not herself. He objects to a temporary separation before the wedding because "his influence over her had been so marked that she had caught his manner and habits, his speech and phrases, his likings and his aversions. And to leave her in farm-land would be to let her slip back again out of accord with him" (chap. 32). She is so easily influenced, so adoring—a potentially perfect Victorian wife. Angel reveals the depth of his condescension when he internally quotes Tennyson's "In Memoriam" as he thinks about her innocent religious faith:

> Leave thou thy sister, when she prays
>   Her early Heaven, her happy views;
>   Nor thou with shadow'd hint confuse
> A life that leads melodious days.

Alec quotes the epic of illicit love, Angel the philosophical poem of advanced Christianity; both quote the poet laureate who opposed Romantic radicalism.

Hardy has thoroughly prepared the reader, if not the heroine, for Angel's vicious reaction to Tess's confession on their wedding night. As soon as he learns she was badgered into a short affair when she was sixteen, farm workers turn into the scum, not the salt, of the earth. When Tess says her mother has told her of cases where husbands forgave worse women than herself, he answers, "Don't, Tess, don't argue. Different societies, different manners. You seem like an unappreciative peasant woman, who has never been initiated into the proportions of things" (chap. 35). The proportions of things apparently include the Victorian double standard, by which a man's short-term affair is forgivable, and hers is not. Angel suddenly reveals his true values: "I thought—any man would have thought—that by giving up all ambition to win a wife with social standing, with fortune, with knowledge of the world, I should secure rustic innocence as surely as I should secure pink cheeks" (chap. 36). His rustic innocence exists in books, not in the true life of the village; what he has really wanted all along is an angel for his house. He is, Hardy's narrator finally says, just a conventional Victorian man, merely the other side of Alec D'Urberville. Both are products of the minister Mr. Clare and Victorian Dissent. "With all his attempted independence of judgment, this advanced and well-meaning young man—a sample product of the last five-and-twenty years—was yet the slave to custom and conventionality when surprised back into his early teachings" (chap. 39). Angel's love for Wordsworth's rural England has been a sham.

His affinity with Shelley, unfortunately, is all too true. "He was, in truth, more spiritual than animal; he had himself well in hand, and was singularly free from grossness. Though not cold-natured, he was rather bright than hot—less Byronic than Shelleyan; and could love desperately, but his love was especially inclined to the imaginative and ethereal; it was a fastidious emotion which could jealously guard the loved one against his very self" (chap. 31). Not all of Angel's affinities with Shelley are bad: he and the intelligent, intellectual narrator share a preference for pagan Greek over repressive Christian culture. But the deepest and most terrible connection is in this sexual imaginativeness, which can also be called an utter lack of kindness, loyalty, warmth, the qualities some people would call love. His cruelty to Tess is built into Shelley's version of Romantic radicalism: the idealism of soaring spiritual love is virtually guaranteed to fall very hard, and to contain no forgiveness. The Shelleyan love that can be distorted into the Victorian ideal of the isolated nuclear family necessarily contains vicious condemnation of a woman's errors. Angel's combination of a fraudulent version of Wordsworth and a decayed version of Shelley dooms Tess.

It is Tess whom the reader must learn to understand as a being who transcends the thoughts of the narrator and the men who destroy her. It is Tess who can lead the reader to a true Romantic radicalism, linked to Wordsworth's in its transformation of England's forgotten rural poor into the best hope for humanity. Hardy's hope is faint, a far cry from Wordsworth's. The only hope in *Tess of the D'Urbervilles* is a hope that can coexist with tragedy, or with what would be tragedy if it were not so profoundly historical, so little the product of eternity.

Like Emily Brontë's Catherine Earnshaw, Tess is implicated in her own destruction. She is drawn to the very culture she actually transcends, and she lacks the self-consciousness, until close to the end, to understand and resist her enemies. As readers, we must go beyond the words and thoughts of the narrator and the modern men who flank Tess, and also beyond her own thoughts, so that we can see in her the living remnant of the rural culture that has already been nearly destroyed. Her final glory is less the qualities that make her the unique, overpowering heroine she is, than those qualities that relate her to the other women of her age and class—Marian, Izz, Retty. Through these women as a group we can begin to glimpse the better culture rural England can still offer to the jaded urban reader.

From the beginning, something almost unimaginably ancient coexists with modernity in Tess. We meet her in a festival of spring; we hear she is educated, much better educated than her ne'er-do-well parents. Modern education and an ancient agricultural life—these are the basis of the internal and external conflicts that destroy Tess. To Hardy's readers, in both the nineteenth and twentieth centuries, the word *education* is likely to have a holy sound, but it is by no means entirely beneficial in Hardy's novel. Trevelyan analyzes the education foisted upon the country people of Tess's generation at the end of the nineteenth century: "As a result of the Education Act of 1870 the agricultural labourer of the next generation and his women folk could all read and write. Unfortunately this power was not directed to foster in them an intelligent and loving interest in country life. The new education was devised and inspected by city folk, intent on producing not peasants but clerks. Before Victoria died, the *Daily Mail* was being read on the village ale bench and under the thatch of the cottage. The distinctive rural mentality was suffering urbanization and local traditions were yielding to nation-wide commonplace."[5] Tess's new education has not turned her into a clerk or a secretary, but it has damaged her, and made her more vulnerable than a woman of an earlier generation would have been to her double nemesis, Alec and Angel.

Though the principal reason why Tess is temporarily enslaved to Alec is economic—after accidentally killing her family's horse, she feels she must keep working for anyone who will pay her—her education has also betrayed her. She would have been better prepared to deal with her lecherous employer and "relative" if she had received her mother's education by way of the ballads and folklore that survived from Elizabethan England, and which tell anyone who cares to know the facts of life. Tess's advanced education, the product of Victorian schoolmasters, has made her refined and also ignorant; at sixteen she comes home pregnant and reproaches her mother for not telling her what men were up to. A sixteen-year-old farm worker of an earlier generation would not have needed telling.

Tess's education is also what makes Angel so attractive to her, when she first sees him at the May dance and also when she sees him again at Richard Crick's dairy farm. Angel, the tourist, stops to dance one dance with the country girls—but not with Tess. Even then she is hurt; she notices him and wants him, not because he is kind or good or handsome but because he *speaks* so much better than the villagers. She herself has learned to speak proper English at school, so she can smell class elevation in a man as surely as Emily Brontë's Catherine Earnshaw, or even Eliot's Rosamond Vincy. Tess, however, is pathetically unconscious of the source of her own feelings.

What was a mild crush in a sixteen-year-old virgin is a passion without end in a nineteen-year-old woman who has suffered. When she meets him again at the dairy, after she has known Alec, she finds his intelligence, his proper Christian upbringing, his delicacy, his chastity irresistible. She does not think she wants to rise in class, but she, like everyone else in England, has been touched by Victorian values. She cannot help herself any more than the other characters in Victorian fiction who have Great Expectations can. "To her sublime trustfulness, he was all that goodness could be—knew all that a guide, philosopher, and a friend should know. She thought every line in the contour of his person the perfection of masculine beauty, his soul the soul of a saint, his intellect that of a seer" (chap. 31). Guide, philosopher, friend, saint, seer—these are Victorian words for the ideal man. Tess is imprisoned by the bookish image of the male saint, like Tennyson's King Arthur, just as Angel is imprisoned by the bookish image of the peasant virgin. It is inevitable that they will find disaster on their wedding night. He has known nothing of real peasants, and she expects a sage and saint and seer to have a bit of normal humanity. Both are riding for a fall. And fall they do, parting in bitterness shortly after their wedding.

In the end they both cut through some of the ideas that have imprisoned them, but too late for happiness. Tess has never entirely lost her true self, but she has been unconscious of her rural identity until she finally rises up in rage against both Angel and Alec. Her true self is her communal self; her true culture is the village culture that supports her when her modern men betray her; her true self and true culture are what Hardy holds up as a radical ideal to the women of late Victorian England. Raymond Williams has written eloquently about the real and continuing value of the communal and customary as opposed to the educated life, in Hardy's fiction, and in the world. "With the offer [of education] again and again comes another idea: that the world of everyday work and ordinary families is inferior, distant; that now we know this world of mind we can have no respect—and of course no affection—for that other and still familiar world."[6] For Williams, both a country man and a radical, Hardy's celebration of the nearly doomed communal life of rural England is still potent in our present. "'Slighted and enduring': not the story of man as he was, distant, limited, picturesque: but slighted in a struggle to grow—to love, to work with meaning, to learn and to teach: enduring in the community of this impulse, which pushes through and beyond particular separations and defeats. It is the continuity not only of a country but of a history and a people.'"[7]

Actually, the continuing life that is Tess Durbeyfield's true culture is older than English culture. Hardy's narrator connects the May dance, our first image of an ancient, surviving rural life, with the life of ancient Greece, a life entirely unknown to his rural characters.

> It was an interesting event to the younger inhabitants of Marlott, though the real interest was not observed by the participators in the ceremony. Its singularity lay less in the fact that there was still retained a custom of walking in procession and dancing on each anniversary than that the members were solely women. In men's clubs such celebrations were, though expiring, less uncommon; but either the natural shyness of the softer sex, or a sarcastic attitude on the part of male relatives, had denuded such women's clubs as remained (if any other did) of this their glory and consummation. The club of Marlott alone lived to uphold the local Cerealia. It had walked for hundreds of years, if not as benefit-club, as votive sisterhood of some sort; and it walked still. (Chap. 2)

A Cerealia is a ceremony that belongs to an older, quieter, earthier Greece than the Greece of the tragedians to whom Hardy's narrator often refers—older, even than Homeric Greece. The unsung agricultural laborers of England and Greece share a secret devotion to Ceres, a secret, ceremonious life, a life whose chthonic deities and mysteries have rarely entered the records of "civilization" or the world of "literature."

Hardy's narrator offers us this agricultural holiness delicately and tentatively throughout *Tess of the D'Urbervilles*, sometimes cheerfully, sometimes mournfully, always skeptically. He speculates longingly about the ancient religion of sun worship with a self-consciousness that no true worshiper could possess: "The sun, on account of the mist, had a curious sentient personal look, demanding the masculine pronoun for its adequate expression. His present aspect, coupled with the lack of all human forms in the scene, explained the old-time heliolatries in a moment. One could feel that a saner religion had never prevailed under the sky. The luminary was a golden-haired, beaming-faced, mild-eyed god-like creature, gazing down in the vigor and intentness of youth upon an earth that was

brimming with interest for him" (chap. 14). We share both the narrator's longing for this worship and his knowledge of his own distance
from it, a distance Tess and her people may not feel. Later, describing
the wretched wandering of Tess and Angel on the day after their
wedding, he imaginatively transforms a mill into a truer, more
ancient holy place than a Christian church whose doctrines have
helped create this couple's misery. "They had rambled round by a
road which led to the well-known ruins of the Cistercian Abbey
behind the mill, the latter having, in centuries past, been attached to
the monastic establishment. The mill still worked on, food being a
perennial necessity; the abbey had perished, creed being transient.
One continually sees the ministration of the temporary outlasting
the ministration of the eternal" (chap. 35). The temporary, of course,
is the truly eternal for this narrator—the world of time, of seasons, of
harvests, of sun. It is the world to which a farm laborer like Tess
belongs.

Tess finds her truest self in agricultural labor itself, not in a world
of spirit. From the time she comes home to Marlott, pregnant, until
she again succumbs, in desperate, homeless poverty to Alec D'Urberville, she is most herself in the company of her own class, people she
intellectually values much less than she values her beloved Angel
Clare. Though she is the subject of an occasional remark in Marlott,
she can still work with her fellows, and can even nurse her short-
lived baby in something like peace, in the field.

The movements of the other women were more or less similar to Tess's,
the whole bevy of them drawing together like dancers in a quadrille at the
completion of a sheaf by each, every one placing her sheaf on end against
those of the rest, till a shock, or "stitch" as it was here called, of ten or a dozen
was formed. . . . "She's fond of that there child, though she did pretend not to
be, and say she wishes the baby and her too were in the churchyard," observed
the woman in the red petticoat.
"She'll soon leave off saying that," replied the one in buff. "Lord, 'tis
wonderful what a body can get used to o' that sort in time." (Chap. 14)

These nameless, kind, working women, less educated than Tess, are
also less infected by Victorian prudishness. They are closer to the
protective village world Wordsworth portrayed almost a hundred
years earlier in "The Thorn," where poor mad Martha Ray, who may
have killed her illegitimate child, is both the subject of village tales
and the object of village protection.

At Richard Crick's dairy farm Tess's companions in work receive names, characters, and nobility. Though the rural communities that Tess inhabits both before and after this, at Marlott, Trantridge, and Flintcomb-Ash, are decaying, being destroyed by industrial progress, in this one part of Tess's life Hardy gives us an almost utopian glimpse of what agricultural life might be. Here she find friends, work, songs, jokes, communal meals, and decent wages. A woman could do worse than milk cows, make butter, and find good-hearted friends like Marion, Izz, and Retty. As educated readers we have to learn to value this life, first as the dilettante Angel does, and then more thoroughly, so that it ceases to be a pastoral and becomes a true and persuasive possibility, a powerful image of what the English might still be if they could make the radical leap away from their learning, their middle-class values, and, especially, their ideas of what women should be.

Men and women, young and old, work together here. Hardy shows their unity most graphically when they search a field for the garlic that has been spoiling the milk. "Differing one from another in natures and moods so greatly as they did, they yet formed a curiously uniform row—automatic, noiseless, and an alien observer passing down the neighboring lane might well have been excused for massing them as 'Hodge'" (chap. 22). This is exactly the kind of scene in which Hardy's contemporary Kropotkin finds the truest humanity: "The communal meadows are mown by the community; and the sight of a Russian commune mowing a meadow—the men rivalling each other in the advance with the scythe, while the women turn the grass over and throw it up into heaps—is one of the most inspiring sights: it shows what human work might be and ought to be."[8]

The three women who rise from the group of workers and become individual characters in Hardy's fiction—Marian, Izz, and Retty—reflect and partake of Tess's grandeur. Her grandeur is inseparable from theirs; only together do they convince the urban, educated, skeptical reader that uneducated laboring women might be heroic women. Although they have all fallen in love with Angel Clare, so passionately in love that Marian becomes an alcoholic from grief, and Retty tries to drown herself, they remain loyal to Tess because the ancient bond is still strong in them. They are not part of the urban world where women assume they must fight other women for their men; they are still part of an older economic world that, in Hardy's opinion, is also a better moral world, and know they must work together, man or no man.

Hardy most clearly reveals his affinity (it is too deep to be called simply a literary debt) with Wordsworth in the language he gives to these women. They speak the same kind of eloquent country language Wordsworth found among England's forgotten workers. For Hardy, as for Wordsworth, country language is best for expressing the simplest and deepest of human feelings. In two of the most moving episodes of *Tess of the D'Urbervilles*, when these women try to help Tess with Angel, their language becomes almost biblical. After leaving Tess, Angel accidentally meets Izz and cynically asks her to go with him to Brazil as a mistress. Though she agrees, she cannot help defending her friend.

> "You love me very, very much, Izz?" he suddenly asked.
> "I do—I have said I do. I loved you all the time we was at the dairy together."
> "More than Tess?"
> She shook her head.
> "No," she murmured, "not more than she."
> "How's that?"
> "Because nobody could love 'ee more than Tess did! . . . She would have laid down her life for 'ee. I could do no more!" (Chap. 40)

These heartbreaking, breathtaking words from a rival touch him; he goes to Brazil alone, with the beginnings of repentance in his heart. Months later, when Alec is again pursuing Tess, Marian and Izz try to bring Angel back from Brazil to save her.

> Honor'd Sir,—
> Look to your wife if you do love her as much as she do love you. For she is sore put to by an Enemy in the shape of a Friend. Sir, there is one near her who ought to be Away. A woman should not be try'd beyond her Strength, and continual dropping will wear away a Stone—ay, more—a Diamond.
>
> From Two Well-Wishers
> (Chap. 52)

Anglo-Saxon vocabulary, rural grammar, and transformed commonplace sayings all become a poetic plea here through which Hardy convinces his readers that Tess is not the only noble-hearted woman in the English countryside.

These heroines stand together, and they also fall together. In *Tess of the D'Urbervilles*, unlike *The Last Chronicle of Barset*, mutual aid among greathearted women cannot stand up to the economic changes threatening rural life. Marian kindly arranges employment for both Tess and Izz at Flintcomb-Ash, a northern turnip farm; the very movement north accelerates the change in time, and Hardy subjects his heroines to the future that awaits rural labor in England. We see what progress means; machines are dominant at Flintcomb-Ash, and the women have become virtual slaves.

Close under the shadow of the stack, and as yet barely visible, was the red tyrant that the women had come to serve—a timber-framed construction, with straps and wheels appertaining—the threshing-machine, which, whilst it was going, kept up a despotic demand upon the endurance of their muscles and nerves. . . . By the engine stood a dark, motionless being, a sooty and grimy embodiment of tallness, in a sort of trance, with a heap of coals by his side; it was the engine-man. The isolation of his manner and color lent him the appearance of a creature from Tophet, who had strayed into the pellucid smokelessness of this region of yellow grain and pale soil, with which he had nothing in common, to amaze and discompose its aborigines.

What he looked he felt. He was in the agricultural world, but not of it. He served fire and smoke; these denizens of the fields served vegetation, weather, frost, and sun. (Chap. 47)

It is this new form of labor and new economic degradation, not anything that could remotely be labeled weakness of character, that drive Tess back to the uncovered Alec. The Durbeyfield family are forced into migration and the new status of propertyless, homeless workers because the rich owners of machines can make more profit from such workers. The business ethics of the city portrayed in *Vanity Fair* and *Dombey and Son* have reached English villages and destroyed them. Here Hardy's narrator rises above philosophical cynicism, above weariness, even above tragedy, into righteous rage.

However, all the mutations so increasingly discernible in village life did not originate entirely in the agricultural unrest. A depopulation was also going on. The village had formerly contained, side by side with the agricultural laborers, an interesting and better-informed class, ranking distinctly above the former—the class to which Tess's father and mother had belonged—and including the carpenter, the smith, the shoe-maker, the huckster, together with the nondescript workers other than farm-laborers; a set of people who owed a certain stability of aim and conduct to the fact of their being life-holders like Tess's father, or copyholders, or, occasionally, small free-holders. But as the long holdings fell in they were seldom again let to similar tenants, and were mostly pulled down, if not absolutely required by the farmer for his hands. Cottagers who were not directly employed on the land were looked upon with disfavor as a rule, and the banishment of some starved the trade of others who were thus obliged to follow. These families, who had formed the backbone of the village life in the past, who were the depositaries of the village traditions, had to seek refuge in the large centres; the process, humorously designated by statisticians as "the tendency of the rural population towards the large towns," being really the tendency of water to flow up-hill when forced by machinery. (Chap. 51)

Hardy takes his stand here, alongside Kropotkin, against the Victorian proponents of "inevitability" and "progress." "In short, to speak of the natural death of the village communities in virtue of economic laws is as grim a joke as to speak of the natural death of soldiers slaughtered on a battlefield."[9]

Tess shares this fury at the end. As a character, she rises above her fellow heroines to full tragic consciousness of the wrong that has been done her. Before she returns to Alec D'Urberville in economic desperation, after her family has been shut out from their expected lodgings, she finally sees that Angel has been the crueler of her modern men. Nothing separates her more decisively from the Victorian angel-in-the-house than the letter she writes to Angel after his desertion, and her subsequent years of devotion: "Oh, why have you treated me so monstrously, Angel! I do not deserve it. I have thought it all over carefully, and I can never, never forgive you! You know that I did not intend to wrong you—why have you so wronged me? You are cruel, cruel indeed! I will try to forget you. It is all injustice I have received at your hands" (chap. 51). This articulate rage is not a departure from Tess's character as a woman laborer, part of the older agricultural England. It is a purgation, a liberation from the Victorian character that has been overlaid on her true self by her progressive education. Now she can finally take her place in nineteenth-century fiction beside Catherine Earnshaw and Hepzibah Pyncheon and Lily Dale as a heroine through whose voice her creator cuts through the expectations of her culture. She is finally a heroine who offers Hardy's readers both an ideal—that of productive, communal labor—and the weapon of anger they would need to change the world.

The horror that awaits Tess in the fictional world of this novel gives terrible emphasis to the need for change. Both she and Angel do change, but not fast enough to avert their doom. Brazil brings Angel not the riches he dreamed of, but sickness, sorrow, poverty, and, a little late, wisdom. With the help of a fellow sufferer, he finally sees that Tess has been good, and he has been bad, that she has been right, and he has been wrong. When he returns to England he is ready to take her back, even though she is being kept by Alec. In this novel, however, years of suffering and suppressed rage do not disappear with mere acts of forgiveness and moments of wrathful truth-telling.

Tess refuses to go with Angel until, in a fit of grief and rage, she has killed Alec. Though Alec has been telling her Angel will not come back, he has not been lying maliciously, but merely saying what any sensible person would say; all she has to do is walk away from him. The murder makes no sense; she knows she will be caught and executed. But it makes terrible, true, emotional sense. She has suffered too much and been angry too long; blood must flow. She is angry at herself for having yielded to Alec not once, but twice; she is angry at Alec for trapping her; and she is angry at Angel for deserting her. She wants to die as much as she wants to live. Her furious letter has erased neither her life as a victim nor her love for Angel nor her lingering feeling of sin. Seeing Angel, she cries, "And he is dying—he looks as if he is dying! . . . And my sin will kill him and not kill me" (chap. 56)! She makes sure she does get killed, by killing Alec; she is caught at Stonehenge, executed by the British legal system.

We do not even have the satisfaction of feeling that though she must die, she has removed some evil from the world by killing. As readers we know that stupid, brutish Alec is no villainous source of wickedness. No one can breathe easier knowing he is dead. What Tess really wants to kill is what no one woman can touch—Victorian progress; Victorian sexual morality; a new economic world where the few men who own machines and corporations are getting richer and more powerful, and many rural laboring women are getting poorer and weaker.

Hardy offers us no hope in *Tess of The D'Urbervilles* through his plot. At the end of the novel we see Angel Clare and 'Liza-Lu Durbeyfield, Tess's sister, walking off hand in hand. But this hint of a possible marriage, a bit of hope, is only another bitter irony. Tess, waiting at Stonehenge for arrest, has asked Angel to marry 'Liza-Lu: "She is so good and simple and pure. O Angel—I wish you would marry her if you lose me, as you will do shortly. O, if you would" (chap. 58)! She disregards Angel's protest, "If I lose you I lose all!" and apparently does not understand his objection, "And she is my sister-in-law." She answers, "That's nothing, dearest. People marry sister-laws continually about Marlott." Angel remains silent, just as he does when she asks him if he thinks they will meet in heaven, just as he did on their wedding night when she asked if he still loved her. Angel's silences mean no.

Angel, the educated modern man, knows what rural Tess does not, that relatively recent English law has forbidden marriage between a man and his deceased wife's sister. The politicians of England had decided that law had to supersede custom in marriage; people of Tess's class had gone on marrying as they did before the new laws of 1835. Angel, of course, would know about the endless debates in Parliament about the Deceased Wife's Sister Marriage Act (which finally passed in 1907 and once again made such marriages legal); he is not about to violate the law. At the beginning of the last chapter Hardy inserts a final reminder for the reader that marriage between Angel and 'Liza-Lu would be illegal, when he identifies Angel's companion as "a tall, slim, budding creature—half girl, half woman—a spiritualized image of Tess, slighter than she, but with the same beautiful eyes—Clare's sister in law, 'Liza-Lu" (chap. 59). We know who 'Liza-Lu is; Hardy reminds us she is Angel's sister-in-law so we will remember that if these two want to marry, they would have to leave England. 'Liza-Lu may be doomed by custom and convention even pettier than those that doomed her sister. Tess is not the only victim of the injustice and irrationality of sexual laws in England. The customs that governed the village where Joan Durbeyfield grew up were saner and more sensible than modern, progressive law.

Though the events of the plot of *Tess of the D'Urbervilles* leave us no hope in the form of marriages, nor ghosts like those of *Wuthering Heights*, the novel as a whole offers radical hope: Hardy has brought back to life Wordsworth's vision of country people and agricultural life. In *Tess of the D'Urbervilles*, as in "Michael," a new economic world of men and machines, promissory notes and progress has won, and the people who grow England's food have lost. But both works still bring to the reader a renewed belief that the forces of destruction are both comprehensible and perhaps stoppable, not cosmic and inexorable. Both leave us with a vision of human grandeur in the laboring people who have been neglected in other literature. The deepest and most radical hope in *Tess of the D'Urbervilles* is that the women of England will be able to recognize not only in Tess, but in

Marian, Izz, and Retty, the possibility that productive work and human faith and fellowship are still alive in England, still possible. We come to recognize our own best, lost selves in Tess and her friends. They offer to women a true alternative to the urban leisure and jealous loneliness of Victorian angels.

11. E. M. Forster: Gasoline and Goddesses

Like Trollope and Hardy, E. M. Forster also asks his readers to discover an unknown rural world as a source of radical hope for women. The difference is that in *Howards End*, unlike the Barsetshire chronicles and *Tess of the D'Urbervilles*, that life has already died, killed by the full-fledged forces of urban culture, machines, and now, in 1910, British imperialism. Rural culture has died—or dies, with Ruth Wilcox, about a third of the way through *Howards End*; however, this culture can be and is reborn, in a strange, apparently unlikely, and ultimately compelling story of the transformation of modern urban liberals into farm women, with the help of a dead woman, who may be, if we believe in her, a ghost, or even a Greek goddess.

Howards End, written just before World War I, is the last great English novel of Romantic radicalism, yet it has been virtually ignored by both feminists and radicals. The best explanation for the general blindness to the radical power of this book is the one Wendell Berry gives for the lightness with which most people read *As You Like It:* "All the characters in the play are *brought down* to better knowledge than they began with. There is now inevitably a 'sophistication' (i. e. ignorance) that will look upon this descent as an 'escape from the real world.' This is apparently because the play has country people in it and takes place mainly in a forest, and most educated people now do not know much about either; they think that country people are stupid and that forests are places where one can be thoughtless and indulge in idle fancies. A 'comedy' that takes place in a forest will, therefore, necessarily be frivolous.'" *Howards End* takes place largely on an abandoned farm, not in a forest, but the rest can remain the same. *Howards End* is not a "liberal" "comedy"; it is a radical, Romantic prophecy. Berry's word "descent" is the right one for what both characters and readers must do in *Howards End*. We must recognize our affinity with the chatty, liberal, modern Victorian narrator and his urban lady friends, the Schlegels—and be prepared to recognize, as they do, a lost, mysterious, redeeming country world.

The vital presence of this lost world separates *Howards End* from Forster's three earlier novels. Like Hardy, Forster moves from a radicalism dominated by Shelley (the title of his second novel, *The Longest Journey*, comes from "Epipsychidion") and concerned with the repressive and arbitrary sexual morality of the English, to a deeper, rural radicalism like Wordsworth's, a radicalism that makes sexual injustice only part of a larger economic injustice. Forster's earlier novels are battles between the pathetic remains of Victorian England—fussiness, class snobbery, sexual fear, philanthropic pretentiousness—and varieties of sexual love—love between upper-class Englishwomen and swaggering Italians, or oddball atheists, or farm workers, and love between men. There are two great changes in *Howards End*: the enemy becomes more economic, more seriously and clearly articulated, as all the forces of English imperialism, which connect all the old fears and follies. The old liberal, personal hope is no longer adequate, but must be replaced by the stronger, deeper, older rural world of Ruth Wilcox and her home.

Forster does not ask his readers to descend through imperialism; he assumes we are allied with his narrator and the Schlegels against the world the Wilcoxes are creating. Though one Wilcox, Henry, turns out to be personally redeemable, as a family they stand for a clearly destructive economic world. We do not have to descend into the knowledge that we do not like the culture of what the Schlegels call "telegrams and anger"; still, Forster gives us a radically new, radically angry look at what liberals oppose as a matter of course. In *Howards End* he lays power bare, and makes us see the totality of what the Wilcoxes are doing, both at home and abroad.

Within this apparently gentle novel there is always the knowledge that England and Germany are about to go to war because they are both empires; the world is not big enough for both of them. Men like the Wilcoxes are making their fortunes from Africa's riches; neither England nor Germany has enough raw materials from which powerful and greedy men can make their money. Men like the Wilcoxes make their money from countries outside England, and what they do with their money changes England as well as the countries they victimize. Henry Wilcox's office contains a map of Africa; he has worked in Cyprus; his son Paul, in Nigeria. By choosing imperialism as the most destructive form of English capitalism, Forster leaves what is commonly called liberalism and allies himself with English radicals like William Morris, who wrote, in his last article: "Look how the whole capitalist world is stretching out long arms towards the barbarous world and grabbing and clutching in eager competition at countries whose inhabitants don't want them. . . . And what is all this for? For the spread of abstract ideas of civilization, for pure benevolence, for the honour and glory of conquest? Not at all. It is for the opening of fresh markets to take in all the fresh profit-producing wealth which is growing greater and greater every day; in other words, to make fresh opportunities for *waste*; the waste of our labour and our lives."[2] What the English and Germans are doing to Africa is not only bad for Africans; it is bad for English and Germans.

In *Howards End* Forster shows us not the suffering of Africans but the wastefulness of the Wilcoxes. Their insensitivity, their lack of appreciation for art and music, their incapacity for personal relationships—these are the flaws liberal women see in them, and these are the least of their faults. Waste is much more important in the action of this novel, the fact that English imperialists are laying waste to both Africa and their own country. At home they are rigid in their assumed superiority to women; they are social Darwinists who believe that the fittest will survive in the business world, "progressives" who believe that bigger is better and more efficient and that there is nothing to value in the village. Henry Wilcox approves entirely of the new economic order. "Take it as a rule that nothing pays on a small scale. Most of the land you see . . . belongs to the people at the Park—they made their pile over copper—good chaps. Avery's Farm, Sishe's—what they call the Common, where you see that ruined oak—one after the other fell in, and so did this, as near as is no matter" (chap. 24). They consciously dismiss the life lived for centuries at Howards End: "The days for small farms are over. It doesn't pay—except with intense cultivation. Small holdings, back to the land—ah! philanthropic bunkum" (chap. 24).

They have a new instrument of disruption in their new means of transportation, the automobile. The narrator keeps the presence, and the meaning, of this new machine, new mode of transportation, new economic fact, and emblematically new attitude toward the earth, before us at all times, perpetually enlarging its meaning. In 1910 automobiles are the exclusive property of rich men, and in this book they become weapons against women and the poor. Very early in the novel, when Helen Schlegel's aunt Juley is rushing from London to Howards End to supervise her niece's short-lived engagement to Paul Wilcox, her railroad train runs beside a road that has now come back into use, since the car has replaced the horse: "at times the Great North Road accompanied her, more suggestive of infinity than any railway awakening, after a nap of a hundred years, to such a life as is conferred by the stench of motor-cars, and to such culture as is implied by the advertisements of antibilious pills" (chap. 3). She finds herself in the Wilcox's automobile when she arrives, and the narrator lets us know what the car is doing to the remaining villagers of Hilton: "Without replying, he turned round in his seat and contemplated the cloud of dust that they had raised in their passage through the village. It was settling again, but not all into the road from which he had taken it. Some of it had percolated through the open windows, some had whitened the roses and gooseberries of the wayside gardens, while a certain proportion had entered the lungs of the villagers" (chap. 3).

Later on the Wilcoxes themselves announce they ran into an old-fashioned horse and cart; they say they and their car were fit as fiddles "as far as Ripon, but there was a wretched horse and cart [with] a fool of a driver" (chap. 10). They run into the same kind of horse and cart Tess Durbeyfield was driving to market when the more modern mail coach ran into her, killing her family's horse; in both novels the horse and cart is an emblem of the ancient life of agricultural labor, which is increasingly vulnerable to the new economic world of machines. Finally, on the way to Evie Wilcox's wedding at Oniton, a car in the wedding party runs over a village girl's cat, usually considered a more "feminine pet than a dog."

Then the car behind them drew up, and the voice of Charles was heard saying: "Get out the women at once." There was a concourse of males, and Margaret and her companions were hustled out and received into the second car. What had happened? As it started off again, the door of a cottage opened, and a girl screamed wildly at them. . . .

The second motor came round the corner. "It is all right, madam," said Crane in his turn. He had taken to call her madam.

"What's all right? The cat?"

"Yes, madam, the girl will receive compensation for it."

"She was a very ruda girla," said Angelo from the third motor thoughtfully. (Chap. 25)

Here the narrator steps forward a little, through Margaret Schlegel, and warns us that this accident, which the men want to dismiss since the victim is not a dog, is serious. "She felt their whole journey from London had been unreal. They had no part with the earth and its emotions. They were dust, and a stink, and cosmopolitan chatter, and the girl whose cat had been killed had lived more deeply than they" (chap. 25).

The presence of the Italian chauffeur is itself part of the meaning of the accident. He is both a male accomplice of the Wilcoxes and their automobile and also a victim, part of the imperialism taking place within Europe itself. The poorer countries are subject to the richer, more developed ones; poor Italians have come to Germany and England to find work as a new servant class. The narrator has already sounded a subtle note of alarm about men like Angelo when he describes Britain's railway stations as entrances to different parts of the country. "Italians realize this, as is natural; those of them who are so unfortunate as to serve as waiters in Berlin call the Anhalt Bahnhof the Stazione d'Italia, because by it they must return to their homes" (chap. 2). Angelo, driven from his home by poverty, is now helping his employers, the Wilcoxes, to invade and plunder the homes of their own countrymen.

The Wilcoxes could not be themselves without their cars. Cars and empire and the destruction of the English village are inseparable. There was no North Sea oil in 1910; the English needed their empire to get the oil to run their cars. And once they had their cars, they could treat their own country as they treated Africa and India. The Wilcoxes travel around England buying and selling houses with new ease and abandon. Places like Ducie Street and Oniton come easy and go easy; the Wilcoxes think nothing of rushing into the country for a wedding and then rushing out. The narrator, however, takes such behavior very seriously and tells us things that cannot begin to enter the minds of the Wilcoxes. After the hurried wedding at Oniton, he says, "But the Wilcoxes have no part in the place, nor in any place. It is not their names that recur in the parish register. It is not their ghosts that sigh among the alders at evening. They have swept into the valley and swept out of it, leaving a little dust and a little money behind" (chap. 29).

The Wilcoxes see themselves, their imperialism and their automobiles, as facts of life, economic necessities, the inevitable results of progress. Forster presents them all as facts, but as alterable and wrong facts, part of an economy to which his two heroines are at least superficially alien. He is supported today not by literary critics, who have almost entirely ignored the meaning of the automobile in *Howards End*, but by radical social critics like Christopher Lasch.

Whatever its power to create new options in theory, in practice industrial technology has developed according to the principle of radical monopoly, as Ivan Illich calls it, whereby new technologies effectively eliminate old technologies, even when the old ones remain demonstrably more efficient for many purposes. Thus the automobile did not simply add another form of transportation to existing forms; it achieved its preeminence at the expense of canals, railways, streetcars, and horse-drawn carriages, thereby forcing the population to depend almost exclusively on automotive transport even for those purposes for which it is obviously unsuited, such as commuting back and forth to work.[3]

Forster's vision of the form economic power would take in our century has proved prophetic, hardly the stuff of wishy-washy liberalism.

Liberalism is exactly what both Forster's narrator and his young heroines, the Schlegels, must learn to recognize as inadequate. The cozy familiarity Forster's narrator establishes among himself, the reader, and the liberal characters begins as a genuine affirmation of shared values, the values of a feminist, intellectual, domestic, personal, benevolent life that exists in articulate but ineffectual opposition to the imperialistic life of the Wilcoxes. The narrator assumes a liberal and literate audience no longer concerned with the nineteenth-century theological issues that were still a burden for Hardy's narrator. Forster's narrator assumes we all have the same cultured, chatty language, the same amusements—concerts, galleries, discussion groups, health food restaurants—"all proteids and body-buildings and people come up to you and beg your pardon, but you have such a beautiful aura" (chap. 17)—and the liberal reformist politics that sometimes even dares to call itself socialism. The narrator begins as a man of letters, an advocate of the life of the Schlegels.

They talked to each other and to other people, they filled the tall thin house at Wickham Place with those whom they liked or could befriend. They even attended public meetings. In their own fashion they cared deeply about politics, though not as politicians would have us care; they desired that the public life should mirror whatever is good in the life within. Temperance, tolerance, and sexual equality were intelligible cries to them; whereas they did not follow our Forward Policy in Thibet with the keen attention that it merits, and would at times dismiss the whole British Empire with a puzzled, if reverent sigh. Not out of them are the shows of history erected: the world would be a grey, bloodless place were it entirely composed of Miss Schlegels. But the world being what it is, perhaps they shine out in it like stars. (Chap. 4)

In both the narrator and the characters Romanticism is still living, but living a feeble, attenuated life as culture instead of radicalism. The Schlegels have lots of books; they like "landscapes"; they believe in the unseen life; they even try to go beyond books a little, when they reproach their protégé Leonard Bast for quoting too much, and praise him for walking all night in the woods in order to experience nature. A walk in the woods is better than nothing, but it is a far cry from *The Lyrical Ballads*.

Both the Schlegels' virtues and their political inadequacy are based on their economic situation, their nice nest eggs of secure stocks about which they and the narrator are refreshingly open. Hobsbawm describes this class:

Rentiers, who lived on the profits and savings of the previous two or three generations' accumulations. By 1871 Britain contained 170,000 'persons of rank and property' without visible occupation—almost all of them women, or rather "ladies," a surprising number of them unmarried ladies. Stocks and shares, including shares in family firms formed into 'private companies' for this purpose, were a convenient way of providing for widows, daughters and other relatives who could not—and no longer needed to be—associated with the management of property and enterprise. The comfortable avenues of Kensington, the villas of spas, and the growing seaside resorts of the middle class, and the environs of Swiss mountains and Tuscan cities welcomed them. The era of railway iron and foreign investment also provided the economic base for the Victorian spinster and the Victorian aesthete.[4]

The Schlegles begin as ladies and travelers, living on their unearned income, both economically comfortable and economically power-less. They are free in that they spend their time and their money as they please; they are certainly not imprisoned in London by patriar-chal ogres, either fathers or husbands. Only gradually do events force them, and us, to understand how little this freedom means.

The first indication of the limitations of their class is an event more serious than they first realize: they lose their lease at Wickham Place and have to move. Travel and movement have been part of their freedom; suddenly they find out that, rich as they are, movement has been thrust upon them as forcibly as it was on the rural laborers of *Tess of the D'Urbervilles.* As individuals, the Schlegels are powerless against what people like the Wilcoxes have set in motion. The narra-tor is reticent, wistful in his condemnation. And since the Schlegels are modern women, they do not understand the true meaning of what has happened to them.

It was absurd, if you came to think of it; Helen and Tibby came to think of it; Margaret was too busy with the house-agents. The feudal ownership of land did bring dignity, whereas the modern ownership of movables is reducing us again to a nomadic horde. We are reverting to the civilization of luggage, and historians of the future will note how the middle classes accreted possessions without taking root in the earth, and may find in this the secret of their imaginative poverty. The Schlegels were certainly the poorer for the loss of Wickham Place. It had helped to balance their lives, and almost to counsel them. Nor is their ground-landlord spiritually the richer. He has built flats on its site, his motor-cars grow swifter, his exposures of Socialism more tren-chant. But he has split the precious distillation of the years, and no chemistry of his can give it back to society again. (Chap. 17)

Neither the narrator nor the characters are ready yet to contemplate a direct economic attack on a culture that makes moving a matter of course, a positive part of a "progressive" society, where people are free to keep changing things in order to make money more efficiently.

The Schlegels cannot understand the true meaning of their forced move until their complacently liberated lives have been repeatedly jolted by two apparently unconnected, but, actually deeply con-nected people—Ruth Wilcox and Leonard Bast. Between them, these two characters will finally force the Schlegels and the reader to recognize that women like them do not offer any resistance to what men like the Wilcoxes stand for, and that real resistance, in the form of a new economy, remains a possibility. The Schlegels must encoun-ter both Ruth Wilcox and Leonard Bast several times before they begin to understand this; neither is fully understood until they come together at Howards End.

Ruth Wilcox is at first merely beautiful, odd, and a little out of place for the Schlegels; they cannot really hear her when she reveals the true importance of their move from Wickham Place: "It is monstrous, Miss Schlegel; it isn't right. I had no idea that this was hanging over you. I do pity you from the bottom of my heart. To be parted from your house, your father's house—it oughtn't to be allowed. It is worse than dying. I would rather die than—Oh, poor girls! Can what they call civilization be right, if people mayn't die in the room where they were born?" (chap. 10). Ruth Wilcox says this early in the novel, when she and Margaret go Christmas shopping; Margaret assumes that such passion over a commonplace occurrence must be due to excessive fatigue. It is not fatigue, but recognition, recognition that what they call civilization is not right.

Margaret cannot understand Ruth Wilcox yet, even though she has already been changed by her. When Margaret meets Ruth in London, months after Helen's disastrous one-night infatuation with Paul Wilcox at Howards End, her first reaction is to cut off the acquaintance; when she finds out Ruth is as worried about renewed pain as she, she makes a hurried gesture that is more significant than she knows. She knows she must see Ruth immediately: "she flung on a hat and shawl, just like a poor woman, and plunged into the fog" (chap. 8). Just like a poor woman! The rich liberal is beginning to change her ways, to leave the insulated London world where a woman can flirt with socialism and yet have no poor friends. Ruth Wilcox, unknown to Margaret, comes from a world where class relations are different, and she has brought Margaret one step toward this world.

Over and over, she unconsciously challenges Margaret's bastion of literary, liberal behavior, the tail end of cultured nineteenth-century Romanticism. She says strange things: "I almost think you forget you're a girl," "There is nothing to get up for in London" (chap. 8). She says almost nothing at the literary luncheon Margaret gives in her honor, and leaves Margaret with the feeling that some undreamed of possibility, something that is more than a single odd woman, exists, though she does not know what it is. "She was not intellectual, nor even alert, and it was odd that, all the same, she should give the idea of greatness. Margaret, zig-zagging with her friends over

Thought and Art, was conscious of a personality that transcended their own and dwarfed their activities. . . . Yet she and daily life were out of focus: one or the other must show blurred. And at lunch she seemed more out of focus than usual, and nearer the line that divides daily life from a life that may be of greater importance" (chap. 9). She spends the rest of the book learning what that life is, that it is not an eerie mystery, but a solid economy.

Margaret finally has a moment of true friendship with Ruth Wilcox, and impulsively, unconsciously, chooses a new life. She comes close to losing her friend when she carelessly answers "Another day" to Ruth's suggestion that they go to Howards End together; soon conquered by her wiser self, she rushes to meet Ruth at the train station and says she will still come if she may. Ruth answers, "You are coming to sleep, dear, too. It is in the morning that my house is most beautiful. You are coming to stop" (chap. 10). Though the trip is cut off by the sudden appearance of the rest of the Wilcox family, the choice has been made. Ruth Wilcox has told Margaret another truth that she cannot yet hear, that she is coming to stop at Howards End. Ruth Wilcox dies soon after, before Margaret can make her trip, but leaves a codicil to her will: "I should like Miss Schlegel (Margaret) to have Howards End" (chap. 11). She knows that Margaret can come to stop, can come to live there as a country woman should. And she knows that no one in her own family has the remotest inkling of what village life should be. Evie and Dolly, the women of the family, are entirely allied with the Wilcox men, and their cars and their empire. Because the family understands neither the house, nor Ruth Wilcox, nor Margaret, they destroy the note without telling Margaret. But Margaret's destiny is settled—she is to begin a new rural life, a life of true Romantic radicalism.

The urgent need for a new life, something different from both the life of the Wilcoxes and the life of the Schlegels, is forced upon the consciousness of both the Schlegels and the reader by the repeated encounters with Leonard Bast. Leonard, unlike Ruth, surprises neither the Schlegels nor the reader with his strangeness, for he is one of the armies of clerks that have been taking over London and appearing with increasing frequency in the novel for fifty years. He surprises only by his suffering. He is the most vivid victim of the Wilcoxes' imperialistic economy, and he is the bearer of bad news to the Schlegels, the news that no social plan available to them can help him. They first meet him at a concert, and Margaret invites him home to retrieve the umbrella Helen has carelessly taken. Good liberals, they hope to be generous to someone of a class below their own. He is uncomfortable, of course, and disappoints them by running away.

He comes back several years later to explain why his bedraggled, pathetic wife had come searching for him at Wickham Place: she had found their card among his books and had been looking for him when he disappeared for a night and a day. The Schlegels are ecstatic when he tells them he spent the night walking out of the city, into the woods; they want to take him a few steps further, to strengthen him, purify him, stop his obeisant references to the inspiring books he has read—the remnants of Romanticism. "But she could not stop him. Borrow was imminent after Jefferies—Borrow, Thoreau, and sorrow" (chap. 14). They cannot stop him because Leonard cannot be strengthened or purified by people like them. He and they are more similar than they want to see or admit. The difference is that the Schlegels have the money and the education to wear their remnants of Romanticism lightly, and Leonard is so degraded by his poverty and the drudgery of his work that his culture is obviously a costume.

Because we, unlike the Schlegels, have seen Leonard at home, we know better than they how little good the remains of Romanticism are doing him.

> "I'll tell you another thing too. I care a good deal about improving myself by means of Literature and Art, and so getting a wider outlook. For instance, when you came in I was reading Ruskin's *Stones of Venice*. I don't say this to boast, but just to show you the kind of man I am. I can tell you, I enjoyed that classical concern this afternoon."
>
> To all his moods Jacky remained equally indifferent. When supper was ready—and not before—she emerged from the bedroom, saying, "But you love me, don't you?"
>
> They began with a soup square, which Leonard had just dissolved in some hot water. It was followed by the tongue—a freckled cylinder of meat, with a little jelly at the top, and a great deal of yellow fat at the bottom— ending with another square dissolved in water (jelly: pineapple) which Leonard had prepared earlier in the day. Jacky ate contentedly enough, occasionally looking at her man with those anxious eyes, to which nothing else in her appearance corresponded, and which yet seemed to mirror her soul. And Leonard managed to convince his stomach that it was having a nourishing meal. (Chap. 6)

Food is just what the Schlegels do not know they have to think about.

But food is at the heart of Leonard's degradation, and food is at the heart of the true, radical Romanticism the Schlegels will have to discover. Hobsbawm says of a man like Leonard, the new urban worker, "His sheer material ignorance of the best way to live in a city, or to eat industrial food (so very different from village food) might actually make his poverty worse than it 'need have been'; that is, than it might have been if he had not been the sort of person he inevitably was."[5] Leonard's terrible food is one of the hidden by-products of the imperialistic capitalism of the Wilcoxes. As Wendell Berry says of the American imperialism that has devastated both our country and the rest of the world, "By now the revolution has deprived the mass of consumers of any independent access to the staples of life: clothing, food, even water. Air remains the only necessity that the average user can still get for himself. And the revolution has imposed a heavy tax on that by way of pollution."[6]

Even though the Schlegels cannot yet comprehend the real meaning of Leonard's life in the English economy, intellectually they recognize him as a problem they cannot solve. After their second meeting with him, they discuss his plight at their women's club. Writing fictional wills for a nonexistent millionaire, they suggest free libraries and tennis courts, free rent, subtle coercion into the colonies, separation from his wife; "he must be assigned a Twin Star, some member of the leisured classes who would watch over him ceaselessly (groans from Helen); he must be given food but no clothes, clothes but no food, a third-return ticket to Venice, without either food or clothes when he arrived there. In short, he might be given anything and everything as long as it was not the money itself" (chap. 15). Margaret does suggest that he be given the money, but the women are unpersuaded—rightly.

The Schlegels discover soon how very worthless all their ideas are to Leonard, how very bankrupt their economic theories are, how very empty their politics have become. In all liberal, helpful good faith, the Schlegels have passed on to Leonard a business tip from Henry Wilcox, now attached to Margaret, that he should clear out of the Porphyrion Fire Insurance company because it was sure to smash. He clears out; the company does not smash; he takes a job in a bank; he gets fired; and he finds himself in a uniquely modern urban class, the unemployable. When Margaret suggests that his luck will change, he knows better. "You don't know what you're talking about.

. . . I shall never get work now. If rich people fail at one profession, they can try another. Not I. I had my groove, and I've got out of it. I could do one particular branch of insurance in one particular office well enough to command a salary, but that's all. . . . I mean if a man over twenty once loses his own particular job, it's all over with him. I have seen it happen to others. Their friends gave them money for a little, but in the end they fall over the edge." (chap. 26). He is right. Neither Henry Wilcox nor the Schlegels meant to hurt him with their advice; having given it, they cannot help him. The very nature of the new forms of urban work has made Leonard unemployable. Henry might have taken him in, but he will not, for the ethics of capitalism do not allow for charity. Henry believes that men like Leonard must fend for themselves, and the Schlegels have no job to give him. Leonard's unemployment, like his food, is a new economic fact, for which neither he nor his would-be benefactors are prepared. Hobsbawm says: "This conflict between the 'moral economy' of the past and the economic rationality of the capitalist present was particularly clear in the realm of social security. The traditional view, which still survived in a distorted way in all classes of rural society and in the internal relations of working-class groups, was that a man had a right to earn a living, and if unable to do so, a right to be kept alive by his community. The view of middle-class liberal economists was that men must take such jobs as the market offered, and that the rational man would, by individual or voluntary collective saving and insurance make provision for accident, illness, and old age."[7] Leonard has made no such provisions, of course, and the Schlegels cannot give him anything that can substitute for the "moral economy" of an older, rural England.

Leonard's difficulties are compounded by another victim of the Wilcox imperialism, his wife. Jacky, sweet, stupid, uneducated, vulgar, a fallen woman, has wheedled poor young Leonard first into sex and then into marriage. This is what the Schlegels know before Helen brings the newly unemployed Basts into Evie Wilcox's country wedding, for a showdown with Henry. At the wedding they find out Jacky's past, for she recognizes and greets Henry as an old lover. On one of his imperialist ventures, a long stay on Cyprus, he had his fling with her; presumably she is the daughter of another Englishman out of England. Helen sums up the life that remained to her after Henry: "Either they sink till the lunatic asylums and the workhouses are full of them, and cause Mr. Wilcox to write letters to the papers complaining of our national degeneracy, or else they entrap a boy into marriage before it is too late" (Chap. 30). Jacky, back in England, has trapped Leonard into marriage, merely from economic desperation. Both are part of the underclass produced by the Wilcox economy; both are problems for which the intellectual politics and intellectual feminism of the Schlegels offer no solution.

The only solution is the revelation to which both the Schlegels and the reader must finally come: the economic radicalism that remains possible at Howards End. There is a secret affinity between the two discordant characters in the Schlegels' life, Leonard Bast and Ruth Wilcox: both still are linked to the old "moral economy" of rural England, though Leonard does not know it. The narrator gives us a hint of this connection when he tells us about Leonard's ancestors: "One guessed him as the third generation, grandson to the shepherd or ploughboy whom civilization had sucked into the town; as one of the thousands who have lost the life of the body and failed to reach the life of the spirit" (chap. 14). When Helen presses him to tell her about his family, on the night of Evie's wedding, "Leonard told her a secret that he had held shameful up to now. 'They were just nothing at all,' he said. '—agricultural labourers and that sort'" (chap. 27). Leonard, a victim of the economy that has been destroying the culture of rural England, has bought that economy's lies, and believes that agricultural laborers are nothing, and that their life was necessarily degraded. Only Ruth Wilcox knows better in this novel, and she is already dead.

Ruth Wilcox triumphs, nevertheless. The strange plot that brings everyone to Ruth's family home must be read in two ways—both as the realistically explicable convergence of people who are in one kind of trouble or another, and then as the workings of a woman who is still a ghost and perhaps a goddess, who is calling people back to an ancient, holy life. That it takes the length of the novel for the Schlegels to understand who Ruth Wilcox is and what kind of life she can bestow is itself historically startling: as we and the Schlegels pick up hints about the life the Howards lived for generations, we recognize that we are finding something that has been lost, and that it became lost in a very short time. What was still alive for Austen and Trollope and Hardy has suddenly, by 1910, entered the realm of mystery.

Neither the Wilcoxes nor the Schlegels have ever thought seriously about the life that Mrs. Wilcox—Ruth Howard—lived as a girl on a small farm outside the village of Hilton. The inhabitants of the modern world—characters, readers, and perhaps even the narrator of the beginning—have forgotten about a life that was recently considered important. The narrator tells us only one clear fact about Ruth Wilcox, and he tells it early in the novel: "She seemed to belong not to the young people and their motor, but to the house and to the tree that overshadowed it. One knew that she worshipped the past, and that the instinctive wisdom the past can alone bestow had descended upon her—that wisdom to which we give the clumsy name of aristocracy. High-born she might not be. But assuredly she cared about her ancestors and let them help her" (chap. 3). It takes us, as readers, a long time to know what that past is, and who those ancestors are. We have to glean our knowledge along with Margaret.

After Ruth dies, and Margaret becomes engaged to Henry, she starts to visit Howards End on various errands; she also starts to gather information that tells her and us how recently Hilton had been a living village, a good place to live. We learn more than the Wilcoxes think they are telling when they start describing old Miss Avery, the farm neighbor who looks after Howards End.

"She really did frighten you," said Henry, who was far from discouraging timidity in females. "Poor Margaret! And very naturally. Uneducated classes are so stupid."

"Is Miss Avery uneducated classes?" Margaret asked, and found herself looking at the decoration scheme of Dolly's drawing room.

"She's just one of the crew at the farm. People like that always assume things. She assumed you'd know who she was. She left all the Howards End keys in the front lobby, and assumed that you'd seen them as you came in, that you'd lock up the house when you'd done, and would bring them on down to her. And there was her niece hunting for them down at the farm. Lack of education makes people very casual. Hilton was full of women like Miss Avery once."

"I shouldn't have disliked it, perhaps."

"Or Miss Avery giving me a wedding present," said Dolly.

Which was illogical but interesting. Through Dolly, Margaret was destined to learn a good deal.

"But Charles said I must try not to mind, because she had known his grandmother."

"As usual, you've got the story wrong, my good Dorothea."

"I mean great-grandmother—the one who left Mrs. Wilcox the house.

Weren't both of them and Miss Avery friends when Howards End, too, was a farm? . . . Then hadn't Mrs. Wilcox a brother—or was it an uncle? Anyhow, he popped the question, and Miss Avery, she said 'No.' Just imagine, if she'd said 'Yes,' she would have been Charles's aunt." (Chap. 24)

Hilton was once full of women like Miss Avery. The old farm woman whom the modern Wilcoxes despise was good enough to be a friend or even a wife to the Howards; she still has enough of the old feeling to give Dolly a wedding present, not expecting Dolly to "mind." She and the Howards were country neighbors, not separated by rank, in a world where rich and poor could associate more lovingly than they do in London. The meaning of Margaret's transformation into a poor woman when she rushes to see Ruth Wilcox in London becomes clearer.

Miss Avery, the last living link with the old life in the novel (her niece is as vulgar and modern as the Wilcoxes, even though she lives in the country), tells Margaret more about the Howards later. "It was a very civil family. Old Mrs. Howard never spoke against anybody, nor let anyone be turned away without food. Then it was never 'Trespassers will be prosecuted' in their land, but would people please not come in" (chap. 33). Miss Avery recognizes that more than such kindness is needed: "Mrs. Howard was never created to run a farm"; "things went on until there were no men" (chap. 33). Neither sex can run a rural, agricultural community alone. Though the Howards were generous, hospitable village women, still living by the code of the "moral economy," they were doomed when men kept leaving the country for the city. Though Henry Wilcox saved what was left of the farm when he married Ruth Howard, he was not about to become a country man. As Henry's wife, Ruth leads a double life, as that of the businessman's wife who has a country place—and, secretly, that of the village woman. Until the end of the novel neither her husband, who is now Margaret's husband, nor the Schlegels understand that her secret life is still a real and good possible life, a genuine basis for an economy, and a radical hope for England. No one makes the intellectual choice of agriculture as the basis of radical change, but all the characters come to Howards End. They come because they have to. They come because they are hurt, wretched, broken. Proud male imperialists, liberated literary women, poor cast-off clerk—none can survive in London.

The person who comes to Howards End most willingly is Margaret, Ruth Wilcox's chosen heir. And even she must learn by stages that she belongs there. On her first visit she begins to recognize the meaning of the land and the house. The land is fertile: "There were the greengage-trees that Helen had once described, there the tennis lawn, there the hedge that would be glorious with dog-roses in June, but the vision now was of black and palest green. Down by the dell-hole more vivid colours were awakening, and Lent Lilies stood sentinel on its margin, or advanced in battalions over the grass. Tulips were a tray of jewels" (chap. 23). And the house is modest and useful, not a palatial monument to Victorian greed. "They were just rooms where one could shelter from the rain. Across the ceiling of each ran a great beam. The dining-room and hall revealed theirs openly, but the drawing-room's was match-boarded—because the facts of life must be concealed from ladies? Drawing-room, dining-room, and hall—how petty the names sounded! Here were simply three rooms where children could play and friends shelter from the rain." (chap. 23). As a piece of architecture, Howards End defies the capitalistic, imperialistic quest for magnitude that has come to dominate both the country and the city. It is a place where people come together, free come from the artificial separations of the hierarchical urban Victorian family; children are not segregated from adults, nor male friends from female friends.

William Morris and Raymond Williams, both country men and both radicals, help us understand the meaning of the cultivated, fertile land and the small house Margaret discovers. Morris writes about the small scale, which the English, at their best, have made into a moral idea: "This land is a little land. . . . All is measured, mingled, varied, gliding easily one thing into another: little rivers, little plains, swelling, speedily changing uplands, all beset with handsome, orderly trees; little hills, little mountains, netted over with the walls of sheep-walks; all is little, yet not foolish and blank, but serious rather, and abundant of meaning, for such as choose to seek it; it is neither prison nor palace, but a decent home."[8] Williams illuminates the meaning of this decent home, the small house, by exposing the meaning of the big house: "Think it through as labour and see how long and systematic the exploitation and seizure must have been, to rear that many houses, on that scale. See by contrast what any ancient, isolated farm, in uncounted generations of labour, has managed to become, by the efforts of any single real family, however prolonged. And then turn, and look at what these other 'families,' these systematic owners, have accumulated and arrogantly declared."[19] Howards End, like Wuthering Heights, is the home of a single agricultural family with enough land to produce its own food. It is the kind of house, with the amount of land, that could easily be made available to large numbers of people in a reordered agricultural economy. It is a shelter for friends; it is a remnant of the ancient "moral economy" of the country.

On Margaret's second visit, ostensibly to admonish old Miss Avery for unpacking their belongings, from Wickham Place, and refurnishing Howards End with them, Margaret first finds herself discomfited and then discovers—as the narrator does—that she can begin to imagine the human life that was lived and might again be lived in rural England. "Here had lived an elder race, to which we look back with disquietude. The country which we visit at week-ends was really a home to it, and the graver sides of life, the deaths, the partings, the yearnings for love, have their deepest expression in the heart of the fields. All was not sadness. The sun was shining without. The thrush sang his two syllables on the budding guelder-rose. Some children were playing uproariously in heaps of golden straw. It was the presence of sadness at all that surprised Margaret, and ended by giving her a feeling of completeness" (chap. 33). Miss Avery's intransigence and this unexpected vision of the *human* life that belongs to the country do for Margaret what none of her books could do: they rekindle the Romanticism of Wordsworth. Still, she tries to persuade Miss Avery to repack her belongings and remains baffled by Miss Avery's insistence that she will come back to live there. Margaret has not yet gone from understanding, emotion, vision to action. Her Romanticism is not yet radical.

Only disaster, an apparently unsolvable problem, brings Margaret to action. She and Helen converge at Howards End because of Helen's illegitimate pregnancy, her violation of England's deepest sexual rules. Neither likes the terms on which they come to Howards End; Helen comes unwillingly, tricked and trapped, and Margaret comes guiltily, part of the trick and the trap. Helen has abruptly left England a few days after Evie's wedding and avoided all contact with her family since; she has come back only because Margaret thinks their Aunt Juley is dying. By the time Helen arrives, Margaret knows her aunt is recovering, but instead of telling Helen, she allows Henry to talk her into plotting to trap her sister, whom they both call "sick." To Henry "the sick had no rights; they were outside the pale; one could lie to them remorselessly. When his first was seized, he had promised to take her down into Hertfordshire, but meanwhile arranged with a nursing-home instead. Helen, too, was ill. And the plan that he sketched out for her capture, clever and well-meaning as it was, drew its ethics from the wolf-pack" (chap. 34). Margaret's intentions are bad, since she is lying to Helen, telling her that she can go to Howards End to get her books without meeting anyone; Henry's intentions are bad, since he wants to lie to his sister-in-law as he lied to his wife, denying her the right to die in the room where she had been born. But Ruth Wilcox is getting her way in spite of all, bringing a pregnant woman to her home to start a new family.

The intellectual radicalism Margaret had felt as a London spinster, but which has grown dormant in her as Henry's wife, reawakens and becomes active as soon as she sees her sister, eight months' pregnant. For the first time, she takes her stand at Howards End and tells Henry and the doctor to leave. "A new feeling came over her; she was fighting for women against men. She did not care about rights, but if men came into Howards End, it should be over her body" (chap. 36). Impulsively and irrationally, she is choosing a sexually radical position. In defending her sister, she is defying the sexual repression of Victorian England, the repression that was so much crueler to women than to men. Victorian families cast women like Helen out; Margaret is standing up for both a saner sexual ethic and a new kind of family.

When Henry denies Helen's request to spend one night at Howards End with her sister, Margaret's anger finally becomes articulate, the rage that has to go along with Romantic, radical hope. Henry claims that Helen's immoral presence will depreciate the value of his property and despoil his dear wife's memory, and insists that her sexual behavior is entirely different from his own with Jacky Bast. "'Not any more of this!' she cried. 'You shall see connection if it kills you, Henry! You have had a mistress—I forgave you. My sister has a lover—you driver her from the house. Do you see the connection? Stupid, hypocritical, cruel—oh, contemptible'" (chap. 38). She leaves Henry, intending to spend one night at Howards End with Helen and then go back with her to Europe. Once there, brought by the most human and painful of causes, they are powerless to leave; they are caught by a power of which they—and we—are only dimly aware.

Henry, Charles, and Leonard must also come to Howards End for the final cataclysm that must precede rebirth. The Wilcox men come to oust the women and to find out how to track the man they call Helen's "seducer." Leonard, meanwhile, has been tracking Margaret, to whom he wants to confess what he, poor self-tormented Victorian, considers his terrible crime against Helen. Everything misguided and wrong in Victorian sexuality brings the men to Howards End, just as it was deception that brought the women. Leonard's shame is unwarranted, for Helen, after all, has seduced him, having the advantages of age, class, and money. And the Wilcoxes' vengefulness against both Helen and her "seducer" is prudery and misogyny masquerading as chivalry. They are not interested in protecting a woman in their family from an exploitive man, or reinstituting an older code of mutually understood sexual rules. What they really feel is unthinking horror at a woman's sexual transgression.

The final bit of British wrongness necessary to keep the new family at Howards End is the blind legal system that condemns Charles Wilcox for the murder of Leonard Bast, even though Leonard was about to die of heart trouble, and misery, and poverty. He dies when Charles exacts his vengeance, by hitting him with the Schlegels' father's sword. "'Yes, murder's enough,' said Miss Avery, coming out of the house with the sword" (chap. 41). In Charles's cruel heart, it has been murder; the English legal system, as Miss Avery foresees, calls it murder too. "The verdict was brought in. Charles was committed for trial. It was against all reason that he should be punished, but the law, being made in his image, sentenced him to three years' imprisonment" (chap. 43). The law is made in Charles's image: the written and unwritten laws of England, the same laws that would condemn Helen for her nonexistent sin, find a true victim in Charles, who does indeed deserve the punishment that has been waiting for him ever since Miss Avery unpacked the sword.

This too has its part in the mysterious plot: Charles's punishment keeps Henry at Howards End, so that it will no longer be inhabited only by women. "Then Henry's fortress gave way. He could bear no one but his wife, he shambled up to Margaret afterwards and asked her to do what she could with him. She did what seemed easiest—she took him down to recruit at Howards End" (chap. 43). At the end he is still sick, broken, afflicted by the hay-fever that has always alienated him from the land, but he is there, part of a new family. Crime, poverty, sexual taboos have brought two women, an old man—and soon, a baby boy—to an abandoned small farm, both to suffer and to begin again. A whole world of wrong, a world run by the Wilcoxes in England, cannot be gently adjusted into ease and comfort; Forster's plot asks us to believe that it will finally begin to precipitate its own destruction. For it has been human, believable, predictable wrong that has brought everyone to the crisis at Howards End. The wrongs seem irremediable to ordinary English ways of thinking, but all along another plot, another narrative, another vision has been working.

Reading through *Howards End,* we can see that the natural disasters built into the English urban economy and Victorian sexual morality have brought everyone together at Howards End; yet upon rethinking and rereading, we have to acknowledge the possibility of a simultaneous supernatural cause; Ruth Wilcox, though dead, has had her way. At the very end we share Margaret's sense of revelation when Dolly reveals a family secret:

"Good-bye, Mr. Wilcox. It does seem curious that Mrs. Wilcox should have left Margaret Howards End, and yet she get it, after all." . . .
At last she said: "Could you tell me, Henry, what was that about Mrs. Wilcox having left me Howards End?"
Tranquilly he replied: "Yes, she did. But that is a very old story. When she was ill and you were so kind to her, she wanted to make you some return, and not being herself at the time, scribbled 'Howards End' on a piece of paper. I went into it thoroughly, and, as it was clearly fanciful, I set it aside, little knowing what my Margaret would be to me in the future."
Margaret was silent. Something shook her life in its inmost recesses, and she shivered.
"I didn't do wrong, did I?" he asked, bending down.
"You didn't, darling. Nothing has been done wrong." (Chap. 44)

Nothing has been done wrong—even though the realistic plot is compounded of wrongs. Nothing has been done wrong because a divinity has been using the Wilcoxes and the Schlegels for her own ends, bringing them back to an ancient agricultural life, not as the fanciful choice of dilettantes, but as an economic and moral necessity.

Forster suggests very slowly, very delicately, the idea that this life might also include a lost divinity, yet he always offers the reader the possibility of rational disbelief, as Emily Brontë and Hawthorne do in *Wuthering Heights* and *The House of the Seven Gables*. The supernatural creatures whom the narrator introduces gradually increase in seriousness and power. He introduces the idea of ghosts with a mere simile: "the fog—we are in November now—pressed against the window like an excluded ghost" (chap. 8). After Ruth Wilcox dies, he keeps suggesting that she may be alive as a ghost. When Henry proposes to Margaret, "Mrs. Wilcox strayed in and out, ever a welcome ghost; surveying the scene, thought Margaret, without one hint of bitterness" (chap. 13). Having learned about Henry's affair with Jacky, Margaret thinks that "Mrs. Wilcox, that unquiet yet kindly ghost, must be left to her own wrong" (chap. 28). After this, we must consider the possibility that the narrator is serious when he says of the Wilcoxes, "It is not their ghosts that sigh among the alders at evening" (chap. 29). All this prepares us for Margaret's final belief that Ruth Wilcox and her house and her farm are both divine and powerful, capable of propelling a group of characters through a painful plot. "I feel that you and I and Henry are only fragments of that woman's mind. She knows everything. She is everything. She is the house, and the tree that leans over it. People have their own deaths as well as their own lives, and even if there is nothing beyond death, we shall differ in our nothingness. I cannot believe that knowledge such as hers will perish with knowledge such as mine" (chap. 40).

Meanwhile, the narrator has been providing another clue to the nature of Ruth Wilcox's divinity, and the plot she is weaving. Both the narrator and the characters keep referring to ancient Greece, first in ways that can be dismissed as more of the literary playfulness with which Forster wrote about gods and Greece in his earlier novels and stories. "The tragedy of preparedness has scarcely been handled, save by the Greeks" (chap. 12). "You mean to keep proportion, and that's heroic, it's Greek" (chap. 23). "Remorse is not among the eternal verities. The Greeks were right to dethrone her" (chap. 40). Even Helen's favorite saying, "Death destroys a man, but the idea of death saves him" (chap. 27), is more Greek than Christian. The Greece of these comments is not Hardy's tragic Greece, reborn among suffering English villagers; it is the Greece of Matthew Arnold's Victorian essays. It is the Greece dearest to young university men, a literary ideal of the balanced, humane, secular life, so much healthier and more sensible than the life of Christian repression.

This may be the only Greece consciously known by characters like the Schlegels. But it is only the introductory edge of Forster's Greece. He gives one hint of the other, older Greece of agricultural deities when he says, "If Drayton were with us again to write a new edition of his incomparable poem, he would sing the nymphs of Hertfordshire as indeterminate of feature, with hair obfuscated by the London smoke. Their eyes would be sad, and averted from their fate towards the Northern flats, their leader not Isis or Sabrina, but the slowly flowing Lea. No glory of raiment would be theirs, no urgency of dance; but they would be real nymphs" (chap. 23). And there is another Greece beyond that inhabited by nymphs—more powerful, more mysterious, a Greece almost lost to literature. It is the Greece of the mystery religions, the Greece of Demeter and Persephone, the Greece to which Hardy alluded with the word "Cerealia."

This is the Greece of Sophocles' last play, *Oedipus at Colonus*, a hidden source of the final magic in *Howards End*. Forster is so subtle, so determined not to alienate his audience of educated, sophisticated, secular people, that he reveals his unfamiliar, shattering source in Sophocles through the familiar, comfortable voice of Matthew Arnold. The narrator speaks repeatedly about "seeing life steadily and seeing it whole," borrowing a phrase from Arnold's "To a Friend." Forster's narrator says of Leonard, "To see life steadily and to see it whole was not for the likes of him" (chap. 6). Commenting on the difference between Margaret and Henry, he says, "It is impossible to see modern life steadily and see it whole, and she had chosen to see it whole. Mr. Wilcox saw steadily" (chap. 18). When Margaret begins to glimpse an ideal unity, in the country, the phrase returns: "In these English farms, if anywhere, one might see life steadily and see it whole, group in one vision its transitoriness and its eternal youth, connect—connect without bitterness until all men are brothers" (chap. 33). Finally, as Leonard goes to Howards End to die, the narrator reminds us once more, "These things were in Hertfordshire; and farther afield lay the house of a hermit—Mrs. Wilcox had known him—who barred himself up, and wrote prophecies, and gave all he had to the poor. While, powdered in between, were the villas of business men, who saw life more steadily, though with the steadiness of the half-closed eye" (chap. 40).

The line sounds so utterly Victorian! But read in context, it offers another way of reading *Howards End*. Arnold gives special thanks in his poem to Sophocles

> whose even-balanced soul
> From first youth tested up to extreme old age,
> Business could not make dull, nor passion wild;
>
> Who saw life steadily, and saw it whole,
> The mellow glory of the Attic stage,
> Singer of sweet Colonus and its child.
>
> (Lines 9–14)

Once we understand the source of Forster's echoing line, we can see that *Howards End* is more than an English novel; it is a Greek drama reborn in England, a drama of magic and salvation. By the end, when joy has emerged from horror, when a silent, ghostly divinity has worked her will, we understand fully what none of the characters can know at the beginning, that empire and intellect, outer life and inner life, Schlegels and Wilcoxes, are not the only elements of which the world is made. Ruth Wilcox, her house, her land, are part of both the English agricultural past and the larger, more ancient past of the earth. The destruction of England's agricultural life, and ancient female divinities, by empire is only a repetition of what has happened before in the Western world, in Rome and in Greece.

There are deep similarities between *Oedipus at Colonus* and *Howards End*. Both reflect the last days of a destructive empire; both are desperate exhortations to a damaged citizenry to come home to their best selves, to the beautiful lands that they are no longer really seeing, and to the old divinities that give both shelter and justice. Just as Ruth Wilcox draws everyone to Howards End to receive justice—blessings and punishments—so the Eumenides, the kindly ones, the transformed Furies, draw everyone to their beautiful fertile shrine at Colonus. Old, blind Oedipus comes there to die and to be transformed, after all his suffering, into a divinity; Theseus, his Athenian host, comes there to welcome him in the best spirit of his city, a place that gives refuge to the wretched of other lands, and to receive Oedipus's blessing in return; Oedipus's brother-in-law and son, who have cruelly banished and repeatedly wronged him, come there to receive his curse. The blessing for both sets of characters and both audiences—ancient Greek and modern English—is the spiritual recovery of a lost life. It is the agricultural life of beautiful fertile lands, sacred places, female goddesses, justice and shelter—the moral economy of the country.

Aubrey de Selincourt's history of Greece makes clear the deep connections between the bad turn imperialistic Athens had taken, and the grove and goddesses of Sophocles' last play. Empire brought Athens certain glories, but it put an end to the people's respect for rural life and for women.

Athens at the beginning of the Peloponnesian War was on top of the world; but for anyone familiar with Herodotus' account of the older Greece, it is hard not to feel that her forward leap, in many ways so remarkable in the history of civilization, was not altogether towards better things. A certain hardness, feverishness almost, has crept into the life of the most civilized community in Greece; the city, now has become all in all. The old country pieties, the old simplicities, are going, or gone. With the almost oriental seclusion of women the graciousness of society has suffered a decline; Greece had always been a man's world, but women within their sphere had nevertheless counted for much; now they counted for nothing whatever—unless like Pericles' Aspasia, they are *hetaerae*, or high-class whores. The age-long conservatism of Greek life, based on the land, the family, the ancient sanctities of place, is being undermined.[10]

The lost ancient sanctity of place and of women, both human and divine, are at the heart of *Oedipus at Colonus*: "Finding that they [Oedipus and Antigone] are at Colonus, near Athens, in a copse thick with laurel, olive, and wild vine and filled with the song of nightingales—a grove which is sacred to the 'dread goddesses, the daughters of Earth and Darkness, the all-seeing Kindly ones'—Oedipus cries out that his destiny is fulfilled, his wanderings are over, for Apollo had foretold that when he came thither he would find rest at last."[11] Rest at last, groves and goddess, antidotes to a male empire—these are also the deepest and most joyful elements of *Howards End*.

The echoes and hints first of ghosts, then of Greek goddesses, lift *Howards End* beyond the realm of the novel into mystery and joyful hope, hope that a world which seems to be going all wrong can still be made right. A female divinity helps make things right, but not as a *dea ex machina*. The divinity of Ruth Wilcox and her sacred place are not, finally, extraordinary. They are an old truth that men have forgotten and that one woman, Miss Avery, remembers, and two others, Margaret and Helen, discover. And this divinity is anything but detached from what we normally consider economic and political reality. People and places become divine in *Howards End* by working together in a productive agricultural economy.

Once we come to believe that the agricultural life awaiting Margaret and Helen is both the beginning of a radical, new economic order that can subvert the Wilcoxes and their empire, and also a reborn, ancient divine order, we can reread or remember the novel, and realize that Forster's narrator has been hinting all along that his heroines are involved in something more than ordinary life. In an inobtrusive subordinate clause he tells us that Howards End is a temple; he also lets us know that Miss Avery, the guardian of the place, sees its destiny. "They went into the dining-room, where the sunlight poured in upon her mother's chiffonier, and upstairs, where many an old god peeped from a new niche. The furniture fitted extraordinarily well. In the central room—over the hall, the room that Helen had slept in four years ago—Miss Avery had placed Tibby's old bassinette. 'The nursery,' she said" (chap. 33). And we have to look twice at the child who will occupy that nursery, Helen's child. First we can see that Howards End is still ruled by the welcoming spirit of Ruth Wilcox's ancestors; it is a shelter and a sanctuary for Helen, the wandering sexual sinner who would be cast out of the prudish world of English imperialists. Our second vision of her reveals that she, like the Greek wandering sexual sinner Oedipus, is bringing the place a blessing. His blessing is spiritual; hers is absolutely material—her baby son, a new *man*, the great-grandson of agricultural laborers. Forster's narrator has hinted, prophetically, that Helen will bear a savior, but the hint is so subtle that we can recognize it only in retrospect. After her night with Leonard, she goes to see her brother Tibby, to ask him to give Leonard five thousand pounds. Tibby understands neither her request nor her state of mind, yet even his dim eyes can see that she has changed in some way. She is "ceaselessly beautiful"—as pregnant women often are; at the last, "her eyes, the hand laid on the mouth, quite haunted him, until they were absorbed into the figure of St. Mary the Virgin, before whom he stopped for a moment on the walk home" (chap. 30). He sees the truth, though he does not recognize it. Unmarried Helen is bringing salvation to a hurt world, not peace but a sword, a new man who will turn the old world upside down.

That these hurt people gathered at Howards End to survive have in fact been saved bursts upon us as a revelation in the last, joyful sunlit chapter. "Tom's father was cutting the big meadow. He passed again and again amid whirring blades and sweet odours of grass, encompassing with narrowing circles the sacred center of the field" (chap. 44). Not even Trollope or Hardy—not even Wordsworth or Emily Brontë—dares say that a field has a sacred center. Forster tosses the idea off lightly, hoping that we have finally understood the holiness of this place, a holiness that the Greeks found in their sacred groves. And it is also a holiness that the old men of Akenfield could still see in 1962. The teacher at the agricultural training center says, "The old men can describe exactly how the ploughing turns over in a particular field. They recognize a beauty and it is this that they really worship. Not with words—with their eyes."[12] The rural dean corroborates: "Fatalism is the real controlling force, this and the nature gods, the spirit of the trees and water and sky and plants. These beliefs seem to have no language, but they rule."[13]

The Schlegels rediscover this holy agricultural economy in *Howards End*, the economy that both liberal women and imperialist men have forgotten. All along it has been alive, waiting for a new family to come and reclaim it. Howards End is more than a beautiful landscape; it is holy because it is productive. The first night Helen and Margaret spend there, Tom, their neighbor, brings milk and eggs—country food, what pregnant women are supposed to eat, country hospitality, no jello and soup cubes. And the last chapter opens with a harvest of hay, a crop to feed animals. This farm is not a retirement home; it is the beginning of a reborn agricultural economy.

The ending is only sketched, suggestive, a utopian hope based on one example of a genuine economic possibility. That this utopian hope is based partly on a life recovered from the past by no means invalidates it. Forster gives Margaret, the transformed liberal, the prophetic voice that can express this hope. "Because a thing is going strong now, it need not go strong for ever. . . . This craze for motion has only set in during the last hundred years. It may be followed by a civilization that won't be a movement, because it will rest on the earth. All the signs are against it now, but I can't help hoping, and very early in the morning in the garden I feel that our house is the future as well as the past" (chap. 44). Forster gives this radical vision to women because in 1910 they are still excluded from the businessman's world. They have nothing to lose but their liberal's liberty and economic powerlessness. And to gain they have economic self-sufficiency and the personal dignity that goes with having a worthwhile job to do.

In 1910 these women must do more than join a village community, for there is virtually nothing left to join. If the only people left in the country are like Miss Avery's niece Madge, the village is going to need a lot of help. Drained of its wealth and its artists, intellectuals, artisans, and proud laborers, the country has become a vacation place for the rich, and a place of drudgery for the poor. The village of Hilton needs the dignity, the intelligence, the culture, and the money that the Schlegels bring; they are restoring what it possessed in the relatively recent past. They are also bringing a hope that belongs to the future, not the past, the kind of hope that can be traced to Shelley, but also to the early Wordsworth, prophet of joy. The Schlegels and Wilcoxes make up an unusual family: an old man, his youngish, childless wife, her younger sister, and the sister's illegitimate son. Unwelcome in the rest of England, at Howards End they suggest the possibilities of both personal transformation and sexual openness. Each person has changed. Henry the charging imperialist is broken and gentle. Margaret the gabbling intellectual has become silent and sews, doing old-fashioned women's labor. Helen the fiery radical has learned to understand why Margaret stood by Henry at Evie's wedding: "Looking back, darling, I know that it was right. It is right to save the man whom one loves. I am less enthusiastic about justice now" (chap. 40). Her former brand of justice was ineffectual; only the justice based on a new economic life can make life better for the Leonard Basts of the world.

Forster's most daring hope for the future of England—especially, of English women—lies beyond economic change. The confessions Margaret and Helen make to each other contain a sexual liberty beyond anything Shelley ever dreamed of. Forster wants to give women their choice of sexual lives. Helen confesses that she no longer wants the love of a man; Margaret, that she does not love children. Margaret says, "It is only that people are far more different than is pretended. All over the world men and women are worrying because they cannot develop as they are supposed to develop. Here and there they have the matter out, and it comforts them" (chap. 44). Forster, a homosexual, dares to combine an ancient economic life of villages and small farms with radical hopes for personal and sexual liberty, liberty for all women and all men who are different. Forster reveals how utopian this hope is in an exchange between Margaret and Helen:

"Men don't know what we want—"
"And never will."
"I don't agree. In two thousand years they'll know." (Chap. 37)

The idea that the world must wait two thousand years is very humbling, a firm reminder that we are a long way from knowing how to make each other happy.

But two thousand years is not forever. It is a figure that gives a kind of mystery to the radical hope of *Howards End*, linking it to *Wuthering Heights* and *The House of the Seven Gables*. These three novels are on the furthest edge of nineteenth-century Romantic radicalism. Emily Brontë, Hawthorne, and Forster bring their heroines beyond economic change, beyond moral change, beyond what we think of as the rules of the real world. The three ghostly heroines beckon us beyond the limits of our own thoughts; they ask us to take the radical leap into hope. The living heroines of each novel embody the radicalism that can be enacted in the present, now, if we dare to move; the ghostly ones remind us that nothing we do in our lives is finite.

12. Conclusion: Suicides and Sanctities

The prophecy of *Howards End* remains a prophecy. It has not come to pass in the twentieth century; it is still true. The dominant voices of the contemporary Western world are the voices of the descendants of the Wilcoxes, and the ever-weaker, though very voluble, descendants of the Schlegels. Those who stand for the Howards remain, however, and recently have been speaking with increasing urgency and power. They are, startlingly, almost all men. Forster's hope that women would lead the way back to an anti-imperialist agricultural life has not been realized; the articulate women of our culture, those who claim "success," have taken other paths, the path of the Wilcoxes and the path of the Schlegels, the path of business, still capitalistic and imperialistic, and the path of private life, intellectual and artistic "fulfillment" and "self-development."

These two dominant paths, which leave the economic suffering of the world untouched between them, were uncannily revealed as dead ends, within a few years of *Howards End*, by women who have become enshrined, along with Charlotte Brontë and George Eliot, as feminist heroines, Kate Chopin and Virginia Woolf. In spite of the two suicides, Woolf's own, and that of Chopin's heroine in *The Awakening*, these two have been anthologized, analyzed, and quoted as sources of liberation. They could be voices of liberation—if they were read as what they are, indications of why the still dominant paths of "feminism" are roads to nowhere.

Chopin wrote *The Awakening* in the United States eleven years before Forster wrote *Howards End*. It can be read as one long elaboration on Ruth Wilcox's declaration to Margaret that there is nothing to get up for in London. Edna Pontellier—urban, rich, pampered, bored—truly has nothing to get up for, and walks into the sea. Her great self-liberation from the oppressions of life as her husband's wife and her children's mother is just what Shelley ordered, about eighty years before: flight from the family, artistic aspiration, and liberated sex. Leaving her husband's house for a cottage of her own, where she thinks she will become an artist, she believes that she is intellectually liberated: "No longer was she content to 'feed upon opinion' when her own soul had invited her" (chap. 32). Soon her careless lover "had detected her latent sensuality, which unfolded under his delicate sense of her nature's requirements like a torpid, torrid, sensitive blossom" (chap. 35). A woman too can aspire to the Shelleyan state of a "sensitive plant."

Disappointed by a possible lover, Edna is reduced to a state of Romantic despair, the total loathing of the world that Shelley and Byron experienced. "Despondency had come upon her there in the wakeful night, and had never lifted. There was no one thing in the world that she desired. There was no human being whom she wanted near her except Robert; and she even realized that the day would come when he, too, and the thought of him would melt out of her existence, leaving her alone. The children appeared before her like antagonists who had overcome her; who had overpowered and sought to drag her into the soul's slavery for the rest of her days. But she knew a way to elude them. She was not thinking of these things when she walked down to the beach" (chap. 39). The new, specifically woman's element in this Romantic agony is the naming of children as the source of enslavement, the enemy to be escaped by a walk into the sea. They are indeed an impediment to a life of artistic freedom, sexual abandon, and endless "self-fulfillment," the life desired by a woman with nothing to get up for, no good work to do, no work that has anything to do with fertility and economic productivity. The spiritual complaint of Chopin's heroine has endless echoes in the feminist writing of the twentieth century.

Virginia Woolf, childless, articulated the absence of work in

"Three Guineas" and recommended a plunge into a river—shortly before she took her own walk into the sea. Writing in 1938, she said,

We, the daughters of educated men, are between the devil and the deep sea. Behind us lies the patriarchal system; the private house, with its nullity, its immorality, its hypocrisy, its servility. Before us lies the public world, the professional system, with its possessiveness, its jealousy, its pugnacity, its greed. The one shuts us up like slaves in a harem; the other forces us to circle like caterpillars head to tail, round and round the mulberry tree, the sacred tree of property. It is a choice of evils. Each is bad. Had we not better plunge off the bridge into the river; give up the game; declare that the whole of human life is a mistake and so end it?[1]

No one can know exactly why Woolf herself so ended it, but she certainly defines the choices in a way that makes the plunge look good. Woolf and Chopin agree in their definition of a woman's domestic life as imprisonment in a patriarchal, and by implication, urban, house; together they define the two alternatives that have dominated women's choices in the twentieth century. Artistic and sexual "liberation" and the men's business world—these have been offered as the choices of a woman who would be free. And together Woolf and Chopin have helped blind women to the other road, that of a reborn, radically independent agricultural life, in which women are not imprisoned in the idle "patriarchal" nuclear families Woolf and Chopin present as the only possible kind of family. The third path they offer is the river and the deep sea, the path that a startling number of famous women have subsequently chosen.

That these two writers explicitly said suicide was the only way out of the bind in which women were caught demands that we reconsider that bind, instead of believing we must choose either business or Shelleyan "liberation." The choices defined to Chopin and Woolf have triumphed, however. The two commandments of both supermarket women's magazines and radical literature like *Powers of Desire* (New York: Monthly Review, 1983) and *Women and Revolution* (Boston: South End, 1981) are: get economic power, and get sexual power. The presuppositions that economic power will remain urban and industrial (whether capitalist or "socialist," as defined in mainstream Marxist circles) and that children are impediments to the getting of both money and sex are virtually unquestioned. If there is one dominant demand in feminist literature across the political spectrum, it is, "Please take care of my children, someone!"

In a sober, mild-mannered academic history of women pioneers in the social sciences, Rosalind Rosenberg concludes:

> Foremost among the difficulties women still face is the fact that belief in the inevitability of separate sexual spheres endures and has even intensified in recent years as a consequence of the writings of sociobiologists. Elsie Clews Parsons' observation that 'to be declassified is very painful to most persons' is still true today, especially with respect to sexual classification, which continues to provide the most important basis ever created for insuring social stability. The fact that motherhood remains an important occurrence in most women's lives makes declassification in the absence of fundamental social reform particularly frightening to women. Since women continue to take private responsibility for most childcare and, more generally, for social welfare, alternative ways of satisfying these social needs must be found if most women are to be both willing and able to claim greater personal freedom.[2]

Barbara Ehrenreich's more politically urgent book, *The Hearts of Men: American Dreams and the Flight from Commitment*, couples an excellent analysis (but no better than Trollope's) of the way men abuse the idea of freedom, with precisely the same demand on behalf of women: "The most obvious and desperately needed service, both for women who are married and joint breadwinners and for those who are sole breadwinners, is reliable, high-quality child care."[3] This is a major demand even in documents on the far feminist left. A resolute cry in *Women and Revolution* is "federally funded non-sexist child care."[4]

Child care *is* the obvious demand for women trapped between choices as defined by Woolf and Chopin: the isolated nuclear family, the business world, the liberated world of art and sex. In a culture that has largely agreed that these are the choices, the most vocal and visible women opposing publicly funded child care seem to be on the far right, women like Phyllis Schlafly, right-to-lifers, and Total Women, who liked both the political status quo and their "nurturing" roles in the patriarchal home. The spate of news stories on sexual abuse in day-care centers is ready-made fuel for the fears of the Right. It suggests that something is wrong, but it need not suggest that women should stay home and play supporting roles in an economy that remains capitalistic and imperialistic.

Sexual abuse in day-care centers should be seen as the dead canary that warns miners poison gas is in the air. It is an indication that the whole system is wrong; it is not an aberration. It can neither be repaired with better legislation nor eliminated by eliminating the day-care centers and sending women back into the imprisoning urban home. As part of the "liberation" of women in a capitalist culture, it is a small, horrifying emblem of what Christopher Lasch describes in *The Culture of Narcissism:* "Strategies of narcissistic survival now present themselves as emancipation from the repressive conditions of the past, thus giving rise to a 'cultural revolution' that reproduces the worst features of the collapsing civilization it claims to criticize."[5] As Thompson demonstrates in *The Making of the English Working Class*, children have been the victims of industrial capitalism for the last two hundred years.

What the prevailing forms of feminism are not addressing adequately is work. What kinds of work are available to women who want to be self-sufficient, self-fulfilling, self-liberating? Not the old kinds, certainly. The production of food and clothing and the care of children are relegated to poor women who work in factories and day-care centers, or—if one is very rich—to chefs, designers, governesses. Even the production of the less necessary goods, art that middle-class women once took for granted, is no longer available. "Amateurism" is disdained, and at the same time women are encouraged to aspire to fame and fortune as artists, actresses, musicians. The work that belonged to women in self-governing, relatively self-sustaining agricultural economies is dismissed as foolish, dull, worthless, mindless. A woman in our culture who wants to *work* has to be earning money, not just making or growing something—even if the product is undeniably necessary.

The economic world is still run by men given fictional representation as Dombeys, Wilcoxes, Pyncheons. They loom over us, not having budged an inch. Women have not moved them; they have moved women—out of their villages, out of their homes, into the business world that Woolf was clear-sighted enough to want to avoid. The presence of women in the economies of the industrialized world has not changed the natures of those economies. Though they allow a few privileged women to be very rich and powerful, they still exploit the natural world, women, and children, just as the industries of the nineteenth century did.

Two books by women illuminate this condition—one indirectly, one directly. Jane Jacobs has inadvertently exposed the true nature of our economy in *Cities and the Wealth of Nations* when she explains

the source of cities' prosperity. "For obvious reasons most city re-
placements of former imports consist of city-made goods and services, but not all. Some of the most momentous instances of city
import-replacing involves former rural goods. A few examples from
the past are replacement of natural ice with the city-originated work
of manufacturing mechanical refrigeration equipment; replacement
of cotton, flax, silk, and fur with artificial, city-devised fibers; replacement of ivory and tortoise-shell with plastics."[6] And what of the
rural workers who used to make the rural goods? And what of the
chemical by-products of all the artificial fibers and plastics, which
present a virtually insoluble problem in the form of toxic waste
dumps? And what of the poor women and children who live near
those dumps? The alleged prosperity of cities is built on many forms
of destruction.

Hilda Scott, who takes a much less cheerful view of the
flourishing cities, particularly of those in the third world, which
Jacobs so admires, says outright that industrial progress has not
helped women as it has helped men. The history she sketches continues Thompson's story of the gradual degradation of both women
and rural laborers by industrial capitalism. Western women have not
been able to keep even the manufacturing jobs that were once theirs.
"Many of the First World women who used to make those pullovers
now labelled 'Made in Hong King' and those stuffed toys marked
'Made in Korea' are now unemployed, the European textile and gar-
ment industry having laid off one million workers during the 1970's.[7]
The people who get these jobs are themselves exploited, and the
transference of jobs to the third world necessitates a quick replaying
of the destruction of rural life like that which took place in
nineteenth-century England. "The free trade zone of Banya-Lepas,
Penang, Malaysia, was established in 1974 on land which had belonged to independent farmers whom the government had resettled
in the interior. It is now occupied exclusively by foreign electronics
firms. When Anne-Marie Münster interviewed workers there in
1980, she found the daily wage to be one-tenth that paid in the
industry in West Germany."[8]

Such industry has not, of course, eliminated agriculture anywhere in the world. But agriculture has increasingly become part of
the industrial world as large farms replace small, and machines
replace horses, and petroleum-based fertilizers replace manure, and

irrigation supplements rainwater. The "efficiency" of the new farms is touted, but in the last few years a lot of unhealthy chickens have come home to roost, and we are being forced to realize that the crisis of work includes a crisis in agriculture. In the sober words of an environmental scientist, describing one of the more benign processes of the new agriculture, "The physical changes wrought by irrigation on formerly dry lands are consequential. Waterlogging and increased salinity and/or alkilinity are problems long associated with artificial irrigation. If not anticipated and corrected, they can defeat the very purpose of the irrigation scheme. Irrigation on a large scale may have unforeseen effects on climate."[9]

The environment, small farmers, children, women, all continue to be victims, all over the world, of what the radical novelists of the nineteenth century attacked through their fictions. They hoped that women would stand up to this economic system, would ally themselves with the threatened agricultural communities where they could be their best, most productive, and freest selves. Their hopes, needless to say, have not been answered. Women in our century have not shared the radical vision of Romanticism. The double dead ends of the Wilcoxes and Schlegels, business world and patriarchal urban home, patriarchal urban home and artistic and sexual liberation, continue to lead us into destruction.

Forster's third road in *Howards End*, the radical tradition that begins with Wordsworth, remains alive in the word of socialists and Christians, farmers and literary critics, historians and poets, ecologists and novelists. This radical tradition kept alive in the novels of the nineteenth century faces two great challenges in the present. It must address itself more clearly to women, as the nineteenth-century novelists did, and try again to convince them that unhappy extremes are not the only choices. And it must still do what has appeared impossible—dismantle the forces of empire.

One true source of hope is that the radical literature, which pushes readers toward what E. P. Thompson calls the "moral economy" of the agricultural community, has remained steady, if not dominant. It has always been a literature that looks both backward and forward, backward to the tradition of common land, common law, custom, ceremony, and forward to liberty and equality, backward to dimly remembered holiness of place, forward to the ever-present possibility Forster expresses through Margaret Schlegel's belief that she can "create new sanctities" (*Howards End*, chap. 26). *Agricultural, sanctities, moral economy,* such words are anathema to the kind of radicalism that has become what the twentieth century calls feminism. Feminists are particularly vulnerable to Christopher Lasch's charge in *The Culture of Narcissism*: "Having trivialized the past by equating it with outmoded styles of consumption, discarded fashions and attitudes, people today resent anyone who draws on the past in serious discussions of contemporary conditions or attempts to use the past as a standard by which to judge the present. Current critical dogma equates every such reference to the past as itself an expression of nostalgia."[10] The radical tradition of English and American Romanticism that descends from Wordsworth has always drawn on the past, and the depth of historical connection has helped it survive into our present.

The vision of the past that has given strength to Romantic radicalism in the nineteenth and twentieth centuries rests on the assumption that what we can find by looking to the past is not merely antiquarian, quaint, interesting, but true and necessary, the power and goodness that belong to us by nature. The belief that sanctities can be re-created, which Forster gives to the heroine of *Howards End,* belongs to this radical tradition because Forster believes that by losing and forgetting the sanctity of place we have violated our natures and our needs. To remember the attachment to place that accompanies the moral economy of agriculture is also take a stand against the destructiveness of imperialism.

Using very different language, and a different idea of sanctity, Forster's contemporary Kropotkin expresses his own belief that new sanctities can be created. He acknowledges that the theories of self-interest (the basis of imperialistic politics, then and now) were destroying his sanctities, the institutions of mutual aid, and affirmed the continual re-creation of those institutions. "Although the destruction of mutual-aid institutions has been going on in practice and theory for full three or four hundred years, hundreds of millions of men continue to live under such institutions; they piously maintain them and endeavour to reconstitute them when they have ceased to exist. In our mutual relations every one of us has his momentary revolt against the fashionable individualistic creed of the day, and actions in which men are guided by their mutual-aid inclinations constitute so great a part of our daily intercourse that if a stop to such actions could be put all further ethical progress would be stopped at once."[11] We rediscover and re-create sanctities because we cannot help it.

The writers who have kept this radical vision alive in the twentieth century have not been quoting past writers as literary authorities; the radicalism based on the moral economy of agriculture keeps being rediscovered and re-created. Evidence can be found everywhere. In 1943 Flora Thompson could look at the erosion of the country life she had known as a child, deplore the spiritual losses of the English village, and still find hope:

> Change came slowly, if surely, and right into the early years of this century many of the old village ways of living remained and those who cherished the old customs were a little more democratic, much as country people had been for generations. A little better educated, a little more prosperous than their parents had been, but still the same unpretentious warm-hearted people, with just enough malice to give point to their wit and a growing sense of injustice which was making them begin to inquire when their turn would come to enjoy a fair share of the fruits of the earth they tilled.
>
> They, too, or rather, their children and grandchildren, were to come in time to the parting of the ways when the choice would have to be made between either merging themselves in the mass standardization of a new civilization or adapting the best of the new to their own needs while still retaining those qualities and customs which have given country life its distinctive character. That choice may not even now have been determined.[12]

Twenty years later, in 1962, Ronald Blythe found the same hopes still living in Akenfield, and in the rest of the world that remained agricultural: "Deep in the nature of such men and elemental to their entire being is the internationalism of the planted earth which makes them, in common with the rice-harvesters of Vietnam or the winemakers of Burgundy, people who are committed to certain basic ideas and actions which progress and politics can elaborate or confuse, but can never alter."[13] This unity is not the passive bond of those trapped in the liberal urban intellectual's imagined version of the idiocy of rural life. It is a bond of earnest choice. "In spite of the sweet reasonableness or dire warnings offered by advocates of bigger units, Britain remains remarkably full of farmers going it alone, or who would go it alone if given half a chance."[14]

Still more recently, British Marxists E. P. Thompson and

Raymond Williams, American anarchist Murray Bookchin, and American Christian Wendell Berry have joined this radical tradition, defying the artificial boundaries of conventional politics in demanding that we save our souls and our bodies and our planet. This radicalism is truly a third road, neither that of the capitalistic state nor that of the imperialist states that call themselves socialist, neither that of business nor that of individual self-development. Raymond Williams picks up the radicalism of the nineteenth century, and the Marxism of William Morris and Kropotkin, when he declares that the image of idiotic rural life has been a destructive element in orthodox Marxism, and that now we need to rediscover one of Marx's neglected ideas—the mutually degrading contrast between the country and the city should be ultimately eliminated.[15]

Williams the twentieth-century Marxist is truly a spiritual son of nineteenth-century Romantic radicals from Wordsworth to Forster. Protesting against the false association that D. H. Lawrence has made between attachment to land and Fascism, an association in which later writers have believed, Williams says, "But as I have watched it settle into what is now a convention—in literary education especially—I have felt it as an outrage, in a continuing crisis and on a persistent border. The song of the land, the song of rural labour, the song of delight in the many forms of life with which we all share our physical world, is too important and too moving to be tamely given up, in an embittered betrayal, to the confident enemies of all significant and actual independence and renewal."[16]

Independence and renewal. These are the best words for the rural radical tradition; they are the deepest values of Wendell Berry, whose Christianity is surprisingly consonant with Williams's Marxism. Describing a well-run marginal farm that did not survive the death of the old man who owned it, he attacks the American agribusinessmen who men themselves conservatives but are in actuality close spiritual cousins of the imperialists whom Forster incarnated as the Wilcoxes.

What do such conservatives wish to conserve? Evidently nothing less than the great corporate blocks of wealth and power, in whose interest is implied the moral degeneracy and economic dependence of the people. They do not esteem the possibility of a prospering, independent class of small owners because they are, in fact, not conservative at all, but the most doctrinaire and disruptive of revolutionaries.

Nevertheless, the old man and his farm made a sort of cultural unit, recognized and valued in this country from colonial times. And it is still a perfectly respectable human possibility. All it requires is the proper humanity.[17]

Proper humanity rightly includes both men and women. But the twentieth-century agricultural radicals have not made the same special plea to women that the radical novelists of the nineteenth century did; women have been hearing another message, that the right choice is that of personal liberty and fulfillment, money, power, sex, art. Logically, it should not need to be stated that the human values that have endured from Wordsworth to Raymond Williams and Wendell Berry mean as much to women as they do to men. But historically, there has been a deadly separation between twentieth-century women and this radical tradition, one reason that the radical novels of the nineteenth century remain an irreplaceably valuable part of this tradition. They offer women heroic images of their own possible best selves, images that invite women to ally themselves with the agricultural world, and with the Romantic, radical tradition of resistance—resistance to the slavery of conformity, the slavery of economic uselessness, the slavery of subjection to an industrial and monopolistic and imperialistic economy.

The final terrible problem for both men and women, a problem nineteenth-century novels cannot address, is how to change the power at the top, power that still belongs to men, the men who own multinational companies and the men who control nuclear weapons. The economic and spiritual crises that writers like Hawthorne and Forster hoped would generate a new radical culture out of necessity, when the old culture began to create its own destruction, are occurring all around us, but the power of the state has remained unshaken in spite of the crises. Is it too absurd to hope that reason might prevail in spite of the clichés, clichés repeated until they start to sound like truth, about the impossibility of stopping progress, the inevitable march of the impersonal forces of history?

Once again, Wendell Berry and a Marxist, the historian William Appleman Williams, agree in their hope. Though most historical evidence supports the idea that empires are intransigent in clinging to their own destructive power, William Appleman Williams has recently reminded us of at least one contrary example—and one example is enough to destroy anything that claims the status of a scientific law. Williams recounts a little-known historical example of an empire that did abandon its own instruments of power—the Chinese Empire in the fifteenth century.

> The responsibilities of commanding such a fleet were equally awesome. Yongle chose Zheng He as his naval chief, a remarkable man who guided the great voyages during the years from 1405 to 1432. Each of them—there were seven in all—had some 300 ships with a combined crew of 27,000. It was the greatest assembly of intercontinental missiles in the history of the world. Clearly enough, had they chosen to do so, the Chinese could have established an empire from Shanghai to the Cape of Good Hope and beyond; but after a major debate among members of the ruling group of the Ming dynasty, that course was rejected. There is no reason to attribute their final decision solely to some special virtue or altruism. Bureaucratic intrigues and the diversion of resources to recapture lands in the north were also factors. Still, in those years there was a revival of idealistic Confucianism, which produced the argument articulated by one thinker of the time:

>> Arms are the instruments of evil which the sage does not use unless he must. The noble rulers and wise ministers of old did not dissipate the strength of the people by deeds of arms. . . . Your minister hopes that your majesty . . . would not indulge in military pursuits nor glorify the sending of expeditions to distant countries. Abandon the barren lands abroad and give the people of China a respite so that they could devote themselves to husbandry and to the schools.

> Emphasize those factors as you will, quantify them if you must, you cannot change the result: in 1433, during the Sung dynasty, the emperor ordered that his nation's great fleet of intercontinental missiles be broken up, burned, or otherwise destroyed. The shipbuilders' records were pulped to prevent others from reviving imperial dreams. And their workers and technicians were reassigned to domestic projects.[18]

Next to this cliché-shattering historical evidence, Wendell Berry's analysis of the wastefulness of the power scythe as an emblem of the wastefulness of heavily industrialized agriculture, and his plea that it could be abandoned, looks very small. But the basic nature of the reasoning is the same: history and power are not immutable exterior forces to which we are subject. The choice remains open, for men and for women, the choice of a different way, neither that of business and empire and machines nor that of narcissistic individualism. "The power scythe—and it is far from being an isolated or unusual example—is not a labor saver or a shortcut. It is a labor maker (you have to pay for it as well as use it) and a long cut.

Apologists for such expensive technological solutions love to say that 'you can't turn back the clock.' But when it makes perfect sense to do so—as when the clock is wrong, of *course* you can!"[19] No clock is preventing women from returning to, growing forward toward, the radical hopes offered in nineteenth-century novels.

Notes
and Index

Notes

Introduction

1. Karl Marx and Friedrich Engels, *Manifesto of the Communist Party*, in *Marx and Engels: Basic Writings on Politics and Philosophy*, ed. Lewis Feuer (New York: Anchor, 1959), 11.
2. Karl Marx, *Capital: A Critique of Political Economy* (New York: International Publishers, 1967), 715.
3. Marx, 724.
4. Marx, 719.
5. Marx, 728.
6. Fernand Braudel, *The Structures of Everyday Life: Civilization and Capitalism*, vol. 1 (New York: Harper and Row, 1979), 437.
7. Dorothy Hartley, *Lost Country Life* (New York: Pantheon, 1979), vii.
8. *The Complete Poems of Emily Dickinson*, ed. Thomas Johnson (Boston: Little, Brown, 1957).
9. Margaret Murray, *The God of the Witches* (New York: Oxford, 1952).
10. Pamela Berger, *The Goddess Obscured: Transformation of the Grain Protectress from Goddess to Saint* (Boston: Beacon, 1985).
11. Lydia Sargent, ed., *Women and Revolution: A Discussion of the Unhappy Marriage of Marxism and Feminism* (Boston: South End, 1981).
12. Adrienne Rich, "*Jane Eyre*: The Temptations of a Motherless Woman," in *Lies, Secrets, and Silence* (New York: Norton, 1979), 106.
13. Hélène Cixous, "The Laugh of the Medusa," in *The "Signs" Reader: Women, Gender, and Scholarship*, ed. Elizabeth Abel and Emily K. Abel (Chicago: University of Chicago Press, 1983), 293.
14. Sandra M. Gilbert and Susan Gubar, *The Madwoman in the Attic: The Woman Writer and the Nineteenth-Century Literary Imagination* (New Haven: Yale University Press, 1979), 71.
15. Nina Auerbach, *Woman and the Demon: The Life of a Victorian Myth* (Cambridge: Harvard University Press, 1982) 1.
16. Erna Hellerstein, Leslie Hume, and Karen Offen, eds., *Victorian Women: A Documentary Account of Women's Lives in Nineteenth*

Century England, France, and the United States (Stanford: Stanford University Press, 1981), 1.

17. Janet Horowitz Murray, ed., *Strong-Minded Women and Other Lost Voices from Nineteenth Century England* (New York: Pantheon, 1982), 4.

18. W. J. T. Mitchell, ed., *Against Theory: Literary Studies and the New Pragmatism* (Chicago: University of Chicago Press, 1985).

19. Michel Foucault, "What Is an Author," in *Textual Strategies: Perspectives in Post-Structuralist Criticism* (Ithaca: Cornell University Press, 1979), 141–61.

20. Roland Barthes, "From Work to Text," in *Textual Strategies*, 77.

21. Jacques Lacan, *The Four Fundamental Concepts of Psycho-Analysis* (New York: Norton, 1977), 207.

22. Catherine Belsey, *Critical Practice* (London: Methuen, 1980), 140.

23. Fredric Jameson, *The Political Unconscious: Narrative as a Socially Symbolic Act* (Ithaca: Cornell University Press, 1981).

24. Elaine Showalter, *A Literature of Their Own* (Princeton: Princeton University Press, 1979).

25. John Drakakis, ed., *Alternative Shakespeares* (London: Methuen, 1985), 25.

26. E. P. Thompson, *The Making of the English Working Class* (1963; reprint, New York: Vintage, 1966), 9.

27. Belsey, *Critical Practice*, 133.

28. Louis Althusser, *Reading Capital* (London: Verso, 1968), 58.

29. Henry Mayhew, *London Labour and the London Poor*, vol. 4 (reprint of 1861–62 ed; New York: Dover, 1968), 281–82.

30. Pierre-Jakez Helias, *The Horse of Pride: Life in a Breton Village* (New Haven: Yale University Press, 1978), 334.

31. Ronald Blythe, *Akenfield: Portrait of an English Village* (New York: Pantheon, 1969), 15.

32. Colin M. Turnbull, *The Forest People* (New York: Simon and Schuster, 1962), 3.

33. Turnbull, 278.

34. Colin M. Turnbull, *The Mountain People* (New York: Simon and Schuster, 1972), 285.

35. Sarah Blaffer Hrdy, *The Woman That Never Evolved* (Cambridge: Harvard University Press, 1982).

36. Philip Kitcher, *Vaulting Ambition: Sociobiology and the Quest for Human Nature* (Cambridge: MIT Press, 1985), 156.

Chapter 1. Romantic Poetry

The important books and articles on Romanticism are far too numerous to be listed here; I shall attempt only a brief acknowledgment and discussion of some of the most important. Before 1970 most critics agreed with Raymond Williams's statement in *Culture and Society, 1780–1950* (1958; reprint, New York: Columbia University Press, 1983): "Than the poets from Blake and Wordsworth to Shelley and Keats there have been few generations of creative writers more deeply interested and more involved in study and criticism of the society of their day" (30). Among the most serious and influential books addressed to the political radicalism of the English Romantics are Crane Brinton, *The Political Ideas of the English Romantics* (Ann Arbor: University of Michigan Press, 1966); Kenneth Neil Cameron, *Young Shelley: The Genesis of a Radical* (New York: Macmillan, 1950); David V. Erdman, *Blake: Prophet against Empire* (Princeton: Princeton University Press, 1969); and Carl Woodring, *Politics in English Romantic Poetry* (Cambridge: Harvard University Press, 1970). These critics and many others have written about the influence of the French Revolution on English Romantic poetry; Woodring has written most fully about the influence of the Enlightenment. I differ with these authors primarily in my belief that the defense of an agricultural economy is a viable form of political radicalism; Wordsworth's poem "Michael" has received surprisingly little critical attention as a poem about the destruction of an agricultural life.

Though the politics of Romantic poetry is my primary concern, I have also been influenced by the many books on the imaginative and aesthetic qualities of Romanticism as a movement. Among the best are Meyer Abrams, *The Mirror and the Lamp* (New York: Oxford University Press, 1953); idem, *Natural Supernaturalism* (New York: Norton, 1971); and idem, *English Romantic Poets: Modern Essays in Criticism* (New York: Oxford University Press, 1960), which contains seminal essays by Lovejoy, Wellek, Wimsatt, Frye, and others. Other indispensable books are Harold Bloom, *The Visionary Company* (New York: Doubleday, 1961); C. M. Bowra, *The Romantic Imagination* (Cambridge: Harvard University Press, 1949); Douglas Bush, *Mythology and the Romantic Tradition* (New York: Oxford University Press, 1937); and Albert Gerard, *English Romantic Poetry: Ethos, Structure, and Symbol in Wordsworth, Coleridge, Shelley, and Keats* (Berkeley: University of California Press, 1968). The most comprehensive book on the new emotional qualities in Romanticism is Mario Praz, *The Romantic Agony* (1951; reprint, New York: Oxford University Press, 1970). A particularly interesting book about the fragmentary quality of much Romantic art is Thomas McFarland, *Romanticism and the Forms of Ruin* (Princeton: Princeton University Press, 1981).

Since 1970 there has been a movement to deny the radicalism of English Romantic poetry. For example, Marilyn Butler argues, in *Romantics, Rebels, and Reactionaries: English Literature and Its Background* (New York: Oxford University Press, 1982), that most of Romanticism is neoclassic and conservative. Jerome McGann, in *The Romantic Ideology: A Critical Investigation* (Chicago: University of Chicago Press, 1983), says that the ideology of Romantic poetry is to be nonideological, and that its political meanings are therefore expressed only unconsciously. Another redefinition of Romantic politics is Heather Glen, *Vision and Disenchantment: Blake's Songs and Wordsworth's Lyrical Ballads* (Cambridge: Cambridge University Press, 1983), which argues that infantile experiences must form the basis of a socialist vision; she looks to emotion rather than economics for political meaning. Both Butler and Glen provide detailed and extremely useful studies of the popular literature on which Romantic poets drew. Another recent book that maintains Wordsworth was reactionary is Donald Stone, *The Romantic Impulse in Victorian Fiction* (Cambridge: Harvard University Press, 1980). Stone sees Byron as the source of the continuing radicalism of Victorian literature, and Wordsworth as the source of Victorian repressiveness.

I have used *The Poetical Works of Wordsworth* (Boston: Houghton, Mifflin, 1982). All references to the poems are included in the text. Among the recent and interesting books specifically on Wordsworth are Geoffrey Hartmann, *Wordsworth's Poetry, 1787–1814* (New Haven: Yale University Press, 1964); and Michael H. Friedman, *The Making of a Tory Humanist: Wordsworth and the Idea of Community* (New York: Columbia University Press, 1979).

All references to Shelley's poems, included in the text, come from *Shelley: Poetical Works* (Oxford: Oxford University Press, 1975). Some useful books are Kenneth Neil Cameron, *Young Shelley: The Genesis of a Radical* (New York: Macmillan, 1950); idem, *Shelley: The Golden Years* (Cambridge: Harvard University Press, 1974); Nathaniel Brown, *Sexuality and Feminism in Shelley* (Cambridge: Harvard University Press, 1975); and Earl Wasserman, *Shelley: A Critical Reading* (Baltimore: Johns Hopkins University Press, 1971).

1. The angry reviews that greeted the publication of *The Lyrical Ballads* are quoted and discussed by Hunter Davies in *William Wordsworth: A Biography* (New York: Atheneum, 1980), 101–2.
2. E. P. Thompson, *The Making of the English Working Class* (1963; reprint New York: Vintage, 1966), 198.
3. Thompson, 405.
4. E. J. Hobsbawm, *Industry and Empire* (reprint, Harmondsworth: Penguin, 1969), 38.
5. Carl Woodring, *Politics in English Romantic Poetry* (Cambridge: Harvard University Press, 1970), 93.
6. Thompson, *Making of the English Working Class*, 219.
7. Raymond Williams, *The Country and the City* (New York: Oxford University Press, 1973), 84.
8. Ronald Blythe, *Akenfield: Portrait of an English Village* (New York: Pantheon, 1969), 218.
9. James Herriot, *All Things Bright and Beautiful* (1974; reprint, New York: Bantam, 1975), 388.
10. Thompson, *Making of the English Working Class*, 198–99.
11. Thompson, 343.
12. Thompson, 232–33.
13. Thompson, 212.
14. Among other books on the influence of Romantic poetry on the nineteenth-century novel, the most important are Robert Kiely, *The Romantic Novel in England* (Cambridge: Harvard University Press, 1972); John Spiers, *Poetry towards Novel* (New York: New York University Press, 1971); and Donald Stone, *The Romantic Impulse in Victorian Fiction* (Cambridge: Harvard University Press, 1980). None of these books is about the political radicalism of Romanticism, but Louis Camazian, in *The Social Novel in England, 1830–1850,* (London: Routledge and Kegan Paul, 1973) attributes the humane vision of Dickens, Gaskell, Kingsley, and Disraeli to Romanticism.
15. Pierre-Jakez Helias, *The Horse of Pride: Life in a Breton Village* (New Haven: Yale University Press, 1978), 330.

Chapter 2. Jane Austen

The amount of published criticism on Jane Austen is voluminous. The single most prevalent assumption in most criticism, and the assumption with which I disagree, is that her novels are all part of a single unified picture of the world—a pleasant and genteel world. This assumption has been almost unquestioned, from 1930 to the present. Some of the preeminent scholars who read Austen as a philosophical whole are Marilyn Butler, *Jane Austen and the War of Ideas* (London: Oxford University Press, 1975); W. A. Craik, *Jane Austen: The Six Novels* (New York: Barnes and Noble, 1965); Barbara Hardy, *A Reading of Jane Austen* (New York: New York University Press, 1976); Sandra Gilbert and Susan Gubar, *The Madwoman in the Attic: The Woman Writer and the Nineteenth-Century Literary Imagination* (New Haven: Yale University Press, 1979); Mary Lascelles, *Jane Austen and Her Art* (Oxford: Clarendon Press, 1939); George Levine, *The Realistic Imagination: English Fiction from Frankenstein to Lady Chatterly* (Chicago: University of Chicago Press, 1981); Lawrence Lerner, *The Truthtellers* (London: Chatto and Windus, 1967); A. Walton Litz, *Jane Austen: A Study of Her Artistic Development* (New York: Oxford University Press, 1965); David Monaghan, *Jane Austen: Structure and Social Vision* (New York: Barnes and Noble, 1980); Marvin Mudrick, *Jane Austen: Irony as Defense and Discovery* (Princeton: Princeton University Press, 1952); Mary Poovey, *The Proper Lady and the Woman Writer: Ideology as Style in the Works of Mary Wollstonecraft, Mary Shelley, and Jane Austen* (Chicago: University of Chicago Press, 1984); Elaine Showalter, *A Literature of Their Own: British Women Novelists from Brontë to Lessing* (Princeton: Princeton University Press, 1977); Patricia Meyer Spacks, *The Female Imagination* (1972; reprint, New York: Avon, 1976); Janet M. Todd, *Women's Friendship in Literature* (New York: Columbia University Press, 1980); Stuart M. Tave, *Some Words of Jane Austen* (Chicago: University of Chicago Press, 1973); and Andrew Wright *Jane Austen's Novels: A Study in Structure* (New York: Oxford University Press, 1961).

The most important critics who have challenged this view of Austen are Lionel Trilling, who discusses the deep philosophical difference between *Mansfield Park* and Austen's other novels, "Mansfield Park," in *The Opposing Self* (New York: Viking, 1955); and Darrell Mansell, in *The Novels of Jane Austen: An Interpretation* (London: Macmillan, 1973). My own essay "Evil and Blunders: Human Nature in *Mansfield Park* and *Emma*" appeared in *Women and Literature*, vol. 4, no. 1: 5–17.

Austen has not fared well among the feminist critics of the last fifteen years. The feminist attack has, in general, repeated Charlotte Brontë's statement in a letter to W. S. Williams, "Jane Austen was a complete and most sensible lady, but a very incomplete and rather insensible (not senseless) woman," in David Lodge, ed., *Emma: A Casebook* (London: Macmillan, 1969). Spacks deprecates Austen because her heroines must win husbands; Showalter, who believes that the preferable literary model is George Sand, implicitly blames Austen because male critics have recommended her to women readers and writers. Todd says that her heroines are cruel to other women, Gilbert and Gubar that she advocates duplicity to her women readers.

The most forceful answer to the objection of female critics that Austen is a trivial writer has been given by Raymond Williams in *The Country and the City* (New York: Oxford University Press, 1973): "Where, it is still asked, are the Napoleonic wars, the real current of history? But history has many currents and the social history of the landed families at that time was among the most important" (113). One critic who has taken Austen most seriously in recent years is Marilyn Butler, who provides an extremely intelligent and thorough discussion of the sentimental and sentimentally radical novels Austen intellectually opposed.

The three novels on which I concentrate, *Mansfield Park, Emma*, and *Persuasion*, have received considerable critical attention. Trilling still stands virtually alone in defending *Mansfield Park* as a book worth taking seriously. Other critics have commented on its difference from Austen's other works, but have called the difference inferiority and have attributed it to tone instead of to a considered philosophical stance. The heroine, Fanny Price, has been particularly difficult for male or female critics to like. Mary Lascelles, Mary Poovey, and Janet Todd have called her so passive that one cannot possibly respect her moral insights. The Crawfords, whose intelligence and liveliness captivate everyone at Mansfield Park except Fanny, have won the majority of the critics; Laurence Lerner and Marvin Mudrick are particularly warm in their defense. The most cogent discussions of the Crawfords as representatives of a historically new economic threat are those of Marilyn Butler, in *Jane Austen and the War of Ideas*, and Warren Roberts, in *Jane Austen and the French Revolution* (New York: St. Martins, 1979).

Though *Emma* has won more praise than *Mansfield Park*, its heroine, too, has been severely criticized. Marvin Mudrick calls her an exploiter; Janet Todd suggests that Austen should have developed the friendship between Emma and Jane Fairfax; Marilyn Butler emphasizes the punishment she must suffer. Many critics have discussed the sexual repression that leads to Emma's interest in Harriet Smith; one of the earliest and most forceful essays is Edmund Wilson's "A Long Talk about Jane Austen," in *Classics and Commercials: A Literary Chronicle of the Forties* (New York: Farror, Straus and Cudahy, 1950). Few critics have emphasized the care with which Austen shows Emma's capacity to heal herself.

The evidence of political radicalism in *Emma* has also gone largely unnoticed. Trilling implicitly lessens the political urgency of the book by calling it an idyll, in "*Emma* and the Legend of Jane Austen," reprinted in *Emma: A Casebook*. The one critic who has noticed the central importance and political meaning of Robert Martin is Ellen Moers, who points out that Mr. Knightley is an active farmer himself and teaches Emma to respect those who take care of the land; cf. *Literary Women: The Great Writers* (1963; reprint, New York: Anchor, 1977). Darrell Mansell and Marilyn Butler also acknowledge that Emma must learn to appreciate the class of farmers but neither makes clear enough that, in a reactionary time, it was a radical act to defend the moral economy of agriculture.

Persuasion has also generated critical disagreement. Stuart Tave has read Anne sensitively and warmly; Poovey and Gilbert and Gubar have called her isolated, alienated, and weak. Among the most thorough treatments of the decay of the gentry in *Persuasion* are those of David Monaghan and Mary Poovey. I believe, however, that these critics miss the sorrow with which Austen says good-bye to the older social world.

I have used the edition of R. W. Chapman (New York: Oxford, 1923) for all three novels, and have cited chapters, rather than pages, in the text for the convenience of readers who have other editions.

1. E. P. Thompson, *The Making of the English Working Class* (reprint New York: Vintage, 1966), 177.
2. E. J. Hobsbawm, *Industry and Empire* (reprint Harmondsworth: Penguin, 1969), 52. Warren Roberts, in *Jane Austen and the French Revolution*, speculates that Sir Thomas left in 1805 and came back in 1807, when Napoleon was blockading the West Indies and when a drop in sugar prices was causing local governments to declare bankruptcy.
3. Lawrence Stone, *The Family, Sex and Marriage in England, 1500–1800* (reprint, abridged New York: Harper and Row, 1979), 250.
4. Hobsbawm, *Industry and Empire*, 50.
5. Stone, *Family, Sex and Marriage*, 168.
6. Stone, 277.
7. Hobsbawm, *Industry and Empire*, 23–24.
8. Thompson, *Making of the English Working Class*, 67.
9. G. M. Trevelyan, *English Social History: A Survey of Six Centuries, Chaucer to Queen Victoria* (New York: David McKay, 1942), 488–89.

Chapter 3. Charlotte and Emily Brontë

In the last fifteen years, critical opinion on Charlotte and Emily Brontë has been sharply divided in several ways: Charlotte Brontë has been in the ascendancy among women but not among men, and Emily Brontë has been almost dismissed by women and often misread by men. Evidence of feminists' warm admiration of Charlotte Brontë, and of *Jane Eyre* especially, can be found in both literary and historical scholarship. Sandra Gilbert and Susan Gubar, authors of one of the most influential feminist readings of nineteenth-century fiction, have made Charlotte Brontë into a virtual paradigm of the nineteenth-century woman writer. Their book *The Madwoman in the Attic: The Woman Writer and the Nineteenth-Century Literary Imagination* (New Haven: Yale University Press, 1979) describes the relationship between Charlotte Brontë, the literary creator, and Bertha Rochester, her ostensible villain, as the model for all other female writers and female characters. Adrienne Rich's important essay "*Jane Eyre*: The Temptations of a Motherless Woman," in *On Lies, Secrets, and Silence*, has also played a major role in elevating Charlotte Brontë (1972; reprint, New York: Norton, 1979). Charlotte Brontë, without her sister, appears as the author of feminist documents in at least three prestigious anthologies of historical writing: Janet Horowitz Murray, *Strong-Minded Women and Other Lost Voices from Nineteenth-Century England* (New York: Pantheon, 1982); Susan Bell and Karen Offen, *Women, the Family, and Freedom: The Debate in Documents*, vol. 1 (Stanford: Stanford University Press, 1983); and Erna Hellerstein, Leslie Hume, and Karen Offen, *Victorian Women: A Documentary Account of Women's Lives in Nineteenth-Century England, France and the United States* (Stanford: Stanford University Press, 1981).

Male critics, on the other hand, have continued to be quite harsh to *Jane Eyre*. Terry Eagleton, the warmest supporter of Emily Brontë in recent years, has written extensively and eloquently about the severe limitations of Charlotte Brontë's Romanticism, in *Myths of Power: A Marxist Study of the Brontës* (London: Macmillan, 1975). Other male critics have also remarked on what most feminist critics appear not to see; for example, Charles Burkhart, in *Charlotte Brontë: A Psychosexual Study* (London: Victor Gollancz, 1973), says she flirts with the sado-masochistic. Both Terry Eagleton, in *Myths of Power*, and Donald Stone, in *The Romantic Impulse in Victorian Fiction* (Cambridge: Harvard University Press, 1980), have discussed Rochester as a Byronic hero. Women, on the other hand, have tended to idealize the relationship between Jane and Rochester. Gilbert and Gubar, in *The Madwoman in the Attic*, call it an equal and ideal marriage; Showalter, in *A Literature of Their Own* (Princeton: Princeton University Press, 1977), virtually justifies Rochester's blindness by saying that this enables him to find out what it is like to be a woman (152).

Male and female critics also differ on the importance of Charlotte Brontë's Christianity in *Jane Eyre*. Male critics such as Burkhart have pointed out that the Victorian audience liked both Helen Burns and St. John Rivers, the most clearly Christian characters in *Jane Eyre*; female critics such as Rich and Showalter have tended to emphasize Jane Eyre's psychological strength more than her Christian orthodoxy.

Feminist critics, on the other hand, have not liked *Wuthering Heights*, Emily Brontë's one novel. Patricia Meyer Spacks, in *The Female Imagination*, (1972; reprint, New York: Avon, 1976), calls it a book about adolescence; Ellen Moers, in *Literary Women: The Great Writers* (1963; reprint, New York: Anchor, 1977), says that "in *Wuthering Heights* these female 'eccentricities' must be called a stronger name: perversities" (153). The most sympathetic critic of Wuthering Heights has been Terry Eagleton, in *Myths of Power*.

The sheer intellectual difficulty of *Wuthering Heights* has led to many critical misinterpretations. Critics who mistakenly see Heathcliff as a straightforwardly Byronic character include Derek Sanford, in *Emily Bronte: Her Life and Work* (London: Peter Owen, 1960), and John Hewish, in *Emily Bronte: A Critical and Biographical Study* (London: Macmillan, 1969). The role of the narrators was a subject of critical discussion in the 1960s; one of the most effective studies is Inga-Stina Ewbank, *Their Proper Sphere: A Study of the Brontë Sisters as Early Victorian Novelists* (Cambridge: Harvard University Press, 1966). Both Ewbank and John Hewish have, however, mistaken Nelly Dean's satanic imagery for that of the author and have, therefore, misread Emily Brontë as another Blake. In *Laughter and Despair* (Berkeley: University of California Press, 1971) U. C. Knoepflmacher conflates Emily Brontë and Blake by calling the heroine's destruction a fall from innocence to experience. *Wuthering Heights* remains one of the most difficult and misread of nineteenth-century novels.

I have used *Jane Eyre* (Harmondsworth: Penguin, 1966) and *Wuthering Heights* (New York: Norton, 1972). For the convenience of readers I have included references to chapters, rather than to pages, within the text.

1. Thorough accounts of the contemporary reactions to the novels of the Brontës are Gilbert and Gubar, *The Madwoman in the Attic: The Woman Writer and the Nineteenth-Century Literary Imagination* (New Haven: Yale University Press, 1979); Muriel Spark and Derek Sanford, *Emily Brontë: Her Life and Work* (London: Peter Own, 1960); and Judith O'Neill, ed., *Critics on Charlotte and Emily Bronte* (London: Allen and Unwin, 1968).

2. Quoted in Winifred Gerin, *Emily Brontë: A Biography* (London: Oxford University Press, 1978), 229.
3. Spark and Sanford, *Emily Brontë*, 145.
4. Eagleton, *Myths of Power*, 8.
5. Eagleton, 3.
6. Winifred Gerin, *Charlotte Brontë: The Evolution of Genius* (reprint, Oxford: Clarendon Press, 1968), 29–30.
7. The fullest history of the Dissenting tradition in Haworth is that of Valentine Cunningham, *Everywhere Spoken Against: Dissent in the Victorian Novel* (Oxford: Clarendon Press, 1975).
8. Gerin, in *Charlotte Brontë*, has discussed the influence of Aunt Branwell.
9. E. P. Thompson, *The Making of the English Working Class* (1963; reprint, New York: Vintage, 1966), 374.
10. Thompson, 370–71.
11. The best study of this connection between love and religion is that of Steven Mintz, *A Prison of Expectations: The Family in Victorian Culture* (New York: New York University Press, 1983).
12. Thompson, *Making of the English Working Class*, 206–7.
13. E. J. Hobsbawm, *Industry and Empire* (reprint, Harmondsworth: Penguin, 1969), 105.
14. Lady Eastlake, under the name E. Rigby, *Quarterly Review* 84 (1848), quoted in O'Neill, *Critics on Charlotte and Emily Brontë*, 49.
15. Thompson, *Making of the English Working Class*, 219.
16. Pierre-Jakez Helias, *The Horse of Pride: Life in a Breton Village* (New Haven: Yale University Press, 1978), 334.
17. Gerin, *Emily Brontë*, 95, 117.
18. Gerin, 35.
19. Gerin, 125.
20. Gerin, 35.
21. Gerin, 55.

Chapter 4. Nathaniel Hawthorne

Because both nineteenth-century American literature and the criticism of that literature have been dominated by men, Hawthorne's feminism has been neglected. Among the major works on Hawthorne that skirt his radical feminism are Richard H. Brodehead, *Hawthorne, Melville, and the Novel* (Chicago: University of Chicago Press, 2nd ed. 1976); Edgar A. Dryden, *Nathaniel Hawthorne: The Poetics of Enchantment* (Ithaca: Cornell University Press, 1977); Charles Fiedelson, *Symbolism and American Literature* (Chicago: University of Chicago Press, 1953); Richard Hunter Fogle, *Hawthorne's Fiction: The Light and the Dark* (Norman: University of Oklahoma Press, 1952, 1964); Edwin Fussell, *Frontier: American Literature and the American West* (Princeton University Press, 1965); Michael Davitt Bell, *Hawthorne and the Historical Romance of New England* (Princeton: Princeton University Press, 1971); Harry Levin, *The Power of Blackness: Hawthorne, Poe, Melville* (New York: Knopf, 1958); F. O. Matthiessen, *American Renaissance: Art and Expression in the Age of Emerson and Whitman* (1941; reprint, New York: Oxford University Press, 1968); Hyatt Waggoner, *Hawthorne: A Critical Study* (Cambridge: Belknap Press of Harvard University Press, 1955).

Taylor Stoehr devotes a chapter of *Hawthorne's Mad Scientists: Pseudoscience and Social Science in Nineteenth Century Life and Letters* (Hamden: Archon, 1978) to Hawthorne's feminism, but he discusses only Zenobia in *The Blithedale Romance* as a representative of the nineteenth-century cult of free love. One of the few feminist writers to mention Hawthorne is Nina Auerbach; in *Woman and the Demon* (Cambridge: Harvard University Press, 1982) she calls Hester Prynne a woman with "self-created potency" (165). Other recent books, such as Gloria Erlich, *Family Themes and Hawthorne's Fiction: The Tenacious Web* (New Brunswick: Rutgers University Press, 1984); and A. G. Lloyd Smith, *Eve Tempted: Writing and Sexuality in Hawthorne's Fiction* (New York: Barnes and Noble, 1984), treat women as sexual beings but not as political forces. An excellent history of women in American life in the mid-nineteenth century is Susan B. Conrad, *Perish the Thought: Intellectual Women in Romantic America, 1830–1860* (New York: Oxford University Press, 1976).

I have used *Nathaniel Hawthorne: Selected Tales and Sketches* (New York: Holt, Rinehart and Winston, 1967) and *The House of the Seven Gables* (New York: Norton, 1967) and have included chapter references within the text.

1. F. O. Matthiessen provides the best account of Hawthorne's wafflings over slavery and over Franklin Pierce's conservative politics, in *American Renaissance: Art and Expression in the Age of Emerson and Whitman* (1941; reprint, New York: Oxford University Press, 1968), 316–32.
2. Alexis de Tocqueville, "How the Americans Understand the Equality of the Sexes," in *Democracy in America*, vol. 2 (New York: Knopf, 1945), bk., 3, chap. 12.
3. Margaret Fuller claims that "the electrical, the magnetic element in Woman has not been fairly brought out at any period," in *Woman in the Nineteenth Century* (New York: Norton, 1971), 103.
4. John Stuart Mill, "On Liberty," in *Three Essays* (New York: Oxford University Press, 1975), 85.
5. Kirkpatrick Sale, *Human Scale* (New York: Putnam, 1980), 392.

Chapter 5. Mary Shelley

The recent trend in criticism by both men and women has been to re-read the reactionary qualities out of Mary Shelley's *Frankenstein*. The enduring power of the story has kept the book alive as a topic for criticism, even though most critics now have ideological objections to the book's political message. For example, George Levine, in *The Realistic Imagination* (Chicago: University of Chicago Press, 1981), says that *Frankenstein* "dramatizes the perversion in myths of male creativity and female dependence" (26). Kate Ellis, in "Monsters in the Garden, Mary Shelley and the Bourgeois Family," in *The Endurance of Frankenstein: Essays on Mary Shelley's Novel*, ed. George Levine and U. C. Knoepflmacher (Berkeley: University of California Press, 1979), calls the book a critique of the bourgeois family (123–42). Both Gilbert and Gubar, in *The Madwoman in the Attic*, and Mary Poovey, in *The Proper Lady and the Woman Writer: Ideology as Style in the Works of Mary Wollstonecraft, Mary Shelley, and Jane Austen* (Chicago: University of Chicago Press, 1984), read the book so metaphorically that the sex of both the monster and his creator are changed, so that *Frankenstein* becomes a parable about the victimization of women.

Excellent work has been done on the relationship between Mary Shelley's difficult life with Shelley and her horror story. In *Ariel Like a Harpy: Shelley, Mary, and Frankenstein* (London: Oxford University Press, 1972), Christopher Small has meticulously traced the similarities between Shelley and Victor Frankenstein (60–120). Peter Dale Scott has explored the implied sexual relationship between the Shelleys, in "Vital Artifice: Mary, Percy, and the Psychopolitical Integrity of Frankenstein," in *The Endurance of Frankenstein*, 172–202. Ellen Moers has written on women's horror of birth, in "Female Gothic," in *The Endurance of Frankenstein*; U. C. Knoepflmacher has written a persuasive essay on the possible influence of Mary Shelley's experience as Godwin's daughter on her fiction, in "Thoughts on the Aggression of Daughters," in *The Endurance of Frankenstein*, 88–119.

The relationship between Shelley's "Prometheus Unbound" and Mary Shelley's modern Prometheus has also received intelligent and exhaustive critical attention. Three of the best analyses of Shelley's poem are those of Gerald McNiece, *Shelley and the Revolutionary Idea* (Cambridge: Harvard University Press, 1969); Carl Woodring, *Politics in English Romantic Poetry* (Cambridge: Harvard University Press, 1970), 278–310; and Earl Wasserman, *Shelley's Prometheus Unbound* (Baltimore: Johns Hopkins University Press, 1965). A good essay on the two readings of the Prometheus myth is George Levine, "The Ambiguous Heritage of Frankenstein," in *The Endurance of Frankenstein*.

I have used *Frankenstein, or, The Modern Prometheus* (London: Oxford University Press, 1969); this is the 1831 edition, the one most readily available. I have cited chapters within the text.

1. Marilyn Butler provides useful surveys of the literary reactions to Romantic radicalism, in both *Jane Austen and the War of Ideas* (London: Oxford University Press, 1975) and *Romantics, Rebels, and Reactionaries* (New York: Oxford University Press, 1982). In "Mary Shelley's Monster: Politics and Psyche in Frankenstein," in *The Endurance of Frankenstein*, 143–72, Lee Sterrenburg also reviews the reactionary politics of the time.

2. *The Letters of Mary Wollstonecraft Shelley* (Baltimore: Johns Hopkins University Press, 1980), 252.

3. Thomas Jefferson Hogg, *The Life of P. B. Shelley* (London: 1858), vol. 1, chap. 2.

4. Small, *Ariel Like a Harpy*, 43.

5. Hogg, *Life of P. B. Shelley*, vol. 1, chap. 3.

6. E. P. Thompson, *The Making of the English Working Class* (1963; reprint, New York: Vintage, 1966), 98–99.

Chapter 6. William Makepeace Thackeray and Charles Dickens

Thackeray and Dickens, like the Romantic poets, have received more critical attention than can be adequately acknowledged. Three of the most important critics of Victorian fiction who have written on both are George Levine, in *The Realistic Imagination* (Chicago: University of Chicago Press, 1981); U. C. Knoepflmacher, in *Laughter and Despair: Readings in Ten*

Novels of the Victorian Era (Berkeley: University of California Press, 1971); and Barbara Hardy, in *The Exposure of Luxury: Radical Themes in Thackeray* (Pittsburgh: University of Pittsburgh Press, 1972), and in *The Moral Art of Dickens* (London: Oxford University Press, 1970). Of the three, Hardy is the most sensitive to Thackeray's radicalism, the least inclined to emphasize his worldliness and cynicism. Donald Stone, in *The Romantic Impulse in Victorian Fiction* (Cambridge: Harvard University Press, 1980), has carefully surveyed the parodies of Romanticism in both Dickens and Thackeray.

The heroines of both Dickens and Thackeray have created problems for many critics. Except U. C. Knoepflmacher, most critics have preferred Becky Sharp to Amelia Sedley in *Vanity Fair*, for the same reasons most have preferred Mary Crawford to Fanny Price in *Mansfield Park*: vitality seems easier to like than passive goodness. Some feminist critics have re-read the angelic heroines so as to make them secretly subversive. For example, Nina Auerbach, in *Woman and the Demon* (Cambridge: Harvard University Press, 1982), says, "The most potent angels of Dickens and Thackeray, Victorian England's two most influential novelists, stand alone. In the alacrity with which they abandon or transcend all houses, they take strength from an older angelology, which the Victorian age feminized but could never quite enclose" (83). Richard Barickman, Susan McDonald, and Myra Stark, the authors of *Corrupt Relations: Dickens, Thackeray, Trollope, Collins and the Victorian Sexual System* (New York: Columbia University Press, 1982), read the angelic heroines as the victims of an eternal patriarchy, rather than as the products of specific economic and social conditions.

The cruelty of Paul Dombey, Dickens's Victorian capitalist, has been hard for many critics to acknowledge fully. In *Dickens: From Pickwick to Dombey* (New York: Basic Books, 1965) Steven Marcus says that Dombey is a victim of "the death of feeling" (338); Fred Schwartzbach claims that Dombey's true error is rejecting the railway as the key to the economic future, in *Dickens and the City* (London: University of London Press, 1979). Arthur A. Adrian has written incisively about child labor, child abuse, and religious ideology, in *Dickens and the Parent-Child Relationship* (Athens: University of Ohio Press, 1984), but still insists that Dombey is not really a bad man (105).

I have used *Vanity Fair* (New York: Modern Library, 1950) and *Dombey and Son* (New York: New American Library, 1964) and have included chapter references in the text. The one quotation from *Pendennis* is from an undated edition (London: Thomas Nelson).

1. E. J. Hobsbawm, *Industry and Empire* (reprint, Harmondsworth: Penguin, 1969), 84.
2. Walter E. Houghton, *The Victorian Frame of Mind* (New Haven: Yale University Press), 191.
3. Houghton, 343–44.
4. Houghton, 352.
5. The topic of Victorian psychiatry has been explored in an excellent collection of essays, Andrew Scull, ed., *Madhouses, Mad-Doctors, and Madmen: The Social History of Psychiatry in the Victorian Era* (Philadelphia: University of Pennsylvania Press, 1981). In "Rejections of Psychological Approaches," Michael T. Clark says that Victorian

psychiatrists considered hysteria bad because it was individualistic and unsociable (294).

6. Barbara Sickerman, "The Paradox of Prudence," in *Madhouses, Mad-Doctors, and Madmen,* points out the inconsistency of Victorian attitudes toward self-control; though self-control was desirable for both men and women, women were not educated in a way that encouraged rationality (223).

7. Elaine Showalter, "Victorian Women and Insanity," in *Madhouses, Mad-Doctors, and Madmen,* 321–22.

8. Showalter, 318.

9. Michel Foucault, *Madness and Civilization: A History of Insanity in the Age of Reason* (New York: Random House, 1965).

10. Raymond Williams, *The Country and the City* (New York: Oxford University Press, 1973), 98.

11. Peter Gay, *The Bourgeois Experience: Education of the Senses* (New York: Oxford University Press, 1984), 644.

12. E. P. Thompson, *The Making of the English Working Class* (1963; reprint, New York: Vintage, 1966), 831.

13. Houghton, *Victorian Frame of Mind,* 79.

Chapter 7. George Eliot

The literature on George Eliot's Romanticism is extensive. The single most ambitious survey of Eliot's debt to Romanticism is Donald Stone, *The Romantic Impulse in Victorian Fiction* (Cambridge: Harvard University Press, 1980); he writes in detail about Eliot's knowledge of Rousseau, the German Romantics, Hegel, Feurbach, Wordsworth, and Shelley. He, however, attributes Victorian conservatism to Wordsworth and a sense of daring to Shelley and Byron. Other general comparisons of Eliot and Wordsworth are those of Humphrey House, in *All in Due Time* (London: Rupert Art-Davis, 1955), 109–15, and U. C. Knoepflmacher, in *George Eliot's Early Novels* (Berkeley: University of California Press, 1968), 14–24. K. M. Newton, in *George Eliot: Romantic Humanist, A Study of the Philosophical Structure of Her Novels* (New York: Barnes and Noble, 1981), argues that Eliot is philosophically Romantic because she is antimetaphysical. Both Stone (235–38) and Newton (135–39) are very good on Will Ladislaw as Eliot's embodiment of Romantic philosophy. Eliot's link between German Romanticism and Judaism is studied most fully in William Baker, *George Eliot and Judaism* (Salzburg: Salzburg Studies in English Literature, 1975).

The most useful book on Eliot's political theories and her debt to contemporary political theory is Suzanne Graver, *George Eliot and Community: A Study in Social Theory and Fictional Form* (Berkeley: University of California Press, 1984). She carefully illuminates Eliot's personal ambivalence toward "The Woman Question" (181–82), one of the social problems that haunts Eliot's fiction. Other critics who have written about the place of women in Eliot's social theories are Ellen Moers, in *Literary Women: The Great Writers* (1963; reprint, New York: Anchor, 1977), and Gilbert and Gubar, in *The Madwoman in the Attic: The Woman Writer and the Nineteenth-Century Literary Imagination.* A sympathetic study of Eliot's life, which necessarily deals with Eliot's difficulties with women, is Ruby V. Redinger, *George Eliot: The Emergent Self* (New York: Knopf, 1975).

There has been surprisingly little criticism on Eliot's historical theory. Many critics have written about Eliot's novels as virtually timeless tragedies, among them, Felicia Bonaparte, *Will and Destiny: Morality and Tragedy in George Eliot's Novels* (New York: New York University Press, 1975); Barbara Hardy, *The Novels of George Eliot: A Study in Form* (New York: Oxford University Press, 1959, 1963); and Jerome Thale, *The Novels of George Eliot* (New York: Columbia University Press, 1959). Many of the male agents of historical change are allied with Evangelical religion in Eliot's fiction; the best book on Eliot's sympathy with Evangelican religion, a sympathy rare among English novelists, is Valentine Cunningham, *Everywhere Spoken Against: Dissent in the Victorian Novel* (Oxford: Clarendon Press, 1975).

Most critics have treated the scientific and highly intellectual narrative voice of *Middlemarch* with great respect. Both George Levine, in *The Realistic Imagination* (Chicago: University of Chicago Press, 1981), and U. C. Knoepflmacher, in *Laughter and Despair* (Berkeley: University of California Press, 1971), praise this voice highly. The most decisive reservations are expressed by Eliot's most radical critic, Raymond Williams, who says, in *The Country and the City* (New York: Oxford University Press, 1973), "There is a new kind of break in the texture of the novel, an evident failure of continuity between the necessary language of the novelist and the recorded language of many of the characters" (169).

I have used *The Mill on the Floss* (New York: New American Library, 1965), *Daniel Deronda* (Harmondsworth: Penguin, 1967), and *Middlemarch* (Boston: Houghton Mifflin, 1968), and have included chapter references in the text.

1. E. P. Thompson, *The Making of the English Working Class* (1963; reprint, New York: Vintage, 1966), 549.
2. Thompson, 408.
3. G. M. Trevelyan, *English Social History: A Survey of Six Centuries, Chaucer to Queen Victoria* (New York: David McKay, 1942), 540.
4. Thompson, *Making of the English Working Class*, 416.
5. Thompson, 345–46.
6. Thompson, 354–55.
7. Thompson, 725.

Chapter 8. Bram Stoker

The critical literature on *Dracula* is much scantier than on most Victorian novels, but there is a body of literature on the group of novels that reflect or comment upon the New Woman movement of the late nineteenth century. Three of the most thorough are Gail Cunningham, *The New Woman and the Victorian Novel* (New York: Barnes and Noble, 1978); Lloyd Fernando, *"New Women" in the Late Victorian Novel* (University Park: Pennsylvania State University Press, 1977); and Patricia Stubbs, *Women and Fiction: Feminism and the Novel, 1880–1920* (Sussex: Harvester, 1979).

The two most effective discussions of Dracula as a demonic figure are those of Mario Praz, in *The Romantic Agony* (1951; reprint, New York: Oxford University Press, 1970), and Nina Auerbach, in *Woman and the Demon* (Cambridge: Harvard University Press, 1982).

I have used *Dracula* (New York: New American Library, 1965) and have included chapter and date references in the text.

1. E. J. Hobsbawm, *Industry and Empire* (reprint, Harmondsworth, Penguin, 1969), 165.
2. James W. Hulse, *Revolutionists in London: A Study of Five Unorthodox Socialists* (Oxford: Clarendon Press, 1970), 2.
3. Hulse, 4.
4. *Karl Marx–Friedrich Engels: Selected Letters*, ed. Fritz J. Raddatz, (Boston: Little, Brown, 1980), 31.
5. Felix Dubois, *The Anarchist Peril*, trans. and enlarged by Ralph Derechef (London: T. Fisher Unwin, 1894), 11.
6. Dubois, 283.
7. Dubois, 83.
8. Ibid.
9. Richard J. Evans, *The Feminists: Women's Emancipation Movements in Europe, America, and Australasia, 1840–1920* (New York: Barnes and Noble, 1979), 68.
10. Quoted in Susan Bell and Karen Offen, eds., *Women, the Family, and Freedom: The Debate in Documents*, vol. 2 (Stanford: Stanford University Press, 1983), 208.
11. Elaine Showalter discusses Brown's case in "Victorian Women and Insanity," in *Madhouses, Mad-Doctors, and Madmen*, ed. Andrew Scull (Philadelphia: University of Pennsylvania Press, 1981), 327–28.
12. Showalter, 328.
13. Thomas Carlyle, *On Heroes, Hero-Worship and the Heroic in History* (reprint, London: Dent, 1965), 239.
14. Carlyle, 253.
15. Friedrich Nietzsche, *The Birth of Tragedy and the Genealogy of Morals* (New York: Doubleday, 1956), 186.
16. Dubois, *Anarchist Peril*, 80.
17. Dubois, 99.
18. Dubois, 232–33.

Chapter 9. Anthony Trollope

Many critics have labeled Trollope a conservative and let the matter of his politics go. This tradition goes as far back as Michael Sadlier's remark in *Trollope—A Commentary* (New York: Farrar Straus, 1947), that "in the tale of English literature he is—to put the matter in a phrase—the supreme novelist of acquiescence" (367). A more extreme version of the theme is John Halperin's, who says in *Trollope and Politics: A Study of the Pallisers and Others* (New York: Barnes and Noble, 1977) that Trollope is not only a conservative, but a racist and an antifeminist. Some recent critics have, however, remarked on the iconoclasm inherent in Trollope's form. John Kincaid, for example, sees in Trollope a conflict "between the closed form inherited from the century before and the open form" of the twentieth century, in *The Novels of Anthony Trollope* (Oxford: Clarendon Press, 1977), 20. George Levine, in *The Realistic Imagination* (Chicago: University of Chicago Press, 1981), has remarked similarly that "It is essential to Trollope's compromised vision of the complexities and disorders of experience that things not be 'done'" (196). Several critics have also remarked on Trollope's tenderness toward his characters, a tenderness so unusual as to be radical. Among the best are Hugh Walpole, in *Anthony Trollope* (New York: Macmillan, 1928), and Bradford Booth, in *Anthony Trollope: Aspects of His Life and Art* (Bloomington: Indiana University Press, 1958).

Critical opinion on Trollope's women has been oddly mixed. The single most common misconception is that Trollope makes no distinction between the women of London and the women of Barsetshire. Richard Barickman, Susan MacDonald, and Myra Stark, in *Corrupt Relations* (New York: Columbia University Press, 1982), see the pernicious effects of Victorian patriarchy on Trollope's urban women, but do not see the freer, better lives of his female characters in Barsetshire. Shirley Robin Letwin, who reads Trollope quite sensitively, also neglects this distinction, in *The Gentleman in Trollope: Individuality and Moral Conduct* (Cambridge: Harvard University Press, 1982). In *The Androgynous Trollope: Attitudes to Women amongst Early Victorian Novelists* (Washington, D.C.: University Press of America, 1982) Rajiva Wijesinha points out that Trollope allows his women characters more variety in marriage than other Victorian novelists do, but by lifting his characters out of their social contexts, she also misses the particular strength of his rural women.

Lily Dale has been the subject of more controversy than any other character, male or female, in the Barsetshire novels. Though the fictional portrait is warm, critics have found this character hard to accept. Bradforth Booth, in *Anthony Trollope*, calls her warped (52); Robert Polhemus, in *The Changing World of Anthony Trollope* (Berkeley: University of California Press, 1968), calls her selfish and perverse (94).

I have used *Barchester Towers and The Warden* (New York: College Library, 1950), *The Small House at Allington* (London: Oxford University Press, 1975), and *The Last Chronicle of Barset* (Boston: Houghton Mifflin, 1964), and have included chapter references in the text.

1. Petr Kropotkin, *Mutual Aid: A Factor of Evolution* (reprint, Boston: Extending Horizons Press, n.d.), 237.
2. Quoted in James Pope Hennessy, *Anthony Trollope* (Boston: Little, Brown, 1972), 140.
3. Ibid.
4. Carroll Smith-Rosenberg, "The Female World of Love and Ritual: Relationships between Women in Nineteenth Century America," in *The "Signs" Reader: Women, Gender, and Scholarship*, ed. Elizabeth Abel and Emily K. Abel (Chicago: University of Chicago Press, 1983), 27–55.
5. G. M. Trevelyan, *English Social History: A Survey of Six Centuries, Chaucer to Queen Victoria* (New York: David McKay, 1942), 535.
6. John Ruskin, "The Nature of the Gothic," in *The Genius of John Ruskin: Selections from His Writings* (Boston: Houghton Mifflin, 1963), 176.
7. Quoted in E. P. Thompson, *William Morris: Romantic to Revolutionary* (New York: Pantheon, 1955), 241–42.
8. Ronald Blythe, *Akenfield: Portrait of an English Village* (New York: Pantheon, 1969), 104.

9. Barbara Ehrenreich, *The Hearts of Men: American Dreams and the Flight from Commitment* (New York: Doubleday, 1983).

Chapter 10. Thomas Hardy

Critical opinion is divided on Hardy's true opinion of English rural life. In 1955 Arnold Kettle said eloquently that *Tess of the D'Urbervilles* is "the most moving expression in our literature—not forgetting Wordsworth—of the destruction of the peasant world," in *An Introduction to the English Novel*, vol. 2 (London: Hutchison, 1955), 62. The most important critic to share this view is Raymond Williams, who pays tribute to Hardy in *The Country and the City* (New York: Oxford University Press, 1973). Others disagree; for example, Reginald James White, in *Thomas Hardy and History* (London: Macmillan, 1974), says that "there is no fuss or foolishness about 'the good old days' in Hardy's picture of the changing world" (6). Merryn Williams, in her thoughtful *Thomas Hardy and Rural England*, describes the degeneration that had taken place before Hardy wrote and concludes that Hardy was, therefore, in favor of modernization (New York: Columbia University Press, 1972).

Hardy's debt to Wordsworth has also been discussed in terms of a way of seeing nature. J. Hillis Miller, in *Thomas Hardy: Distance and Desire* (Cambridge: Harvard University Press, 1976), writes about the double vision in Hardy's fiction, the disjunction between characters and narrators. George Levine, in *The Realistic Imagination* (Chicago: University of Chicago Press, 1981), has said that Hardy resembles Wordsworth in that both look to the universal character existing below the veneer of civilization. Some recent critics have said it is impossible to find or define a coherent philosophy of nature in Hardy. Bruce Johnson calls *Tess of the D'Urbervilles* a cruelly Darwinian novel, different from the others, in *True Correspondence: A Phenomenology of Thomas Hardy's Novels* (Tallahassee: University Presses of Florida, 1983); Penny Boumelha says that even within *Tess of the D'Urbervilles* no coherent philosophy of nature can be constructed, in *Thomas Hardy and Women: Sexual Ideology and Narrative Form* (Sussex: Harvester, 1982).

Recently a great deal of attention has been given to Hardy and to the late nineteenth-century sexual debates. J. W. Beach, in *The Technique of Thomas Hardy* (1922; reprint, New York: Russell and Russell, 1962), was one of the first to point out that *Tess of the D'Urbervilles* was written at a time "when, in serious literature, especially in plays, a great deal of attention was being paid to the subject of the déclassée—the woman who would come back, the woman who lives with 'the shadow of a sin,' the woman who has to pay for 'one false step'" (20). Merryn Williams devotes a whole chapter of *Thomas Hardy and Rural England* to the theme of seduction in country novels before Hardy (79–99). Lloyd Fernando, in *New Women in the Late Victorian Novel* (University Park: Pennsylvania State University Press, 1977), has written about Hardy's concern with the difficulty of producing sensible rules for sexual relationships. Gail Cunningham, in *The New Woman and the Victorian Novel* (New York: Barnes and Noble, 1978), mentions his interest in divorce. Patricia Stubbs, in *Women and Fiction: Feminism and the Novel, 1880–1920* (Sussex: Harvester, 1979), writes about Hardy's interest in sexual incompatibility. Sylvia Strauss, in *"Traitors to the Masculine Cause": The Men's Campaign for Women's Rights* (Westport, Conn.: Greenwood, 1982), has a long discussion of the feminism of *Jude the Obscure*, but does not mention *Tess of the D'Urbervilles*. Probably the most exhaustive study of the sexual controversies in which Hardy was embroiled, and the popular novels by women he would have known, is Penny Boumelha, *Thomas Hardy and Women*.

Another aspect of Hardy's treatment of women is his treatment of the men who hurt women. Opinion has been divided on how to judge Tess and her two men, Alec and Angel. Ian Gregor has written well on Alec's power as an economic intruder, a representative of laissez-faire capitalism, in *The Great Web: The Form of Hardy's Major Fiction* (Totowa, N. J.: Roman and Littlefield, 1970). Critics have tended to exculpate Angel instead of seeing him too as an intruder. Virginia Hyman, in *Ethical Perspectives in the Novels of Thomas Hardy* (Port Washington, N. Y.: Kennikat, 1975), blames him only for not following through on his beliefs, but remaining intellectual rather than progressing to what she calls the "sociological" state (121). Rosemary Sumner writes about Angel's failure in purely psychological terms, in *Thomas Hardy, Psychological Novelist* (New York: St. Martin's, 1981).

I have used the fifth edition of *Tess of the D'Urbervilles* (New York: New American Library, 1962) and have included chapter references in the text.

1. G. M. Trevelyan, *English Social History* (New York: David McKay, 1942), 552.
2. Trevelyan, 554.
3. E. P. Thompson, *The Making of the English Working Class* (1963; reprint, New York: Vintage, 1966), 403–4.
4. Michael Millgate, *Thomas Hardy: A Biography* (New York: Random House, 1982), 295.
5. Trevelyan, *English Social History*, 576.
6. Raymond Williams, *The Country and the City* (New York: Oxford University Press, 1973). 198.
7. Williams, 214.
8. Petr Kropotkin, *Mutual Aid* (reprint, Boston: Extending Horizons Press, n.d.), 128.
9. Kropotkin, 236.

Chapter 11. E. M. Forster

Both Forster's radicalism and his feminism have been given short shrift by critics. Forster's most loving and perceptive reader remains Lionel Trilling, in *E. M. Forster* (1943; reprint, New York: Harcourt Brace, 1971). Unfortunately Trilling has set the tone for too much of late criticism, which has called Forster a "liberal" and concerned itself primarily with "personal relationships." This mode of criticism tends to dismiss Ruth Wilcox as a piece of literary fancy, and Leonard Bast as a hopeless, irredeemable victim; it tends to condemn the ending of the book as escapist. Some of the most important books in this vein are Frederick Crews, *E. M. Forster: The Perils of Humanism* (Princeton: Princeton University Press, 1962); Barbara Rosecrance, *Forster's Narrative Vision* (Ithaca: Cornell University Press, 1982); and Wilfred Stone, *The Cave and the Mountain: A Study of E. M. Forster* (Stanford: Stanford University Press, 1966).

I have used *Howards End* (New York: Random House, 1921) and have included chapter references within the text.

1. Wendell Berry, "Poetry and Place," in *Standing by Words* (San Francisco: North Point Press, 1983), 184.
2. E. P. Thompson, *William Morris* (New York: Pantheon, 1955), 632.
3. Christopher Lasch, *The Minimal Self: Psychic Survival in Troubled Times* (New York: Norton, 1984), 43–44.
4. E. J. Hobsbawm, *Industry and Empire* (reprint, Harmondsworth: Penguin, 1969), 119.
5. Hobsbawm, 87.
6. Wendell Berry, *The Unsettling of America: Culture and Agriculture* (New York: Avon, 1977), 6.
7. Hobsbawm, *Industry and Empire*, 87–88.
8. Thompson, *William Morris*, 728.
9. Raymond Williams, *The Country and the City* (New York: Oxford University Press, 1973), 105.
10. Aubrey de Selincourt, *The World of Herodotus* (reprint, San Francisco: North Point Press, 1982), 366.
11. Selincourt, 324.
12. Ronald Blythe, *Akenfield: Portrait of an English Village* (New York: Pantheon, 1969), 198–99.
13. Blythe, 75.

Chapter 12. Conclusion

A few brave feminist critics have resisted the adulation of Virginia Woolf and Kate Chopin. Patricia Meyer Spacks, in *The Female Imagination* (1972; reprint, New York: Avon, 1976), and Elaine Showalter, in *A Literature of Their Own* (Princeton: Princeton University Press, 1977), have both condemned the idealization of suffering, suicidal heroines.

I have used *The Awakening* (1899; reprint, New York: Norton, 1976) and included references in the text.

1. Virginia Woolf, "Three Guineas," quoted in *Women, the Family, and Freedom*, ed. Susan Bell and Karen Offen, vol. 2 (Stanford: Stanford University Press, 1983), 362.
2. Rosalind Rosenberg, *Beyond Separate Spheres: The Intellectual Roots of Modern Feminism* (New Haven: Yale University Press, 1982), 245–46.
3. Barbara Ehrenreich, *The Hearts of Men* (New York: Doubleday, 1983), 177.
4. Lydia Sargent, ed., *Women and Revolution* (Boston: South End, 1981), 349.
5. Christopher Lasch, *The Culture of Narcissism* (New York: Norton, 1979), xxv.
6. Jane Jacobs, *Cities and the Wealth of Nations: Principles of Economic Life* (New York: Random House, 1984), 41.
7. Hilda Scott, *Working Your Way to the Bottom: The Feminization of Poverty* (Boston: Pandora, 1984), 49.
8. Scott, 50.
9. John F. Richards, "Documenting Environmental History: Global Patterns of Land Conversion," in *Environment*, vol. 26, no. 9 (November 1984), 34.
10. Lasch, *Culture of Narcissism*, xxvii.

11. Petr Kropotkin, *Mutual Aid* (reprint, Boston: Extending Horizons Press, n.d.), 229.
12. Flora Thompson, *Lark Rise to Candleford* (reprint, Harmondsworth: Penguin, 1973), 535–36.
13. Ronald Blythe, *Akenfield: Portrait of an English Village* (New York: Pantheon, 1969), 15.
14. Blythe, 235.
15. Raymond Williams, *The Country and the City* (New York: Oxford, 1973), 304.
16. Williams, 271.
17. Wendell Berry, *The Unsettling of America, Culture and Agriculture* (New York: Avon, 1978), 191.
18. William Appleman Williams, "Missile Ban in Washington, 1921," *The Nation*, 26 November 1983, 530–31.
19. Wendell Berry, "A Good Scythe," in *The Gift of Good Land* (San Francisco: North Point Press, 1981), 175.

Index

About the Author

JUDITH WEISSMAN is associate professor of English at Syracuse University, where she has taught since 1972. A graduate of Washington University (B.A. 1967) and the University of California at San Diego (Ph.D. 1972), she is the author of numerous articles in journals, including *The Sewanee Review, The Georgia Review, Women & Literature,* and *The Midwest Quarterly.* In 1967 she received a Woodrow Wilson fellowship. She lives in Syracuse, New York.

About the Book

Half Savage and Hardy and Free was composed in Granjon by Modern Type & Design, Inc. of Clearwater, Florida. It was printed on 60 lb. Warren's Olde Style and bound by Maple-Vail Book Manufacturing Group of Binghamton, New York. Design by Joyce Kachergis Book Design and Production, Inc. of Bynum, North Carolina.

Wesleyan University Press, 1987